The Encyclopedia of
Asian Cooking

The Encyclopedia of
Asian Cooking

Introduction: Madame Grace Zia Chu
General Editor: Jeni Wright

OCTOPUS

Contents

Introduction: Madame Grace Zia Chu
General Editor: Jeni Wright
Authors: Khalid Aziz
  Sri Owen
  Patricia Herbert
  Ornsiri Selby-Lowndes
  Gloria Zimmerman
  Bach Ngo
  Deh-ta Hsiung
  Kay Shimizu
  Jan Leeming
Consultants: Gloria Zimmerman
  Kitty Sham

First published 1980 by
Octopus Books Limited
59 Grosvenor Street
London W1

© 1980 Octopus Books Limited
Reprinted 1982

ISBN 0 7064 0990 6

Produced by
Mandarin Publishers
Limited
22a Westlands Road,
Quarry Bay, Hong Kong

Printed in Hong Kong

Introduction

My interest in Asian cooking stems from a thirty-year career in teaching Chinese cooking, a rigorous intellectual training that insisted I must know ten times as much about a subject as I hoped to teach my students, and a lifelong itchy foot that set me wandering all over the globe, questioning, looking, tasting and making new friends.

Whenever I go to a country that I have never visited, I like to set out on my own or with friends, wandering through streets and bazaars, tasting the food from the stalls. It is in these direct encounters with the native cooking and produce that you get a feel for the way the people really live.

One afternoon in Tokyo I sat on a tall stool at a counter; behind the counter there was a cauldron of cooked rice; nearby were hundreds of short bamboo skewers of seafood and meat marinating in a dark sauce. I chose clams and prawns (shrimp) and the serving girl cooked them over a small *hibachi,* then set them over the hot rice to finish cooking in the steam.

Another time I found myself in Singapore, where the days are blazing hot but the nights are pleasantly cooled by sea breezes. Every night we would sit down to a sumptuous banquet. Later, around midnight, we would wander through the market stalls tasting the delicacies they offered. At one stall, we nibbled tiny packages of lightly-spiced (prawns) shrimp rolled in leaves; at another, we drank fresh coconut milk; somewhere else, there were spicy skewers of satay. It was like attending a wonderful bazaar.

One midwinter, I visited Korea, surely one of the coldest places on the face of the earth at that time of year! In a simple restaurant, we sat on the floor at low tables, as one does in Japan. In the centre of the table there was a heavy brass-lidded stove full of charcoal. Not only did it heat the room, but it was used to cook the dinner. Each guest chose a piece of marinated beef with his chopsticks and laid it, sizzling, on the griddle over the brass. When cooked to taste, the beef was transferred to a rice bowl, before eating.

On my most recent trip to Asia, I took several members of my family to Kweilin in South China. On a trip down the Li-Kiang river, we stopped at an open-air restaurant famous for its seafood and sat at long wooden tables to enjoy the fish dishes. After lunch I went to the primitive kitchen and introduced myself to the chef. He made for me the most delicious dish I have ever eaten. A fish was pulled from the river behind his kitchen, filetted on the spot, chopped, seasoned, formed into balls and cooked with vegetables. It was the freshest, most delicious dish I had tasted in China, and it was completely new to me.

How is it that I, a so-called expert on Chinese food, could still be surprised by something new to eat in China? In just such a way, no matter how knowledgeable you may be about aspects of Asian cooking, you will find many surprises in this encyclopedia. The subject is so rich and varied, the scope so vast, and the treatment so complete.

Each chapter begins with an introduction about the people, their culture and their food. The recipes are well-chosen to represent each cuisine and the accompanying photographs are not only appetizing, they guide the reader to the proper presentation of unfamiliar foods, by showing which dishes to choose and how to combine the foods on the plate. The glossary is an ideal reference source for the special Asian ingredients.

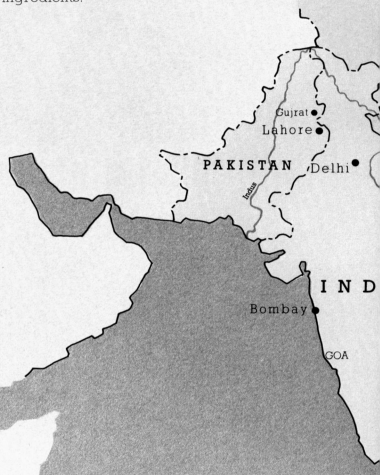

NOTES

Standard spoon measurements are used in all recipes:
1 tablespoon = one 15 ml spoon
1 teaspoon = one 5 ml spoon
All spoon measures are level.

Fresh herbs are used unless otherwise stated. If unobtainable substitute a bouquet garni of the equivalent dried herbs, or use dried herbs instead but halve the quantities stated.

Quantities are given in both metric and imperial measures. For each recipe, follow either set of measures but not a mixture of both because they are not interchangeable.

Details of specialist ingredients, marked with an asterisk, are given in the glossary (pages 216–219).

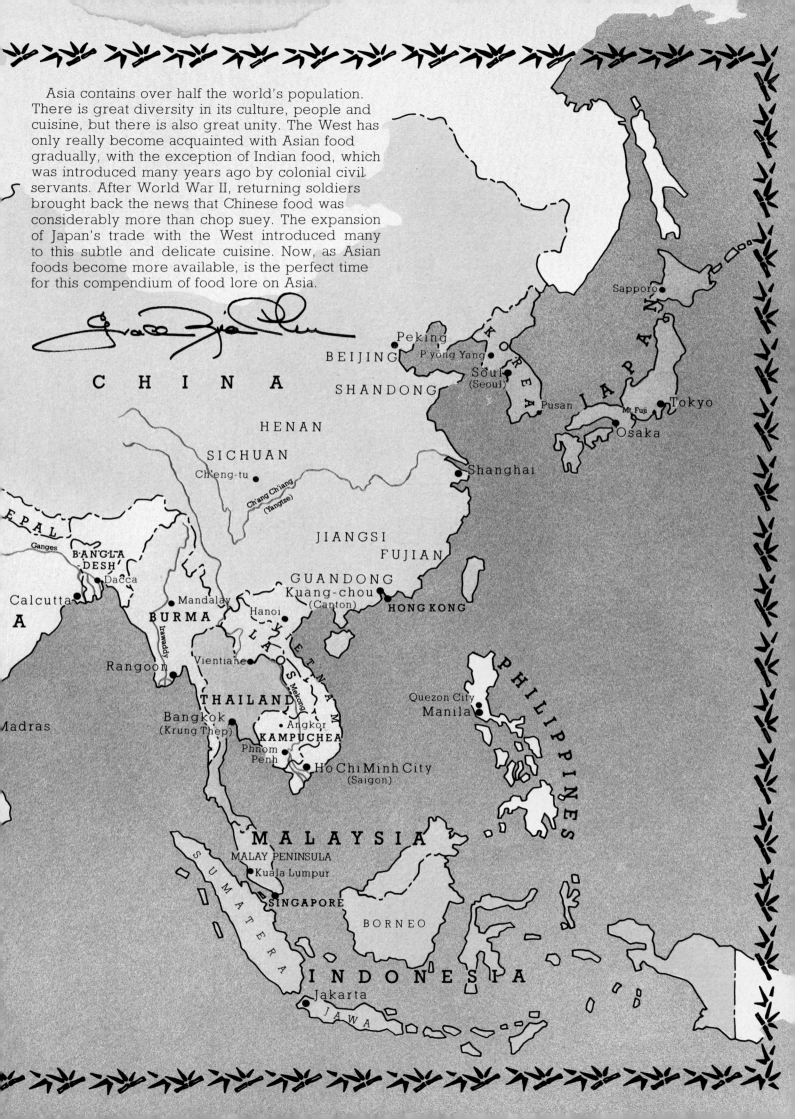

Asia contains over half the world's population. There is great diversity in its culture, people and cuisine, but there is also great unity. The West has only really become acquainted with Asian food gradually, with the exception of Indian food, which was introduced many years ago by colonial civil servants. After World War II, returning soldiers brought back the news that Chinese food was considerably more than chop suey. The expansion of Japan's trade with the West introduced many to this subtle and delicate cuisine. Now, as Asian foods become more available, is the perfect time for this compendium of food lore on Asia.

India, Pakistan and Bangladesh

Khalid Aziz

For most people living in the Indian sub-continent the pleasure of eating is, unfortunately, no more than an expression of the will to survive. Food is very much a necessity of life and little more for the majority of the 600 million or so who inhabit the land from the Indus to the Ganges. The average peasants' main meal today probably consists of a little rice, with perhaps a thick *dal** enlivened by a *tarka* of garlic and chillis. Not a meal of deep gastronomic significance, but simply a repast designed to keep body and soul together. However, beyond this simple peasant diet lies a history of culinary skill and expertise.

To speak of Indian food as one indivisible style would be wrong. There is, most would agree, a common thread which links all styles of Indian cooking, but it is a drawstring which encompasses widely spaced points. Looking at the Indian sub-continent one will see that the first culinary differences correspond to the political boundaries between the countries which make up the area. Pakistan, when it became a state in its own right in 1948, was divided into East and West Pakistan and populated by Muslims. These two areas were separated by a thousand miles of India, populated by Hindus.

It is said that there are as many differences between Hindu and Muslim cooking as there are between the religions themselves. Muslims do not eat pork, but other meat is acceptable and widely incorporated into the Muslim cuisine, as long as it is butchered in the prescribed manner (to allow as much blood as possible to drain from the carcass). However, many Hindus, particularly those from Gujrat in the south, make vegetarianism an inexorable part of their faith. For them cooking is an art indeed, designed to turn out not only tasty dishes, but a balanced diet based on vegetables, suited to the needs of an arduous life. What was East Pakistan is now Bangladesh. Predominantly Muslim, the Bangladeshi style of cooking revolves largely around the fish that inhabit the thousands of miles of waterway that make up the Ganges delta. Fish is acceptable to Muslims, as it is believed to have already been sacrificially slaughtered by virtue of the gill slits which appear to cut the neck of the creature!

Meat, sacrificed in the proper manner for Muslims, assumes an even greater role in cuisine for Sikhs. Traditionally, Sikhs are a warlike people who make the possession of a dagger an article of faith. Their beasts have to be killed by *jhutka* – the complete decapitation of the animal, which ideally should be achieved in one blow.

Availability of raw materials is as important as religious beliefs in determining the Indian diet. In the north, temperate climes prevail. In Pakistan and Nepal, the Himalayan foothills provide lush grassy slopes for grazing. Here, broad-leaved vegetables, including spinach and cauliflower are grown. Further south on the plains of India, a combination of baking sun and irrigation permits peas, lentils and other pulses (legumes), and tropical vegetables, such as green peppers, aubergine (eggplant) and bhindi (okra) to be cultivated. It is here too that the spices and strong flavourings are grown – especially turmeric and chillis. Around the Indian coastline, as yet unspoilt by pollution – seafood including all manner of shellfish, is abundant. In Bangladesh, the rivers teem with every kind of fish, including the huge *Ma Sher*, which is large enough to provide a feast for a village.

There are almost as many different styles of eating in the Indian sub-continent as there are styles of cooking. Throughout the sub-continent, the hand is used to eat with. Traditionally the right hand is used, never the left. Muslims in particular seem to make great play of this – the left hand being considered ungodly in the extreme. In polite society it is considered incorrect to allow the fingers to be soiled beyond the second knuckle point. Traditionally, Hindus serve a meal on a *thali* – a tray-like plate usually made of metal. Each item of the meal is placed in a discreet pile around the edge of the *thali* – the centre being reserved as the area for eating off. In this way the diner can use the *thali* as a kind of artist's palette, mixing and blending flavours like colours. Today in modern India, convenience has obviated the use of the *thali*, but even when confronted with a plateful of curry and rice, many Indians will maintain a traditional *thali*-based style of eating.

The eating of both bread and rice in the same meal is frowned upon in some quarters. Usually such a choice does not arise – those in paddy growing areas use rice to provide their carbohydrate; where wheat grows in abundance, bread is the order of the day. Whilst day in, day out, the average peasant has to content himself with a simple meal of rice and vegetables, on holidays no expense is spared to eat the best available. During festivals, the emphasis is on abundance and flavour, and it is this festival cooking that plays the major part in the development of Indian cuisine. Rice is still the staple food, but it will be combined with meat and stock to make sumptuous pilaus, with cardamoms

8

and cloves adding aromatic piquancy. In the north, lamb dishes such as *Korma* (see page 22) and *Roghan Gosht* (see page 32) are made.

Throughout the sub-continent, the giving and receiving of sweets has always marked celebration. Chief among these is perhaps *Halwa* (see page 48) – a fudge-like concoction which, being easily carried, is today sent over great distances to expatriates so that they may indulge with their families on great occasions. Much use is made of milk in the preparation of sweets. In the days leading up to a festival, kitchens in sweetmeat shops and homes alike are dominated by huge bubbling cauldrons of milk being

reduced to make *khoa* – a kind of evaporated milk. *Khoa* is then used to make all manner of sweetmeats – *Kulfi* (see page 49) and *Gulab Jamun* (see page 51), for example.

Milk is also used to make puddings for high days and holidays. On the Muslim festival days or *Ids* – particularly *Id-ul-Fitr* which follows the thirty days of fasting in the month of Ramadan – Muslims dress in their best clothes and visit one another. They offer and receive milk puddings decorated with finely beaten silver leaf, known as *varak*.* The most popular dishes are *Sewaiian* (see page 48), made with vermicelli, and *Kheer* (see page 52), made with rice flour.

Regional Cooking Styles

In the north, particularly northern Pakistan, tandoori cooking has dominated for centuries. A *tandoor* is a clay oven, conically shaped like a beehive. Three hours before cooking, a charcoal fire is lit in the *tandoor* and, when searing temperatures are reached inside, cooking can begin. Tandoori recipes depend on quick cooking. Meat is cut into chunks and marinated, then cooked on skewers in a matter of minutes. Poultry is dealt with in the same way, either whole or cut into serving pieces.

As the *tandoor* is an oven and not merely a charcoal barbecue, it offers one of the few opportunities for making leavened bread. Normally, Indian bread is a simple griddle-cooked dough of flour and water. Naan however, makes full use of yeast to provide a product that, cooked on the inside walls of the *tandoor* is lighter than most unleavened bread.

Advanced though tandoori cooking is, it is not a complete cuisine. It has developed hand in glove with the Mughal style of cooking, after the fashion of the Mughal emperors who laid great emphasis on presentation. It is within this style, which extends down towards central India, that food appears to be at its most appetizing. From Mughal cooking a new and differing style developed around Delhi. This Delhi style is today much revered and many of the best recipes are ubiquitous throughout the sub-continent. Bombay, being a major port, developed a more cosmopolitan style, with such delicacies as cutlets and sweet and sour dishes – learnt from the Chinese. Also on the west coast, Indian Christians developed their own styles, particularly in Goa. Further south on the Keralanese coast, the use of fenugreek has been developed to a fine art, mainly to absorb odour in fish dishes.

The Tamils, further inland and on the east coast, make use of the plentiful supplies of coconut available – hardly a main dish is prepared without coconut in one form or another! A type of coconut paste is made by holding half a coconut against the rotating blade of a crude scraper, often co-owned by many families, and the resulting pasty milk is used to give substance to Tamili curries.

It seems to be a rule that the hotter the temperature, the hotter the food. Certainly the Madrasis, who live in constantly high temperatures, prove the point. Vindaloo, cooked with the addition of vinegar, has been treated with reverence by generations of restaurant goers in the West. Yet, it is the Bengalis who have been mainly responsible for bringing Indian food to the West. Certainly in Britain, and to a lesser extent in North America, the majority of so-called Indian restaurants are, in fact, today run by Bangladeshis. Bengali cooking is perhaps the epitome of good fish cooking. A rather muddy tasting river-bed fish, with the addition of Bengali *masalas*, is turned into a delicious meal.

Inevitably, with time and the levelling effect of

the British Raj, many recipes have crossed traditional regional boundaries and their antecedents have been transformed during five thousand years of cooking.

Cooking Utensils

It is a fallacy that lack of utensils is a major hurdle to the Westerner setting out to cook Indian food. The sub-continent is poor, and food often has to be prepared and cooked in primitive conditions. The average Western kitchen is more than equipped to cope with the demands of Indian food. For example, using a grinder or pestle and mortar to grind spices is far easier than using the traditional stone and slab! Currying is basically a stewing process, so a large heavy saucepan is all that is needed. *Bhoona* is similar to the Chinese method of stir-frying, performed in a wok. A deep-sided frying pan (skillet) can normally be used for this or, where larger quantities are called for, a heavy saucepan.

Obviously a *tandoor* can present problems, but a charcoal barbecue will cook marinated meat on skewers. Chicken is best started in a conventional oven and finished on the barbecue. Naan is more difficult, but reasonable results can be obtained in a hot oven. Unleavened breads, such as chapattis, are traditionally cooked on a dome-shaped disc known as a *tawa*, which is heated over a fire. This utensil is perhaps worth investing in, although good results can be obtained by using any flat metal plate. When deep-frying – pakoras, puri, hoppers – for example, use normal deep-frying equipment.

Serving

When serving Indian food, balance must be borne in mind. Starters or hors d'oeuvre are not generally served as such, but there is no reason why some small dish should not be served as an appetizer. Similarly, sweets are not normally taken with everyday meals, but again, serve them if you wish. Bread or rice are served as part of the main course, being generally preferred. Main meat dishes are best accompanied by a vegetable curry and perhaps a *dal*.* Guests will also appreciate the coolness of a salad; green salad is more authentic because good tomatoes are generally few and far between in the sub-continent. A refreshing yogurt dish will also be appreciated.

Use hot spices cautiously: there is little point in bombarding a digestion accustomed to a Western diet with fiery hot food. To quench the thirst most Indians take water, usually well iced and sometimes flavoured with sandalwood or rose. Muslims, of course, shun alcohol although some Hindus and Sikhs take beer. Lager or wine can be served with Indian food, but it is doubtful that subtle vintages will be appreciated.

The golden rule with Indian food is to remember that it is not static; it changes every time a cook adds a little extra something, be that cook in Bombay or Calcutta, Lahore or Madras, or even London or New York.

Garam Masala

Garam Masala forms the base for much of the cuisine of India, and many people regard it as the philosopher's stone that turns ordinary cooking into golden cuisine. Consequently, there are almost as many recipes for Garam Masala as there are cooks in India. For this recipe, use either bleached or green cardamoms. Measure the spices with teaspoons or larger spoons, depending on the quantity you wish to make. If stored in an airtight jar, Garam Masala should keep for 3 to 6 months.

METRIC/IMPERIAL

1½ spoons whole cardamoms
5 spoons coriander seeds
1 spoon cumin seeds
1½ spoons whole cloves
6 spoons whole black peppercorns

AMERICAN

1½ spoons whole cardamoms
5 spoons coriander seeds
1 spoon cumin seeds
1½ spoons whole cloves
6 spoons whole black peppercorns

METHOD

Remove the seeds from the cardamoms, then place on a baking (cookie) sheet with the remaining ingredients.

Bake in a preheated very hot oven (240°C/475°F, Gas Mark 9) for 10 minutes, then leave to cool. Grind to a fine powder using a pestle and mortar, coffee mill or electric blender. Store in an airtight jar.

Bombay Duck

This is the common name applied to the Bummaloe fish, which swims in coastal waters around the sub-continent. The fish is a scavenger and is said to have derived its doubtful name from one of its better known habitats, the docks at Bombay. The fish are usually netted and then hung up to dry in the sun; salt is added later. The taste, not to mention the smell, is an acquired experience, but they are available here and are worth trying. They should be grilled (broiled) for a minute or so on each side and served warm. A useful starter, but out of consideration for guests, alternatives are usually offered!

Curry Sauce

It is useful to know the basics of curry cookery before proceeding further with Indian food. This curry sauce is not a dish in itself, but is useful for currying leftovers.

METRIC/IMPERIAL

100 g/4 oz ghee*
1 large onion, peeled and sliced
2 garlic cloves, peeled and sliced
1 teaspoon coriander powder
1 teaspoon turmeric powder
1 teaspoon chilli powder
½ teaspoon salt
1 teaspoon freshly ground black
    pepper
300 ml/½ pint water
1 teaspoon Garam Masala (see
    opposite page)

AMERICAN

½ cup ghee*
1 large onion, peeled and sliced
2 garlic cloves, peeled and sliced
1 teaspoon coriander powder
1 teaspoon turmeric powder
1 teaspoon chili powder
½ teaspoon salt
1 teaspoon freshly ground black
    pepper
1¼ cups water
1 teaspoon Garam Masala (see
    opposite page)

METHOD

Melt the ghee in a pan, add the onion and garlic and fry gently until soft but not brown. Stir in the coriander, turmeric, chilli, salt and pepper, then add the ingredients to be curried – meat, fish, poultry or vegetables, etc. Fry for 5 minutes, then add the water and bring to the boil.

Lower the heat and simmer for 10 minutes, then add the Garam Masala and simmer for a further 5 minutes. Serve hot with vegetables, or simply spooned over a bowl of rice.

SERVES 4

Poppadoms

Poppadoms are one of the best known Indian foods in the world. Originally they were designed as appetizers in the strictest sense of the word. With the British Raj in India the poppadom came into its own, and no colonel's table would have been complete without a pile of fresh ones. Some of the British in India developed the habit of crumbling the poppadom over a plate laden with curry and rice; but most Indians prefer to eat them from a side plate so as to savour their crispness.

Poppadoms are available both plain and spiced. The spicing is achieved mostly with crushed black pepper, but hotter poppadoms are made using chilli powder. The process of making poppadoms is so complicated that it is best to buy them ready, prepared. The dough, made from besan* (chick pea (garbanzos) flour), is very sensitive to humidity, so it is important to store poppadoms in a cool, dry place. Deep-frying is the best method of cooking.

Heat the oil or fat in a deep fryer until a small piece of poppadom, dropped into the oil or fat, immediately sizzles and rises to the surface. Before cooking, beat the poppadoms on a table to get rid of the dust.

Using a slotted spoon and a fish slice, fry the poppadoms, two at a time, for about 10 to 15 seconds, then turn them over and fry the other side. (Frying two together prevents them curling up.) Drain the poppadoms and stack them upright in a rack so any excess fat can drain away.

To enjoy poppadoms at their best, eat within a few hours of frying.

Preparing Garam Masala from the basic spices: bleached and green cardamoms, coriander seeds, cloves, black peppercorns and cumin seeds

Dosas; Somosas; Pakoras

Samosas
Curried Pastries

Samosas are often referred to as curry puffs by occidentals. In fact, they are deep-fried envelopes of crisp pastry filled with a dry curry. In India they are usually eaten as a snack – often served with tea – but they also make a good dinner party starter.

METRIC/IMPERIAL

Pastry:
225 g/8 oz plain flour
50 g/2 oz ghee*
½ teaspoon salt
200 ml/⅓ pint milk (approximately), soured with a little lemon juice
vegetable oil for deep-frying
Filling:
Keema (see page 27), or Aloo Gobi (see page 36)

AMERICAN

Pastry:
2 cups all-purpose flour
¼ cup ghee*
½ teaspoon salt
1 cup milk (approximately), soured with a little lemon juice
vegetable oil for deep-frying
Filling:
Keema (see page 27), or Aloo Gobi (see page 36)

METHOD

Sift the flour into a bowl, rub in the ghee, then add the salt. Stir in the soured milk gradually, to form a hard dough which is velvety to the touch. Chill in the refrigerator until required.

Break the dough into pieces, about 2.5 cm/1 inch in diameter. Roll out into very thin circles, then cut each circle in half. Spoon a little of the chosen filling in the centre of each semi-circle, then fold in half to make a triangular cone shape, enclosing the filling. Moisten the edges of the dough with soured milk, then press together to seal.

Deep-fry in hot oil for about 1 minute until the pastry is golden brown. Drain well and serve warm.
MAKES ABOUT 25
Note: Samosas keep quite well in an airtight container; reheat under a preheated grill (broiler) before serving.

Hoppers
Crisp Rice Pancakes (Crêpes)

Hoppers are fine rice pancakes. Traditionally, they are cooked in round-bottomed earthenware *chatties* in the ashes of a charcoal fire. Rice flour batter is poured into a hot *chatty* and immediately spun so that the batter flies to the curved sides of the vessel and sizzles into a delicate filigree. In Western kitchens, a deep frying pan (skillet) with curved sides can be used instead.

METRIC/IMPERIAL

2 tablespoons desiccated coconut
200 ml/⅓ pint water
225 g/8 oz rice
½ teaspoon bicarbonate of soda
½ teaspoon salt
25 g/1 oz butter

AMERICAN

2 tablespoons shredded coconut
1 cup water
1 cup rice
½ teaspoon baking soda
½ teaspoon salt
2 tablespoons butter

METHOD

Soak the coconut in the water for 4 hours. Meanwhile, grind the rice using a mortar and pestle, coffee mill or electric blender.

Strain the coconut water into the ground rice, then add the soda and salt. Beat to make a smooth batter, then leave to stand for 12 hours to allow the ground rice to absorb the liquid.

Beat the batter until well aerated. Lightly grease a hot frying pan (skillet) with a little butter. Pour in a little batter, tilting the pan so that the batter spreads to the edge. Cook for about 30 seconds or until the centre of the hopper is solid. Do not turn over. Repeat with the remaining batter. Serve hot and fresh.
MAKES 25 to 30

Pakoras
Savoury Fritters

Pakoras are made from a thick batter of *besan* (chick pea (garbanzos) flour)*. Sometimes the batter is simply deep-fried to a deep golden brown and served on its own, but more often it is used as a coating for fresh vegetables, particularly spinach. Pakoras make a very easy starter for a dinner party.

METRIC/IMPERIAL

100 g/4 oz besan*
½ teaspoon chilli powder
½ teaspoon salt
150 ml/5 fl oz natural yogurt
1 teaspoon lemon juice
vegetable oil for deep-frying

AMERICAN

1 cup besan*
½ teaspoon chili powder
½ teaspoon salt
⅔ cup unflavored yogurt
1 teaspoon lemon juice
vegetable oil for deep-frying

METHOD

Sift the flour into a bowl, rubbing any lumps through the sieve (strainer) with the back of a spoon. Add the chilli powder and salt and mix well. Stir in the yogurt and lemon juice gradually. Cover and leave in a cool place for 2 hours until the batter is thick; it should be much thicker than a pancake (crêpe) batter.

Heat the oil in a deep-fat fryer until a little of the batter, dropped into the oil, sizzles and rises to the surface. Deep-fry the batter in spoonfuls, or use to coat fresh spinach leaves or very thin slices of aubergine (eggplant) and deep-fry. Drain on kitchen paper towels, then serve fresh and warm.
SERVES 4
Note: Pakoras will keep in an airtight container for a few days; reheat under a preheated grill (broiler) before serving.

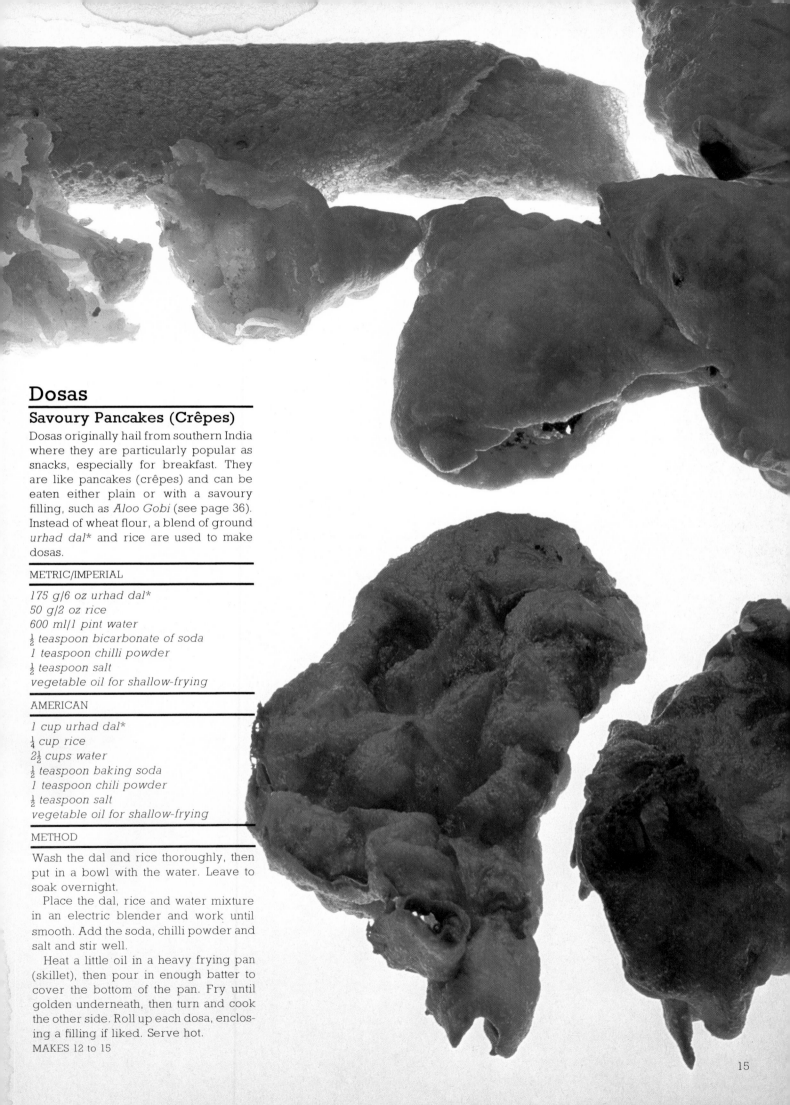

Dosas

Savoury Pancakes (Crêpes)

Dosas originally hail from southern India where they are particularly popular as snacks, especially for breakfast. They are like pancakes (crêpes) and can be eaten either plain or with a savoury filling, such as *Aloo Gobi* (see page 36). Instead of wheat flour, a blend of ground *urhad dal** and rice are used to make dosas.

METRIC/IMPERIAL

175 g/6 oz urhad dal*
50 g/2 oz rice
600 ml/1 pint water
½ teaspoon bicarbonate of soda
1 teaspoon chilli powder
½ teaspoon salt
vegetable oil for shallow-frying

AMERICAN

1 cup urhad dal*
¼ cup rice
2½ cups water
½ teaspoon baking soda
1 teaspoon chili powder
½ teaspoon salt
vegetable oil for shallow-frying

METHOD

Wash the dal and rice thoroughly, then put in a bowl with the water. Leave to soak overnight.

Place the dal, rice and water mixture in an electric blender and work until smooth. Add the soda, chilli powder and salt and stir well.

Heat a little oil in a heavy frying pan (skillet), then pour in enough batter to cover the bottom of the pan. Fry until golden underneath, then turn and cook the other side. Roll up each dosa, enclosing a filling if liked. Serve hot.

MAKES 12 to 15

Mulligatawny

Mulligatawny soup has no history in India before the British Raj – it was simply an invention to satisfy the needs of army officers who demanded a soup course at dinner. The literal translation of *mulligatawny* is 'pepper water'!

METRIC/IMPERIAL

50 g/2 oz dried tamarind*
1.2 litres/2 pints beef stock (made with cubes)
50 g/2 oz ghee*
1 large onion, peeled and sliced
2 garlic cloves, peeled and sliced
1 teaspoon ground ginger
2 teaspoons freshly ground black pepper
2 teaspoons coriander powder
½ teaspoon fenugreek powder
½ teaspoon chilli powder
½ teaspoon turmeric powder
½ teaspoon salt

AMERICAN

¼ cup tamarind pulp*
5 cups beef stock (made with cubes)
¼ cup ghee*
1 large onion, peeled and sliced
2 garlic cloves, peeled and sliced
1 teaspoon ginger powder
2 teaspoons freshly ground black pepper
2 teaspoons coriander powder
½ teaspoon fenugreek powder
½ teaspoon chili powder
½ teaspoon turmeric powder
½ teaspoon salt

METHOD

Put the tamarind in a pan, add just enough stock to cover, then bring to the boil. Remove the pan from the heat and leave the tamarind to soak for 4 hours.

Melt the ghee in a heavy pan, add the onion and garlic and fry gently until soft. Add the spices and salt. Fry for 3 minutes, stirring constantly, then stir in the remaining stock. Strain the tamarind liquid, discarding the seeds, then add to the pan and simmer for 15 minutes. Taste and adjust the seasoning. Serve hot.
SERVES 4

Ekoori
Spiced Scrambled Eggs

This dish traditionally belongs to the Parsees, a religious order that trace their origins back several millenia. They have always been one of the most adaptable of races, and have therefore endured. One of their principles is simplicity – and certainly Ekoori is simplicity itself.

METRIC/IMPERIAL

8 eggs
4 tomatoes, chopped
1 teaspoon salt
50 g/2 oz ghee*
1 medium onion, peeled and sliced
2 green chillis, chopped
1 teaspoon turmeric powder
1 teaspoon coriander powder

8 eggs
4 tomatoes, chopped
1 teaspoon salt
¼ cup ghee*
1 medium onion, peeled and sliced
2 green chilis, chopped
1 teaspoon turmeric powder
1 teaspoon coriander powder

METHOD

Put the eggs, tomatoes and salt in a bowl and beat well. Melt the ghee in a pan, add the onion and fry gently until soft. Add the chillis and spices and fry for 2 minutes, stirring constantly. Add the beaten egg mixture and stir with a wooden spoon until the eggs are scrambled. Serve hot on toast for breakfast, or as an inexpensive starter for a dinner party.
SERVES 4

Jhinga Sambal, served with poppadoms

Jhinga Sambal
Prawn (Shrimp) and Egg Sambal

This dish is good for a light buffet or cocktail party. It is simple to make, but full of flavour.

METRIC/IMPERIAL

450 g/1 lb peeled prawns
4 hard-boiled eggs, quartered
300 ml/½ pint coconut milk*
1 small onion, peeled and minced
1 garlic clove, peeled and crushed
1 green chilli, chopped
juice of ½ lemon
pinch of chilli powder
½ teaspoon salt
To garnish:
50 g/2 oz cooked green peas
chopped coriander leaves*

AMERICAN

1 lb shelled shrimp
4 hard-cooked eggs, quartered
1¼ cups coconut milk*
1 small onion, peeled and ground
1 garlic clove, peeled and crushed
1 green chili, chopped
juice of ½ lemon
pinch of chili powder
½ teaspoon salt
To garnish:
⅓ cup green peas
chopped coriander leaves*

METHOD

Arrange the prawns (shrimp) and eggs in a serving dish, then chill in the refrigerator.

Work the coconut milk, onion, garlic, green chilli, lemon juice, chilli powder and salt in an electric blender until evenly blended. Pour over the prawns (shrimp) and eggs. Garnish with the peas and coriander. Serve well chilled, with poppadoms if liked.
SERVES 4

Saag Jhinga (above); Jhinga Pathia;
Jhinga Kari Madras

Saag Jhinga

Prawns (Shrimp) and Spinach

The combination of spinach and prawns
(shrimp) is unusual, yet the two flavours
complement each other very well.

METRIC/IMPERIAL

50 g/2 oz ghee*
1 large onion, peeled and sliced
2 garlic cloves, peeled and sliced
1 tablespoon tomato purée
½ teaspoon Garam Masala (see page 12)
1½ teaspoons coriander powder
½ teaspoon turmeric powder
½ teaspoon chilli powder
½ teaspoon ground ginger
1 teaspoon salt
450 g/1 lb frozen whole leaf spinach
450 g/1 lb peeled prawns

AMERICAN

¼ cup ghee*
1 large onion, peeled and sliced
2 garlic cloves, peeled and sliced
1 tablespoon tomato paste
½ teaspoon Garam Masala (see page 12)
1½ teaspoons coriander powder
½ teaspoon turmeric powder
½ teaspoon chili powder
½ teaspoon ginger powder
1 teaspoon salt
1 lb frozen whole leaf spinach
1 lb shelled shrimp

METHOD

Melt the ghee in a heavy pan, add the
onion and garlic and fry gently until soft.
Stir in the tomato purée (paste) and fry,
stirring, for 1 minute. Add the spices and
salt and fry for a further 5 minutes,
stirring constantly.

Add the frozen spinach and break up
with a wooden spoon. Cook until the
spinach has thawed, stirring frequently,
then add the prawns (shrimp). Cook for a
further 5 minutes, turning the prawns
(shrimp) gently to coat with the spinach.
Serve immediately.
SERVES 4

Jhinga Pathia

Spiced Prawns (Shrimp) in Coconut Milk

This is an interesting dish in which
coconut is used both to bring out the
flavour of the prawns (shrimp) and to add
texture to the sauce. It is popular in
southern India, where fresh coconuts are
readily available.

METRIC/IMPERIAL

100g /4 oz ghee*
1 medium onion, peeled and sliced
3 garlic cloves, peeled and sliced
2 teaspoons coriander powder
1 teaspoon turmeric powder
1 teaspoon chilli powder
½ teaspoon ground ginger
½ teaspoon salt
½ teaspoon freshly ground black
   pepper
2 tablespoons vinegar
200 ml/⅓ pint coconut milk*
450 g/1 lb peeled prawns
2 tablespoons tomato purée

18

AMERICAN

½ cup ghee*
1 medium onion, peeled and sliced
3 garlic cloves, peeled and sliced
2 teaspoons coriander powder
1 teaspoon turmeric powder
1 teaspoon chili powder
½ teaspoon ginger powder
½ teaspoon salt
½ teaspoon freshly ground black
   pepper
2 tablespoons vinegar
1 cup coconut milk*
1 lb shelled shrimp
2 tablespoons tomato paste

METHOD

Melt the ghee in a heavy pan, add the onion and garlic and fry gently until soft. Mix the spices and seasonings to a paste with the vinegar, add to the pan and fry for a further 3 minutes, stirring continuously.

Stir in the coconut milk and simmer, stirring, for 5 minutes. Add the prawns (shrimp) and tomato purée (paste) and simmer for 2 minutes until the prawns (shrimp) are fully coated with a thick sauce. Serve immediately.
SERVES 4

Jhinga Kari Madrasi

Madras Dry Prawn (Shrimp) Curry

Many people think a curry has to be swimming with sauce. This is not so, as many Indians have a taste for dishes free of excessive juice. However, it must be remembered that lack of liquid tends to concentrate the spices, therefore be very careful when altering the liquid quantity in recipes.

METRIC/IMPERIAL

50 g/2 oz ghee*
1 small onion, peeled and sliced
2 garlic cloves, peeled and sliced
1 teaspoon coriander powder
½ teaspoon turmeric powder
pinch of ground ginger
½ teaspoon cumin powder
½ teaspoon salt
450 g/1 lb peeled prawns
1 tablespoon vinegar
pinch of chilli powder to garnish

AMERICAN

¼ cup ghee*
1 small onion, peeled and sliced
2 garlic cloves, peeled and sliced
1 teaspoon coriander powder
½ teaspoon turmeric powder
pinch of ginger powder
½ teaspoon cumin powder
½ teaspoon salt
1 lb shelled shrimp
1 tablespoon vinegar
pinch of chili powder to garnish

METHOD

Melt the ghee in a heavy pan, add the onion and garlic and fry gently until soft. Add the spices and salt and fry for a further 3 minutes, stirring constantly.

Reduce the heat to very low, then add the prawns (shrimp) and toss lightly for 1 minute until coated with the spices. Stir in the vinegar, then increase the heat and cook for 30 seconds.

Sprinkle with the chilli powder and serve immediately.
SERVES 4

19

Kookarh Korma

Chicken Korma

This is one of the most famous Indian dishes, which makes good use of the marinating process. The *korma* method can also be applied to meat; lamb korma is particularly popular in northern India.

METRIC/IMPERIAL

175 ml/6 fl oz natural yogurt
2 teaspoons turmeric powder
3 garlic cloves, peeled and sliced
1 chicken, weighing 1.5 kg/3 lb,
   skinned and cut into 8 pieces
100 g/4 oz ghee*
1 large onion, peeled and sliced
1 teaspoon ground ginger
5 cm/2 inch piece of cinnamon stick
5 whole cloves
5 whole cardamoms
1 tablespoon crushed coriander seeds
1 teaspoon cumin powder
½ teaspoon chilli powder
1 teaspoon salt
1½ tablespoons desiccated coconut
2 teaspoons roasted almonds

AMERICAN

¾ cup unflavored yogurt
2 teaspoons turmeric powder
3 garlic cloves, peeled and sliced
1 chicken, weighing 3 lb, skinned and
   cut into 8 pieces
½ cup ghee*
1 large onion, peeled and sliced
1 teaspoon ginger powder
2 inch piece of cinnamon stick
5 whole cloves
5 whole cardamoms
1 tablespoon crushed coriander seeds
1 teaspoon cumin powder
½ teaspoon chili powder
1 teaspoon salt
1½ tablespoons shredded coconut
2 teaspoons roasted almonds

METHOD

Work the yogurt, turmeric and 1 garlic clove in an electric blender, then pour over the chicken. Cover and leave to marinate overnight.

Melt the ghee in a heavy pan, add the onion and remaining garlic and fry gently until soft. Add the spices and salt and fry for a further 3 minutes, stirring constantly.

Add the chicken with the marinade and coconut, then cover with a tight-fitting lid and simmer for 45 minutes or until the chicken is tender. Scatter the almonds over the chicken. Serve hot.

SERVES 4

Note: The chicken may alternatively be cooked whole; allow an extra 20 to 30 minutes cooking time.

Murgh Dhansak

Chicken with Lentils

The Parsees are a people who trace their origins back to antiquity and Chicken Dhansak is a dish which dates almost as far back. Literally translated, it means 'wealthy chicken'. Strictly speaking, it should be made from two types of pulses (dried beans) – *chenna dal** and *moong dal.** If these are not available, use whichever *dal** is most readily obtainable.

METRIC/IMPERIAL

225 g/8 oz chenna dal*
225 g/8 oz moong dal*
1.2 litres/2 pints water
175 g/6 oz ghee*
2 large onions, peeled and sliced
4 garlic cloves, peeled and sliced
6 whole cloves
6 whole cardamoms
1½ teaspoons ground ginger
2 teaspoons Garam Masala (see page
   12)
2½ teaspoons salt
1 chicken, weighing 1.5 kg/3 lb,
   skinned, boned and cut into 8 pieces
450 g/1 lb frozen whole leaf spinach
4 large tomatoes, chopped

Murgh Hyderabad
Hyderabad-Style Chicken

This recipe, from Hyderabad, Deccan, uses coconut, and it is well worth obtaining a fresh one to make it, if at all possible.

METRIC/IMPERIAL

100 g/4 oz ghee*
1 large onion, peeled and sliced
2 garlic cloves, peeled and sliced
4 whole cardamoms
4 whole cloves
2.5 cm/1 inch piece of cinnamon stick
2 teaspoons Garam Masala (see page 12)
1 teaspoon turmeric powder
1 teaspoon chilli powder
1 teaspoon salt
1 chicken, weighing 1.5 kg/3 lb, skinned, boned and cut into 8 pieces
flesh of ½ fresh coconut, thinly sliced
1 tablespoon tomato purée
300 ml/½ pint water

AMERICAN

½ cup ghee*
1 large onion, peeled and sliced
2 garlic cloves, peeled and sliced
4 whole cardamoms
4 whole cloves
1 inch piece of cinnamon stick
2 teaspoons Garam Masala (see page 12)
1 teaspoon turmeric powder
1 teaspoon chili powder
1 teaspoon salt
1 chicken, weighing 3 lb, skinned, boned and cut into 8 pieces
flesh of ½ fresh coconut, thinly sliced
1 tablespoon tomato paste
1¼ cups water

METHOD

Melt the ghee in a heavy pan, add the onion and garlic and fry gently until soft. Add the spices and salt and fry for a further 3 minutes, stirring constantly. Add the chicken and fry for 10 minutes until browned on all sides, then add the coconut, tomato purée (paste) and water. Stir well, then bring to the boil.

Lower the heat, cover with a tight-fitting lid and simmer for 45 minutes or until the chicken is tender. Serve hot.
SERVES 4

AMERICAN

½ lb chenna dal*
½ lb moong dal*
5 cups water
¾ cup ghee*
2 large onions, peeled and sliced
4 garlic cloves, peeled and sliced
6 whole cloves
6 whole cardamoms
1½ teaspoons ginger powder
2 teaspoons Garam Masala (see page 12)
2½ teaspoons salt
1 chicken, weighing 3 lb, skinned, boned and cut into 8 pieces
1 lb frozen whole leaf spinach
4 large tomatoes, chopped

METHOD

Wash the dals, place in a saucepan and add the water. Bring to the boil and simmer, covered, for 15 minutes.

Meanwhile, melt the ghee in a heavy pan, add the onions and garlic and fry gently until soft. Add the spices and salt and fry for a further 3 minutes, stirring constantly. Add the chicken and fry until browned on all sides, then remove from the pan and drain on kitchen paper towels.

Add the spinach and tomatoes to the pan and fry gently for 10 minutes, stirring occasionally.

Mash the dals in the cooking water, then stir into the spinach mixture. Return the chicken to the pan, cover with a tight-fitting lid and simmer for 45 minutes or until the chicken is tender. Serve hot.
SERVES 4

Murgh Dhansak; Kookarh Korma; Murgh Hyderabad

Tandoori Murgh
Tandoori Chicken

In recent years, an increasing number of Indian restaurants in the West have been offering tandoori-style food and these dishes have become increasingly well known. The *tandoor* oven is usually about 1 metre/3 feet high and is made of clay. Searing temperatures are maintained by a charcoal fire at the base of the oven, and the cooking is so efficient that whole *poussins* (young chickens) can be cooked in minutes. *Naan* (see page 45) is cooked on the wall of the oven and skewered meat and poultry in the centre.

One of the secrets of tandoori chicken is the marinade – the longer the chicken is left in the marinade, the more authentic will be the finished dish. It is quite usual for the chicken to be marinated in a cool place for 3 days, sometimes for as long as 1 week.

This recipe has been adapted so that it can be made successfully in a conventional oven.

METRIC/IMPERIAL

1 chicken, weighing 1.5 kg/3 lb,
   skinned and cut into 4 pieces
juice of 2 lemons
4 teaspoons salt
2 garlic cloves, peeled and sliced
1 large onion, peeled and sliced
1 teaspoon coriander powder
$\frac{1}{2}$ teaspoon red food colouring
$\frac{1}{2}$ teaspoon chilli powder
1 teaspoon ground ginger
To garnish:
1 lettuce
1–2 tomatoes, sliced
$\frac{1}{2}$ onion, sliced into rings
few lemon wedges

AMERICAN

1 chicken, weighing 3 lb, skinned and
   cut into 4 pieces
juice of 2 lemons
4 teaspoons salt
2 garlic cloves, peeled and sliced
1 large onion, peeled and sliced
1 teaspoon coriander powder
$\frac{1}{2}$ teaspoon red food color
$\frac{1}{2}$ teaspoon chili powder
1 teaspoon ginger powder
To garnish:
1 head of lettuce
1–2 tomatoes, sliced
$\frac{1}{2}$ onion, sliced into rings
few lemon wedges

METHOD

Make 3 deep cuts in each piece of chicken with a sharp knife. Rub the flesh all over with half the lemon juice, then rub in the salt. Mix the remaining ingredients to a paste with the remaining lemon juice, using an electric blender if available. Put the chicken in a baking dish lined with foil, then pour over the marinade. Cover and leave to marinate for at least 12 hours.

Roast in a preheated moderate oven (180°C/350°F, Gas Mark 4) for $1\frac{1}{4}$ hours or until the chicken is tender. Increase the heat to moderately hot (200°C/400°F, Gas Mark 6) and roast for a further 15 to 20 minutes until browned on top. Serve hot on a bed of lettuce leaves, garnished with tomato slices, onion rings and lemon wedges. Serve *Naan* (see page 45) as an accompaniment.
SERVES 4

Tandoori Murgh, served with Naan (see page 45)

Kukul Curry
Chicken Curry

There are a multitude of recipes for chicken curry; this one is from Sri Lanka.

METRIC/IMPERIAL

100 g/4 oz ghee*
1 large onion, peeled and sliced
3 garlic cloves, peeled and sliced
4 green chillis, chopped
2 teaspoons coriander powder
1½ teaspoons turmeric powder
1 chicken, weighing 1.5 kg/3 lb, skinned and cut into 8 pieces
600 ml/1 pint coconut milk*
juice of ½ lemon

AMERICAN

½ cup ghee*
1 large onion, peeled and sliced
3 garlic cloves, peeled and sliced
4 green chilis, chopped
2 teaspoons coriander powder
1½ teaspoons turmeric powder
1 chicken, weighing 3 lb, skinned and cut into 8 pieces
2½ cups coconut milk*
juice of ½ lemon

METHOD

Melt the ghee in a heavy pan, add the onion and garlic and fry gently until soft. Add the chillis and spices and fry for a further 3 minutes, stirring constantly.

Add the chicken pieces to the pan and fry gently until browned on all sides. Stir in the coconut milk, then simmer gently for 45 minutes or until the chicken is tender. Add the lemon juice and simmer for a further 10 minutes, stirring occasionally. Serve hot.
SERVES 4

Murgh Mussalam
Spiced Baked Chicken

METRIC/IMPERIAL

1 chicken, weighing 1.5 kg/3 lb, skinned and cut into 8 pieces
175 ml/6 fl oz natural yogurt
1 large onion, peeled and chopped
3 garlic cloves, peeled and sliced
3 green chillis
1 teaspoon coriander powder
175 g/6 oz ghee*
2.5 cm/1 inch piece of cinnamon stick
10 whole cardamoms
10 whole cloves
1 teaspoon ground ginger
1 teaspoon salt
1 teaspoon freshly ground black pepper
½ teaspoon saffron threads, soaked in 1 tablespoon boiling water for 30 minutes

AMERICAN

1 chicken, weighing 3 lb, skinned and cut into 8 pieces
¾ cup unflavored yogurt
1 large onion, peeled and chopped
3 garlic cloves, peeled and sliced
3 green chilis
1 teaspoon coriander powder
¾ cup ghee*
1 inch piece of cinnamon stick
10 whole cardamoms
10 whole cloves
1 teaspoon ginger powder
1 teaspoon salt
1 teaspoon freshly ground black pepper
½ teaspoon saffron threads, soaked in 1 tablespoon boiling water for 30 minutes

METHOD

Make 3 deep cuts in each piece of chicken with a sharp knife. Work the yogurt, onion, garlic, chillis and coriander in an electric blender, then pour over the chicken. Cover and leave to marinate overnight.

Drain the chicken, reserving the marinade. Melt the ghee in a flameproof casserole, add the chicken and fry for about 15 minutes until browned on all sides. Add the spices and seasonings, except the saffron, and fry for a further 3 minutes, stirring constantly. Add the saffron with its liquid, then add the reserved marinade.

Cover the casserole and cook in a preheated moderately hot oven (190°C/375°F, Gas Mark 5) for about 30 minutes or until the chicken is tender and the sauce is very thick. Serve hot.
SERVES 4

Shikar Vindaloo
Vinegared Pork Curry

Pork dishes are few and far between in India. This recipe comes from the south where it is said to be best made with the pork from the wild boar that roam the area. The *vindaloo* method can be applied to any meat; it makes a very hot curry which should be served with plenty of yogurt.

METRIC/IMPERIAL

½ teaspoon cardamom seeds
½ teaspoon ground cloves
½ teaspoon ground ginger
1 tablespoon coriander powder
2 teaspoons turmeric powder
4 teaspoons chilli powder
1 teaspoon cumin powder
1 teaspoon salt
½ teaspoon freshly ground black
    pepper
200 ml/⅓ pint vinegar
450 g/1 lb boned pork, cut into
    4 cm/1½ inch cubes
50 g/2 oz ghee*
5 garlic cloves, peeled and sliced

AMERICAN

½ teaspoon cardamom seeds
½ teaspoon powdered cloves
½ teaspoon ginger powder
1 tablespoon coriander powder
2 teaspoons turmeric powder
4 teaspoons chili powder
1 teaspoon cumin powder
1 teaspoon salt
½ teaspoon freshly ground black
    pepper
1 cup vinegar
1 lb boneless pork, cut into 1½ inch
    cubes
¼ cup ghee*
5 garlic cloves, peeled and sliced

METHOD

Mix the spices and seasonings to a thick paste with a little of the vinegar, then rub into the pork.

Melt the ghee in a heavy pan, add the garlic and fry for 1 to 2 minutes, stirring frequently. Add the pork to the pan and cover with the remaining vinegar.

Bring to the boil, then lower the heat, cover and simmer for about 1 hour or until the meat is tender. Serve hot with *Chappattis* (see page 44) and plenty of natural (unflavored) yogurt.
SERVES 4

Keema; Shika Vindaloo, served with Chappattis (see page 45) and Dahi (see page 34)

Shikar Kari
Pork Curry

The tamarind water in this recipe counteracts the fattiness of pork.

METRIC/IMPERIAL

100g /4 oz dried tamarind*
200 ml/⅓ pint boiling water
50 g/2 oz ghee*
1 large onion, peeled and sliced
3 garlic cloves, peeled and chopped
2 green chillis, chopped
1 teaspoon ground ginger
3 whole cloves
5 cm/2 inch piece of cinnamon stick
1 tablespoon coriander powder
1 teaspoon turmeric powder
½ teaspoon chilli powder
½ teaspoon cumin seeds
450 g/1 lb boned pork, cut into
    2.5 cm/1 inch cubes

AMERICAN

½ cup tamarind pulp*
1 cup boiling water
¼ cup ghee*
1 large onion, peeled and sliced
3 garlic cloves, peeled and chopped
2 green chilis, chopped
1 teaspoon ginger powder
3 whole cloves
2 inch piece of cinnamon stick
1 tablespoon coriander powder
1 teaspoon turmeric powder
½ teaspoon chili powder
½ teaspoon cumin seeds
1 lb boneless pork, cut into 1 inch
    cubes

METHOD

Soak the tamarind in the water for 2 hours.

Melt the ghee in a heavy pan, add the onion and garlic and fry gently until soft. Add the chillis and spices and fry for a further 3 minutes, stirring constantly. Add the pork and fry for a further 5 minutes, stirring until each piece of meat is coated with the spice mixture.

Strain the tamarind, discarding the seeds, and stir the water into the pan. Bring to the boil, then lower the heat, cover and simmer for about 1 hour or until the meat is tender. Serve hot.
SERVES 4

Keema
Spiced Minced (Ground) Beef

This dish is easy to prepare, and is often used for banquets and other functions. Use the best quality minced (ground) beef available. If liked, peas or diced boiled potatoes can be added.

METRIC/IMPERIAL

50 g/2 oz ghee*
2 large onions, peeled and sliced
2 garlic cloves, peeled and sliced
1 teaspoon turmeric powder
2 teaspoons chilli powder
½ teaspoon coriander powder
½ teaspoon cumin seeds
1 teaspoon salt
1 teaspoon freshly ground black pepper
450 g/1 lb minced beef

AMERICAN

¼ cup ghee*
2 large onions, peeled and sliced
2 garlic cloves, peeled and sliced
1 teaspoon turmeric powder
2 teaspoons chili powder
½ teaspoon coriander powder
½ teaspoon cumin seeds
1 teaspoon salt
1 teaspoon freshly ground black pepper
1 lb ground beef

METHOD

Melt the ghee in a pan, add the onions and garlic and fry gently until soft. Add the spices and seasonings and fry for a further 3 minutes, stirring constantly. Add the beef and fry, stirring, until browned. Continue frying until the meat is cooked and the curry is dry. Serve hot.
SERVES 4

Kofta Kari
Meatball Curry

Minced (ground) beef is often used in Indian cooking, and *kofta* is a classic method. In this recipe the meatballs are sealed by deep-frying; although this takes a little extra time, it reduces the risk of the meatballs falling apart.

METRIC/IMPERIAL

450 g/1 lb minced beef
2 large onions, peeled and chopped
4 garlic cloves, peeled and chopped
2 teaspoons turmeric powder
2 teaspoons chilli powder
2 teaspoons coriander powder
1½ teaspoons cumin powder
1 teaspoon ground ginger
2 teaspoons salt
1 egg, beaten
vegetable oil for deep-frying
100 g/4 oz ghee*
200 ml/⅓ pint water
mint or coriander leaves* to garnish

AMERICAN

1 lb ground beef
2 large onions, peeled and chopped
4 garlic cloves, peeled and chopped
2 teaspoons turmeric powder
2 teaspoons chili powder
2 teaspoons coriander powder
1½ teaspoons cumin powder
1 teaspoon ginger powder
2 teaspoons salt
1 egg, beaten
vegetable oil for deep-frying
½ cup ghee*
1 cup water
mint or coriander leaves* to garnish

METHOD

Put the beef in a bowl and add half the onions, garlic, spices and salt. Stir well, then bind the mixture together with the beaten egg.

Form the mixture into 12 small balls. Heat the oil in a pan until very hot, add the meatballs a few at a time and deep-fry for 5 minutes. Remove from the pan with a slotted spoon, drain on kitchen paper towels and set aside.

Melt the ghee in a heavy pan, add the remaining onions and garlic and fry gently until soft. Add the remaining spices and salt and fry for a further 3 minutes, stirring constantly. Add the meatballs and turn gently to coat with the spices, then add the water and bring to the boil. Lower the heat and simmer gently for 30 minutes.

Serve hot, garnished with mint or coriander leaves. *Baigan Tamatar* (see page 36) is an ideal accompaniment.
SERVES 4

Calcutta Kari
Calcutta Beef Curry

There are any number of recipes for beef curry, but perhaps the best known are Madras Beef Curry and Calcutta Beef Curry.

METRIC/IMPERIAL

300 ml/½ pint water
450 g/1 lb beef, cut into 2.5 cm/1 inch cubes
1½ teaspoons coriander powder
1 teaspoon turmeric powder
1 teaspoon cumin powder
1½ teaspoons salt
1 teaspoon freshly ground black pepper
1 tablespoon milk
50 g/2 oz ghee*
1 small onion, peeled and sliced
1 garlic clove, peeled and sliced
chopped mint or coriander leaves* to garnish

AMERICAN

1¼ cups water
1 lb beef, cut into 1 inch cubes
1½ teaspoons coriander powder
1 teaspoon turmeric powder
1 teaspoon cumin powder
1½ teaspoons salt
1 teaspoon freshly ground black pepper
1 tablespoon milk
¼ cup ghee*
1 small onion, peeled and sliced
1 garlic clove, peeled and sliced
chopped mint or coriander leaves* to garnish

METHOD

Bring the water to the boil in a pan, add the beef and simmer for about 30 minutes.

Meanwhile, mix the spices and seasonings to a paste with the milk. Melt the ghee in a pan, add the onion and garlic and fry gently until soft. Stir in the paste and fry for a further 1 minute. Add the meat and half its cooking liquid, bring to the boil, then lower the heat and simmer for 1½ hours or until the meat is tender. Sprinkle with mint or coriander and serve hot.
SERVES 4

Madrasi Kari
Madras Beef Curry

One of the hottest beef curries.

METRIC/IMPERIAL

100 g/4 oz ghee*
450 g/1 lb beef, cut into 2.5 cm/1 inch cubes
1 large onion, peeled and sliced
3 garlic cloves, peeled and sliced
1½ teaspoons coriander powder
2 teaspoons turmeric powder
1 teaspoon ground ginger
1 teaspoon cumin powder
2½ teaspoons chilli powder
2 teaspoons Garam Masala (see page 12)
1 teaspoon salt
1½ teaspoons freshly ground black pepper
200 ml/⅓ pint water

AMERICAN

½ cup ghee*
1 lb beef, cut into 1 inch cubes
1 large onion, peeled and sliced
3 garlic cloves, peeled and sliced
1½ teaspoons coriander powder
2 teaspoons turmeric powder
1 teaspoon ginger powder
1 teaspoon cumin powder
2½ teaspoons chili powder
2 teaspoons Garam Masala (see page 12)
1 teaspoon salt
1½ teaspoons freshly ground black pepper
1 cup water

METHOD

Melt the ghee in a heavy pan, add the beef and fry briskly until browned on all sides. Remove from the pan with a slotted spoon and set aside. Add the onion and garlic and fry gently until soft. Add the spices and seasonings and fry for a further 3 minutes, stirring constantly.

Return the beef to the pan and fry for a further 3 minutes, stirring to coat the beef with the spices. Stir in the water and bring to the boil, then lower the heat and simmer gently for 1½ hours or until the meat is tender. Serve hot.
SERVES 4

Calcutta Kari; Kofta Kari, served with Baigan Tamatar (see page 36) and Kesari Chawal (see page 45)

Bhuna Gosht
Dry Beef Curry

Bhuna is a system of cooking by frying. It can be used with meat and vegetables, although it is usual to pre-cook meat unless it is cut into small thin pieces. Usually *bhuna* dishes are dry with little sauce, and the skill in cooking them lies in not using water. However, if this proves too difficult and the meat shows signs of sticking, then you may cheat just a little and add water – as long as it is boiled off before serving.

METRIC/IMPERIAL

50 g/2 oz ghee*
450 g/1 lb beef steak, sliced into strips
1 small onion, peeled and sliced
2 garlic cloves, peeled and sliced
1 teaspoon chilli powder
1 teaspoon cumin powder
1 teaspoon Garam Masala (see page 12)
½ teaspoon freshly ground black pepper
1 red chilli, cored, seeded and sliced
½ teaspoon salt

AMERICAN

¼ cup ghee*
1 lb flank or round steak, sliced into strips
1 small onion, peeled and sliced
2 garlic cloves, peeled and sliced
1 teaspoon chili powder
1 teaspoon cumin powder
1 teaspoon Garam Masala (see page 12)
½ teaspoon freshly ground black pepper
1 red chili, cored, seeded and sliced
½ teaspoon salt

METHOD

Melt the ghee in a large frying pan (skillet) until smoking hot, add the beef and fry briskly for 30 seconds, turning the meat constantly to prevent sticking and burning. Remove the meat from the pan with a slotted spoon and set aside.

Add the onion and garlic to the pan and fry gently until soft. Stir in the spices and black pepper and fry for 3 minutes, stirring constantly. Return the meat to the pan, stir in the sliced chilli and salt and fry for a further 5 minutes or until the meat is tender. Serve hot, with rice and *Raeta* (see page 35).

SERVES 4

Pasanda
Spiced Beef in Yogurt

This is a fine northern dish. Usually beef is used, although lamb may be substituted.

METRIC/IMPERIAL

450 g/1 lb beef, thinly sliced
1 teaspoon salt
300 ml/½ pint natural yogurt
175 g/6 oz ghee*
1 large onion, peeled and sliced
3 garlic cloves, peeled and sliced
1½ teaspoons ground ginger
2 teaspoons coriander powder
2 teaspoons chilli powder
½ teaspoon cumin powder
1½ teaspoons turmeric powder
1 teaspoon Garam Masala (see page 12)

AMERICAN

1 lb beef, thinly sliced
1 teaspoon salt
1¼ cups unflavored yogurt
¾ cup ghee*
1 large onion, peeled and sliced
3 garlic cloves, peeled and sliced
1½ teaspoons ginger powder
2 teaspoons coriander powder
2 teaspoons chili powder
½ teaspoon cumin powder
1½ teaspoons turmeric powder
1 teaspoon Garam Masala (see page 12)

METHOD

Put the beef between 2 sheets of greaseproof (waxed) paper and tenderize with a mallet. Rub the beef with the salt, then put in a bowl and cover with the yogurt. Leave to marinate overnight.

Melt the ghee in a heavy pan, add the onion and garlic and fry gently until soft. Add the spices and fry for a further 3 minutes, stirring constantly.

Add the beef and marinade to the pan, stir well, then cover the pan with a tight-fitting lid and simmer for 1½ hours or until the meat is tender. Serve hot.

SERVES 4.

Mhaans Kari

Lamb Curry

In most parts of the Indian sub-continent, goat meat is eaten as much, if not more, than lamb and mutton. Certainly with most recipes the two are interchangeable. If you happen to come across a butcher selling goat meat, have no hesitation in using this recipe!

METRIC/IMPERIAL

100 g/4 oz ghee*
450 g/1 lb boned lamb shoulder or leg, cut into 2.5 cm/1 inch cubes
1 large onion, peeled and sliced
2 garlic cloves, peeled and sliced
2 teaspoons coriander powder
1 teaspoon turmeric powder
1 teaspoon cumin powder
½ teaspoon freshly ground black pepper
1 green chilli, chopped
½ teaspoon chilli powder
300 ml/½ pint water
1 teaspoon salt

AMERICAN

½ cup ghee*
1 lb boneless lamb shoulder or leg, cut into 1 inch cubes
1 large onion, peeled and sliced
2 garlic cloves, peeled and sliced
2 teaspoons coriander powder
1 teaspoon turmeric powder
1 teaspoon cumin powder
½ teaspoon freshly ground black pepper
1 green chili, chopped
½ teaspoon chili powder
1¼ cups water
1 teaspoon salt

METHOD

Melt the ghee in a heavy pan, add the lamb and fry briskly until browned on all sides. Remove from the pan with a slotted spoon, drain well and set aside.

Add the onion and garlic to the pan and fry gently until soft. Stir in the remaining ingredients except the water and salt and fry for a further 3 minutes, stirring constantly. Return the lamb to the pan, add the salt and water, then simmer for 45 minutes to 1 hour or until the meat is tender. Cover the pan if a curry with plenty of sauce is preferred; cook uncovered for a dry curry. Serve hot.
SERVES 4

Pasanda; Bhuna Gosht, served with Raeta (see page 35)

31

Roghan Gosht

Spiced Lamb with Yogurt

This dish from northern India brings out the best of the well-flavoured lamb that grazes on the temperate slopes there.

METRIC/IMPERIAL

450 g/1 lb boned lamb shoulder or leg,
  cut into 2.5 cm/1 inch cubes
juice of 1 lemon
2 teaspoons salt
200 ml/⅓ pint natural yogurt
175 g/6 oz ghee*
2 large onions, peeled and sliced
4 garlic cloves, peeled and sliced
1 teaspoon ground ginger
½ teaspoon chilli powder
1 teaspoon cumin powder
1 teaspoon coriander powder
½ teaspoon freshly ground black
  pepper
1 × 142 g/5 oz can tomato purée
200 ml/⅓ pint water

AMERICAN

1 lb boneless lamb shoulder or leg, cut
  into 1 inch cubes
juice of 1 lemon
2 teaspoons salt
1 cup unflavored yogurt
¾ cup ghee*
2 large onions, peeled and sliced
4 garlic cloves, peeled and sliced
1 teaspoon ginger powder
½ teaspoon chili powder
1 teaspoon cumin powder
1 teaspoon coriander powder
½ teaspoon freshly ground black
  pepper
½ cup tomato paste
1 cup water

METHOD

Put the lamb in a bowl and sprinkle with the lemon juice and salt. Add the yogurt and mix well, then cover and leave to marinate overnight.

Melt the ghee in a heavy pan, add the onions and garlic and fry gently until soft. Add the spices and seasoning and fry for a further 3 minutes, stirring constantly. Stir in the meat and marinade and fry for a further 10 minutes, stirring occasionally, then add the tomato purée (paste) and water.

Cover the pan with a tight-fitting lid and simmer for 45 minutes to 1 hour or until the meat is tender and the sauce is fairly thick. Boil off any excess liquid if necessary, then serve hot.
SERVES 4

Illustrated above: Cooking Tikka Kabab over a charcoal barbecue

Dopiazah

Spiced Lamb with Onions

Dopiazah is the term applied to a dish which contains double the normal amount of onions – if not more! *Doh* means two or twice, and *piazah* means onions. The main feature of the *dopiazah* is that half the onions are cooked with the meat; the other half are added at a later stage to give a contrast in texture.

METRIC/IMPERIAL

175 g/6 oz ghee*
1 kg/2 lb onions, peeled and sliced
2 teaspoons cumin powder
1 teaspoon fenugreek powder
1 tablespoon turmeric powder
2 teaspoons Garam Masala (see page
  12)
3 green chillis, chopped
450 g/1 lb boned lamb shoulder or leg,
  cut into 2.5 cm/1 inch cubes
300 ml/½ pint water

AMERICAN

¾ cup ghee*
2 lb onions, peeled and sliced
2 teaspoons cumin powder
1 teaspoon fenugreek powder
1 tablespoon turmeric powder
2 teaspoons Garam Masala (see page
  12)
3 green chilis, chopped
1 lb boneless lamb shoulder or leg, cut
  into 1 inch cubes
1¼ cups water

METHOD

Melt the ghee in a heavy pan, add the onions and fry gently until soft. Remove half the onions from the pan and set aside. Add the spices to the onions remaining in the pan and fry for 3 minutes, stirring constantly. Add the chillis, then the lamb, and fry until the lamb is browned on all sides.

Stir in the water and bring to the boil, then lower the heat and simmer for 45 minutes to 1 hour or until the meat is tender. Add the reserved onions and cook for a further 5 minutes until the curry is fairly dry. Serve hot.
SERVES 4

Tikka Kabab
Spiced Lamb Kebabs

A fine northern Indian delicacy, Tikka Kabab are to be found over charcoal barbecues at virtually every street corner. Ideally they should be cooked over a charcoal griddle, but satisfactory results can be obtained by grilling (broiling).

METRIC/IMPERIAL

450 g/1 lb boned lamb shoulder or leg, cut into 2.5 cm/1 inch cubes
juice of 1 lemon
150 ml/5 fl oz natural yogurt
4 small onions, peeled and quartered
3 garlic cloves, peeled and chopped
½ teaspoon turmeric powder
1 tablespoon vinegar
½ teaspoon salt
1 teaspoon freshly ground black pepper
1 green pepper, cored, seeded and cut into 2.5 cm/1 inch squares
1 lemon, quartered, to garnish

AMERICAN

1 lb boneless lamb shoulder or leg, cut into 1 inch cubes
juice of 1 lemon
⅔ cup unflavored yogurt
4 small onions, peeled and quartered
3 garlic cloves, peeled and chopped
½ teaspoon turmeric powder
1 tablespoon vinegar
½ teaspoon salt
1 teaspoon freshly ground black pepper
1 green pepper, cored, seeded and cut into 1 inch squares
1 lemon, quartered, to garnish

METHOD

Put the lamb in a bowl and sprinkle with the lemon juice. Put the yogurt, half the onion, the garlic, turmeric, vinegar and seasoning in an electric blender and work until the mixture is evenly blended. Pour over the lamb and stir well. Cover and leave to marinate overnight.

Thread the cubes of meat on kebab skewers, alternating with the green pepper and remaining onion quarters. Barbecue or grill (broil) the kebabs, turning frequently, until tender.

Serve hot, garnished with lemon quarters, and accompanied by *Naan* (see page 45) and salad.
SERVES 4

Padina Chatni
Mint Chutney

The word 'chutney' in India describes anything which brings out flavour and adds piquancy to food. Chutneys are usually freshly made and not bottled as in the West – bottled accompaniments are known as pickles in India. This chutney, made with mint, is very refreshing and goes well with most dishes.

METRIC/IMPERIAL

150 ml/5 fl oz natural yogurt
100 g/4 oz chopped mint
2 green chillis, finely chopped
juice of 1 lemon
½ teaspoon salt
pinch of chilli powder to garnish

AMERICAN

⅔ cup unflavored yogurt
3 cups chopped mint
2 green chilis, finely chopped
juice of 1 lemon
½ teaspoon salt
pinch of chili powder to garnish

METHOD

Put all the ingredients in a serving bowl and stir well. Chill in the refrigerator, then sprinkle with the chilli powder before serving.
SERVES 4

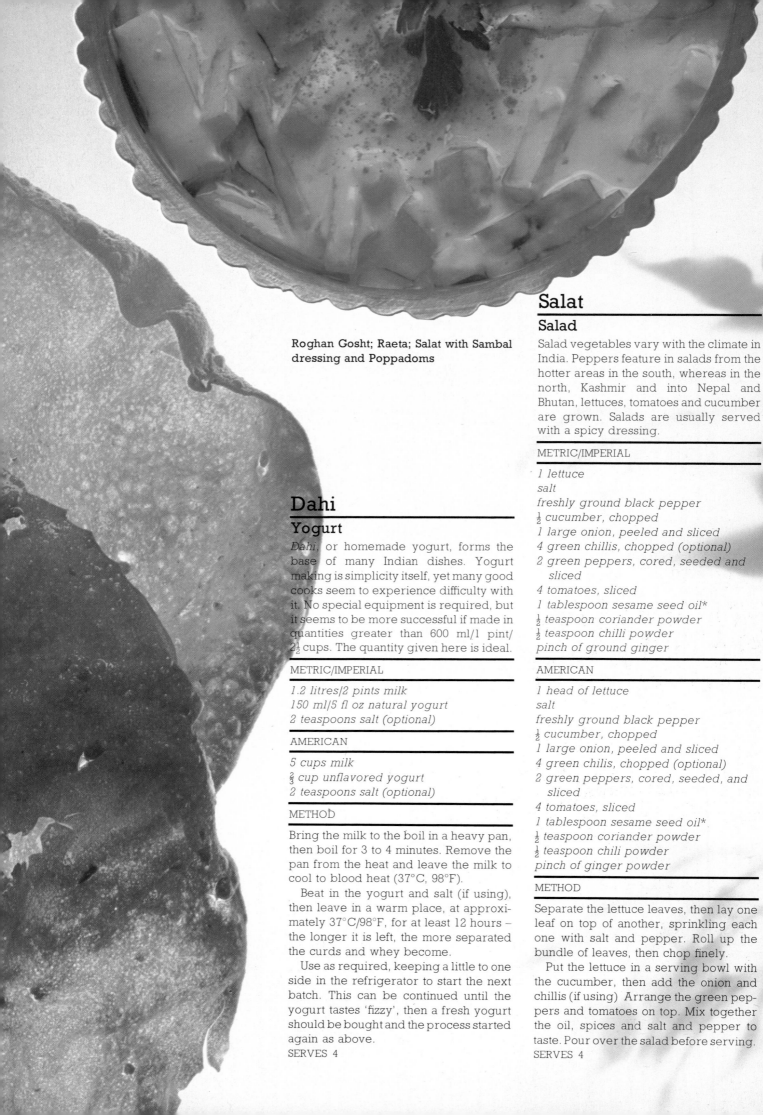

Roghan Gosht; Raeta; Salat with Sambal dressing and Poppadoms

Salat
Salad

Salad vegetables vary with the climate in India. Peppers feature in salads from the hotter areas in the south, whereas in the north, Kashmir and into Nepal and Bhutan, lettuces, tomatoes and cucumber are grown. Salads are usually served with a spicy dressing.

METRIC/IMPERIAL

1 lettuce
salt
freshly ground black pepper
½ cucumber, chopped
1 large onion, peeled and sliced
4 green chillis, chopped (optional)
2 green peppers, cored, seeded and sliced
4 tomatoes, sliced
1 tablespoon sesame seed oil*
½ teaspoon coriander powder
½ teaspoon chilli powder
pinch of ground ginger

AMERICAN

1 head of lettuce
salt
freshly ground black pepper
½ cucumber, chopped
1 large onion, peeled and sliced
4 green chilis, chopped (optional)
2 green peppers, cored, seeded, and sliced
4 tomatoes, sliced
1 tablespoon sesame seed oil*
½ teaspoon coriander powder
½ teaspoon chili powder
pinch of ginger powder

METHOD

Separate the lettuce leaves, then lay one leaf on top of another, sprinkling each one with salt and pepper. Roll up the bundle of leaves, then chop finely.

Put the lettuce in a serving bowl with the cucumber, then add the onion and chillis (if using) Arrange the green peppers and tomatoes on top. Mix together the oil, spices and salt and pepper to taste. Pour over the salad before serving.
SERVES 4

Dahi
Yogurt

Dahi, or homemade yogurt, forms the base of many Indian dishes. Yogurt making is simplicity itself, yet many good cooks seem to experience difficulty with it. No special equipment is required, but it seems to be more successful if made in quantities greater than 600 ml/1 pint/ 2½ cups. The quantity given here is ideal.

METRIC/IMPERIAL

1.2 litres/2 pints milk
150 ml/5 fl oz natural yogurt
2 teaspoons salt (optional)

AMERICAN

5 cups milk
⅔ cup unflavored yogurt
2 teaspoons salt (optional)

METHOD

Bring the milk to the boil in a heavy pan, then boil for 3 to 4 minutes. Remove the pan from the heat and leave the milk to cool to blood heat (37°C, 98°F).

Beat in the yogurt and salt (if using), then leave in a warm place, at approximately 37°C/98°F, for at least 12 hours – the longer it is left, the more separated the curds and whey become.

Use as required, keeping a little to one side in the refrigerator to start the next batch. This can be continued until the yogurt tastes 'fizzy', then a fresh yogurt should be bought and the process started again as above.
SERVES 4

Raeta
Yogurt with Cucumber

When Westerners have problems with Indian food because of its spicyness, this is invariably because they have never been offered Raeta as an accompaniment to their meal – this yogurt-based dish is the perfect antidote to stung palates! There is virtually no end to the combination of vegetables that can be blended with yogurt to make Raeta, but the following recipe is a good all-rounder.

METRIC/IMPERIAL

300 ml/½ pint natural yogurt
½ cucumber, cut into matchstick strips
1 small onion, peeled and chopped
1 small tomato, chopped (optional)
1 teaspoon salt
To garnish:
2 teaspoons chopped coriander
  leaves*
½ teaspoon chilli powder

AMERICAN

1¼ cups unflavored yogurt
½ cucumber, cut into matchstick strips
1 small onion, peeled and chopped
1 small tomato, chopped (optional)
1 teaspoon salt
To garnish:
2 teaspoons chopped coriander
  leaves*
½ teaspoon chili powder

METHOD

Put all the ingredients in a serving bowl and stir well to mix. Sprinkle with the coriander leaves and chilli powder, then chill in the refrigerator before serving.
SERVES 4

Sambal
Spiced Dressing

Sambal is typically southern Indian in origin, and is usually served as an accompaniment to a main dish. This recipe is for a basic sambal, which can be used on its own or with other ingredients added to it – finely shredded lettuce or cabbage, for example. If you add 2 tablespoons coconut milk* or fresh milk, this will make a sambal sauce which can be used to coat prawns (shrimp). Aloo Sambal is made by adding diced cooked potatoes to the basic sambal dressing.

METRIC/IMPERIAL

50 g/2 oz ghee*
1 large onion, peeled and chopped
2 garlic cloves, peeled and chopped
2 green chillis, chopped
1 teaspoon turmeric powder
½ teaspoon ground ginger
½ teaspoon cumin powder
½ teaspoon chilli powder

AMERICAN

¼ cup ghee*
1 large onion, peeled and chopped
2 garlic cloves, peeled and chopped
2 green chilis, chopped
1 teaspoon turmeric powder
½ teaspoon ginger powder
½ teaspoon cumin powder
½ teaspoon chili powder

METHOD

Melt the ghee in a frying pan (skillet), add the onion and garlic and fry gently until soft. Add the chillis and spices and fry for a further 3 minutes, stirring constantly. Use as required.
SERVES 4

Aloo Gobi

Spiced Potatoes and Cauliflower

Potatoes and cauliflowers are both available in India, although they tend to be found only in the more temperate climes. Aloo Gobi is a good example of the way in which Indian cuisine can adapt itself to utilize vegetables originally foreign to the area.

METRIC/IMPERIAL

175 g/6 oz ghee*
1 kg/2 lb potatoes, peeled and
    chopped into 2.5 cm/1 inch pieces
2 large onions, peeled and sliced
4 garlic cloves, peeled and sliced
2 teaspoons chilli powder
1 teaspoon turmeric powder
1 teaspoon coriander powder
2 teaspoons salt
½ teaspoon freshly ground black
    pepper
1.2 litres/2 pints water
450 g/1 lb cauliflower florets
2 teaspoons Garam Masala (see page
    12)

AMERICAN

¾ cup ghee*
2 lb potatoes, peeled and chopped into
    1 inch pieces
2 large onions, peeled and sliced
4 garlic cloves, peeled and sliced
2 teaspoons chili powder
1 teaspoon turmeric powder
1 teaspoon coriander powder
2 teaspoons salt
½ teaspoon freshly ground black
    pepper
5 cups water
8 large cauliflower florets
2 teaspoons Garam Masala (see page
    12)

METHOD

Melt the ghee in a heavy pan, add the potatoes and fry gently for exactly 1 minute. Remove from the pan with a slotted spoon and set aside.

Add the onions and garlic to the pan and fry gently until soft. Add the spices and seasonings, except the Garam Masala, and fry for a further 3 minutes, stirring constantly.

Return the potatoes to the pan, add the water and bring to the boil. Lower the heat and simmer for 10 minutes, then add the cauliflower. Simmer for a further 15 minutes until the vegetables are tender and the sauce is thick.

Increase the heat to boil off any excess liquid if necessary. Stir in the Garam Masala and serve hot.
SERVES 4

Baigan Tamatar

Spiced Aubergines (Eggplant) and Tomatoes

The aubergine (eggplant) is a popular vegetable in Indian cuisine; there is nothing finer than its shining, purple firmness at the peak of ripening. When making any aubergine (eggplant) dish, select the vegetables with care; reject any that are soft and past their best.

Baigan Tamatar goes well with any tandoori meal.

METRIC/IMPERIAL

175 g/6 oz ghee*
1 large onion, peeled and sliced
2 garlic cloves, peeled and sliced
1 teaspoon coriander powder
2.5 cm/1 inch piece of cinnamon stick
1 teaspoon chilli powder
1 teaspoon salt
1 teaspoon freshly ground black
    pepper
450 g/1 lb aubergines, chopped into
    2.5 cm/1 inch pieces
450 g/1 lb tomatoes, chopped into
    2.5 cm/1 inch pieces
3 tablespoons tomato purée
200 ml/⅓ pint water

AMERICAN

¾ cup ghee*
1 large onion, peeled and sliced
2 garlic cloves, peeled and sliced
1 teaspoon coriander powder
1 inch piece of cinnamon stick
1 teaspoon chili powder
1 teaspoon salt
1 teaspoon freshly ground black
    pepper
1 lb eggplant, chopped into 1 inch
    pieces
1 lb tomatoes, chopped into 1 inch
    pieces
3 tablespoons tomato paste
1 cup water

METHOD

Melt the ghee in a heavy pan, add the onion and garlic and fry gently until soft. Add the spices and seasonings and fry for 3 minutes, stirring constantly.

Add the aubergines (eggplant), tomatoes and tomato purée (paste) and toss gently to coat with the spice mixture.

Stir in the water and bring to the boil. Lower the heat and simmer for 25 to 30 minutes until the aubergines (eggplant) are tender and the sauce is quite thick. Increase the heat to boil off any excess liquid, if necessary. Serve hot.
SERVES 4

Baigan Tamatar; Aloo Gobi; Saag

Saag

Spinach

Spinach is a much-prized vegetable in India. As it is very delicate, both in structure and taste, a particularly gentle spicing is used. This recipe calls for frozen spinach; if using fresh spinach, double the quantity given here.

METRIC/IMPERIAL	AMERICAN	METHOD
50 g/2 oz ghee* 1 small onion, peeled and sliced 1 teaspoon Garam Masala (see page 12) 1 teaspoon salt 450 g/1 lb frozen whole leaf spinach	¼ cup ghee* 1 small onion, peeled and sliced 1 teaspoon Garam Masala (see page 12) 1 teaspoon salt 1 lb frozen whole leaf spinach	Melt the ghee in a heavy pan, add the onion and fry gently until soft. Add the Garam Masala and salt and fry for a further 3 minutes, stirring constantly. Add the frozen spinach and cook for about 5 minutes until defrosted, stirring constantly. Serve hot. SERVES 4

Matar Panir

Peas and Indian Cheese Curry

This is a basic recipe for a *panir* curry. The spices used are light so as not to mask the flavour of the cheese. Other vegetables can be used rather than peas and tomatoes, if liked.

METRIC/IMPERIAL

100 g/4 oz ghee*
450 g/1 lb Panir (see opposite page), cubed
1 onion, peeled and sliced
1 teaspoon ground ginger
½ teaspoon cumin powder
½ teaspoon chilli powder
½ teaspoon salt
450 g/1 lb frozen peas
2 tomatoes, chopped

AMERICAN

½ cup ghee*
1 lb Panir (see opposite page), cubed
1 onion, peeled and sliced
1 teaspoon ginger powder
½ teaspoon cumin powder
½ teaspoon chili powder
½ teaspoon salt
3 cups frozen peas
2 tomatoes, chopped

METHOD

Melt the ghee in a frying pan (skillet), add the panir and fry until brown. Remove from the pan with a slotted spoon, drain on kitchen paper towels and set aside.

Add the onion to the pan and fry gently until soft. Add the spices and salt and fry for a further 3 minutes, stirring constantly.

Add the peas and tomatoes and stir gently until the peas are coated with the spice mixture. Stir in the panir and heat through, taking care not to break up the cubes of cheese. Serve hot.
SERVES 4

Panir
Indian Curd Cheese

Cheese has never really had a following in the Indian sub-continent, and certainly no really distinctive varieties have developed, as in the West. However, panir – a simple curd cheese – is a well-established dish in its own right; it is also used in vegetable curries.

METRIC/IMPERIAL

1.2 litres/2 pints milk
250 ml/8 fl oz natural yogurt
2 teaspoons lemon juice
1½ teaspoons salt

AMERICAN

5 cups milk
1 cup unflavored yogurt
2 teaspoons lemon juice
1½ teaspoons salt

METHOD

Put the milk in a pan and bring to the boil. Remove from the heat, leave to cool to blood heat, then beat in the yogurt, lemon juice and salt. Leave in a warm place, at approximately 37°C/98°F, for 12 hours.

Strain the curds and whey through a piece of muslin (cheesecloth) placed over a bowl – draw up the corners of the muslin (cheesecloth) and allow the whey to drip through. Leave for 30 minutes, then squeeze out as much liquid as possible.

Shape the cloth into a rectangle around the cheese, then place under a heavy weight. Leave for 3 hours, then remove the weight and cloth and cut the panir into cubes. Serve raw, or use in vegetable curries.
MAKES ABOUT 450 g/1 lb

Bhindi Foogath
Braised Okra (Ladies' Fingers) with Chillis

Originally from southern India, a foogath is very similar to a *sambal* in that it is a savoury dish made from vegetables. The difference between the two is that a foogath is cooked and is often made with leftover cooked vegetables. Also, the flavour of ginger is predominant.

METRIC/IMPERIAL

50 g/2 oz ghee*
1 large onion, peeled and sliced
3 garlic cloves, peeled and sliced
2.5 cm/1 inch piece of fresh root
    ginger,* peeled and finely chopped
2 green chillis, finely chopped or
    minced
½ teaspoon chilli powder
450 g/1 lb bhindi, topped and tailed
200 ml/⅓ pint water
salt
2 teaspoons desiccated coconut

AMERICAN

¼ cup ghee*
1 large onion, peeled and sliced
3 garlic cloves, peeled and sliced
1 inch piece of fresh ginger root,*
    peeled and finely chopped
2 green chilis, finely chopped or
    ground
½ teaspoon chili powder
1 lb bhindi, topped and tailed
1 cup water
salt
2 teaspoons shredded coconut

METHOD

Melt the ghee in a heavy pan, add the onion, garlic, ginger, chillis and chilli powder. Fry gently for 5 minutes until soft, stirring occasionally.

Add the bhindi, water and salt to taste. Bring to the boil, then lower the heat, cover and simmer for 5 to 10 minutes until the bhindi are just tender, but still firm to the bite. Stir in the coconut and serve hot.
SERVES 4

Bhindi Bhaji
Spicy Fried Okra (Ladies' Fingers)

Okra (ladies' fingers) are grown throughout the Indian sub-continent. They are considered to be a delicacy and a worthy accompaniment to any meal. Canned okra (ladies' fingers) tends to be rather stringy and for most dishes, particularly this one, it is preferable to use the fresh vegetable.

METRIC/IMPERIAL

100 g/4 oz ghee*
1 large onion, peeled and sliced
2 garlic cloves, peeled and sliced
1 tablespoon coriander powder
1 teaspoon turmeric powder
½ teaspoon salt
½ teaspoon freshly ground black
    pepper
450 g/1 lb fresh bhindi, topped, tailed
    and cut into 1 cm/½ inch pieces
150 ml/¼ pint water
½ teaspoon Garam Masala (see page 12)

AMERICAN

½ cup ghee*
1 large onion, peeled and sliced
2 garlic cloves, peeled and sliced
1 tablespoon coriander powder
1 teaspoon turmeric powder
½ teaspoon salt
½ teaspoon freshly ground black
    pepper
1 lb fresh bhindi, topped, tailed and
    cut into ½ inch pieces
⅔ cup water
½ teaspoon Garam Masala (see page 12)

METHOD

Melt the ghee in a heavy pan, add the onion and garlic and fry gently until soft. Add the spices and seasonings, except the Garam Masala, and fry for a further 3 minutes, stirring constantly. Add the bhindi, then stir gently to coat with the spice mixture, taking care not to break them.

Stir in the water and bring to the boil. Lower the heat, cover and simmer for 5 to 10 minutes until the bhindi are just tender, but still firm to the bite. Stir in the Garam Masala and serve hot.
SERVES 4

Matar Panir;Bhindi Bhaji

Sabzi Pilau

Pilau

Savoury Rice

Pilau rice differs from *Biryani* in that the rice is sautéed in *ghee** with onion and garlic before boiling. Nowadays, the term *pilau* is often incorrectly applied to rice that has been simply boiled in stock instead of water. This recipe is for a traditional pilau.

During the initial frying, the rice must be stirred constantly to ensure that every grain is evenly saturated with *ghee**. The finished pilau should be perfectly dry, each grain of rice being separate and all liquid absorbed.

METRIC/IMPERIAL

450 g/1 lb rice
225 g/8 oz ghee*
50 g/2 oz blanched almonds (optional)
1 onion, peeled and sliced
2 garlic cloves, peeled and sliced
10 whole cloves
10 whole cardamoms
5 cm/2 inch piece of cinnamon stick
1 teaspoon salt
1.2 litres/2 pints boiling water

AMERICAN

2 cups rice
1 cup ghee*
½ cup blanched almonds (optional)
1 onion, peeled and sliced
2 garlic cloves, peeled and sliced
10 whole cloves
10 whole cardamoms
2 inch piece of cinnamon stick
1 teaspoon salt
5 cups boiling water

METHOD

Wash the rice thoroughly, then put in a bowl and cover with water. Leave to soak for 2 hours.

Melt the ghee in a heavy pan, add the almonds, if using, and fry until lightly coloured, stirring constantly. Remove from the pan with a slotted spoon, then leave to drain on kitchen paper towels. Add the onion and garlic to the pan and fry gently until soft.

Drain the rice, then add to the pan with the spices and salt. Fry for 3 minutes, stirring constantly until each grain of rice is coated with the mixture. Add the water and bring back to the boil, then lower the heat, cover and simmer for 20 to 25 minutes until the rice has absorbed all of the water. Stir in the almonds, if used, and serve hot.

SERVES 4

Kitcheri

Savoury Rice with Lentils

This is an Indian dish which has become truly international, and nowadays it is hard to think of *kitcheri* or kedgeree as anything other than a means of using up leftovers – usually fish. However, it is a highly regarded dish in India, particularly on the Keralonese coasts where the seafood kitcheris are famous. The following recipe is a basic kitcheri with lentils.

METRIC/IMPERIAL

350 g/12 oz rice
175 g/6 oz lentils
100 g/4 oz ghee*
1 large onion, peeled and sliced
2 garlic cloves, peeled and sliced
1½ teaspoons turmeric powder
10 whole cloves
6 whole cardamoms
7.5 cm/3 inch piece of cinnamon stick
salt
1 teaspoon freshly ground black pepper
900 ml/1½ pints boiling water

AMERICAN

1½ cups rice
¾ cup lentils
½ cup ghee*
1 large onion, peeled and sliced
2 garlic cloves, peeled and sliced
1½ teaspoons turmeric powder
10 whole cloves
6 whole cardamoms
3 inch piece of cinnamon stick
salt
1 teaspoon freshly ground black pepper
3¾ cups boiling water

METHOD

Wash the rice and lentils thoroughly, then put in a bowl and cover with water. Leave to soak for 2 hours.

Melt the ghee in a heavy pan, add the onion and garlic and fry gently until soft. Add the spices and seasonings and fry for a further 3 minutes, stirring constantly.

Drain the rice and lentils, add to the pan and toss for 5 minutes until every grain is coated. Add the water and bring to the boil. Lower the heat, cover with a tight-fitting lid and simmer for 20 to 30 minutes until the rice and lentils are cooked.

Remove the lid and boil off any excess liquid before serving, turning constantly to prevent sticking. Serve immediately. SERVES 4

Sabzi Pilau

Vegetable Pilau

In poorer areas, vegetables are often substituted for meat in traditional dishes, and for millions in the Indian sub-continent, Vegetable Pilau is very much the dominant 'special' rice dish. Other vegetables, such as potatoes and cauli-flower, may be added if liked.

METRIC/IMPERIAL

50 g/2 oz ghee*
1 large onion, peeled and sliced
2 garlic cloves, peeled and sliced
1 teaspoon chilli powder
½ teaspoon cumin seeds
2 teaspoons coriander powder
1 teaspoon salt
1 teaspoon crushed black peppercorns
100 g/4 oz carrots, peeled and diced
100 g/4 oz runner beans, trimmed and diced
100 g/4 oz turnips, peeled and diced
600 ml/1 pint water (approximately)
100 g/4 oz shelled or frozen peas
Pilau, made with 450 g/1 lb rice (see opposite page)

AMERICAN

¼ cup ghee*
1 large onion, peeled and sliced
2 garlic cloves, peeled and sliced
1 teaspoon chili powder
½ teaspoon cumin seeds
2 teaspoons coriander powder
1 teaspoon salt
1 teaspoon crushed black peppercorns
¾ cup peeled and diced carrots
½ cup trimmed and diced string beans
⅔ cup peeled and diced turnip
2½ cups water (approximately)
¾ cup shelled or frozen peas
Pilau, made with 2 cups rice (see opposite page)

METHOD

Melt the ghee in a heavy pan, add the onion and garlic and fry gently until soft. Add the spices and seasonings and fry for a further 3 minutes, stirring constantly. Add the vegetables, except the peas, and stir until evenly coated with the spice mixture.

Stir in just enough water to cover the vegetables and bring to the boil. Lower the heat and simmer for 10 to 15 minutes until the vegetables are just tender and the sauce is thick but not dry, adding the peas for the last 5 minutes. Add more water during cooking if necessary.

Divide the curry in two. Fold one half gently into the hot pilau, then pile into a warmed serving dish. Pour the remaining curry over and serve immediately.

SERVES 4

Tarka Dal
Spiced Lentil Purée

Dal* is the collective name applied to a variety of pulses which form the staple diet for millions of people in the Indian sub-continent. Many are vegetarians, and these pulses – with a high vitamin content – are an important part of their daily food intake. The most common *dal** in the Western world is *masoor* or lentils, although many other varieties are available in Indian food shops. Be careful when making the *tarka* – sesame seed oil* reaches a higher temperature than most other oils.

METRIC/IMPERIAL	AMERICAN
2 teaspoons coriander powder	2 teaspoons coriander powder
1 teaspoon turmeric powder	1 teaspoon turmeric powder
1 teaspoon cumin powder	1 teaspoon cumin powder
½ teaspoon chilli powder	½ teaspoon chili powder
1 teaspoon salt	1 teaspoon salt
1 teaspoon freshly ground black pepper	1 teaspoon freshly ground black pepper
1 tablespoon vinegar	1 tablespoon vinegar
225 g/8 oz lentils	1 cup lentils
50 g/2 oz ghee*	¼ cup ghee*
1 large onion, peeled and sliced	1 large onion, peeled and sliced
2 garlic cloves, peeled and sliced	2 garlic cloves, peeled and sliced
600 ml/ 1 pint water (approximately)	2½ cups water (approximately)
Tarka:	**Tarka:**
1 tablespoon sesame seed oil*	1 tablespoon sesame seed oil*
1 garlic clove, peeled and sliced	1 garlic clove, peeled and sliced
1 green chilli, sliced	1 green chili, sliced
1 teaspoon coriander seeds	1 teaspoon coriander seeds

METHOD

Mix the spices and seasonings to a paste with the vinegar. Wash the lentils thoroughly and drain. Melt the ghee in a heavy pan, add the onion and garlic and fry gently until soft. Add the spice paste and fry for 3 minutes, stirring. Add the lentils and cook, stirring, for 1 minute.

Stir in the water and bring to the boil. Lower the heat and simmer for 10 to 15 minutes until a yellow broth is obtained, adding more water if necessary.

To make the tarka: Heat the oil in a small frying pan (skillet) until on the point of smoking, then immediately add the remaining ingredients. Fry until the garlic has turned black, pour into the hot dal and serve immediately.

SERVES 4

Biryani
Savoury Rice with Meat

In India, biryanis often steam for hours over the embers of a charcoal fire, although this is usually more for convenience than necessity, and the intrinsic flavour of the dish is the same when cooked by the following method.

The Mughal emperors demanded very high standards in all aspects of their cuisine, and such lowly dishes as rice were not exempt. Biryani was perfected as an attempt to raise the humble rice grain to a higher culinary status – and make it the king of rice dishes fit for kings!

METRIC/IMPERIAL

350 g/12 oz rice
750 ml/1¼ pints water
2 teaspoons salt
450 ml/¾ pint Curry Sauce (see page 13)
350 g/12 oz cooked meat (beef, chicken, lamb), cut into 2.5 cm/1 inch cubes
1½ teaspoons turmeric powder
½ teaspoon coriander powder

To garnish:
1 green or red pepper, cored, seeded and cut into rings
2 hard-boiled eggs, sliced
2–3 firm tomatoes, sliced
coriander leaves* (optional)
varak,* finely beaten (optional)

AMERICAN

1½ cups rice
3 cups water
2 teaspoons salt
2 cups Curry Sauce (see page 13)
¾ lb cooked meat (beef, chicken, lamb), cut into 1 inch cubes
1½ teaspoons turmeric powder
½ teaspoon coriander powder

To garnish:
1 green or red pepper, cored, seeded and cut into rings
1–2 hard-cooked eggs, sliced
2–3 firm tomatoes, sliced
coriander leaves* (optional)
varak,* finely beaten, (optional)

METHOD

Wash the rice thoroughly. Bring the water to the boil in a large pan, add the rice and salt and bring back to the boil. Simmer for exactly 10 minutes, then drain off the excess water and set the rice aside.

Put the curry sauce in a pan with the cooked meat and heat until bubbling. Add the turmeric and coriander and cook over high heat for 2 minutes, stirring constantly. Add the rice and stir thoroughly and gently until the rice has absorbed the colour of the turmeric evenly. Cover the pan, lower the heat and cook gently until the rice is completely cooked.

Transfer the biryani to a warmed serving platter. Garnish with the pepper rings, egg and tomato slices. Top with coriander leaves and sprinkle with varak, if liked. Serve immediately.

SERVES 4

Biryani

Chawal
Plain Rice

The successful cooking of rice is crucial to mastering the art of Indian cuisine. The best rice is undoubtedly *basmati*, although patna comes a close second. There are almost as many methods of cooking rice as there are varieties. One of the most important points to remember is that rice must be thoroughly washed under cold running water before cooking; this prevents the grains of rice from sticking together during cooking.

METRIC/IMPERIAL

225 g/8 oz rice
450 ml/¾ pint boiling water
pinch of salt
coriander leaves and varak* to garnish (optional)

AMERICAN

1 cup rice
2 cups boiling water
pinch of salt
coriander leaves and varak* to garnish (optional)

METHOD

Wash the rice thoroughly to remove rice dust and other impurities. Bring the water to the boil in a large pan, then add the salt and rice. Bring back to the boil, then lower the heat and simmer for 15 to 20 minutes until the rice is *al dente* – tender but firm to the bite. Transfer the rice to a casserole, draining off any excess water; some varieties of rice will absorb more water than others. Cover with a moist cloth or kitchen paper towels, then cover the casserole with a tight-fitting lid. Bake in a preheated hot oven (200°C/400°F, Gas Mark 6) for about 30 minutes. Serve hot, plain or garnished with coriander leaves and varak.
SERVES 4

Chappatti
Unleavened Bread

Traditionally, chappattis are cooked on a convex griddle known as a *tawa*. If this is not available, use an upturned cast-iron frying pan (skillet).

METRIC/IMPERIAL

225 g/8 oz ata*
½ teaspoon salt
200 ml/⅓ pint water (approximately)

AMERICAN

2 cups ata*
½ teaspoon salt
1 cup water (approximately)

METHOD

Sift the flour and salt into a bowl, then add the water gradually and mix to a firm dough. Turn onto a lightly floured surface and knead well until smooth and elastic. Break the dough into 8 to 10 pieces, then form into balls. Roll out on a lightly floured surface as thinly as possible; the dough must be less than 3 mm/⅛ inch thick.

Dust the upturned frying pan (skillet) lightly with flour and place over high heat. Put a chappatti in the pan and cook for 3 to 4 minutes until blisters begin to appear. Turn the chappatti over and cook the other side for 3 to 4 minutes.

Remove the chappatti from the pan with tongs, then place directly on the heat and cook for a few seconds until black blisters form and the chappatti swells up. Keep hot in the oven or under the grill (broiler) while cooking the remainder. Serve hot, as soon as possible after cooking.
MAKES 8 to 10

Tarka Dal (see page 42); Chawal; Naan

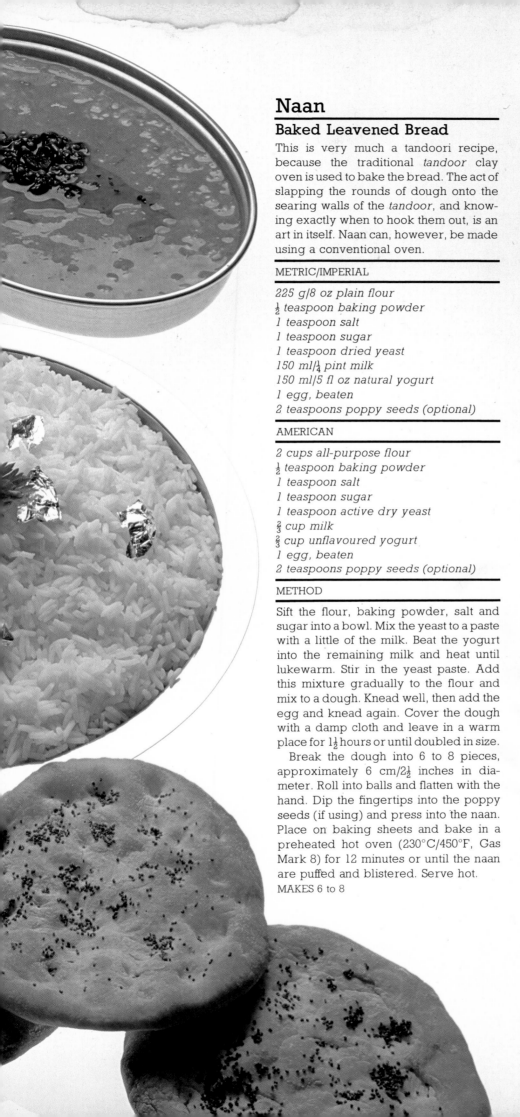

Naan
Baked Leavened Bread

This is very much a tandoori recipe, because the traditional *tandoor* clay oven is used to bake the bread. The act of slapping the rounds of dough onto the searing walls of the *tandoor*, and knowing exactly when to hook them out, is an art in itself. Naan can, however, be made using a conventional oven.

METRIC/IMPERIAL

225 g/8 oz plain flour
½ teaspoon baking powder
1 teaspoon salt
1 teaspoon sugar
1 teaspoon dried yeast
150 ml/¼ pint milk
150 ml/5 fl oz natural yogurt
1 egg, beaten
2 teaspoons poppy seeds (optional)

AMERICAN

2 cups all-purpose flour
½ teaspoon baking powder
1 teaspoon salt
1 teaspoon sugar
1 teaspoon active dry yeast
⅔ cup milk
⅔ cup unflavoured yogurt
1 egg, beaten
2 teaspoons poppy seeds (optional)

METHOD

Sift the flour, baking powder, salt and sugar into a bowl. Mix the yeast to a paste with a little of the milk. Beat the yogurt into the remaining milk and heat until lukewarm. Stir in the yeast paste. Add this mixture gradually to the flour and mix to a dough. Knead well, then add the egg and knead again. Cover the dough with a damp cloth and leave in a warm place for 1½ hours or until doubled in size.

Break the dough into 6 to 8 pieces, approximately 6 cm/2½ inches in diameter. Roll into balls and flatten with the hand. Dip the fingertips into the poppy seeds (if using) and press into the naan. Place on baking sheets and bake in a preheated hot oven (230°C/450°F, Gas Mark 8) for 12 minutes or until the naan are puffed and blistered. Serve hot.
MAKES 6 to 8

Kesari Chawal
Saffron Rice

Saffron is the most delicate of condiments, unique if only for the fact that, although used in very small quantities, its power is unrivalled. Saffron threads come from the stamens of a type of crocus which abounds on the temperate slopes of the Himalayan foothills. It is common throughout northern India, particularly in Nepal and Bhutan where it is used to colour the robes of the Buddhist priests a deep yellow.

It takes 75,000 crocus blooms to make 450 g/1 lb saffron, but then this delicate spice can colour several thousand times its own weight. Today, synthetic food colouring is often used in place of saffron, but there is no substitute for the flavour of the real spice.

METRIC/IMPERIAL

175 g/6 oz ghee*
2 large onions, peeled and sliced
350 g/12 oz rice
1 teaspoon whole cloves
4 whole cardamoms
1 teaspoon salt
1 teaspoon freshly ground black pepper
½ teaspoon saffron threads, soaked in 1 tablespoon boiling water for 30 minutes
750 ml/1¾ pints boiling water
varak* to garnish (optional)

AMERICAN

¾ cup ghee*
2 large onions, peeled and sliced
1½ cups rice
1 teaspoon whole cloves
4 whole cardamoms
1 teaspoon salt
1 teaspoon freshly ground black pepper
½ teaspoon saffron threads, soaked in 1 tablespoon boiling water for 30 minutes
3 cups water
varak* to garnish (optional)

METHOD

Melt the ghee in a heavy pan, add the onions and fry gently until soft.

Wash the rice thoroughly, then drain. Add to the pan with the spices and seasonings, then fry for 3 minutes, stirring frequently.

Add the saffron with its liquid and stir well, then add the water and bring to the boil. Lower the heat and simmer for 15 to 20 minutes until cooked. Drain.

Transfer to a warmed serving dish and garnish with varak, if liked. Serve hot.
SERVES 4

Besani Roti

Fried Besan Bread

This is a kind of fried bread which has an irresistible taste. *Besan** is a flour made from chick peas (garbanzos) and its properties are therefore somewhat different from ordinary wheat flour. It is more aromatic and less starchy. It is also quite difficult to knead into a smooth dough, but this is essential for a good result.

METRIC/IMPERIAL

225 g/8 oz besan*
1 teaspoon salt
200 ml/⅓ pint water
100 g/4 oz ghee*
175 g/6 oz butter, melted

AMERICAN

2 cups besan*
1 teaspoon salt
1 cup water
½ cup ghee*
¾ cup melted butter

METHOD

Sift the flour into a bowl, rubbing the lumps through the sieve (strainer) with the back of a spoon. Stir in the salt. Add the water gradually and mix to a stiff dough, then knead in the ghee and work until smooth.

Break the dough into 4 to 6 pieces, approximately 7.5 cm/3 inches in diameter, then form into balls. Roll out on a lightly floured surface to a 5 mm/¼ inch thickness.

Spread a little melted butter over the base of a frying pan (skillet), then cook the roti one at a time over low heat for about 3 minutes on each side. Keep hot in the oven while cooking the remainder. Serve hot, brushed with the remaining melted butter.
MAKES 4 to 6

Paratha

Flaky Wholewheat Bread

A paratha is essentially a fried *chappatti*. A good paratha depends on the layering of fat in the dough. Some Indian cooks prefer to combine the fat in the dough-making process but, although this is easier, the final result is not so good.

Parathas are very satisfying, so allow no more than 1½ per person.

METRIC/IMPERIAL

225 g/8 oz ata*
½ teaspoon salt
200 ml/⅓ pint water
100 g/4 oz ghee* or butter, melted

AMERICAN

2 cups ata*
½ teaspoon salt
1 cup water
½ cup melted ghee* or butter

Prepare the dough as for Chappattis (see page 45). Break the dough into 4 to 6 pieces and roll into balls, approximately 7.5 cm/3 inches, in diameter. Roll each out on a lightly floured surface to a 3 mm/⅛ inch thickness. Brush with melted ghee or butter, then roll up from one side and reform into a ball. Repeat this rolling process 5 times, then roll out to a 5 mm/¼ inch thickness.

Warm a lightly greased frying pan (skillet) over high heat, place a paratha in the pan and fry over moderate heat for about 1 to 1½ minutes on each side until lightly browned. Keep hot in the oven or under the grill (broiler) while frying the remainder. Serve hot, as soon as possible after cooking.

MAKES 4 to 6

Puri

Deep-Fried Wholewheat Bread

A traditional Indian breakfast will often include puris; they are eaten simply – with plenty of chutney. Many people send to the bazaar for them, rather than cook them at home, as they are more easily prepared in bulk. As with all Indian breads, the secret is to serve them hot.

METRIC/IMPERIAL

175 g/6 oz ata*
½ teaspoon salt
150 ml/¼ pint water
50 g/2 oz ghee* or butter, melted
vegetable oil for deep-frying

AMERICAN

1½ cups ata*
½ teaspoon salt
⅔ cup water
¼ cup melted ghee* or butter
vegetable oil for deep-frying

METHOD

Sift the flour and salt into a bowl, then add the water gradually to make a firm dough. Add the ghee or butter, kneading it in well, then leave to rest for 20 minutes.

Break the dough into 8 to 10 pieces, approximately 2.5 cm/1 inch in diameter, then form into balls. Roll out on a lightly floured surface into rounds, just less than 3 mm/⅛ inch thick.

Heat the oil in a pan until moderately hot. Deep-fry the puris, one at a time, for about 1½ minutes until they puff up and float to the surface, spooning the oil over them as they fry. Remove from the pan, drain and keep hot in the oven while deep-frying the remaining puris. Serve hot.

MAKES 8 to 10

Illustrated above: Preparing Puris, Besani Roti and Parathas

Sewaiian
Vermicelli and Nut Dessert

There are a number of variations of this dish, some using large quantities of milk and cream. This is a very basic recipe, which can be made richer by adding cream as the dish is cooling.

METRIC/IMPERIAL

225 g/8 oz vermicelli
75 g/3 oz ghee*
1 tablespoon sultanas
1 tablespoon slivered almonds
1 tablespoon pistachio nuts
1 tablespoon rose water
To finish:
600 ml/1 pint cream (optional)
2 tablespoons desiccated coconut
caster sugar for sprinkling (optional)
varak,* finely beaten

AMERICAN

½ lb vermicelli
⅓ cup ghee*
1 tablespoon seedless white raisins
1 tablespoon slivered almonds
1 tablespoon pistachios
1 tablespoon rose water
To finish:
2½ cups cream (optional)
2 tablespoons shredded coconut
sugar for sprinkling (optional)
varak,* finely beaten

METHOD

Put the vermicelli in a pan and cover with water. Bring to the boil, then lower the heat and simmer for about 10 minutes until the vermicelli softens and sinks to the bottom of the pan.

Drain off enough water to leave the vermicelli just covered, then add the ghee and bring to the boil. Lower the heat, cover the pan and simmer for a further 10 minutes until thoroughly cooked; do not stir the vermicelli or it will break.

Fold in the sultanas (seedless white raisins) and nuts, taking care not to break the vermicelli. Add the rose water, then transfer the mixture to a serving dish. Pour over the cream, if using. Sprinkle with the coconut and sugar, if using. Serve hot or cold, decorated with varak.
SERVES 4

Halwa
Spiced Semolina Dessert

There are as many halwas in India as there are cities, and each centre of population guards the reputation of its sweet-meat. Often halwa is used as a kind of culinary envoy – being sent all over the world. It is well worth making at home, although it is said that the art of the *halwai* (halwa maker) is inherited and cannot be learnt!

METRIC/IMPERIAL

225 g/8 oz semolina
4 tablespoons desiccated coconut
450 g/1 lb sugar
1 tablespoon poppy seeds
seeds of 6 cardamoms
600 ml/1 pint water
100 g/4 oz ghee,* melted

Sewaiian; Kulfi; Chaat; Halwa

AMERICAN

1⅓ cups semolina flour
¼ cup shredded coconut
2 cups sugar
1 tablespoon poppy seeds
seeds of 6 cardamoms
2½ cups water
½ cup melted ghee*

METHOD

Put the semolina in a heavy pan with the coconut, sugar, poppy and cardamom seeds. Mix well then stir in the water. Bring to the boil, stirring, then lower the heat and simmer for at least 1 hour until every ingredient is soft, stirring frequently. Add the ghee gradually and mix well.

Transfer the mixture to a shallow tray and spread evenly. Leave to cool, then cut into triangles or diamond shapes. Store in an airtight container in a cool place.
SERVES 4

Chaat
Spiced Fruit Salad

Chaat is served either as an appetizer or as an accompaniment to a main course. In the central and northern parts of India, *chaat* houses abound, where for a few *annas*, this chilled spiced dessert can be taken with a little tea. There is no limit to the variety of fruit that can be used in chaat, but this recipe uses fruit which is easily obtainable in the West.

METRIC/IMPERIAL

2 oranges
2 bananas
2 pears
1 apple
2 guavas (optional)
juice of 1 lemon
2 teaspoons chilli powder
1 teaspoon ground ginger
1 teaspoon Garam Masala (see page 12)
1 teaspoon salt
½ teaspoon freshly ground black pepper
varak,* finely beaten, to decorate (optional)

AMERICAN

2 oranges
2 bananas
2 pears
1 apple
2 guavas (optional)
juice of 1 lemon
2 teaspoons chili powder
1 teaspoon ginger powder
1 teaspoon Garam Masala (see page 12)
1 teaspoon salt
½ teaspoon freshly ground black pepper
varak,* finely beaten, to decorate (optional)

METHOD

Peel the oranges and bananas and chop roughly. Core the pears and apple and chop roughly with the guavas, if using. (Do not discard the guava seeds.)

Put the fruit in a bowl and sprinkle with the lemon juice. Mix together the spices and seasonings, sprinkle over the fruit, then toss lightly until each piece of fruit is coated. Chill in the refrigerator for 2 hours. Serve decorated with varak, if liked.
SERVES 4

Kulfi
Ice Cream with Pistachios and Almonds

For centuries, ice cream has been made and sold in the streets of every major city in India. Traditionally, it is frozen in metal cones immersed in a freezing mixture of chopped ice and salt, but it can be frozen in containers used for ordinary ice cream.

METRIC/IMPERIAL

900 ml/1½ pints milk
50 g/2 oz rice flour*
300 ml/½ pint single cream or evaporated milk
100 g/4 oz sugar
1 tablespoon chopped pistachio nuts
1 tablespoon chopped blanched almonds
green food colouring (optional)
pistachio nuts and varak* to decorate (optional)

AMERICAN

3¾ cups milk
½ cup rice flour*
1¼ cups light cream or evaporated milk
½ cup sugar
1 tablespoon chopped pistachios
1 tablespoon chopped blanched almonds
green food color (optional)
pistachio nuts and varak* to decorate (optional)

METHOD

Bring the milk to the boil in a pan, then simmer until reduced to two thirds of its original volume. Stir in the rice flour gradually, then the cream or evaporated milk. Bring to the boil again, then lower the heat and simmer for a further 15 minutes. Add the sugar, stirring well to dissolve.

Leave to cool, then stir in the nuts and food colouring, if using. Transfer the mixture to suitable freezing containers and freeze until partially frozen. Beat vigorously to break down the ice crystals, then freeze until firm. Serve decorated with pistachios and varak, if liked.
SERVES 4

Rasgullah
Cream Cheese Balls in Syrup

Rasgullah is similar to Gulab Jamun, but it is made with *Panir* (Indian curd cheese) rather than ground almonds.

METRIC/IMPERIAL

Panir made with 600 ml/1 pint milk (see page 39)
75 g/3 oz blanched almonds, chopped
100 g/4 oz semolina
Syrup:
900 ml/1½ pints water
1 kg/2 lb sugar
pinch of cream of tartar
½ teaspoon rose water

AMERICAN

Panir made with 2½ cups milk (see page 39)
¾ cup chopped almonds
⅔ cup semolina flour
Syrup:
3¾ cups water
4 cups sugar
pinch of cream of tartar
½ teaspoon rose water

METHOD

Stir the panir to a smooth paste, then add the almonds and semolina and mix until smooth. Break the dough into 12 to 15 pieces, about the size of walnuts, then shape into balls.

To make the syrup: Put all the ingredients, except the rose water, in a heavy pan and heat gently until the sugar has dissolved, stirring occasionally. Bring to the boil, add the balls of dough, then lower the heat and simmer very gently for 2 hours. Stir in the rose water, then serve hot or cold.
MAKES 12 to 15

Gajjar Kheer
Carrot Pudding

Carrots are not the usual kind of ingredient for a sweet pudding, but in this dish they are used with great effect. It is very rich and sweet, and few people will have room for a second helping!

METRIC/IMPERIAL

450 g/1 lb carrots, peeled and grated
225 g/8 oz sugar
1.5 litres/2½ pints milk
6 whole cardamoms
1 tablespoon sultanas
1 tablespoon slivered almonds

AMERICAN

1 lb carrots, peeled and grated
1 cup sugar
6¼ cups milk
6 whole cardamoms
1 tablespoon seedless white raisins
1 tablespoon slivered almonds

METHOD

Put the carrots in a bowl and sprinkle with the sugar. Set aside.

Put the milk in a pan with the cardamoms. Bring to the boil and boil steadily for 45 minutes or until the milk is reduced by half. Add the carrots, then simmer until the mixture thickens.

Remove the pan from the heat, leave to cool slightly, then stir in the sultanas (seedless white raisins) and almonds. Serve hot or cold.
SERVES 4

Jallebi
Doughnut Spirals in Syrup

These pretzel-like sweets are a joy if eaten fresh and warm. In Indian cities they are sold at open stalls where, by the light of a hissing Petromax lamp, the Jallebi are deep-fried especially for you.

METRIC/IMPERIAL

Batter:
275 g/10 oz plain flour
25 g/1 oz rice flour*
pinch of baking powder
½ teaspoon salt
400 ml/⅔ pint water
vegetable oil for deep-frying
Syrup:
900 ml/1½ pints water
1 kg/2 lb sugar
pinch of cream of tartar
½ teaspoon rose water
½ teaspoon yellow or red food colouring (optional)

AMERICAN

Batter:
2½ cups all-purpose flour
¼ cup rice flour*
pinch of baking powder
½ teaspoon salt
1¾ cups water
vegetable oil for deep-frying
Syrup:
3¾ cups water
4 cups sugar
pinch of cream of tartar
½ teaspoon rose water
½ teaspoon yellow or red food color (optional)

METHOD

Sift the flours, baking powder and salt into a bowl. Add the water gradually and beat to a smooth batter. Cover and leave in the refrigerator overnight.

The next day, make the syrup: Put the water, sugar and cream of tartar in a heavy pan and heat gently until the sugar has dissolved, stirring occasionally.

Gulab Jamun
Almond Balls in Syrup

This is the name given to a classic sweet in Indian cuisine. Essentially, it is dumplings infused with a rose-flavoured syrup.

METRIC/IMPERIAL

250 g/8 oz plain flour
250 g/8 oz ground almonds
100 g/4 oz butter
1 teaspoon baking powder
150 ml/¼ pint natural yogurt
vegetable oil for deep-frying
Syrup:
900 ml/1½ pints water
1 kg/2 lb sugar
pinch of cream of tartar
5 whole cloves
5 whole cardamoms
½ teaspoon rose water

AMERICAN

2 cups all-purpose flour
2 cups ground almonds
½ cup butter
1 teaspoon baking powder
⅔ cup unflavored yogurt
vegetable oil for deep-frying
Syrup:
3¾ cups water
4 cups sugar
pinch of cream of tartar
5 whole cloves
5 whole cardamoms
½ teaspoon rose water

METHOD

Sift the flour and almonds into a bowl, then rub in the butter. Stir in the baking powder, then add the yogurt gradually and mix to a firm dough. Cover and leave to stand for 2 hours.

Meanwhile, make the syrup: Put all the ingredients, except the rose water, in a heavy pan and heat gently until the sugar has dissolved, stirring occasionally. Bring to just below boiling point, then remove from the heat and stir in the rose water.

Break the dough into 20 to 25 pieces, approximately 2.5 cm/1 inch in diameter, then roll into balls. Heat the oil in a deep-fat fryer or deep heavy-based frying pan, then deep-fry the balls until they turn a rich golden brown. Remove from the pan with a slotted spoon and drain on kitchen paper towels. Immerse the balls in the syrup while still warm. Serve hot or cold.
MAKES 20 to 25

Bring to just below boiling point, then remove from the heat and stir in the rose water and food colouring, if using. Leave to cool.

Heat the oil in a deep-fat fryer or deep heavy-based frying pan until a little of the batter, dropped into the hot oil, sizzles and turns crisp. Put the batter into a piping bag, fitted with a 2.5 cm/1 inch plain nozzle, and pipe spirals, about 10 cm/4 inches in diameter, into the hot oil. Deep-fry for about 3 minutes until crisp, then remove from the pan with a slotted spoon and drain on kitchen paper towels. Immerse the jallebi in the syrup for 30 seconds while still warm, then serve hot or cold.
SERVES 4

Rasgullah; Jallebi; Gajjar Kheer

Kesar Pilau
Sweet Rice

This dish can be made richer by adding more fruit or nuts, or both. It is traditionally served on special feast days in India.

METRIC/IMPERIAL

450 g/1 lb rice
350 g/12 oz ghee*
175 g/6 oz sultanas
100 g/4 oz pistachio nuts
100 g/4 oz blanched almonds
10 whole cloves
10 whole cardamoms
2.5 cm/1 inch piece of cinnamon stick
1 teaspoon ground allspice
1 teaspoon saffron threads, soaked in
  1 tablespoon boiling water for 30
  minutes
900 ml/1½ pints boiling water
100 g/4 oz sugar
varak* to decorate

AMERICAN

2 cups rice
1½ cups ghee*
1 cup seedless white raisins
1 cup pistachios
1 cup blanched almonds
10 whole cloves
10 whole cardamoms
1 inch piece of cinnamon stick
1 teaspoon ground allspice
1 teaspoon saffron threads, soaked in
  1 tablespoon boiling water for 30
  minutes
3¾ cups boiling water
½ cup sugar
varak* to decorate

METHOD

Wash the rice thoroughly, then put in a bowl and cover with cold water. Leave to soak for 2 hours.

Melt 100 g/4 oz/½ cup ghee in a pan, add the sultanas (seedless white raisins) and nuts and fry gently for 3 minutes. Remove from the pan with a slotted spoon and set aside.

Melt the remaining ghee in the pan. Add the cloves, cardamoms, cinnamon and allspice and fry gently for 5 minutes, stirring frequently. Drain the rice, add to the spice mixture and mix well. Stir in the saffron with its liquid, then the boiling water.

Cover the pan and simmer for 20 to 25 minutes until the rice is tender and has absorbed the liquid. Drain off any excess liquid if necessary, then add the sugar and the fried sultanas (seedless white raisins) and nuts. Serve hot or cold, decorated with varak.
SERVES 4

Kheer
Creamed Rice Pudding

At any Muslim festival – such as *Id-ul-Fitr*, which is held to celebrate the end of a month of fasting – certain sweet dishes prevail. Muslims wear their best clothes and visit friends, where they will be invited to take tea and either of the traditional sweet dishes – *Sewaiian* or kheer.

Kheer is based on rice flour,* which is not always easily obtainable; it can however be made at home, by simply grinding rice in a coffee mill, electric blender or by using a pestle and mortar.

METRIC/IMPERIAL

600 ml/1 pint milk
100 g/4 oz sugar
50 g/2 oz rice flour*
2 teaspoons chopped pistachio nuts
2 teaspoons blanched slivered
  almonds
½ teaspoon rose water

AMERICAN

2½ cups milk
½ cup sugar
½ cup rice flour*
2 teaspoons chopped pistachios
2 teaspoons blanched slivered
  almonds
½ teaspoon rose water

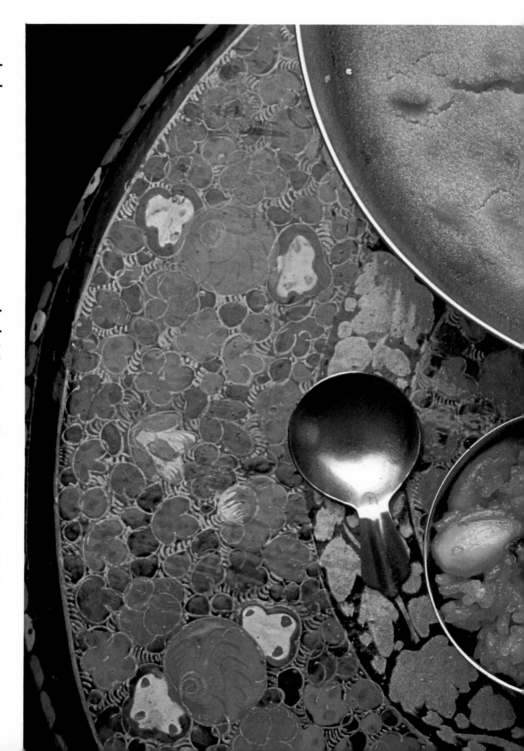

METHOD

Put the milk in a pan and bring to the boil. Stir in the sugar, then sprinkle in the rice flour, stirring constantly. Add the nuts and cook until the mixture begins to thicken, stirring constantly. Remove the pan from the heat and stir in the rose water. Serve cold.
SERVES 4

Beveca; Kesar Pilau; Kheer

Beveca
Coconut Pudding

METRIC/IMPERIAL

2 coconuts
450 ml/¾ pint boiling water
225 g/8 oz caster sugar
175 g/6 oz rice flour*
2 eggs, beaten
50 g/2 oz slivered almonds

AMERICAN

2 coconuts
2 cups boiling water
1 cup sugar
1½ cups rice flour*
2 eggs, beaten
½ cup slivered almonds

METHOD

Break the coconuts in half, extract the thin milk and reserve. Scrape (grate) the flesh into a bowl, then pour on the boiling water. Leave to steep for 15 minutes, then strain the liquor through muslin (cheesecloth), squeezing out the last drop of thick coconut milk. Mix with the thin milk from the coconut, then beat in the remaining ingredients.

Put the mixture in a pan and bring to the boil. Lower the heat and simmer until the mixture thickens, stirring constantly. Pour into a greased 20 cm/8 inch round baking tin (pan) and bake in a preheated moderate oven (180°C/350°F, Gas Mark 4) for about 30 minutes until the top is browned. Serve hot.
SERVES 4

Malaysia, Singapore and Indonesia

Sri Owen

This area comprises such a variety of races, landscapes and cultures that a common tradition of cooking and eating seems unlikely. However, there is a certain unity among the recipes of the region. Many dishes also show how this South-East Asian cuisine has been affected by travellers and immigrants; there is evidence of Indian, Chinese, Dutch and even British influence but all dishes are essentially local in origin and flavour; in the Indonesian word – asli.

There are other common factors. The Malay Peninsula and the islands share a tropical monsoon climate and large areas are extremely fertile. The South China Sea contains plenty of fish and seafood. It is also fairly easy to navigate, which has encouraged goods and culinary ideas, including spices and recipes, to circulate freely around the islands. The staple food is rice, which is harvested with appropriate ceremony from the flooded fields or sawah which make a mosaic of the contours of every hillside. Rice is the mainstay of South-East Asian cooking. Spices are also important, especially cumin, galingale, lemon grass, ginger, cloves, tamarind, cinnamon and turmeric. These are the spices which first brought Europeans to the Indies. Some of them have been familiar in the Western kitchens ever since, others remain exotic or little used, but today nearly all of them can be obtained here quite easily.

Cooking Techniques and Utensils

Broadly speaking, people cook in the same way throughout the area. Charcoal stoves are used to provide the intense heat needed for rapid frying or grilling (broiling). Ovens are almost unknown, although for convenience some of the recipes in this chapter have been adapted for oven-cooking.

Meat and vegetables are usually cut into small pieces before cooking, either to enable them to be cooked very quickly, or to increase the absorption of spice and sauce flavourings during slow-simmering. Another reason for this is probably because in the past all solid food had to be eaten gracefully with the fingers of the right hand alone.

Almost all the essential utensils needed for Indonesian and Malaysian cooking can be found in any kitchen anywhere in the world. There are three special items, however, that are worth buying if Indonesian and Malaysian dishes are to be cooked often. The first is a wajan, a round-bottomed frying pan (skillet), which is more generally known by its Chinese name of wok. It sits comfortably on a charcoal stove or gas ring and is ideally shaped to spread heat evenly while stir-frying – which is as important in Indonesian cooking as it is in Chinese. It is also easy to clean. A wajan is however unsuitable for cooking on an electric hotplate so a wide flat-bottomed heavy pan, such as a Spanish paella dish, should be used instead.

The second item is a rice steamer, which is a very useful piece of equipment if rice is to be cooked often because it practically guarantees perfectly cooked rice every time. The rice is first boiled in an ordinary pan, then transferred to the steamer when it has absorbed all the water and cooked for a further 10 minutes. Leftover rice can be reheated in the steamer.

The third item, which is perhaps the most important is an ulek-ulek (pestle) and a cobek (mortar), made of wood or stone. Many of the recipes in this chapter require garlic, chillis and other ingredients to be pounded to a paste and, although this can be achieved in an electric blender, there is always the risk that the resulting paste will be too watery. A conventional mortar and pestle is satisfactory, but there is nothing quite like the genuine ulek-ulek and cobek.

Ingredients

Apart from rice and spices, many other specialist ingredients are widely used throughout the Indonesian-Malaysian world. Coconut palms grow everywhere and the coconut flesh and oil are added to many meat dishes and sweets. Santen,* made by pressing the natural oils out of the flesh of the coconut and mixing them in water, is used constantly. It imparts a distinctive but delicate flavour to dishes, and acts as a thickening agent.

Another ingredient widely used is the pungent, dark-coloured shrimp paste which the Indonesians call terasi,* but which is elsewhere known as blacan or balachan. It has a very strong flavour and should therefore be used in tiny quantities.

Three different chillis give Indonesian food its hot reputation; lombok hijau* (green), lombok merah* (red) and lombok rawit.* Florists often sell lombok rawit as decorative houseplants, but they are, in fact, the hottest of all chillis. It is true that Indonesians are accustomed to eating hot peppers and find it hard to go without them, but this does not mean that all Indonesian food has to be hot; any of the recipes given here can equally well be made with little or no chilli. The quantity of chilli given is in any case small and will do no more than give the dish a slight kick, which should not offend even the most sensitive of mouths! It is the seeds of the chilli which are the hottest part, and these can be discarded, if preferred. Boiled rice

or a few slices of raw cucumber will cool the mouth quickly if too much chilli has been eaten – far more quickly than water.

Serving

Although an everyday family meal may simply consist of rice, served with one or two dishes of vegetables and possibly a little meat or fish, even the most minor social occasion in Indonesia, Malaysia or Singapore calls for plenty of good food. Any celebration is likely to be accompanied by an elaborate array of side dishes, relishes, sauces, *Serundeng* (see page 60), *Krupuk* (see page 60) and huge amounts of rice. The Dutch in the islands adapted the custom for their own use and called it *rijsttafel*, or rice table. There are no separate courses at a meal of this kind, but the sweet usually appears some time towards the end of the meal. All the main dishes are served together and everyone helps themselves.

Almost all the dishes in this chapter can be eaten simply with a fork. A spoon is useful when eating dishes which have a sauce, or large quantities of rice. Chopsticks are not used for Indonesian or Malaysian food; they are however, used for dishes of Chinese origin, such as the noodle dishes from Singapore.

China tea – without milk or sugar – is a good drink to take with food of this kind, although cold lager or a full-bodied wine may alternatively be served.

Spelling and pronunciation

The Indonesian and Malaysian national languages are already very similar, and are likely to grow closer still. Within the last decade or so, the spelling of both languages has been standardized, and the revised spelling is used in this chapter. The letter *j* is now pronounced as *j* in the English word 'judge'. The letter *c* is pronounced as *ch* as in the English 'church'. *Cobek* is therefore pronounced *cho-bek* with a very short final *k*, and *kencur* is *k'n-choor*. Apart from these exceptions, Indonesian and Malaysian words can be pronounced roughly as they are spelt.

Origins

Many of the dishes described in this chapter will be familiar to anyone who has been to South-East Asia, or has eaten his way through the menu in an Indonesian or Malaysian restaurant! Others I have recalled from my early life in Sumatra and Java, or have collected from members of my family and friends. The country of origin of a recipe is given wherever I have felt this was justified. If no origin is given, the dish belongs about equally to Singapore, Malaysia and Indonesia.

Soto Ayam
Spiced Chicken Soup

METRIC/IMPERIAL

1.5 litres/2½ pints water
1 small chicken, quartered
4 Dublin Bay (king) prawns, cleaned,
    deveined and halved
salt
freshly ground black pepper
2 kemiri,* chopped
4 shallots, peeled and chopped
2 garlic cloves, peeled and chopped
1 teaspoon ground ginger
pinch of turmeric powder
pinch of chilli powder
vegetable oil for frying
1 tablespoon light soy sauce
75 g/3 oz bean sprouts, cleaned
1 potato, peeled and sliced into very
    thin rounds
To garnish:
few lemon slices
coriander leaves*

AMERICAN

6¼ cups water
1 small chicken, quartered
4 jumbo shrimp, cleaned, deveined
    and halved
salt
freshly ground black pepper
2 kemiri,* chopped
4 shallots, peeled and chopped
2 garlic cloves, peeled and chopped
1 teaspoon ginger powder
pinch of turmeric powder
pinch of chili powder
vegetable oil for frying
1 tablespoon light soy sauce
1¼ cups bean sprouts, cleaned
1 potato, peeled and sliced into very
    thin rounds
To garnish:
few lemon slices
coriander leaves*

METHOD

Bring the water to the boil in a large pan.
Add the chicken, prawns (shrimp) and
salt and pepper to taste, then cover and
simmer for 40 minutes.

Strain and reserves 1.2 litres/2 pints/
5 cups of the cooking liquid. Shred the
meat from the chicken. Peel the prawns
(shrimp) and discard the heads, then cut
each one into 4 or 5 pieces.

Put the kemiri, shallots and garlic in a
cobek or mortar and pound to a very
smooth paste. Add the ginger, turmeric
and chilli powder and mix well.

Heat 2 tablespoons oil in a wok or deep
frying pan (deep-fat fryer), add the spice
paste and fry for a few seconds. Stir in
300 ml/½ pint/1¼ cups of the reserved

cooking liquid, the soy sauce, chicken
and prawns (shrimp). Simmer for 10
minutes, then add the remaining cooking
liquid and simmer for a further 10 minutes. Add the bean sprouts, taste and
adjust the seasoning, then continue cooking for 3 minutes.

Meanwhile, heat a little oil in a frying
pan (skillet), add the potato slices and fry
until crisp on both sides.

Divide the potato slices equally between 4 to 6 warmed soup bowls. Ladle
the soup into the bowls, then garnish with
the lemon slices and coriander. Serve
hot.
SERVES 4 to 6

Laksa Lemak
Prawn (Shrimp) and
Vermicelli Soup
Singapore

This soup is traditionally garnished with
Sambal Bajak (see page 82), but since this
is hot and spicy, you may prefer to serve
it in a separate bowl so that guests can
help themselves according to taste.

METRIC/IMPERIAL

600 ml/1 pint water
100 g/4 oz pork fillet or chicken breast
    meat
salt
freshly ground black pepper
175 g/6 oz laksa*
1½ tablespoons vegetable oil
5 shallots, peeled and finely sliced
4 spring onions, cut into 1 cm/½ inch
    lengths
2 garlic cloves, peeled and crushed
1 teaspoon ground ginger
1 teaspoon coriander powder
½ teaspoon turmeric powder
175 g/6 oz peeled frozen prawns
300 ml/½ pint thick santen*
2 blocks yellow tahu,* cut into thick
    strips
75 g/3 oz bean sprouts, cleaned
1–2 teaspoons Sambal Bajak (see page
    82) to garnish (optional)

AMERICAN

2½ cups water
¼ lb pork loin or chicken breast meat
salt
freshly ground black pepper
6 oz laksa*
1½ tablespoons vegetable oil
5 shallots, peeled and finely sliced
4 scallions, cut into ½ inch lengths
2 garlic cloves, peeled and crushed
1 teaspoon ginger powder
1 teaspoon coriander powder
½ teaspoon turmeric powder
1 cup shelled frozen shrimp
1¼ cups thick santen*
2 blocks yellow tahu,* cut into thick
    strips
2 cups bean sprouts, cleaned
1–2 teaspoons Sambal Bajak (see page
    82) to garnish (optional)

METHOD

Bring the water to the boil in a large pan.
Add the pork or chicken and salt and
pepper to taste. Cover and simmer for 40
minutes.

Strain and reserve the cooking liquid.
Cut the meat into small cubes.

Put the laksa in a pan and cover with
boiling water. Cover and leave to stand
for 5 minutes. Drain thoroughly.

Heat the oil in a wok or deep frying pan
(deep-fat fryer), add the shallots and fry
for 1 minute, then add the spring onions
(scallions), garlic and spices. Fry for 30
seconds, stirring constantly, then add the
meat and prawns (shrimp). Stir-fry for 1
minute, then add the reserved cooking
liquid and simmer for 25 minutes.

Add the laksa and santen and bring
very slowly to the boil, stirring gently to
prevent the santen from curdling. Add
the tahu and bean sprouts and simmer for
5 to 8 minutes, stirring occasionally.

Pour into a warmed soup tureen, then
garnish with the Sambal Bajak, if using.
Serve hot.
SERVES 4 to 6

Soto Ayam; Laksa Lemak; Mie Bakso

Mie Bakso

Noodle Soup with Meatballs

Indonesia

Bakso or *baso*, is a cake or ball made of meat, fish, prawns (shrimp) or bean curd, or a combination of these. In this recipe, the *Bakso* is made with beef. If liked, you can make the meatballs in advance to avoid preparing and cooking just before serving.

METRIC/IMPERIAL

Soup:

100 g/4 oz egg noodles
salt
2 tablespoons vegetable oil
3 shallots, peeled and finely sliced
2 garlic cloves, peeled and finely sliced
pinch of ground ginger
1 tablespoon light soy sauce
1.5 litres/2½ pints beef stock
4 spring onions, cut into thin rounds
2 carrots, peeled and cut into thin rounds
50 g/2 oz mange tout peas, topped and tailed
3 Chinese cabbage leaves
freshly ground black pepper

Meatballs:

225 g/8 oz lean beef
3 tablespoons cornflour
1 egg white
2 teaspoons sea salt

AMERICAN

Soup:

¼ lb egg noodles
salt
2 tablespoons vegetable oil
3 shallots, peeled and finely sliced
2 garlic cloves, peeled and finely sliced
pinch of ginger powder
1 tablespoon light soy sauce
6¼ cups beef stock
4 scallions, cut into thin rounds
2 carrots, peeled and cut into thin rounds
15–18 snow peas, topped and tailed
3 stalks bok choy
freshly ground black pepper

Meatballs:

½ lb lean beef
3 tablespoons cornstarch
1 egg white
2 teaspoons coarse salt

METHOD

Bring a large pan of water to the boil. Add the noodles and ½ teaspoon salt and boil for 5 minutes. Drain, rinse under cold running water, then drain and set aside.

To make the meatballs: Work the beef through the fine blade of a mincer (grinder) several times, then chop with a heavy knife until it is almost a paste. Transfer to a bowl, add the cornflour (cornstarch), egg white and salt and pepper to taste. Mix well, then shape into small balls, about the size of marbles. Drop them one by one into a bowl containing 600 ml/1 pint/2½ cups water and the coarse sea salt.

Bring 600 ml/1 pint/2½ cups water to the boil in a large pan. Add a pinch of salt, then remove the meatballs from the salted water with a slotted spoon and drop them one at a time into the boiling water. Boil for 5 to 8 minutes, then drain and set aside.

Just before serving, heat the oil in a large pan. Add the shallots and garlic and fry for 1 minute, stirring constantly. Add the ginger, soy sauce, stock, spring onions (scallions) and carrots. Simmer for 5 minutes, then add the mange tout (snow peas) and cabbage (bok choy). Taste and adjust the seasoning, then simmer for a further 3 to 4 minutes.

Add the noodles and meatballs, increase the heat and cook for a further 1 minute. Serve immediately.

SERVES 6 to 8

Sayur Lodeh Jakarta
Creamy Vegetable Soup
Indonesia

This soup becomes a rich vegetable stew if more vegetables are added and the quantity of water decreased. It can then be served as one of the side dishes at a *rijsttafel.**

METRIC/IMPERIAL

1 medium aubergine, sliced
salt
4 kemiri, chopped*
4 shallots, peeled and chopped
*1 slice terasi**
2 garlic cloves, peeled and chopped
   (optional)
1 red or green chilli, chopped
   (optional)
*25 g/1 oz ebi**
1.2 litres/2 pints water
2 teaspoons coriander powder
*pinch of sereh powder**
*2 daun jeruk purut**
½ teaspoon brown sugar
50 g/2 oz French or runner beans,
   topped, tailed and cut into
   2.5 cm/1 inch lengths
50 g/2 oz white cabbage or cauliflower
   florets, shredded or finely chopped
50 g/2 oz bamboo shoot, finely sliced
50 g/2 oz watercress, stalks discarded
   (optional)
*50 g/2 oz creamed coconut**

AMERICAN

1 medium eggplant, sliced
salt
4 kemiri, chopped*
4 shallots, peeled and chopped
*1 slice terasi**
2 garlic cloves, peeled and chopped
   (optional)
1 red or green chili, chopped
   (optional)
*⅓ cup ebi**
5 cups water
2 teaspoons coriander powder
*pinch of sereh powder**
*2 daun jeruk purut**
½ teaspoon brown sugar
15 string beans, topped, tailed and cut
   into 1 inch lengths
¾ cup shredded cabbage or 1 large
   cauliflower floret, finely chopped
½ cup bamboo shoot, finely sliced
½ bunch watercress, stalks discarded
   (optional)
*¼ cup thick santen**

METHOD

Sprinkle the aubergine (eggplant) slices with salt, leave to stand for 30 minutes, then rinse under cold running water.

Meanwhile, put the kemiri in a *cobek* or mortar with the shallots, terasi, garlic and chilli, if using. Pound to a very smooth paste, then transfer to a small pan. Add the ebi and 120 ml/4 fl oz/½ cup water and boil for 2 to 3 minutes.

Strain the liquid into a clean pan. Add the remaining water, coriander, sereh, daun jeruk purut and sugar. Bring to the boil, then add the vegetables except the watercress. Simmer for 5 minutes.

Add the watercress, if using, and the creamed coconut (santen) and simmer until the coconut has dissolved, stirring constantly. Taste and adjust the seasoning, then pour into a warmed soup tureen. Serve hot.
SERVES 4

Soto Madura
Spicy Beef Soup
Indonesia

This is a rich, meaty soup which can be served as a starter, or with other dishes as part of a main course.

METRIC/IMPERIAL

1.5 litres/2½ pints water
450 g/1 lb boned brisket of beef,
   trimmed
salt
freshly ground black pepper
75 g/3 oz peeled frozen prawns
*4 kemiri**
6 shallots, peeled
3 garlic cloves, peeled
2 tablespoons corn oil
1 teaspoon ground ginger
1 teaspoon turmeric powder
½ teaspoon chilli powder (optional)
To garnish:
1 tablespoon chopped coriander
   *leaves**
1 tablespoon chopped onion, fried
4 lemon slices

AMERICAN

6¼ cups water
1 lb boneless brisket of beef, trimmed
salt
freshly ground black pepper
2 medium frozen shrimp, shelled
4 kemiri*
6 shallots, peeled
3 garlic cloves, peeled
2 tablespoons corn oil
1 teaspoon ginger powder
1 teaspoon turmeric powder
½ teaspoon chili powder (optional)
To garnish:
1 tablespoon chopped coriander
    leaves*
1 tablespoon chopped onion, fried
4 lemon slices

METHOD

Bring the water to the boil in a large pan. Add the beef with a little salt and pepper, then cover and simmer for 40 minutes.

Strain and reserve the cooking liquid. Cut the beef into small cubes, discarding any fat and gristle.

Mince (grind) together the prawns (shrimp), kemiri, 3 shallots and the garlic. Heat 1 tablespoon of the oil in a pan, add the minced (ground) mixture and fry for 1 minute. Stir in the ginger, turmeric and half the reserved cooking liquid. Cover and simmer for 15 minutes.

Meanwhile, finely chop the remaining shallots. Heat the remaining oil in a large pan, add the shallots and fry until golden brown. Add the beef, 2 tablespoons of the reserved cooking liquid, a little salt and the chilli powder, if using. Cover and simmer for 2 minutes.

Strain the prawn (shrimp) and kemiri liquid into the beef mixture, then add the remaining reserved cooking liquid. Bring to the boil, then lower the heat, cover and simmer for 40 to 50 minutes.

Taste and adjust the seasoning, then pour into a warmed soup tureen. Garnish with the coriander, onion and lemon slices. Serve hot.
SERVES 6

Rempeyek Kacang
Savoury Peanut Brittle

These little peanut snacks are delicious at any time of day, but they go particularly well with pre-dinner drinks. It is advisable to use very fine rice powder* to make them – ordinary rice flour does not give the best results. If stored in an airtight container, Rempeyek will keep for at least two weeks.

METRIC/IMPERIAL

2 kemiri,* chopped
1 garlic clove, peeled and chopped
2 teaspoons coriander powder
1 teaspoon salt
100 g/4 oz rice powder*
250 ml/8 fl oz water
175 g/6 oz whole shelled peanuts,
    halved if large
300 ml/½ pint vegetable oil

AMERICAN

2 kemiri,* chopped
1 garlic clove, peeled and chopped
2 teaspoons coriander powder
1 teaspoon salt
1 cup rice powder*
1 cup water
1 cup whole shelled peanuts, halved if
    large
1¼ cups vegetable oil

METHOD

Put the kemiri and garlic in a *cobek* or mortar and pound to a very smooth paste. Add the coriander and salt and stir well, then mix in the rice powder and water to make a smooth, liquid batter. Stir in the peanuts.

Heat 5 tablespoons of the oil in a non-stick frying pan (skillet). Place spoonfuls of the batter in the pan. Fry each one for 1 minute, then remove from the pan with a slotted spoon and drain on kitchen paper towels. Repeat until all the batter is used up, adding more oil to the pan as necessary. Stir the uncooked batter from time to time, adding a little water if it becomes dry while standing.

Pour the remaining oil into a wok or deep-fryer. Add any remaining oil from the pan and heat to 180°C/350°F. Add about 8 rempeyek to the pan and fry for about 1 minute until golden brown, turning them several times during frying. Drain and leave until cold before serving.
MAKES 50 to 55

Pergedel Jagung
Corn Fritters

These can be served as a snack on their own, or as part of a meal with other vegetables.

METRIC/IMPERIAL

6 corn on the cob, or 1 × 326 g/11½ oz
    can sweetcorn, drained
75 g/3 oz peeled prawns (optional)
4 shallots, peeled
2 garlic cloves, peeled (optional)
1 red chilli, or ½ teaspoon chilli powder
1 teaspoon coriander powder
salt
1 large egg, beaten
vegetable oil for shallow-frying

AMERICAN

6 corn on the cob, or 1 × 12 oz can corn
    kernels, drained
2 medium shrimp, shelled (optional)
4 shallots, peeled
2 garlic cloves, peeled (optional)
1 red chilli, or ½ teaspoon chili powder
1 teaspoon coriander powder
salt
1 large egg, beaten
vegetable oil for shallow-frying

METHOD

If you are using corn on the cob, grate the kernels off the cobs. Mince (grind) the prawns (shrimp), shallots, garlic and red chilli, if using. Mix with the corn, then add the coriander and salt to taste. Add the egg and beat thoroughly.

Heat 5 tablespoons oil in a frying pan (skillet), then drop a heaped tablespoonful of the mixture into the pan. Flatten with a fork, then repeat this process until there are 5 or 6 fritters in the pan. Fry for about 2½ minutes, then turn over and cook the other side. Remove from the pan with a slotted spoon and drain on kitchen paper towels. Repeat until all the mixture is used, adding more oil to the pan as necessary. Serve hot or cold.
SERVES 4

Rempeyek Kacang

Serundeng

**Roast Grated Coconut
with Peanuts**

Indonesia

Serundeng is an Indonesian side dish which has both a delicious taste and texture. Serve guests with a very small quantity as a little goes a long way. If stored in an airtight container, Serundeng will keep for several weeks.

METRIC/IMPERIAL

7 tablespoons vegetable oil
75 g/3 oz whole shelled peanuts
3 kemiri,* chopped
3 shallots, peeled and chopped
2 garlic cloves, peeled and chopped
1 slice terasi*
2 teaspoons coriander powder
pinch of cumin powder
pinch of laos powder*
175 g/6 oz desiccated coconut
1 teaspoon brown sugar
2 tablespoons tamarind water*
1 salam leaf*
salt
150 ml/¼ pint water

60

AMERICAN

7 tablespoons vegetable oil
½ cup whole shelled peanuts
3 kemiri,* chopped
3 shallots, peeled and chopped
2 garlic cloves, peeled and chopped
1 slice terasi*
2 teaspoons coriander powder
pinch of cumin powder
pinch of laos powder*
1 cup shredded coconut
1 teaspoon brown sugar
2 tablespoons tamarind water*
1 salam leaf*
salt
⅔ cup water

METHOD

Heat 5 tablespoons of the oil in a small frying pan (skillet), add the peanuts and fry for about 5 minutes until just brown, shaking the pan constantly. Remove from the pan and leave to cool. Put the kemiri, shallots, garlic and terasi in a *cobek* or mortar and pound to a smooth paste. Stir in the coriander, cumin and laos.

Heat the remaining oil in a wok or deep frying pan (deep-fat fryer). Add the spice paste and fry for 1 minute, stirring constantly. Stir in the coconut, then the sugar, tamarind water, salam leaf and salt to taste. Stir-fry for a few minutes, then add the water and simmer until the water is completely absorbed. Cover and cook gently for 50 minutes to 1 hour until golden brown, stirring frequently.

Add the peanuts, then remove from the heat and cool before serving.
SERVES 4
Illustrated on page 62.

Krupuk

Shrimp Crackers (Crisps)

Krupuk, or Krupuk Udang, are sold in Chinese shops and supermarkets, and sometimes in delicatessens. They are uncooked and look like thin, flat, pink tongues, about 10 cm/4 inches long. When cooked, they are light and crisp and similar to the shrimp slices served in Chinese restaurants, although they are larger, brighter pink and, in most people's opinion, have more flavour. The Chinese name for them is *kapeng*.

METHOD

To cook shrimp crackers: Heat about 300 ml/½ pint/1¼ cups vegetable oil in a wok or deep frying pan (deep-fat fryer). Drop the crackers into the pan, one at a time; they will immediately swell to several times their original size. Try to press the crackers reasonably flat with a fish slice during the first 1 to 2 seconds of frying, while they are still soft, otherwise they will buckle and twist and not cook properly. Fry for a few seconds further, then remove from the pan and drain off the excess oil. Leave to cool, then serve immediately, or store in an airtight container and eat within 24 hours. Serve with drinks or as part of a meal.

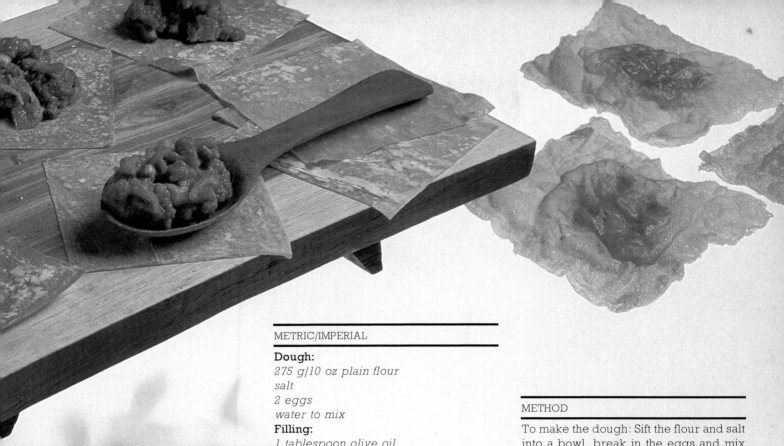

Preparing Martabak

Martabak

Stuffed Savoury Pancakes (Crêpes)

Indonesia/Singapore

Strictly speaking, Martabak are not pancakes (crêpes) at all, but quick-fried envelopes of very thin dough, stuffed with minced (ground) meat and spices. They are very popular as snacks to be eaten in the open air; you can buy them at Indonesian market stalls or from street vendors who will make them especially for you, absolutely fresh and with ingredients to suite your taste.

If you are making them at home, they can accompany a meal, or be served with drinks beforehand, or they can be eaten as a snack at any time of day. Cold Martabak are excellent as part of a packed lunch.

This recipe gives instructions for making your own dough, but if preferred you can buy packets of *wun tun* (wonton skins)* from Chinese supermarkets and use them for the casing instead – 100 g/ 4 oz/¼ package is the right quantity for this amount of filling.

METRIC/IMPERIAL

Dough:
275 g/10 oz plain flour
salt
2 eggs
water to mix

Filling:
1 tablespoon olive oil
1–2 large onions, peeled and finely sliced
2 garlic cloves, peeled and crushed
1 teaspoon coriander powder
½ teaspoon cumin powder
½ teaspoon ground ginger
½ teaspoon chilli powder
½ teaspoon turmeric powder
1 teaspoon sereh powder*
salt
450 g/1 lb cooked lamb or beef, minced

To finish:
2–3 eggs, according to taste
50 g/2 oz spring onions, chopped
25 g/1 oz coriander leaves,* chopped
vegetable oil for shallow-frying

AMERICAN

Dough:
2½ cups all-purpose flour
salt
2 eggs
water to mix

Filling:
1 tablespoon olive oil
1–2 large onions, peeled and finely sliced
2 garlic cloves, peeled and crushed
1 teaspoon coriander powder
½ teaspoon cumin powder
½ teaspoon ginger powder
½ teaspoon chili powder
½ teaspoon turmeric powder
1 teaspoon sereh powder*
salt
1 lb cooked lamb or beef, ground

To finish:
2–3 eggs, according to taste
5 medium scallions, chopped
¾ cup chopped coriander leaves*
vegetable oil for shallow-frying

METHOD

To make the dough: Sift the flour and salt into a bowl, break in the eggs and mix well. Knead thoroughly, adding enough water to make a smooth, firm dough.

Roll the dough into a ball on a board lightly sprinkled with cornflour (cornstarch). Flatten the ball with a rolling pin and very carefully pull it out into the thinnest possible sheet. Cut the dough into 7.5 cm/3 inch squares, then chill in the refrigerator until required.

To make the filling: Heat the olive oil in a wok or deep frying pan (deep-fat fryer), add the onions and garlic and fry gently until soft. Add the spices and salt and fry for 30 seconds, stirring constantly. Add the meat, stir well and fry for 1 to 2 minutes, stirring constantly. Leave to cool for 30 minutes to 1 hour.

To finish: Break the eggs into the filling. Add the spring onions (scallions) and coriander and stir well. Place a few squares of dough on a board, lightly sprinkled with cornflour (cornstarch). Place a heaped tablespoon of filling on each square and put another square on top, then press the edges of the dough together firmly to seal.

Heat 5 tablespoons oil in a frying pan (skillet). When the oil is very hot, add the martabak and press down with a fish slice for a few seconds. Fry for about 1 minute on each side, turning them once only. Remove from the pan with a slotted spoon and drain on kitchen paper towels. Repeat with the remaining ingredients, adding more oil to the pan as required. Serve hot or cold, cut into triangles if preferred.

SERVES 6 to 8

Note: When cooked, the martabak should be flat and evenly filled with meat; the casing should be quite crisp around the edges, but soft in the centre.

Rempah-Rempah

Prawn (Shrimp) and Bean Sprout Fritters

Malaysia

These are normally made without prawns (shrimp), but their addition certainly makes the fritters tastier. Serve as a side dish with a rice meal, or as a snack with drinks.

METRIC/IMPERIAL

100 g/4 oz peeled prawns, chopped or minced
225 g/8 oz bean sprouts
4 spring onions, thinly sliced
2 shallots, peeled and finely sliced
2 garlic cloves, peeled and crushed
2 tablespoons chopped coriander leaves* (optional)
2 tablespoons coarsely grated white coconut flesh (optional)
50 g/2 oz rice flour* or self-raising flour
1 teaspoon baking powder
1 teaspoon coriander powder
1 teaspoon ground ginger
½ teaspoon chilli powder
3 tablespoons water
1 egg, beaten
salt
freshly ground black pepper
vegetable oil for deep-frying
lemon slices to garnish

AMERICAN

3 medium shrimp, shelled and chopped or ground
½ lb bean sprouts
4 scallions, thinly sliced
2 shallots, peeled and finely sliced
2 garlic cloves, peeled and crushed
2 tablespoons chopped coriander leaves* (optional)
2 tablespoons coarsely grated white coconut flesh (optional)
½ cup rice flour* or self-rising flour
1 teaspoon baking powder
1 teaspoon coriander powder
1 teaspoon ginger powder
½ teaspoon chili powder
3 tablespoons water
1 egg, beaten
salt
freshly ground black pepper
vegetable oil for deep-frying
lemon slices to garnish

METHOD

Put all the ingredients for the fritters in a bowl and mix well. Form the mixture into small balls about the size of walnuts, or flatten them into burger shapes.

Heat the oil in a wok or deep-fryer and fry the rempah-rempah for 1½ to 2 minutes until golden brown. Remove from the pan with a slotted spoon and drain on kitchen paper towels. Transfer to a serving dish and garnish with lemon slices. Serve hot or cold.

SERVES 6 to 8 as a side dish

Sambal Goreng Udang dan Telur

Prawns (Shrimp) and Eggs in Spicy Coconut Sauce

Indonesia

METRIC/IMPERIAL

575 g/1¼ lb Dublin Bay (king) prawns, peeled
5 kemiri,* chopped
3 red chillis, seeded and chopped, or 2 teaspoons sambal ulek*
1 small onion, peeled and chopped
2 garlic cloves, peeled and chopped
1 slice terasi*
2 teaspoons coriander powder
1 teaspoon ground ginger
½ teaspoon sereh powder*
pinch of laos powder*
2 tablespoons vegetable oil
3 ripe tomatoes, skinned, seeded and chopped
salt
1 salam leaf*
2 daun jeruk purut* (optional)
150 ml/¼ pint water
150 ml/¼ pint very thick santen*
4 hard-boiled eggs, shelled and halved
75 g/3 oz mange tout peas, topped and tailed

To garnish:
1 cooked, unpeeled Dublin Bay (king) prawn
lemon twist

AMERICAN

1¼ lb jumbo shrimp, shelled
5 kemiri,* chopped
3 red chilis, seeded and chopped, or
   2 teaspoons sambal ulek*
1 small onion, peeled and chopped
2 garlic cloves, peeled and chopped
1 slice terasi*
2 teaspoons coriander powder
1 teaspoon ginger powder
½ teaspoon sereh powder*
pinch of laos powder*
2 tablespoons vegetable oil
3 ripe tomatoes, skinned, seeded
and chopped
salt
1 salam leaf*
2 daun jeruk purut* (optional)
⅔ cup water
⅔ cup very thick santen*
4 hard-cooked eggs, shelled and
   halved
22–25 snow peas, topped and tailed
To garnish:
1 cooked, unshelled jumbo shrimp
lemon twist

METHOD

Discard the heads from the prawns (shrimp), then cut each one in half.

Put the kemiri, chillis or sambal ulek, onion, garlic and terasi in a *cobek* or mortar and pound to a very smooth paste. Add the spices and mix well.

Heat the oil in a pan, add the spice paste and fry for 1 minute, stirring constantly. Add the prawns (shrimp), tomatoes and salt to taste. Stir, then cover and simmer gently for 2 minutes.

Stir in the salam leaf, daun jeruk purut, if using, and water, then increase the heat and boil, uncovered, for 5 minutes.

Lower the heat, add the santen and eggs, and simmer for 8 minutes, stirring frequently. Add the mange tout (snow peas) and simmer for 3 minutes until they are quite tender and the sauce is thick. Taste and adjust the seasoning, then transfer to a serving dish and garnish with the prawn (shrimp) and lemon twist. Serve hot, with *Serundeng* (see page 60). SERVES 4

Gerinting Udang
Spiced Fried Prawns (Shrimp)
Singapore

This dish should really be made with freshly boiled prawns (shrimp), but it is still delicious with precooked prawns (shrimp) from the fishmonger. Serve as a side dish with rice, or as a snack.

METRIC/IMPERIAL

450 g/1 lb peeled prawns
2 tablespoons tamarind water*
pinch of turmeric powder
½ teaspoon ground ginger
2 shallots, peeled and sliced
2 garlic cloves, peeled and crushed
1 tablespoon light soy sauce
150 ml/¼ pint vegetable oil
Batter:
7 tablespoons rice powder* or plain
   flour
5 tablespoons water
salt
freshly ground black pepper
1 small egg, beaten

AMERICAN

1 lb shelled shrimp
2 tablespoons tamarind water*
pinch of turmeric powder
½ teaspoon ginger powder
2 shallots, peeled and sliced
2 garlic cloves, peeled and crushed
1 tablespoon light soy sauce
⅔ cup vegetable oil
Batter:
½ cup rice powder* or all-purpose
   flour
⅓ cup water
salt
freshly ground black pepper
1 small egg, beaten

METHOD

Discard the heads from the prawns (shrimp), but leave on the tails. Place in a bowl with the tamarind water, turmeric, ginger, shallots, garlic and soy sauce. Stir well, then leave to marinate for at least 30 minutes.

Meanwhile, make the batter. Put the rice powder or flour in a bowl, then gradually stir in the water. Add salt and pepper to taste, then beat in the egg.

Drain the marinade from the prawns (shrimp) and shallots. Dip the prawns (shrimp) and shallots into the batter.

Heat the oil in a frying pan (skillet), then add the prawns (shrimp) and shallots, one at a time until the bottom of the pan is covered. Fry until golden brown and crisp, then turn over and fry the underside. Serve hot or cold. SERVES 4

**Gerinting Udang; Sambal Goreng
Udang dan Telur; Rempah-Rempah**

Bola-Bola Tahu
Fried Prawn (Shrimp) and Bean Curd Balls
Malaysia

METRIC/IMPERIAL

3 blocks tahu*
225 g/8 oz peeled prawns
2 garlic cloves, peeled and crushed (optional)
1 tablespoon cornflour
1 egg, beaten
salt
freshly ground black pepper
vegetable oil for deep-frying
Sauce:
3 large ripe tomatoes, chopped
2 shallots, peeled and sliced
1 garlic clove, peeled and crushed
150 ml/¼ pint water
1 tablespoon light soy sauce
2 teaspoons lemon juice or vinegar
2 teaspoons sugar
50 g/2 oz mange tout peas, topped and tailed (optional)
To garnish:
few fried onion rings
chopped coriander leaves*

AMERICAN

3 blocks tahu*
½ lb shelled shrimp
2 garlic cloves, peeled and crushed (optional)
1 tablespoon cornstarch
1 egg, beaten
salt
freshly ground black pepper
vegetable oil for deep-frying
Sauce:
3 large ripe tomatoes, chopped
2 shallots, peeled and sliced
1 garlic clove, peeled and crushed
⅔ cup water
1 tablespoon light soy sauce
2 teaspoons lemon juice or vinegar
2 teaspoons sugar
15–18 snow peas, topped and tailed (optional)
To garnish:
few fried onion rings
chopped coriander leaves*

METHOD

Put the tahu in a bowl and mash to a smooth paste. Mince (grind) the prawns (shrimp), then add to the tahu, together with the garlic if using, the cornflour (cornstarch), egg and salt and pepper to taste. Mix well, then form into small balls, about the size of walnuts.

Heat the oil in a wok or deep frying pan (deep-fat fryer) to 180°C/350°F. Add the prawn balls and deep-fry until golden brown. Remove from the pan with a slotted spoon and drain on kitchen paper towels.

Meanwhile, make the sauce. Put the tomatoes, shallots, garlic and water in a pan. Bring to the boil, and boil for 5 minutes. Strain the mixture into a clean pan, then add the remaining sauce ingredients, with salt and pepper to taste. Return to the heat and simmer for 3 minutes.

Add the prawn balls to the sauce and simmer for about 1 minute until heated through, stirring gently. Garnish with onion rings and coriander and serve immediately.
SERVES 4

Kepiting Pedas
Crab with Chilli
Singapore

This dish is better without the soft meat from the shell of the crab, so reserve this for another dish if you are using whole crabs. In Singapore, the crab is eaten with the fingers, but a fork can be used to help extract the crabmeat from its shell.

METRIC/IMPERIAL

2 medium crabs, boiled, or 8 large crab claws
3 tablespoons vegetable oil
1 tablespoon lemon juice
salt
Sauce:
5 red chillis, seeded and chopped
1 onion, peeled and chopped
2 garlic cloves, peeled and chopped
1 teaspoon ground ginger
2 tablespoons vegetable oil
2 ripe tomatoes, skinned, seeded and chopped, or 2 teaspoons tomato purée
1 teaspoon sugar
1 tablespoon light soy sauce
3 tablespoons water

AMERICAN

2 medium crabs, boiled, or 8 large
  crab claws
3 tablespoons vegetable oil
1 tablespoon lemon juice
salt
Sauce:
5 red chilis, seeded and chopped
1 onion, peeled and chopped
2 garlic cloves, peeled and chopped
1 teaspoon ginger powder
2 tablespoons vegetable oil
2 ripe tomatoes, skinned, seeded and
  chopped, or 2 teaspoons tomato
  paste
1 teaspoon sugar
1 tablespoon light soy sauce
3 tablespoons water

METHOD

Clean the crabs thoroughly, then cut each body into 2 or 4 pieces. Chop the claws into 2 or 3 pieces if they are very large.

Heat the oil in a frying pan (skillet), add the crab pieces and fry for 5 minutes, stirring constantly. Add the lemon juice and salt to taste, then remove from the heat and keep hot.

To make the sauce: Put the chillis, onion and garlic in a *cobek* or mortar and pound to a very smooth paste. Add the ginger and stir well to mix.

Heat the oil in a wok or deep frying pan (deep-fat fryer). Add the spice paste and fry for 1 minute, stirring constantly. Add the tomatoes, sugar and soy sauce and stir-fry for 2 minutes, then stir in the water. Add salt if necessary and simmer for a further 1 minute.

Add the crab and stir to coat each piece in the sauce. Serve hot.
SERVES 4

Kepiting Pedas; Bola-Bola Tahu; Sambal Sotong

Goreng Sotong
Fried Squid
Singapore

The secret of this dish is the marinade, which needs at least 2 hours to be effective – preferably longer. Serve Goreng Sotong as a side dish with rice, or by itself as a starter.

METRIC/IMPERIAL

750 g/1½ lb squid
4 tablespoons tamarind water*
½ teaspoon turmeric powder
1 teaspoon ground ginger
pinch of chilli powder
4 shallots, peeled and sliced
3 garlic cloves, peeled and crushed
½ teaspoon salt
1 teaspoon dark soy sauce (optional)
vegetable oil for deep-frying

AMERICAN

1½ lb squid
¼ cup tamarind water*
½ teaspoon turmeric powder
1 teaspoon ginger powder
pinch of chili powder
4 shallots, peeled and sliced
3 garlic cloves, peeled and crushed
½ teaspoon salt
1 teaspoon dark soy sauce (optional)
vegetable oil for deep-frying

METHOD

Clean the squid, discarding the ink sac and head. Chop the tentacles into 2.5 cm/1 inch lengths, then slice the squid into thin rings.

Put the squid in a bowl with the remaining ingredients. Leave to marinate for at least 2 hours.

Drain the squid and discard the marinade. Heat the oil in a wok or deep frying pan (deep-fat fryer) to 180°C/350°F. Deep-fry the squid for 5 to 6 minutes, stirring occasionally. Remove from the pan with a slotted spoon and drain on kitchen paper towels. Serve hot.
SERVES 4

Sambal Sotong
Squid in Red Chilli Sauce
Singapore

Despite its name, this is a main dish, not a relish. The chillis give a good red colour, but if you find they make it too hot, use paprika or sweet red peppers instead.

METRIC/IMPERIAL

1 kg/2 lb squid
1 tablespoon white vinegar
750 ml/1¼ pints water
5 kemiri,* chopped
6 large red chillis, seeded and
  chopped
6 shallots, peeled and chopped
1 slice terasi* (optional)
2 teaspoons ground ginger
pinch of cumin powder
pinch of turmeric powder
pinch of sereh powder*
2 tablespoons vegetable oil
3 tablespoons tamarind water*
1 teaspoon brown sugar
salt

AMERICAN

2 lb squid
1 tablespoon white vinegar
3 cups water
5 kemiri,* chopped
6 large red chilis, seeded and
  chopped
6 shallots, peeled and chopped
1 slice terasi* (optional)
2 teaspoons ginger powder
pinch of cumin powder
pinch of turmeric powder
pinch of sereh powder*
2 tablespoons vegetable oil
3 tablespoons tamarind water*
1 teaspoon brown sugar
salt

METHOD

Clean the squid, discarding the ink sac and head. Chop the tentacles into 1 cm/½ inch lengths, then cut the squid into small squares. Mix the vinegar with 600 ml/1 pint/2½ cups of the water, then use to rinse the squid. Drain immediately.

Put the kemiri, chillis, shallots and terasi in a *cobek* or mortar and pound to a very smooth paste. Add the spices and mix well.

Heat the oil in a pan, add the spice paste and fry for 1 minute, stirring constantly. Add the squid and tamarind water and fry for a further 3 minutes. Stir in the sugar, salt and remaining water and simmer for 5 to 6 minutes, stirring frequently. Serve hot.
SERVES 4 to 6

Pais Ikan
Aromatic Baked Fish
Indonesia

There are variations of this dish all over Indonesia, and it has many different names. This version is from Sunda, in West Java. If preferred, the *santen** can be omitted, in which case the spice mixture (*bumbu**) should be scraped off the fish after baking, and the fish grilled (broiled) simply with oil or butter.

METRIC/IMPERIAL

1.5 kg/3–3½ lb conger eel, or 2 large mackerel, cleaned
salt
10 shallots, peeled and finely sliced
4 garlic cloves, peeled and finely sliced
1 cm/½ inch piece of fresh root ginger,* peeled and cut into thin strips
4 sereh stalks,* cut into thin rounds or 1½ teaspoons sereh powder*
3 green chillis, seeded and cut into thin rounds, or 1 teaspoon chilli powder
1½ teaspoons turmeric powder
3 daun jeruk purut*
3 tablespoons chopped mint
3 whole cloves
pinch of grated nutmeg
pinch of cumin powder
pinch of laos powder*
2 teaspoons brown sugar
1 tablespoon dark soy sauce
juice of 1 small lime or ½ lemon
300 ml/½ pint thick santen*
1 tablespoon olive oil or melted butter

AMERICAN

3–3½ lb conger eel, or 2 large mackerel, cleaned
salt
10 shallots, peeled and finely sliced
4 garlic cloves, peeled and finely sliced
½ inch slice of fresh ginger root,* peeled and cut into thin strips
4 sereh stalks,* cut into thin rounds, or 1½ teaspoons sereh powder*
3 green chilis, seeded and cut into thin rounds, or 1 teaspoon chili powder
1½ teaspoons turmeric powder
3 daun jeruk purut*
3 tablespoons chopped mint
3 whole cloves
pinch of grated nutmeg
pinch of cumin powder
pinch of laos powder*
2 teaspoons brown sugar
1 tablespoon dark soy sauce
juice of 1 small lime or ½ lemon
1¼ cups thick santen*
1 tablespoon olive oil or melted butter

METHOD

If using conger eel, rub it with a little salt. Make several shallow cuts on each side, spacing them fairly wide apart. If using mackerel, discard the heads, score the skin and rub with a little salt.

Put the remaining ingredients, except the santen and oil or butter, in a bowl. Mix well, then rub all over the fish. Wrap in foil and cook in a preheated moderate oven (180°C/350°F, Gas Mark 4) for 45 minutes.

Remove the foil from the fish, then scrape the spice mixture into a small pan. Add the santen, bring to the boil, then lower the heat and simmer until the mixture is quite thick.

Put the fish in a shallow flameproof dish. Strain the spice and santen mixture over the top, then add the oil or butter. Grill (broil) under a preheated hot grill (broiler), turning the fish once, until golden brown on both sides. Serve hot or cold.

SERVES 4

Pangek Ikan
Spiced Poached Trout
Indonesia

This way of cooking river fish is well known in West Sumatra. *Paku** or *pakis* – young fern shoots (fiddleheads) – are used to add an alluring, quite indefinable flavour to the dish. In Indonesia, large quantities of fish are cooked at the same time in a deep earthenware pot and the fish are removed from the pot as and when required. It is possible to keep the dish in the refrigerator for as long as 1 week, but the whole dish must be re-heated before serving – even if you wish to serve only part of it.

METRIC/IMPERIAL

8 small river trout, cleaned
salt
8 kemiri,* chopped
4 red chillis, chopped, or 1 tablespoon sambal ulek*
8 shallots, peeled and chopped
4 garlic cloves, peeled and chopped
2 teaspoons ground ginger
1 teaspoon turmeric powder
½ teaspoon laos powder*
750 ml/1¼ pints very thick santen*
7 tablespoons tamarind water*
575 g/1¼ lb paku*
2 salam leaves*
40 g/1½ oz mint sprigs

AMERICAN

8 small river trout, cleaned
salt
8 kemiri,* chopped
4 red chilis, chopped, or 1 tablespoon sambal ulek*
8 shallots, peeled and chopped
4 garlic cloves, peeled and chopped
2 teaspoons ginger powder
1 teaspoon turmeric powder
½ teaspoon laos powder*
3 cups very thick santen*
7 tablespoons tamarind water*
1¼ lb fiddlehead ferns*
2 salam leaves*
¾ cup mint sprigs

Pangek Ikan; Pais Ikan

Ikan Bakar
Grilled (Broiled) Fish
Indonesia

Both freshwater and sea fish can be cooked in this way – the secret is simply that the fish must be absolutely fresh. For optimum flavour, cook the fish over a charcoal barbecue.

METRIC/IMPERIAL

4 fresh rainbow trout or mackerel, cleaned
juice of 1 lime, or 1 tablespoon white vinegar
2 garlic cloves, peeled and crushed
salt
Sauce:
2 tomatoes, skinned
2 red chillis
1 slice terasi*
2 shallots, peeled
1 teaspoon dark soy sauce (optional)

AMERICAN

4 fresh rainbow trout or mackerel, cleaned
juice of 1 lime, or 1 tablespoon white vinegar
2 garlic cloves, peeled and crushed
salt
Sauce:
2 tomatoes, skinned
2 red chilis
1 slice terasi*
2 shallots, peeled
1 teaspoon dark soy sauce (optional)

METHOD

Make several shallow cuts on both sides of the fish, then rub with the lime juice or vinegar, the garlic and salt. Leave to stand for 30 minutes.

Grill (broil) the fish under a preheated hot grill (broiler) for 10 to 15 minutes until cooked through, turning them over once during cooking. Transfer to a baking (cookie) sheet lined with foil, arranging them side by side in a single layer.

To make the sauce: Put the tomatoes, chillis, terasi and shallots under the grill (broiler) for 2 minutes. Transfer the chillis, terasi and shallots to a cobek or mortar and pound to a paste.

Put the paste in a pan with the tomatoes and soy sauce, if using. Heat gently for 1 minute, breaking the tomatoes down with a wooden spoon.

Pour the sauce over the fish, then return to the hot grill (broiler) and grill (broil) for 1 minute. Serve immediately.
SERVES 4

METHOD

Rub the fish with salt. Put the kemiri, chillis, if using, shallots and garlic in a cobek or mortar and pound to a very smooth paste. Add the spices, santen, tamarind water and 1 teaspoon salt and mix well.

Line a flameproof casserole with a layer of paku (fiddleheads). Arrange a single layer of trout on top, then cover with more paku (fiddleheads). Repeat these layers until all the trout and paku (fiddleheads) have been used, finishing with a layer of paku (fiddleheads).

Arrange the salam leaves and mint on top, then pour over the spice mixture. Cover with a tight-fitting lid and simmer gently for 1 hour Serve hot.
SERVES 4

Ayam Goreng Jawa
Fried Chicken Javanese-style
Indonesia

Before frying chicken, the Javanese boil it first, either in water or *santen** with plenty of spices.

METRIC/IMPERIAL

1 chicken, weighing 1.5 kg/3–3½ lb, cut into serving pieces
5 shallots, peeled and finely sliced
4 garlic cloves, peeled and finely sliced
2 teaspoons coriander powder
½ teaspoon cumin powder
pinch of sereh powder*
pinch of laos powder*
pinch of grated nutmeg
1 small cinnamon stick (optional)
1 bay leaf
1 teaspoon brown sugar (optional)
salt
900 ml/1½ pints water
vegetable oil for deep-frying

AMERICAN

1 chicken, weighing 3–3½ lb, cut into serving pieces
5 shallots, peeled and finely sliced
4 garlic cloves, peeled and finely sliced
2 teaspoons coriander powder
½ teaspoon cumin powder
pinch of sereh powder*
pinch of laos powder*
pinch of grated nutmeg
1 small cinnamon stick (optional)
1 bay leaf
1 teaspoon brown sugar (optional)
salt
3¾ cups water
vegetable oil for deep-frying

METHOD

Put all the ingredients in a heavy pan. Bring to the boil, then lower the heat, cover and simmer for about 1 hour until the chicken is tender and almost all the stock has been absorbed, turning occasionally during cooking.

Remove the chicken from the pan and leave to cool. Heat the oil in a deep-fat fryer to 180°C/350°F. Add the chicken and deep-fry for about 10 minutes until golden brown. Remove from the pan with a slotted spoon and drain on kitchen paper towels. Serve hot.
SERVES 4

Ayam Panggang Kecap
Roast and Grilled (Broiled) Chicken with Soy Sauce
Malaysia

METRIC/IMPERIAL

1 chicken, weighing 1.5 kg/3–3½ lb
salt
2 tablespoons dark soy sauce
2 shallots, peeled and finely sliced
2 garlic cloves, peeled and crushed
½ teaspoon chilli powder
juice of ½ lemon or lime
2 teaspoons sesame seed oil*
oil for basting (optional)

AMERICAN

1 chicken, weighing 3–3½ lb
salt
2 tablespoons dark soy sauce
2 shallots, peeled and finely sliced
2 garlic cloves, peeled and crushed
½ teaspoon chili powder
juice of ½ lemon or lime
2 teaspoons sesame seed oil*
oil for basting (optional)

METHOD

Rub the chicken with salt, then roast in a preheated moderately hot oven (190°C/375°F, Gas Mark 5) for 45 minutes or until golden brown. Leave to cool.

Cut the chicken into 4 pieces, then beat the flesh to loosen the fibres. Mix together the remaining ingredients and rub over the chicken. Cover and leave to marinate for 1 hour, turning the chicken pieces occasionally.

Just before serving, reheat the chicken under the grill (broiler), brushing it first with oil, if liked. Serve hot.
SERVES 4

Kelia Ayam
Indonesian Chicken Curry
Indonesia

This dish can be cooked in advance and reheated just before serving.

METRIC/IMPERIAL

8 shallots, peeled and chopped
2 garlic cloves, peeled and chopped
4 kemiri,* chopped
2 tablespoons water
600 ml/1 pint thick santen*
1 teaspoon ground ginger
1 teaspoon chilli powder
1 teaspoon turmeric powder
1 salam leaf*
salt
1 chicken, weighing 1.5 kg/3–3½ lb, cut into serving pieces

AMERICAN

8 shallots, peeled and chopped
2 garlic cloves, peeled and chopped
4 kemiri,* chopped
2 tablespoons water
2½ cups thick santen*
1 teaspoon ginger powder
1 teaspoon chili powder
1 teaspoon turmeric powder
1 salam leaf*
salt
1 chicken, weighing 3–3½ lb, cut into serving pieces

METHOD

Place the shallots, garlic, kemiri and water in an electric blender and work until smooth. Transfer the liquid to a wok or deep frying pan (deep-fat fryer) and add the santen, spices, salam leaf, salt and chicken. Simmer for 1 to 1½ hours until the sauce is thick, then taste and add more salt if necessary. Serve hot.
SERVES 4

Saté Ayam

Chicken Saté

This is one of the easiest and most versatile kinds of *saté** to prepare, as well as being one of the most popular. It is equally good served with rice, eaten as a snack with drinks, or as a starter with cucumber salad and *Lontong* (see page 81). Use bamboo skewers if available.

If you have a charcoal barbecue, use this for cooking *saté**; otherwise an ordinary gas or electric stove will give satisfactory results.

Saté Ayam can either be served on its own or with the sauces for *Saté Kambing* (see page 74). If serving without sauce, double the marinade quantities and brush over the meat during grilling (broiling).

Ayam Goreng Jawa; Kelia Ayam; Ayam Panggang Kecap

METRIC/IMPERIAL

1 kg/2 lb boned chicken, skinned (preferably from breast and thigh)
1 tablespoon dark soy sauce
2 shallots, peeled and finely sliced
1 garlic clove, peeled and crushed
pinch of chilli powder (optional)
1 tablespoon lemon juice (optional)

AMERICAN

2 lb boned chicken, skinned (preferably from breast and thigh)
1 tablespoon dark soy sauce
2 shallots, peeled and finely sliced
1 garlic clove, peeled and crushed
pinch of chili powder (optional)
1 tablespoon lemon juice (optional)

METHOD

Cut the chicken into 2.5 cm/1 inch cubes. Mix together the remaining ingredients in a bowl. Add the chicken and stir to coat thoroughly, then cover and leave to marinate for at least 1 hour.

Divide the chicken pieces equally between 4 skewers and grill (broil) for 5 to 8 minutes, turning frequently. Serve hot.
SERVES 4
Illustrated on page 81.

Babi Kecap
Pork in Soy Sauce
Singapore

METRIC/IMPERIAL

4 garlic cloves, peeled
2 tablespoons plain flour
1 tablespoon light soy sauce
750 g/1½ lb pork fillet, cut into cubes
75 g/3 oz Chinese dried mushrooms,*
    soaked in warm water for 30
    minutes, or 100 g/4 oz button
    mushrooms, sliced
7 tablespoons vegetable oil or melted
    pork fat
1 teaspoon ground ginger
5 spring onions, thinly sliced
freshly ground black pepper
3 tablespoons dark soy sauce
1 teaspoon white vinegar
2 tablespoons rice wine* (optional)

AMERICAN

4 garlic cloves, peeled
2 tablespoons all-purpose flour
1 tablespoon light soy sauce
1½ lb pork loin, cut into cubes
3 oz Chinese dried mushrooms,*
    soaked in warm water for 30 minutes,
    or 1 cup sliced button mushrooms
7 tablespoons vegetable oil or melted
    pork fat
1 teaspoon ginger powder
5 scallions, thinly sliced
freshly ground black pepper
3 tablespoons dark soy sauce
1 teaspoon white vinegar
2 tablespoons rice wine* (optional)

METHOD

Crush 2 garlic cloves and mix with the flour and light soy sauce. Coat the pork with this mixture, then leave to stand for at least 30 minutes. Meanwhile, drain the Chinese mushrooms, if used, then discard the hard stalks and cut each mushroom cap into 4 pieces.

Heat the oil or fat in a wok or deep frying pan (deep-fat fryer). Add half the meat and fry for 6 to 8 minutes until browned on all sides, turning frequently. Fry the remaining meat in the same way. Remove from the pan with a slotted spoon and drain on kitchen paper towels.

Pour off all but 2 to 3 tablespoons oil from the pan, then add the mushrooms and fry for 3 minutes. Slice the remaining garlic and add to the pan with the ginger. Stir, then add the meat, spring onions (scallions), pepper, soy sauce and vinegar. Stir-fry for 2 minutes, then add the rice wine, if using. Serve hot, with accompaniments, such as *Tumis Buncis* (see page 77).
SERVES 4

Bebek Hijau
Duck in Green Chilli Sauce
Indonesia

This dish improves if it is prepared 24 hours before required so the fat can be skimmed off. If a milder sauce is preferred, use green peppers instead of chillis.

METRIC/IMPERIAL

10 green chillis, seeded and chopped
8 kemiri,* chopped
3 tablespoons coconut oil or peanut oil
10 shallots, peeled and finely sliced
4 garlic cloves, peeled and finely sliced
2 teaspoons ground ginger
½ teaspoon turmeric powder
pinch of laos powder*
1 sereh stalk,* bruised, or ½ teaspoon
    sereh powder*
1 duck, weighing 1.75 kg/4–4¼ lb,
    skinned and cut into 8 pieces
3 tablespoons tamarind water*
1 daun kunyit* (optional)
3 daun jeruk purut* (optional)
1 bay leaf
salt
freshly ground black pepper
300 ml/½ pint water
2 tablespoons snipped chives

AMERICAN

10 green chilis, seeded and chopped
8 kemiri,* chopped
3 tablespoons coconut oil or peanut oil
10 shallots, peeled and finely sliced
4 garlic cloves, peeled and finely sliced
2 teaspoons ginger powder
½ teaspoon turmeric powder
pinch of laos powder*
1 sereh stalk,* bruised or ½ teaspoon
    sereh powder*
1 duck, weighing 4–4¼ lb, skinned and
    cut into 8 pieces
3 tablespoons tamarind water*
1 daun kunyit* (optional)
3 daun jeruk purut* (optional)
1 bay leaf
salt
freshly ground black pepper
1¼ cups water
2 tablespoons snipped chives

METHOD

Put the chillis and kemiri in a *cobek* or mortar and pound to a very smooth paste.

Heat the oil in a pan, add the shallots and garlic and fry gently until lightly browned. Add the chilli and kemiri paste, stir-fry for 1 minute, then stir in the spices and sereh. Add the remaining ingredients, except the water and chives. Stir well, then cover and simmer gently for 45 minutes.

Remove the lid, increase the heat and boil for 10 minutes, stirring occasionally. Add the water and chives and cook for 15 minutes.

Discard the sereh stalk, if used, daun kunyit, daun jeruk purut and bay leaf. Correct the seasoning. Leave to cool, then chill in the refrigerator overnight.

Skim off the fat, reheat and serve hot with rice and accompaniments, such as *Oseng-Oseng Wortel dan Bloemkool* (see page 75).
SERVES 4

Saté Babi
Pork Saté
Singapore

There are endless *saté** variations, using different meat and marinade ingredients.

Try to include a little fat with each piece of meat, or the *saté** will become dry when cooked. For optimum flavour, use a charcoal barbecue for cooking. Use bamboo skewers if available.

METRIC/IMPERIAL

750 g/1½ lb pork fillet
2 tablespoons light soy sauce
2 garlic cloves, peeled and crushed
2 shallots, peeled and chopped
2 teaspoons five spice powder*
1 tablespoon clear honey
freshly ground black pepper

AMERICAN

1½ lb pork loin
2 tablespoons light soy sauce
2 garlic cloves, peeled and crushed
2 shallots, peeled and chopped
2 teaspoons five spice powder*
1 tablespoon honey
freshly ground black pepper

METHOD

Cut the pork into 2.5 cm/1 inch cubes, then slice each cube in half so that the chunks of meat are quite thin. Put the pork in a bowl with the remaining ingredients and mix well. Leave to marinate for 2 to 3 hours.

Divide the pork pieces equally between 4 kebab skewers, then place the skewers on a wire rack. Put the rack on a baking (cookie) sheet and roast in a preheated moderate oven (180°C/350°F, Gas Mark 4) for 30 minutes. Transfer to a preheated hot grill (broiler) and grill (broil) for 5 to 8 minutes, turning frequently. Serve immediately.
SERVES 4
Illustrated on page 81.

Bebek Hijau, served with Nasi Putih (see page 80) and Oseng-Oseng Wortel dan Bloemkool (see page 75); Babi Kecap, served with Tumis Buncis (see page 77)

Rendang Padang
A Traditional Sumatran Beef Dish
Indonesia

METRIC/IMPERIAL

1.5 kg/3–3½ lb brisket of beef or chuck
   steak, cut into large chunks
1.75 litres/3 pints thick santen*
10 shallots, peeled and sliced
4 garlic cloves, peeled and crushed
2 teaspoons ground ginger
4 teaspoons chilli powder, or 2
   tablespoons sambal ulek*
1 teaspoon laos powder*
1½ teaspoons turmeric powder
2 salam leaves*
1 daun kunyit* (optional)
salt

AMERICAN

3–3½ lb brisket or chuck steak, cut into
   large chunks
7½ cups thick santen*
10 shallots, peeled and sliced
4 garlic cloves, peeled and crushed
2 teaspoons ginger powder
4 teaspoons chili powder, or 2
   tablespoons sambal ulek*
1 teaspoon laos powder*
1½ teaspoons turmeric powder
2 salam leaves*
1 daun kunyit* (optional)
salt

METHOD

Put all the ingredients in a wok or deep frying pan (deep-fat fryer). Simmer, uncovered, for 1 to 1½ hours or until the sauce becomes very thick, stirring occasionally.

Taste and add more salt if necessary, then simmer for a further 1½ hours until the meat becomes dark brown and has absorbed almost all the liquid in the pan, stirring frequently. Serve hot or cold, with rice and accompaniments, such as *Urap* (see page 77).

SERVES 8 to 10

Dendeng Pedas
Fried Steak with Chilli
Indonesia

In Indonesia, *dendeng* is thinly sliced meat which is coated in spices, then dried in the sun. The slices are coated with crushed red chillis, which make the meat *pedas* – chilli-hot. *Dendeng* should be tender and brittle as a result of its exposure to many hours of hot sunshine. It is sold ready to cook in packets in Indonesian shops and markets, but outside Indonesia a good Dendeng Pedas can be made using this recipe.

METRIC/IMPERIAL

575 g/1¼ lb rump steak or topside of
   beef
2 teaspoons coriander powder
2 tablespoons tamarind water*
1 teaspoon brown sugar
salt
freshly ground black pepper
8 red chillis, seeded and chopped
4 shallots, peeled and chopped
2 garlic cloves, peeled and chopped
6 tablespoons vegetable oil
1 teaspoon lemon juice

AMERICAN

1¼ lb New York sirloin, hip or top
   round steak
2 teaspoons coriander powder
2 tablespoons tamarind water*
1 teaspoon brown sugar
salt
freshly ground black pepper
8 red chilis, seeded and chopped
4 shallots, peeled and chopped
2 garlic cloves, peeled and chopped
6 tablespoons vegetable oil
1 teaspoon lemon juice

METHOD

Slice the meat thinly across the grain, then cut the slices into 5 cm/2 inch squares. Arrange in a single layer on a plate and sprinkle with the coriander, tamarind water, sugar, and salt and pepper to taste.

Press each piece with your hands so that the spices are thoroughly absorbed into the meat, then spread the slices out on the plate again. Leave to stand for 2 to 3 hours (in the sun if possible).

Put the chillis, shallots and garlic in a *cobek* or mortar and pound until broken, but not reduced to a paste.

Heat the oil in a heavy frying pan (skillet). Add the meat and fry until evenly browned and cooked through. Remove from the pan with a slotted spoon and keep hot.

Add the pounded mixture to the oil remaining in the pan and fry for 2 to 3 minutes, stirring constantly. Return the meat to the pan and stir to coat with the spice mixture. Add the lemon juice and salt to taste and stir well. Serve hot, with rice and accompaniments, such as *Acar Kuning* (see page 78), *Serundeng* (see page 60), *Krupuk* (see page 60) and *Sambal* (see page 83).

SERVES 4
Illustrated on page 78.

Kambing Korma (above); Rendang Padang, served with Urap (see page 77) and Nasi Putih (see page 80)

Kambing Korma
Lamb Curry
Malaysia

METRIC/IMPERIAL

4 shallots, peeled
3 garlic cloves, peeled
6 kemiri*
450 ml/¾ pint thick santen*
575 g/1¼ lb boned leg of lamb, cut into small cubes
salt
3 tablespoons vegetable oil
1 small onion, peeled and finely sliced
1½ teaspoons coriander powder
½ teaspoon cumin powder
1 teaspoon ground ginger
pinch of laos powder*
4 whole cloves
2.5 cm/1 inch piece of cinnamon stick
3 whole cardamoms
1 salam leaf*
1 sereh stalk,* bruised, or ½ teaspoon sereh powder*
3 tablespoons tamarind water*
½ teaspoon freshly ground white pepper

AMERICAN

4 shallots, peeled
3 garlic cloves, peeled
6 kemiri*
2 cups thick santen*
1¼ lb boneless leg of lamb, cut into small cubes
salt
3 tablespoons vegetable oil
1 small onion, peeled and finely sliced
1½ teaspoons coriander powder
½ teaspoon cumin powder
1 teaspoon ginger powder
pinch of laos powder*
4 whole cloves
1 inch piece of cinnamon stick
3 whole cardamoms
1 salam leaf*
1 sereh stalk,* bruised, or ½ teaspoon sereh powder*
3 tablespoons tamarind water*
½ teaspoon freshly ground white pepper

METHOD

Mince (grind) the shallots, garlic and kemiri, then transfer to an electric blender, add 2 tablespoons santen and work to a smooth paste.

Put the mixture in a bowl, add the lamb and a little salt and mix well. Leave to marinate for 30 minutes.

Heat the oil in a pan, add the onion and fry gently until soft. Add the spices, salam leaf and sereh. Stir-fry for a few seconds, then add the meat and marinade and fry for 2 minutes. Add the tamarind water, salt and pepper. Cover and cook gently for 15 minutes, stirring every 5 minutes to prevent burning. Stir in the remaining santen and simmer for 40 minutes or until the meat is tender and the sauce is quite thick.

Discard the salam leaf, sereh stalk, if using, cloves, cinnamon stick and cardamoms. Taste and adjust the seasoning. Serve hot.
SERVES 4

Gulé Kambing

Aromatic Lamb Stew

Indonesia

This is a very liquid stew, which can be served as a spicy, meaty soup.

METRIC/IMPERIAL

4 kemiri,* chopped
1 small onion, peeled and chopped
3 garlic cloves, peeled and chopped
2 teaspoons coriander powder
1 teaspoon ground ginger
½ teaspoon turmeric powder
pinch of white pepper
pinch of cayenne pepper
pinch of chilli powder
pinch of laos powder*
2 tablespoons vegetable oil
1 kg/2–2¼ lb boned leg or shoulder of
   lamb, cut into small cubes
1 teaspoon brown sugar
4 tablespoons tamarind water*
salt
1 sereh stalk,* bruised
1 small cinnamon stick
3 whole cloves
1 salam leaf*
450 ml/¾ pint water
450 ml/¾ pint thick santen*

AMERICAN

4 kemiri,* chopped
1 small onion, peeled and chopped
3 garlic cloves, peeled and chopped
2 teaspoons coriander powder
1 teaspoon ginger powder
½ teaspoon turmeric powder
pinch of white pepper
pinch of cayenne pepper
pinch of chili powder
pinch of laos powder*
2 tablespoons vegetable oil
2–2¼ lb boneless leg or shoulder of
   lamb, cut into small cubes
1 teaspoon brown sugar
¼ cup tamarind water*
salt
1 sereh stalk,* bruised
1 small cinnamon stick
3 whole cloves
1 salam leaf*
2 cups water
2 cups thick santen*

METHOD

Put the kemiri, onion and garlic in a cobek or mortar and pound to a very smooth paste. Add the spices and mix well.

Heat the oil in a pan, add the spice paste and fry for 1 minute, stirring constantly. Add the lamb and stir-fry for 1 to 2 minutes, then stir in the sugar, tamarind water and salt to taste. Cover and simmer for 4 minutes.

Add the remaining ingredients except the santen. Cover and simmer for a further 20 minutes. Add the santen and a little salt if necessary, then cover and simmer for 20 to 25 minutes, stirring occasionally.

Discard the sereh, cinnamon, cloves and salam leaf. Pour into a warmed soup tureen. Serve hot, with rice and accompaniments, such as Urap (see page 77).
SERVES 6 to 8

Saté Kambing

Lamb Saté

Make sure that some fat is included with the meat or the saté* will be dry. Use bamboo skewers if available.

As with all satés,* a charcoal barbecue should ideally be used for cooking, but an ordinary gas or electric stove will give satisfactory results.

This recipe gives two sauces – either or both may be served with saté* – in separate bowls so that guests can help themselves. Saté Kambing is particularly good served with Lontong (see page 81).

METRIC/IMPERIAL

1 kg/2–2¼ lb boned leg or shoulder of
   lamb, cut into small cubes
Marinade:
2 tablespoons dark soy sauce
2 tablespoons tamarind water*
4 shallots, peeled and finely chopped
3 garlic cloves, peeled and crushed
½ teaspoon chilli powder
1 teaspoon ground ginger
½ teaspoon coriander powder
1 teaspoon brown sugar
Peanut sauce:
5 tablespoons vegetable oil
100 g/4 oz whole shelled peanuts
3 shallots, peeled and chopped
1 garlic clove, peeled and chopped
1 slice terasi*
pinch of chilli powder
salt
1 tablespoon peanut oil
300 ml/½ pint water
1 tablespoon tamarind water*
1 teaspoon brown sugar
Chilli sauce:
3 tablespoons dark soy sauce
2 shallots, peeled and finely sliced
1 garlic clove, peeled and crushed
1 green chilli, finely chopped, or
   ¼ teaspoon chilli powder
juice of ½ lemon
1 teaspoon olive oil (optional)
½ teaspoon brown sugar

AMERICAN

2–2¼ lb boneless leg or shoulder of
   lamb, cut into small cubes
Marinade:
2 tablespoons dark soy sauce
2 tablespoons tamarind water*
4 shallots, peeled and finely chopped
3 garlic cloves, peeled and crushed
½ teaspoon chili powder
1 teaspoon ginger powder
½ teaspoon coriander powder
1 teaspoon brown sugar
Peanut sauce:
⅓ cup vegetable oil
½ cup whole shelled peanuts
3 shallots, peeled and chopped
1 garlic clove, peeled and chopped
1 slice terasi*
pinch of chili powder
salt
1 tablespoon peanut oil
1¼ cups water
1 tablespoon tamarind water*
1 teaspoon brown sugar
Chili sauce:
3 tablespoons dark soy sauce
2 shallots, peeled and finely sliced
1 garlic clove, peeled and crushed
1 green chili, finely chopped, or
   ¼ teaspoon chili powder
juice of ½ lemon
1 teaspoon olive oil (optional)
½ teaspoon brown sugar

METHOD

Put the lamb in a bowl with the marinade ingredients. Stir well, then leave to marinate for at least 2 hours, preferably overnight.

Divide the lamb cubes equally between 6 skewers. Grill (broil) for 5 to 8 minutes, turning frequently.

To make the peanut sauce: Heat the vegetable oil in a small frying pan (skillet), add the peanuts and fry for about 5 minutes until just brown, shaking the pan constantly. Remove from the pan and leave to cool, then work to a powder in an electric grinder, or using a cobek or mortar.

Put the shallots, garlic and terasi in a cobek or mortar and pound to a very smooth paste. Add the chilli powder and salt to taste and mix well.

Heat the peanut oil in a pan, add the spice paste and fry gently for a few seconds, stirring constantly. Add the water and bring to the boil, then add the ground peanuts, tamarind water and sugar. Stir, then taste and add more salt if necessary. Continue boiling until the sauce is thick, stirring constantly.

To make the chilli sauce: Put all the ingredients in a bowl and mix well.
SERVES 6
Illustrated on page 81.

74

Oseng-Oseng Wortel dan Bloemkool

Sauté of Carrots and Cauliflower

Indonesia

METRIC/IMPERIAL

6 carrots, peeled and sliced diagonally
175 g/6 oz cauliflower florets
2 tablespoons vegetable oil or melted
    butter
1 garlic clove, peeled and crushed
1 slice terasi,* crushed (optional)
4 spring onions, chopped into
    1 cm/½ inch lengths
1 tablespoon light soy sauce
pinch of chilli powder
pinch of ground ginger
salt

AMERICAN

6 carrots, peeled and sliced diagonally
3 large cauliflower florets
2 tablespoons vegetable oil or melted
    butter
1 garlic clove, peeled and crushed
1 slice terasi,* crushed (optional)
4 scallions, cut into ½ inch lengths
1 tablespoon light soy sauce
pinch of chili powder
pinch of ginger powder
salt

METHOD

Add the carrots and cauliflower to a pan of boiling water. Boil for 3 minutes, then drain.

Heat the oil or butter in a wok or deep frying pan (deep-fat fryer). Add the garlic and terasi and fry for a few seconds. Stir in the spring onions (scallions) and soy sauce, then add the carrots and cauliflower. Add the remaining ingredients and cook for 2 minutes, stirring constantly. Serve hot.

SERVES 4

Illustrated on page 71.

Gulé Kambing, served with Urap (see page 77) and Nasi Putih (see page 80)

Gado-Gado

Cooked Mixed Salad with Peanut Dressing

Like *saté*,* you will find Gado-Gado wherever you go in Malaysia, Singapore or Indonesia. For those who are fond of peanut sauce, this is an ideal dish to have by itself for a light lunch, or serve at any meal with rice and meat.

METRIC/IMPERIAL	AMERICAN
Sauce:	**Sauce:**
vegetable oil for deep-frying	*vegetable oil for deep-frying*
100 g/4 oz whole shelled peanuts	*½ cup whole shelled peanuts*
*1 slice terasi**	*1 slice terasi**
2 shallots, peeled and chopped	*2 shallots, peeled and chopped*
1 garlic clove, peeled and chopped (optional)	*1 garlic clove, peeled and chopped (optional)*
salt	*salt*
*½ teaspoon chilli powder or sambal ulek**	*½ teaspoon chili powder or sambal ulek**
½ teaspoon brown sugar	*½ teaspoon brown sugar*
400 ml/14 fl oz water	*1¾ cups water*
25 g/1 oz creamed coconut (optional)*	*2 tablespoons thick santen* (optional)*
1 tablespoon lemon juice	*1 tablespoon lemon juice*
Salad:	**Salad:**
75 g/3 oz cabbage, shredded	*1 cup shredded cabbage*
2 medium carrots, peeled and sliced	*2 medium carrots, peeled and sliced*
75 g/3 oz cauliflower florets	*2 small cauliflower florets*
75 g/3 oz French or runner beans, topped, tailed and sliced	*20–24 string beans, topped, tailed and sliced*
100 g/4 oz bean sprouts	*2 cups bean sprouts*
1 medium potato, peeled and sliced	*1 medium potato, peeled and sliced*
¼ cucumber, sliced	*¼ cucumber, sliced*
To garnish:	**To garnish:**
1–2 hard-boiled eggs, shelled and sliced	*1–2 hard-cooked eggs, shelled and sliced*
Krupuk, broken into pieces (see page 60)	*Krupuk, broken into pieces (see page 60)*
few fried onion slices	*few fried onion slices*
1 lettuce	*1 head of lettuce*

METHOD

To make the sauce: Heat the oil in a wok or deep frying pan (deep-fat fryer) and fry the peanuts for 5 to 6 minutes. Drain thoroughly on kitchen paper towels. Allow to cool, then work to a fine powder in an electric grinder, or with a pestle and mortar.

Put the terasi, shallots and garlic, if using, in a *cobek* or mortar. Pound to a very smooth paste, then add a little salt. Heat 1 tablespoon vegetable oil in a pan, add the paste and fry for 1 minute, stirring constantly. Add the chilli powder or sambal ulek, sugar and water, bring to the boil, then add the ground peanuts. Stir well, then simmer until thick, stirring occasionally. Add the creamed coconut (santen) if using, and stir until dissolved. Keep hot.

76

Gado-Gado; Urap; Tumis Buncis

Urap
Cooked Salad with Coconut Dressing
Indonesia

For this salad, you can vary the combination of vegetables as you wish. Do not overcook them or they will lose their crispness and flavour.

METRIC/IMPERIAL

1 slice terasi,* grilled
2 garlic cloves, peeled and chopped
1 shallot, peeled and chopped
½ teaspoon chilli powder
1 teaspoon brown sugar
1 tablespoon tamarind water*
salt
100 g/4 oz grated white coconut flesh
100 g/4 oz cabbage, shredded
100 g/4 oz French or runner beans,
    topped and tailed
2 medium carrots, peeled and sliced
100 g/4 oz bean sprouts
To garnish:
few watercress sprigs
few cucumber slices

AMERICAN

1 slice terasi,* broiled
2 garlic cloves, peeled and chopped
1 shallot, peeled and chopped
½ teaspoon chili powder
1 teaspoon brown sugar
1 tablespoon tamarind water*
salt
2 cups grated white coconut flesh
1½ cups shredded cabbage
¼ lb string beans, topped and tailed
2 medium carrots, peeled and sliced
2 cups bean sprouts
To garnish:
few watercress sprigs
few cucumber slices

METHOD

Put the terasi, garlic and shallot in a *cobek* or mortar and pound to a very smooth paste. Add the chilli powder, sugar, tamarind water and salt and mix well. Combine with the coconut.

Cook the cabbage, beans, carrots and bean sprouts separately in boiling water for 3 to 5 minutes; they should still be crisp. Drain thoroughly.

Just before serving, toss the vegetables in the coconut mixture and pile the salad into a serving bowl. Garnish with watercress and cucumber slices. Serve warm.
SERVES 4

Tumis Buncis
Spiced French Beans
Indonesia

METRIC/IMPERIAL

2 tablespoons vegetable oil
3 shallots, peeled and finely sliced
1 garlic clove, peeled and crushed
    (optional)
1 teaspoon ground ginger
pinch of chilli powder
pinch of grated nutmeg
450 g/1 lb French beans, topped,
    tailed and halved
salt
freshly ground black pepper
6 tablespoons strong-flavoured chicken
    stock, or 1 chicken stock cube
    dissolved in 6 tablespoons water

AMERICAN

2 tablespoons vegetable oil
3 shallots, peeled and finely sliced
1 garlic clove, peeled and crushed
    (optional)
1 teaspoon ginger powder
pinch of chili powder
pinch of grated nutmeg
1 lb string beans, topped, tailed and
    halved
salt
freshly ground black pepper
6 tablespoons strong-flavored
chicken stock, or 1 chicken bouillon
cube dissolved in 6 tablespoons
water

METHOD

Heat the oil in a pan, add the shallots and garlic and fry gently for 1 minute. Stir in the remaining ingredients, except the stock, and cook for 2 minutes.

Stir in the stock, cover and simmer gently for 5 minutes. Remove the lid and cook for a further 2 to 3 minutes, stirring constantly. Correct the seasoning. Serve hot.
SERVES 4

Cook the cabbage, carrots, cauliflower, beans, bean sprouts and potato separately in boiling water for 3 to 5 minutes; they should still be crisp. Drain thoroughly.

Arrange the vegetables on a large serving dish; place the cabbage on the dish first, then the carrots, cauliflower, beans and bean sprouts. Arrange the cucumber and potato slices around the edge, then garnish with the egg slices, krupuk and fried onion. Garnish the edge of the dish with lettuce leaves.

Stir the lemon juice into the sauce, then, either pour over the vegetables, or hand separately. Serve warm.
SERVES 6 to 8

Nasi Putih

Boiled White Rice

For cooking rice, choose a saucepan with a thick, heavy base. During the final stage of cooking, a thin layer of rice will stick to the bottom of the pan, unless you invest in a rice steamer.

A rice steamer is simply a pan with holes in it, which is placed inside a pan of boiling water. The rice is first boiled in an ordinary pan as described below, then transferred to the steamer, when it has absorbed all the water. Leftover rice can be kept in a steamer for up to 24 hours after boiling, then reheated by gentle steaming.

METRIC/IMPERIAL

350 g/12 oz long-grain rice
600 ml/1 pint water

AMERICAN

1½ cups long-grain rice
2½ cups water

METHOD

Wash the rice thoroughly under cold running water. Drain, then place in a pan with the water; do not add salt. Bring to the boil, stirring once or twice, then lower the heat and simmer, uncovered, until all the water has been absorbed into the rice. Stir once, then lower the heat and cover the pan with a tight-fitting lid – it should be as near airtight as possible. Cook very gently for 10 minutes. Serve hot.
SERVES 4 to 6

Nasi Goreng

Fried Rice

The ingredients in this basic recipe can be varied according to taste and availability. Fried rice may be served as an alternative to Nasi Putih, or as a satisfying meal in itself – if suitably garnished. It is usually eaten with meat or fish and vegetables and is particularly popular served with baked or grilled (broiled) fish, or any kind of saté*

The chillis or chilli powder in this recipe give the rice a good red colour, but they do make it hot – substitute paprika if you prefer milder rice.

On a restaurant menu, Nasi Goreng Istimewa usually indicates that the rice is well-garnished and topped with a fried egg.

METRIC/IMPERIAL

275 g/10 oz long-grain rice
450 ml/¾ pint water
2 tablespoons vegetable oil, clarified butter or pork fat
4 shallots, peeled and thinly sliced
2 red chillis, seeded and thinly sliced, or 2 teaspoons sambal ulek*
50 g/2 oz pork, beef or bacon, chopped
1 tablespoon light soy sauce
1 teaspoon tomato ketchup or tomato purée (optional)
salt

To garnish:

few fried onion slices
1 plain omelet made with 1 egg, cut into strips
few coriander leaves* or parsley sprigs
few cucumber slices

AMERICAN

1¼ cups long-grain rice
2 cups water
2 tablespoons vegetable oil, clarified butter or pork fat
4 shallots, peeled and thinly sliced
2 red chilis, seeded and thinly sliced, or 2 teaspoons sambal ulek*
¼ cup chopped pork, beef or bacon, firmly packed
1 tablespoon light soy sauce
1 teaspoon tomato ketchup or tomato paste (optional)
salt

To garnish:

few fried onion slices
1 plain omelet, made with 1 egg, cut into strips
few coriander leaves* or parsley sprigs
few cucumber slices

METHOD

At least 2 hours before the dish is required, wash the rice thoroughly, then cook in the water as for Nasi Putih.

Heat the oil in a wok or deep frying pan (deep-fat fryer), add the shallots and chillis, if using, and fry for 1 to 2 minutes. Add the meat or bacon and fry for 3 minutes, stirring constantly, then add the rice, soy sauce, tomato ketchup or purée (paste) and sambal ulek, if using. Fry, stirring, for 5 to 8 minutes, then taste and add salt if necessary.

Transfer to a warmed serving dish and garnish with the onion, omelet, coriander or parsley and cucumber. Serve immediately.
SERVES 4

Nasi Kuning

Savoury Yellow Rice

This is a brightly coloured dish which is often served at feasts and celebrations. It can be served simply as an alternative to Nasi Putih, or garnished with the same ingredients as Nasi Goreng.

METRIC/IMPERIAL

350 g/12 oz long-grain rice
2 tablespoons vegetable oil or clarified butter
1 teaspoon turmeric powder
600 ml/1 pint chicken stock
1 teaspoon coriander powder
½ teaspoon cumin powder
1 cinnamon stick
1 whole clove
1 salam leaf*

AMERICAN

1½ cups long-grain rice
2 tablespoons vegetable oil or clarified butter
1 teaspoon turmeric powder
2½ cups chicken stock
1 teaspoon coriander powder
½ teaspoon cumin powder
1 cinnamon stick
1 whole clove
1 salam leaf*

METHOD

Soak the rice in cold water for 1 hour, wash thoroughly under cold running water, then drain.

Heat the oil or butter in a pan, add the rice and fry for 2 minutes. Stir in the turmeric and fry for 2 minutes, then add the remaining ingredients and boil until the rice has absorbed all the liquid. Continue cooking for 10 minutes as for Nasi Putih, either in a rice steamer or pan with a tight-fitting lid. Serve hot.
SERVES 4 to 6

Nasi Lemak

White Rice in Santen

In Indonesia this kind of rice is called Nasi Uduk or Nasi Gurih.

METRIC/IMPERIAL

350 g/12 oz long-grain rice
600 ml/1 pint santen*
½ teaspoon salt

AMERICAN

1½ cups long-grain rice
2½ cups santen*
½ teaspoon salt

Saté Ayam (see page 69); Saté Babi (see page 70); Saté Kambing (see page 74); served with Lontong

METHOD

Wash and cook the rice as for *Nasi Putih*, boiling it with the santen and salt instead of the water; stir several times during boiling. When all the santen has been absorbed by the rice, continue cooking for 10 minutes as for *Nasi Putih*, either in a rice steamer or pan with a tight-fitting lid. Serve hot.

SERVES 4 to 6

Lontong

Compressed Boiled Rice

Indonesia

Traditionally, people in Java eat lontong as part of their celebration of the Muslim New Year; but it is a popular way of cooking rice at any time all over Indonesia.

The grains of rice are compressed by prolonged boiling inside a casing or packet. In the tropics, this casing is usually a banana leaf; another variation, called *ketupat*, is made in a similar way in a casing woven from palm fronds.

Plastic freeze-and-boil bags make a perfectly satisfactory substitute, or boil-in-the-bag rice can be used with equally good results. Lontong must be served cold, therefore the cooking needs to begin at least 8 hours before the meal is to be eaten.

METRIC/IMPERIAL

350 g/12 oz long-grain rice, or
  3 × 100 g/4 oz packets boil-in-the-bag rice
water
pinch of salt

AMERICAN

1½ cups long-grain rice
water
pinch of salt

METHOD

If using long-grain rice, divide the rice equally between 3 freeze-and-boil bags (approx 20 cm/8 inches square). Close the bags by sewing a seam 14 cm/5½ inches from the bottom to make rectangular packets, each about one third full of rice. Pierce a few very small holes in each bag.

Put the bags of rice into a large saucepan of boiling water, making sure that the rice is completely submerged. Add the salt and simmer for 1¼ hours, topping up with more boiling water as necessary to ensure that the rice is always covered. The rice is ready when compressed into a firm mass. Remove from the pan and leave to cool for at least 6 hours. Strip off the bags and slice the lontong into chunks. Serve cold.

SERVES 4 to 6

Sambal Bajak

Hot Relish

Indonesia

This sambal will keep for a long time, and is one of the most popular of the hot relishes.

METRIC/IMPERIAL

20 red chillis, seeded and chopped
10 shallots, peeled and chopped
2 garlic cloves, peeled and chopped
5 kemiri,* chopped
1 slice terasi*
2 tablespoons vegetable oil
1 teaspoon ground ginger
1 teaspoon brown sugar
3 tablespoons tamarind water*
salt
150 ml/¼ pint thick santen*

AMERICAN

20 red chilis, seeded and chopped
10 shallots, peeled and chopped
2 garlic cloves, peeled and chopped
5 kemiri,* chopped
1 slice terasi*
2 tablespoons vegetable oil
1 teaspoon ginger powder
1 teaspoon brown sugar
3 tablespoons tamarind water*
salt
⅔ cup thick santen*

METHOD

Put the chillis, shallots, garlic, kemiri and terasi in a *cobek* or mortar and pound to a very smooth paste.

Heat the oil in a pan, add the paste and fry for 2 minutes. Add the ginger, sugar, tamarind water and salt to taste, stir well, then add the santen. Simmer for about 15 minutes until the sambal is thick and oily, stirring occasionally. Stir-fry for a further 2 to 3 minutes, then serve hot or cold.
SERVES 4

Sambal Kelapa
Coconut Relish

This sambal should be eaten on the day it is made.

METRIC/IMPERIAL

1 slice terasi,* fried or grilled
2 garlic cloves, peeled and chopped
3–5 lombok rawit,* chopped
1 small piece gula Jawa*
1 tablespoon tamarind water*
7 tablespoons freshly grated white
    coconut flesh
salt

AMERICAN

1 slice terasi,* fried or broiled
2 garlic cloves, peeled and chopped
3–5 lombok rawit,* chopped
1 small piece gula Jawa*
1 tablespoon tamarind water*
7 tablespoons freshly grated white
    coconut flesh
salt

METHOD

Put the terasi, garlic, lombok rawit and gula Jawa in a *cobek* or mortar and pound to a very smooth paste. Add the remaining ingredients, with salt to taste, and mix well. Serve cold.
SERVES 4

Sambal Terasi or Blacan
Hot Relish

Indonesia/Malaysia

This sambal should be eaten on the day it is made.

METRIC/IMPERIAL

6–8 green or red chillis
1 shallot, peeled and chopped
1 garlic clove, peeled and chopped
1 slice terasi,* grilled
½ teaspoon brown sugar
2 teaspoons lemon juice
salt

AMERICAN

6–8 green or red chilis
1 shallot, peeled and chopped
1 garlic clove, peeled and chopped
1 slice terasi,* broiled
½ teaspoon brown sugar
2 teaspoons lemon juice
salt

METHOD

Cook the chillis in boiling water for 6 to 8 minutes, then drain. Discard the seeds and chop the flesh, then pound in a *cobek* or mortar, with the shallot, garlic and terasi. Add the sugar, lemon juice and salt to taste. Mix well. Serve cold.
SERVES 4

Pisang Goreng
Fried Bananas

Do not use over-ripe bananas for this accompaniment dish.

METRIC/IMPERIAL

75 g/3 oz rice flour*
25 g/1 oz butter, melted
175 ml/6 fl oz santen*
pinch of salt
4 medium bananas
3 tablespoons clarified butter

AMERICAN

¾ cup rice flour*
2 tablespoons melted butter
¾ cup santen*
pinch of salt
4 medium bananas
3 tablespoons clarified butter

METHOD

Put the flour, melted butter, santen and salt in a bowl and stir well to make a smooth, liquid batter.

Peel the bananas and cut each one in half lengthways or slice into rounds. Roll the banana pieces in the batter until they are well coated. Heat the clarified butter in a large frying pan (skillet), add the banana pieces and fry until golden brown on all sides, turning frequently. Serve hot.
SERVES 4

Sambal Kelapa; Sambal Bajak; Sambal Terasi

Agar-Agar Dengan Serikaya

Seaweed Pudding

METRIC/IMPERIAL

7 g/¼ oz agar-agar strands*
1.2 litres/2 pints water
75 g/3 oz caster sugar
Serikaya:
3 small eggs
50 g/2 oz gula Jawa*
salt
600 ml/1 pint thick santen*

AMERICAN

30–35 agar-agar strands*
5 cups water
6 tablespoons superfine sugar
Serikaya:
3 small eggs
⅓ cup gula Jawa*
salt
2½ cups thick santen*

METHOD

Soak the agar-agar in just enough cold water to cover for at least 2 hours, preferably overnight.

Drain the agar-agar then put in a large pan with the water. Add the sugar and simmer for a few minutes until the agar-agar and sugar have dissolved, stirring occasionally. Strain through a fine nylon sieve (strainer) or muslin (cheesecloth), then pour into a 1 litre/2 pint/5 cup mould. Leave to cool, then store in the refrigerator until required.

To make the serikaya: Put the eggs and gula Jawa in a bowl over a pan and whisk until thick and fluffy. Add the salt and santen and whisk thoroughly. Pour into a pudding basin (heatproof bowl). Place in a steamer or large pan, containing 2.5 cm/1 inch boiling water, and steam for 10 to 15 minutes until thick.

Turn the agar-agar out onto a serving plate. Serve accompanied by the hot or cold serikaya.
SERVES 8 to 10

Lepat Bugis; Rujak; Kue Dadar

Kue Dadar

Coconut Pancakes (Crêpes)

Singapore

METRIC/IMPERIAL

Filling:
175 g/6 oz gula Jawa*
300 ml/½ pint water
225 g/8 oz freshly grated white coconut flesh
pinch of ground cinnamon
pinch of grated nutmeg
pinch of salt
2 teaspoons lemon juice
Pancakes:
100 g/4 oz plain flour
1 egg, beaten
300 ml/½ pint milk
lard for shallow-frying

AMERICAN

Filling:
1 cup gula Jawa*
1¼ cups water
4 cups freshly grated white coconut flesh
pinch of ground cinnamon
pinch of grated nutmeg
pinch of salt
2 teaspoons lemon juice
Crêpes:
1 cup all-purpose flour
1 egg, beaten
1¼ cups milk
lard for shallow-frying

METHOD

To make the filling: Put the gula Jawa and water in a pan and heat gently until the sugar has dissolved. Add the remaining ingredients, except the lemon juice, and mix well. Simmer gently for a few minutes until the coconut has absorbed all the water, yet is still moist.

To make the pancakes (crêpes): Sift the flour and a pinch of salt into a bowl. Add the egg, then gradually beat in the milk to make a smooth batter.

Grease an 18 cm/7 inch frying pan (skillet) and place over moderate heat. Pour in just enough batter to cover the base thinly, tilting the pan to spread it. Cook for 1 minute, then turn the pancake (crêpe) and cook the other side. Repeat with the remaining batter, to make 8 pancakes (crêpes).

Add the lemon juice to the filling and divide equally between the pancakes (crêpes). Roll up and serve warm or cold.

SERVES 4 or 8

Rujak
Spiced Fruit Salad

Kedondong is a tropical fruit with firm, crisp flesh. If unobtainable, use crisp dessert apples instead. *Jeruk Bali* is a large citrus fruit with red flesh. It is only available in Asia; ugli fruit or Texas grapefruit may be used as a substitute in the West.

METRIC/IMPERIAL

1 under-ripe mango
2 kedondong, or crisp dessert apples
$\frac{1}{2}$ fresh pineapple
$\frac{1}{2}$ teaspoon salt
$\frac{1}{2}$ jeruk Bali, or 1 ugli fruit or Texas grapefruit
$\frac{1}{4}$ cucumber, peeled and sliced
Bumbu:
1 lombok rawit,* chopped, or pinch of chilli powder
1 slice terasi,* grilled (optional)
100 g/4 oz gula Jawa*
pinch of salt
1 tablespoon tamarind water*

AMERICAN

1 under-ripe mango
2 kedondong or crisp dessert apples
$\frac{1}{2}$ fresh pineapple
$\frac{1}{2}$ teaspoon salt
$\frac{1}{2}$ jeruk Bali, or 1 ugli fruit or Texas grapefruit
$\frac{1}{4}$ cucumber, peeled and sliced
Bumbu:
1 lombok rawit,* chopped, or pinch of chili powder
1 slice terasi,* broiled (optional)
$\frac{2}{3}$ cup gula Jawa*
pinch of salt
1 tablespoon tamarind water*

METHOD

Wash, peel and slice the mango, kedondong or apples and pineapple, then place in a bowl. Add just enough cold water to cover and stir in the salt. Peel the jeruk Bali, or other fruit, and divide into segments.

To make the bumbu: Put the lombok rawit, terasi and gula Jawa in a *cobek* or mortar, and pound until smooth. Add the salt and tamarind water and stir well.

Drain the fruit and arrange in a serving bowl with the jeruk Bali, or other fruit, and cucumber. Pour the bumbu over the fruit and fold gently to mix.

SERVES 4 to 6

Lepat Bugis
Coconut Cream Cups
Indonesia

In Malaysia and Indonesia, these cups are usually made from banana leaves (as illustrated). If fresh coconut is not available, desiccated (shredded) coconut may be substituted.

METRIC/IMPERIAL

225 g/8 oz rice flour*
350 ml/12 fl oz santen*
pinch of salt
Filling:
75 g/3 oz brown sugar
250 ml/8 fl oz water
100 g/4 oz freshly grated white coconut flesh
1 tablespoon glutinous rice flour*
Coconut cream:
250 ml/8 fl oz very thick santen*
pinch of salt

AMERICAN

2 cups rice flour*
$1\frac{1}{2}$ cups santen*
pinch of salt
Filling:
$\frac{1}{2}$ cup brown sugar, firmly packed
1 cup water
2 cups freshly grated white coconut flesh
1 tablespoon sweet rice flour*
Coconut cream:
1 cup very thick santen*
pinch of salt

METHOD

Put the rice flour in a pan, pour in the santen and mix well. Add the salt and cook until the mixture begins to thicken, stirring occasionally. Cook for a further 5 minutes, stirring constantly, then remove from the heat.

To make the filling: Put the sugar and water in a pan and heat gently until dissolved. Stir in the coconut, then simmer for a few minutes until it has absorbed all the water. Stir in the glutinous (sweet) rice flour and cook for 2 minutes, stirring constantly.

To make the coconut cream: Put the santen and salt in a heavy pan and boil for 3 minutes, stirring constantly.

Spoon about 2 teaspoons of this cream into 8 ramekins or individual heatproof dishes. Put 1 tablespoon of the rice flour mixture on top, then spoon over the filling. Divide the remaining rice flour mixture between the dishes, then top with the remaining coconut cream. Steam for 10 to 15 minutes, then serve hot or cold.

SERVES 4

Burma

Patricia Herbert

Burma is probably one of the least well-known of all Asian countries and many people have no idea what Burmese food is like. Burmese restaurants are few and far between – even, surprisingly, in Burma itself. There is really nothing mysterious or different about Burmese cooking, and the best way to sample the food is to learn to cook it yourself. Burmese food is distinctive, although it incorporates certain elements from the cooking of neighbouring India and China, and shares some common features with other South-East Asian cuisines.

The Burmese have taken their food seriously for a long time. In the thirteenth century, a certain King Narathihapate ruled Pagan, a great Buddhist city whose thousands of stone temples can still be seen today. This King's nickname was 'Eater of Three Hundred Curries', because, in the words of the Burmese chronicles: 'Whensoever the King partook of food, there must always be three hundred dishes, salted and spiced, sweet and sharp, bitter and hot, luscious and parching.'

A typical Burmese meal will include a wide range of tastes, each designed to balance, contrast or complement the others. A Burmese menu is quite different from a Western one. A soup is nearly always included; this is not taken separately as a first course, but served at the same time as the main dish and sipped at intervals throughout the meal. Soups are usually light and refreshing to the palate. Sharp or slightly sour tasting soup is particularly popular.

The main dish will usually be a curry of meat, fish or vegetables. In general Burmese curries are not overpoweringly hot; those who crave extra hotness will nonchalantly nibble fiery green chillies dipped in salt! With very few exceptions, a Burmese meal is considered incomplete without a huge bowl of white boiled rice. This is usually cooked without salt or oil as the main dish provides the seasoning. Sometimes *Coconut Rice* (see page 97) is served instead of plain boiled rice. Vegetables are also served with each meal, cooked or served raw and either dipped in a sharp shrimp or vinegar sauce, or assembled into a salad. Burmese salads are made from a wide range of exotic ingredients, including banana bud flowers, green mangoes and all sorts of strange leaves, but more ordinary ingredients like tomatoes and cucumbers are also used. Various condiments accompany the meal, one of the most popular being *Ngapi-gyaw* (see page 96).

Burmese people rarely eat desserts, but at the end of a meal they might serve a plate of sliced, fresh fruit. The Burmese have many recipes for delicious cake or pudding-type snacks called *món*, which they either make at home or, more frequently, buy from a roadside stall. Three recipes for Burmese *món* are given in this chapter – they are all easy to make and would make good desserts to finish a Burmese meal. Traditionally, wines and spirits are not served, but nowadays many people enjoy beer or wine with a Burmese meal.

One of Burma's most famous dishes, *O-nó Kauk-swè* (see page 92) is a one-course meal served without rice. Basically it consists of noodles and soup, with plenty of accompaniments mixed in at the time of eating. Families in Burma often cook this dish for large numbers on special occasions,

Burmese kitchen is a large stone mortar and pestle. Dawn breaks in Burma to the accompaniment of the pounding of pestle on mortar! The Burmese usually pound the onions, garlic, ginger and chillies that make up the basic flavouring of their curries. To simplify matters, the recipes in this chapter specify crushed garlic and chilli powder, but the onions and ginger should be pounded. In true Burmese style, you can of course, pound dried red chillies instead of using chilli powder. If you do not have a pestle and mortar, an electric grinder can be used instead.

Ingredients

The Burmese use either peanut oil or sesame seed oil for cooking, but as these are quite heavy and rich for Western palates, corn, sunflower or vegetable oil can be used instead. Many Burmese dishes use salted shrimp paste, dried shrimps or shrimp sauce, and this is a feature shared with nearly all of the South-East Asian cuisines. Many Western people find shrimp paste a difficult taste to acquire and for this reason it is only included in the condiment *Ngapi-gyaw* (see page 96) for which it is essential. Dried shrimps and shrimp sauce impart a very pleasant flavour to soups and other dishes.

Another unusual Burmese ingredient is the fruit of the tamarind tree. This adds a sharpness to food which is more subtle than the taste of lemon or vinegar. Creamed coconut is added to certain special dishes; in Burma this is made by scraping the coconut flesh, then squeezing it in hot water to extract the cream and flavour.

Serving

The Burmese usually sit at a round, low dining table for meals; the aim being to give a convivial atmosphere and to make sure that every dish is within reach. No ornaments or flowers are put on the table, as this would detract from the food. Each place on the table is laid with a plate and a soup bowl. A china soup spoon is provided for the soup, but the other dishes are usually eaten, very neatly and deftly, with the fingers, though the habit of eating with a fork and spoon is now becoming more widespread. The Burmese use small round serving dishes, except for one-course noodle dishes and the rice; these are put in large bowls in the centre of the table. The small dishes are constantly refilled and never allowed to become less than half full.

Burmese people like to keep their conversation to a minimum during a meal and concentrate on eating. In common with many Oriental cultures, it can be considered discourteous to the food to talk too much. Above all, the Burmese are a very tolerant people and they would be the first to say that you need not follow rigidly their way of serving the food. The main thing is to eat and enjoy it!

such as a baby's name giving day, or the day a son enters a monastery for his novitiate period. On these occasions, Buddhist monks are invited to the house to have a special meal and to recite prayers and blessings. Friends are invited too, but they will be fed a little later than the monks who eat first thing in the morning before returning to the monastery for the rest of the day. In Buddhist terms, it is an honour to feed monks and a way of earning merit which will ensure a better rebirth in one's next life.

Cooking Utensils

Burmese cooking is usually over open wood fires or kerosene stoves. The cooking process is quite simple – usually a combination of frying and simmering – and no special cooking utensils are needed. However, an essential item in every

Soup with Fresh Greens

Hìn-nú-nwe Hìn-gyo

This is an everyday soup which is quick and very easy to make. The dried shrimps can be pounded at home or bought ready-powdered and the soup can be varied from day to day by adding different fresh green vegetables: watercress, sorrel, spinach, cabbage, pea leaves or mustard leaves.

METRIC/IMPERIAL

1.2 litres/2 pints water
1 medium onion, peeled and sliced
3 garlic cloves, peeled and sliced
3 tablespoons pounded dried shrimps*
½ teaspoon shrimp paste* (optional)
2 teaspoons soy sauce
1 teaspoon salt
225 g/8 oz fresh green leaves, washed

AMERICAN

5 cups water
1 medium onion, peeled and sliced
3 garlic cloves, peeled and sliced
3 tablespoons pounded dried shrimps*
½ teaspoon shrimp paste* (optional)
2 teaspoons soy sauce
1 teaspoon salt
½ lb fresh green leaves, washed

METHOD

Put the water, onion and garlic in a pan and bring to the boil. Lower the heat, then add the shrimps, shrimp paste, if using, soy sauce and salt. Stir well, then add the green leaves.

Boil for 5 minutes, taste and adjust the seasoning, then pour into a warmed soup tureen. Serve hot.
SERVES 4

Clear Soup

Hìn-gyo Yò-yò

This soup is usually served with rather oily dishes such as *Wet-thani* (see page 93). Its base is pork stock, made by boiling pork bones in water, but a stock made from a chicken or duck carcass can be used instead.

The soup can be made more substantial by adding cabbage, cauliflower, carrots, bean sprouts or noodles, and simmering the soup for 5 to 10 minutes longer than the time given below.

METRIC/IMPERIAL

350 g/12 oz pork bones
5 peppercorns, crushed
3 garlic cloves, peeled and crushed
2 teaspoons soy sauce
1.5 litres/2½ pints water
salt
freshly ground black pepper
To garnish:
2 tablespoons finely chopped celery
  (optional)
3 tablespoons finely chopped spring
  onions, including green tops

AMERICAN

¾ lb pork bones
5 peppercorns, crushed
3 garlic cloves, peeled and crushed
2 teaspoons soy sauce
6¼ cups water
salt
freshly ground black pepper
To garnish:
2 tablespoons finely chopped celery
  (optional)
3 tablespoons finely chopped scallions,
  including green tops

METHOD

Put the pork bones, peppercorns, garlic, soy sauce and water in a large pan. Bring to the boil, then lower the heat and simmer for about 30 minutes.

Remove the bones from the soup with a slotted spoon. Add salt and pepper to taste, then transfer to a warmed soup tureen and sprinkle with the celery, if using, and spring onions (scallions). Serve hot.
SERVES 4

Radish and Fish Soup; Soup with Fresh
Greens; Clear Soup

Radish and Fish Soup

Mon-la-ú Hìn-gyo

This is a fairly rich soup, with a distinctive flavour which is imparted by the tamarind. It is usually made with long white radishes, but it can alternatively be made with spinach or sorrel leaves, or with sliced aubergine (eggplant) or okra.

METRIC/IMPERIAL

225 g/8 oz filleted white fish (cod, haddock, etc.), cut into chunks
1 teaspoon salt
½ teaspoon turmeric powder
2 tablespoons vegetable oil
1 medium onion, peeled and pounded
3 garlic cloves, peeled and crushed
1 cm/½ inch piece of fresh root ginger,* peeled and pounded
½ teaspoon chilli powder
4 tomatoes, chopped
½ teaspoon shrimp paste* (optional)
1 tablespoon shrimp-flavoured soy sauce*
5 sprigs coriander leaves*
3 tablespoons dried tamarind pulp*
350 g/12 oz long white radish,* including green tops, peeled and thinly sliced

AMERICAN

½ lb filleted white fish (cod, haddock, etc.), cut into chunks
1 teaspoon salt
½ teaspoon turmeric powder
2 tablespoons vegetable oil
1 medium onion, peeled and pounded
3 garlic cloves, peeled and crushed
½ inch piece of fresh ginger root,* peeled and pounded
½ teaspoon chili powder
4 tomatoes, chopped
½ teaspoon shrimp paste* (optional)
1 tablespoon shrimp-flavored soy sauce*
5 sprigs coriander leaves*
3 tablespoons dried tamarind pulp*
¾ lb long white radish,* including green tops, peeled and thinly sliced

METHOD

Put the fish in a bowl and rub with the salt and turmeric. Set aside.

Heat the oil in a large pan. Mix together the onion, garlic, ginger and chilli powder. Add to the pan and fry gently until lightly coloured, then add the fish. Stir-fry for a few minutes, then add the tomatoes, shrimp paste, if using, soy sauce, 1.2 litres/2 pints/5 cups cold water and the coriander. Bring to the boil, then lower the heat and simmer for 15 minutes.

Meanwhile, put the tamarind in a bowl, pour over 6 tablespoons hot water, then knead to extract the flavour. Strain the liquid, discarding the tamarind pulp.

Add the tamarind liquid and radish to the pan and simmer for 15 minutes or until the radish is clear and tender. Taste and adjust the seasoning, then leave to stand for about 30 minutes to allow the full flavour to develop.

Reheat, then pour into a warmed soup tureen. Serve hot.
SERVES 4

Prawn (Shrimp) Curry with Tomatoes
Pazun Hìn

In Burma, large prawns (shrimp), are used to make this dish. If possible, try to use Dublin Bay or Pacific prawns (king shrimp), but if these are not obtainable, then ordinary prawns (shrimp) may be used instead.

METRIC/IMPERIAL

575 g/1¼ lb peeled prawns
2 tablespoons shrimp-flavoured soy
   sauce*
½ teaspoon salt
½ teaspoon turmeric powder
4 tablespoons vegetable oil
1 large onion, peeled and pounded
4 garlic cloves, peeled and crushed
1 cm/½ inch piece of fresh root ginger,*
   peeled and pounded
½ teaspoon chilli powder
3 tomatoes, roughly chopped
2 tablespoons chopped coriander
   leaves*
4 tablespoons water
coriander leaves* to garnish

AMERICAN

1¼ lb shelled shrimp
2 tablespoons shrimp-flavored soy
   sauce
½ teaspoon salt
½ teaspoon turmeric powder
¼ cup vegetable oil
1 large onion, peeled and pounded
4 garlic cloves, peeled and crushed
½ inch piece of fresh ginger root,*
   peeled and pounded
½ teaspoon chili powder
3 tomatoes, roughly chopped
2 tablespoons chopped coriander
   leaves*
¼ cup water
coriander leaves* to garnish

METHOD

Put the prawns (shrimp) in a bowl with the soy sauce, salt and turmeric. Mix well, then set aside.

Heat the oil in a pan, add the onion, garlic, ginger and chilli powder and stir-fry until fragrant but not dry.

Add the prawns (shrimp), tomatoes and coriander, increase the heat slightly, then cover the pan and cook for 5 minutes. Stir in the water, lower the heat, cover and simmer for 10 to 15 minutes until the prawns are cooked and the water has been absorbed.

Transfer to a warmed serving dish and garnish with coriander leaves. Serve hot.
SERVES 4

Spiced Fried Fish with Onions
Ngà-gyaw

METRIC/IMPERIAL

750 g/1½ lb white fish fillets (cod, haddock, etc.), cut into 10 cm/4 inch squares
½ teaspoon turmeric powder
1 tablespoon shrimp-flavoured soy
   sauce*
2 tablespoons dried tamarind pulp*
6 tablespoons hot water
7 tablespoons vegetable oil
2 medium onions, peeled and sliced
1½ teaspoons chilli powder

AMERICAN

1½ lb white fish fillets (cod, haddock, etc.), cut into 4 inch squares
½ teaspoon turmeric powder
1 tablespoon shrimp-flavored soy
   sauce*
2 tablespoons dried tamarind pulp*
6 tablespoons hot water
7 tablespoons vegetable oil
2 medium onions, peeled and sliced
1½ teaspoons chili powder

METHOD

Put the fish in a bowl and rub lightly with the turmeric and soy sauce. Set aside.

Put the tamarind in a bowl, cover with the hot water, then knead to extract the flavour. Strain the liquid, discarding the tamarind pulp.

Heat the oil in a large frying pan (skillet), add the onions and fry over brisk heat until golden and crisp. Remove from the pan with a slotted spoon and drain the onions on kitchen paper towels.

Pour off half the oil from the pan, then add the chilli powder. Increase the heat slightly, add the fish and fry quickly for 1 minute.

Add the tamarind liquid, cover and simmer for about 20 minutes until the fish is cooked and the liquid has almost all been absorbed. (If necessary, add a little more oil during cooking, to prevent sticking.)

Transfer to a warmed serving dish and sprinkle the fried onions over the fish. Serve hot.
SERVES 4

Steamed Fish Parcels
Ngà-baung-dok

In Burma, this subtly-flavoured dish is steamed in banana leaves (as illustrated), but in the West, foil may be substituted. If liked, spinach or lettuce may be used instead . of the Chinese cabbage (bok choy) suggested here.

METRIC/IMPERIAL

575 g/1¼ lb thick white fish fillets (cod, haddock, etc.), cut into
   7.5×3.5 cm/3×1½ inch pieces
2 teaspoons salt
½ teaspoon turmeric powder
3 small onions, peeled
2 garlic cloves, peeled and crushed
2.5 cm/1 inch piece of fresh root
   ginger,* peeled and pounded
½ teaspoon chilli powder
1 tablespoon rice flour*
50 g/2 oz creamed coconut,* roughly
   chopped
7 tablespoons boiling water
2 teaspoons vegetable oil
½ teaspoon powdered lemon grass*
10 Chinese cabbage leaves, washed
   and cut in half

1¼ lb thick white fish fillets (cod, haddock, etc.), cut into 3 × 1½ inch pieces
2 teaspoons salt
½ teaspoon turmeric powder
3 small onions, peeled
2 garlic cloves, peeled and crushed
1 inch piece of fresh ginger root,* peeled and pounded
½ teaspoon chili powder
1 tablespoon rice flour*
⅔ cup coconut milk*
2 teaspoons vegetable oil
½ teaspoon powdered lemon grass*
10 bok choy leaves, washed and cut in half

METHOD

Put the fish in a bowl and rub lightly with half the salt and turmeric. Set aside.

Thinly slice 1 onion, then pound the remaining onions. Mix the pounded onions to a paste with the remaining salt and turmeric, the garlic, ginger, chilli powder and rice flour.

If using creamed coconut, place in a bowl, add the water and stir until the coconut melts. Add (coconut milk) to the onion paste with the oil, sliced onion and the lemon grass. Mix well.

Cut ten 18 cm/7 inch squares of foil. Place 1 piece of Chinese cabbage (bok choy) on each foil square, then top with a little of the paste mixture. Place a piece of fish and a little more paste mixture on top of this, then cover with another piece of Chinese cabbage (bok choy). Fold the foil, enclosing the filling, to form parcels. Fold the edges together to seal.

Steam the parcels for 20 minutes or until the fish is cooked through. Serve hot.

MAKES 10

Burmese Chicken Curry

Chet-thà Hsi-byan

This is a typical Burmese curry, cooked in such a way that the 'oil returns' (hsi-byan in Burmese) to the top of the dish at the end of cooking. For the best flavour, chop the chicken into small pieces across the joints, as in Chinese cooking. As a variation, omit the bay leaves and cinnamon and substitute 4 tomatoes, roughly chopped, and ½ teaspoon powdered lemon grass.*

METRIC/IMPERIAL

1 chicken, weighing 1.5 kg/3–3½ lb, chopped into pieces
2 tablespoons soy sauce
1 teaspoon salt
½ teaspoon turmeric powder
3 medium onions, peeled
4 garlic cloves, peeled
2.5 cm/1 inch piece of fresh root ginger,* peeled and pounded
1–2 teaspoons chilli powder, according to taste
5 tablespoons vegetable oil
3 bay leaves
1 piece of cinnamon stick

Prawn (Shrimp) Curry with Tomatoes; Steamed Fish Parcels; Fried Spiced Fish with Onions

1 chicken, weighing 3–3½ lb, chopped into pieces
2 tablespoons soy sauce
1 teaspoon salt
½ teaspoon turmeric powder
3 medium onions, peeled
4 garlic cloves, peeled
1 inch piece of fresh ginger root,* peeled and pounded
1–2 teaspoons chili powder, according to taste
⅓ cup vegetable oil
3 bay leaves
1 piece of cinnamon stick

METHOD

Put the chicken in a bowl with the soy sauce, salt and turmeric; mix well.

Pound 1 onion and 3 garlic cloves, mix with the ginger and chilli powder, then rub into the chicken.

Slice the remaining onions and garlic thinly. Heat the oil in a large pan, add the onions and garlic and fry gently for 5 to 10 minutes until soft and fragrant. Add the chicken and any remaining pounded mixture. Fry for 10 minutes until the chicken is brown on all sides, stirring occasionally.

Add the bay leaves and cinnamon and enough water to just cover the chicken (about 600 ml/1 pint/2½ cups). Increase the heat and bring to the boil, then cover and simmer for about 35 minutes until the oil has risen to the surface, leaving a thick curry sauce underneath. If there is too much liquid towards the end of the cooking time, increase the heat and boil, uncovered, until reduced and thickened. Serve hot with plain boiled rice or Coconut Rice (see page 97).
SERVES 4

Chicken with Noodles and Coconut

On-nó Kauk-swè

This is probably the most famous of all Burmese dishes: it is something of a feast, but it is not too difficult to prepare at home. Try to use the special split pea and lentil flours, as these give the dish its authentic Burmese flavour. Chick pea (garbanzos) flour may be substituted for the split pea flour, if this is more easily obtainable.

In Burma, the dish is served in wide soup bowls or plates – the noodles are placed in the bottom of the bowls, then a little of each of the accompaniments is sprinkled on top, followed by the hot chicken mixture. Each diner squeezes lemon juice over his serving just before eating.

METRIC/IMPERIAL

1 chicken, weighing 1.5 kg/3–3½ lb, cut into large pieces
salt
½ teaspoon turmeric powder
3 litres/6 pints water
7 tablespoons vegetable oil
4 medium onions, peeled and pounded
4 garlic cloves, peeled and crushed
2.5 cm/1 inch piece of fresh root ginger,* peeled and pounded
2 teaspoons chilli powder
5 tablespoons split pea flour*
5 tablespoons lentil flour*
150 g/5 oz creamed coconut,* roughly chopped
1 kg/2 lb fresh or dried egg noodles
To serve:
6 tablespoons oil
12 garlic cloves, peeled and sliced crossways
3 hard-boiled eggs, shelled and quartered
2 onions, peeled and sliced
5 spring onions, including green tops, finely chopped
1 tablespoon chilli powder (optional)
2 lemons, quartered

AMERICAN

1 chicken, weighing 3–3½ lb, cut into large pieces
salt
½ teaspoon turmeric powder
3 quarts water
7 tablespoons vegetable oil
4 medium onions, peeled and pounded
4 garlic cloves, peeled and crushed
1 inch piece of fresh ginger root,* peeled and pounded
2 teaspoons chili powder
5 tablespoons split pea flour*
5 tablespoons lentil flour*
1⅔ cups thick coconut milk*
2 lb fresh or dried egg noodles
To serve:
6 tablespoons oil
12 garlic cloves, peeled and sliced crossways
3 hard-cooked eggs, shelled and quartered
2 onions, peeled and sliced
5 scallions, including green tops, finely chopped
1 tablespoon chili powder (optional)
2 lemons, quartered

METHOD

Rub the chicken with 1 tablespoon salt and the turmeric, then place in a very large pan. Add the water, bring to the boil, then lower the heat and simmer for about 25 minutes until the chicken is just cooked, but still firm. Remove the chicken from the pan; leave the cooking liquid to simmer gently over low heat.

Remove the skin and bones from the chicken and add them to the simmering cooking liquid. (For maximum flavour the chicken bones should be cracked, but this is not essential.) Cut the chicken meat into chunks.

Meanwhile, heat the oil in a large pan, add the onions, garlic, ginger and chilli powder and stir-fry for 5 minutes. Add the chicken meat and stir-fry for 5 to 10 minutes. Turn off the heat.

Mix the flours to a paste with about 200 ml/⅓ pint/1 cup cooking liquid and set aside. Strain the remaining cooking liquid into the pan containing the chicken meat.

Stir in the flour paste and bring to the boil. Lower the heat, add the creamed

Chicken with Noodles and Coconut

coconut (coconut milk) and simmer for about 20 minutes until the mixture has the consistency of thick pea soup, stirring frequently. If the mixture becomes too thick, add a little more water; if it is too thin, add a little more lentil flour paste. Turn off the heat, taste and adjust the seasoning, then cover the pan and set aside.

Cook the noodles in boiling salted water for about 7 minutes; drain and keep hot.

To serve: Heat the oil in a small frying pan (skillet), add a handful of the boiled noodles and fry over brisk heat until crisp. Remove from the pan with a slotted spoon and drain on kitchen paper towels, then place in a serving bowl.

Add the garlic to the pan, fry over brisk heat until golden and crisp, then transfer to a small serving bowl.

Reheat the chicken mixture, then pile into a warmed serving dish. Serve the remaining ingredients in separate small bowls as accompaniments to the chicken and noodles. Serve hot.

SERVES 6 to 8

Red Pork
Wet-thani

This dish is called 'Red or Golden Pork' because the oil in the dish is coloured by the chilli powder. The Burmese like to use fatty pork – either shoulder or belly – for this recipe, but if this is not to your taste, then pork fillet (tenderloin) may be used instead.

METRIC/IMPERIAL

1 kg/2–2¼ lb boned pork, cut into
   2.5 cm/1 inch cubes
3 tablespoons soy sauce
1 teaspoon freshly ground black
   pepper
5 cm/2 inch piece of fresh root
   ginger,* peeled
3 medium onions, peeled and pounded
3 garlic cloves, peeled and crushed
200 ml/⅓ pint boiling water
1 teaspoon chilli powder
5 tablespoons vegetable oil

AMERICAN

2–2¼ lb boneless pork, cut into 1 inch
   cubes
3 tablespoons soy sauce
1 teaspoon freshly ground black
   pepper
2 inch piece of fresh ginger root,*
   peeled
3 medium onions, peeled and pounded
3 garlic cloves, peeled and crushed
1 cup boiling water
1 teaspoon chili powder
⅓ cup vegetable oil

METHOD

Put the pork in a bowl with 2 tablespoons soy sauce and the pepper; mix well.

Pound half the ginger, then mix with the onions and garlic. Stir in all but 1 tablespoon of the boiling water, then strain the mixture and retain both the liquid and the pounded ingredients.

Stir the chilli powder into the reserved boiling water. Cut the remaining ginger into thin strips. Heat the oil in a large heavy pan, add the ginger and fry until just sizzling, then add the pork and stir-fry until brown.

Add the liquid reserved from the pounded ingredients, cover the pan and simmer for about 10 minutes or until the liquid has almost all been absorbed. Add the chilli water, the remaining soy sauce and the reserved pounded mixture.

Cover and cook over low heat for about 40 minutes or until the pork is tender, stirring occasionally to prevent sticking. (If lean pork has been used, it may be necessary to add a little water during cooking.) Serve hot.

SERVES 4 to 6

Beef Curry
Amè-thà Hìn

The beef in this recipe needs to be marinated for at least 4 hours, preferably overnight. It is then cooked slowly with very little liquid, so it is best cooked in a heavy-based pan. Adjust the cooking time according to the quality of the meat.

METRIC/IMPERIAL

1 kg/2–2¼ lb braising steak, cut into
   2.5 cm/1 inch cubes
1 tablespoon shrimp-flavoured soy
   sauce*
½ teaspoon turmeric powder
1 tablespoon malt vinegar
2 medium onions, peeled and pounded
4 garlic cloves, peeled and crushed
2.5 cm/1 inch piece of fresh root
   ginger,* peeled and pounded
1 teaspoon chilli powder
4 tablespoons vegetable oil
3 bay leaves
2 pieces of cinnamon stick
5 peppercorns
salt

AMERICAN

2–2¼ lb chuck steak, cut into 1 inch
   cubes
1 tablespoon shrimp-flavored soy
   sauce*
½ teaspoon turmeric powder
1 tablespoon malt or cider vinegar
2 medium onions, peeled and pounded
4 garlic cloves, peeled and crushed
1 inch piece of fresh ginger root,*
   peeled and pounded
1 teaspoon chili powder
¼ cup vegetable oil
3 bay leaves
2 pieces of cinnamon stick
5 peppercorns
salt

METHOD

Put the meat in a bowl with the soy sauce, turmeric and vinegar. Mix well, then leave to marinate for at least 4 hours, preferably overnight.

Mix together the onions, garlic, ginger and chilli powder. Heat the oil in a large heavy pan, add the pounded mixture and stir-fry for 10 minutes or until the mixture begins to brown.

Add the beef, bay leaves, cinnamon and peppercorns and enough water to half cover the beef. Cover and simmer over low heat for about 45 minutes or until the meat is tender; stir in a little water if necessary during cooking.

Taste and adjust the seasoning towards the end of the cooking time, adding a little salt according to taste. Serve hot.

SERVES 4 to 6

Vegetable Curry

Hìn-thì Hìn ywet Hìn-tamyò

The proportion of vegetables can be varied to suit individual tastes and availability.

METRIC/IMPERIAL

3 medium potatoes, peeled and cut into 3.5 cm/1½ inch cubes

1 medium aubergine, cut into 2.5 cm/1 inch slices

4 carrots, peeled and diced

1 medium cauliflower, divided into florets

225 g/8 oz okra cut into 2.5 cm/1 inch lengths

4 tablespoons vegetable oil

1 medium onion, peeled and pounded

3 garlic cloves, peeled and crushed

1 cm/½ inch piece of fresh root ginger,* peeled and pounded

1 teaspoon chilli powder

½ teaspoon turmeric powder

75 g/3 oz dried salt fish,* roughly sliced (optional)

3 tomatoes, roughly chopped

3 tablespoons chopped coriander leaves*

1 fresh green chilli (optional)

AMERICAN

3 medium potatoes, peeled and cut into 1½ inch cubes

1 medium eggplant, cut into 1 inch slices

4 carrots, peeled and diced

1 medium cauliflower, divided into florets

½ lb okra, cut into 1 inch lengths

¼ cup vegetable oil

1 medium onion, peeled and pounded

3 garlic cloves, peeled and crushed

½ inch piece of fresh ginger root,* peeled and pounded

1 teaspoon chili powder

½ teaspoon turmeric powder

3 oz dried salt fish,* roughly sliced (optional)

3 tomatoes, roughly chopped

3 tablespoons chopped coriander leaves*

1 fresh green chili (optional)

METHOD

Put the potatoes, aubergine (eggplant), carrots, cauliflower and okra in a bowl. Cover with cold water and set aside.

Heat the oil in a large pan, add the onion, garlic, ginger, chilli powder and turmeric and stir-fry until fragrant.

Add the salt fish, if using, stir-fry for 2 minutes, then stir in one third of the tomatoes and the coriander. Add the potatoes and just enough water to cover. (Add a little salt if salt fish is not used.) Bring to the boil, then lower the heat and simmer for 10 minutes.

Add the aubergine (eggplant) and carrots, simmer for 5 minutes, then add the cauliflower and a little more water, if necessary. Bring back to the boil, add the remaining tomatoes and the chilli, if using. Simmer for 5 minutes, then add the okra.

Lower the heat and simmer for 5 minutes or until the vegetables are cooked, but still firm, and most of the liquid has been absorbed. Discard the chilli, if used. Serve hot.

SERVES 4

Vegetable Curry; Right: Ingredients for Assorted Vegetable Salad

Assorted Vegetable Salad

Thanat-son-Thok

Although called a salad, the vegetables in this dish are blanched or quickly cooked first. The choice of vegetables can be varied according to taste and availability.

METRIC/IMPERIAL

4 carrots, scraped
salt
175 g/6 oz French beans, topped and tailed
100 g/4 oz okra
100 g/4 oz fresh bean sprouts
100 g/4 oz cauliflower florets
100 g/4 oz bamboo shoot (optional)
50 g/2 oz sesame seeds*
2 tablespoons vegetable oil
1 medium onion, peeled and sliced

AMERICAN

4 carrots, scraped
salt
1½ cups string beans, topped and tailed
1 cup okra
2 cups fresh bean sprouts
2 large cauliflower florets
1 cup bamboo shoot (optional)
5 tablespoons sesame seeds*
2 tablespoons vegetable oil
1 medium onion, peeled and sliced

METHOD

Cook the carrots in boiling salted water for about 7 minutes, then remove from the pan and leave to cool.

Cook the remaining vegetables separately in boiling salted water, allowing about 3 minutes for each vegetable – they should remain crunchy. Leave to cool.

Put the sesame seeds in a small, heavy frying pan (skillet) and fry over dry heat until 'toasted' golden brown, shaking the pan constantly. Remove from the pan and set aside.

Add the oil to the pan, heat gently, then add the onion. Fry over brisk heat until golden and crisp, then remove from the pan with a slotted spoon and drain on kitchen paper towels. Reserve 1 tablespoon of the oil.

Slice the carrots into thin matchstick strips. Slice the beans and okra diagonally into 1 cm/½ inch pieces. Arrange the vegetables in separate piles on a long serving dish.

Stir a pinch of salt into the reserved oil, drizzle over the vegetables, then sprinkle with the sesame seeds and fried onion. Serve cold or chilled.
SERVES 6 to 8

Fried Aubergine (Eggplant)

Hkayàn-thì Gyaw

This vegetable dish can be served as a side dish to a main meal of curry and rice, or eaten on its own. The aubergine (eggplant) can be baked in advance and the dish completed when required.

METRIC/IMPERIAL

1 large aubergine
2 tablespoons vegetable oil
1 medium onion, peeled and sliced
1 garlic clove, peeled and crushed
1 cm/½ inch piece of fresh root ginger,* peeled and pounded
½ teaspoon salt
2 spring onions, including green tops, finely chopped, to garnish

AMERICAN

1 large eggplant
2 tablespoons vegetable oil
1 medium onion, peeled and sliced
1 garlic clove, peeled and crushed
½ inch piece of fresh ginger root,* peeled and pounded
½ teaspoon salt
2 scallions, including green tops, finely chopped, to garnish

METHOD

Put the aubergine (eggplant) on a lightly oiled baking (cookie) sheet and bake in a preheated hot oven (220°C/425°F, Gas Mark 7) for about 1 hour or until soft to the touch, turning occasionally. Remove from the oven and leave to cool.

Heat the oil in a frying pan (skillet), add the onion and garlic and fry gently until beginning to brown.

Meanwhile, peel off the aubergine (eggplant) skin, scoop out the flesh and mash with a fork. Add to the pan with the ginger and salt, then stir-fry for 5 to 10 minutes.

Transfer to a warmed serving dish and garnish with the spring onions (scallions). Serve hot or cold.
SERVES 4

Cucumber Salad
Thanhat

This salad can also be made with carrots, cauliflower, runner (string) beans or fresh bean sprouts.

METRIC/IMPERIAL

2 medium cucumbers, peeled, seeded and cut into 7.5 cm/3 inch long strips
3 tablespoons vinegar
1 teaspoon salt
6 tablespoons vegetable oil
2 medium onions, peeled and sliced
8 garlic cloves, peeled and sliced
½ teaspoon turmeric powder
1 teaspoon sugar
2 tablespoons sesame seeds*

AMERICAN

2 medium cucumbers, peeled, seeded and cut into 3 inch long strips
3 tablespoons vinegar
1 teaspoon salt
6 tablespoons vegetable oil
2 medium onions, peeled and sliced
8 garlic cloves, peeled and sliced
½ teaspoon turmeric powder
1 teaspoon sugar
2 tablespoons sesame seeds*

METHOD

Put the cucumber in a pan with 2 tablespoons of the vinegar and just enough water to cover. Bring to the boil, then lower the heat and simmer for about 4 minutes until the cucumber becomes transparent. Drain, sprinkle with ½ teaspoon salt, then leave to cool.

Heat the oil in a frying pan (skillet), add the onions and fry over brisk heat until golden and crisp. Remove from the pan with a slotted spoon and drain on kitchen paper towels. Add the garlic to the pan, fry until golden, then remove and drain.

Add the turmeric, sugar and remaining salt to the pan, stir, then add half the sesame seeds. Stir-fry for 1 to 2 minutes, remove from the heat and leave to cool in the pan.

Stir the remaining vinegar into the mixture in the pan, then add the cucumber and toss well. Drain off the excess oil and vinegar, then pile the cucumber into a pyramid shape on a serving plate. Sprinkle with the onion, garlic and remaining sesame seeds. Serve cold or chilled.
SERVES 4

Tomato Salad
Hkayàn-chin-thì Let-thok

This salad is best made with under-ripe tomatoes.

METRIC/IMPERIAL

4 tablespoons vegetable oil
1 medium onion, peeled and sliced
4 medium tomatoes, thinly sliced
1 tablespoon pounded, roasted shelled peanuts (see page 129)
3 tablespoons chopped coriander leaves*
1 teaspoon shrimp-flavoured soy sauce*
juice of ½ lemon
coriander leaves* to garnish

AMERICAN

¼ cup vegetable oil
1 medium onion, peeled and sliced
4 medium tomatoes, thinly sliced
1 tablespoon pounded, roasted shelled peanuts (see page 129)
3 tablespoons chopped coriander leaves*
1 teaspoon shrimp-flavored soy sauce*
juice of ½ lemon
coriander leaves* to garnish

METHOD

Heat 3 tablespoons of the oil in a small frying pan (skillet), add the onion and fry over brisk heat until golden and crisp. Remove from the pan with a slotted spoon and drain on kitchen paper towels.

Put the tomatoes in a bowl, then add the peanuts, coriander, soy sauce and remaining oil and toss lightly to mix.

Arrange the tomato mixture on a serving plate, sprinkle with the lemon juice and top with the onion. Garnish with coriander. Serve cold or chilled.
SERVES 4

Burmese Balachaung — Shrimp Condiment
Ngapi-gyaw

Every household in Burma has its own special recipe for making this spicy shrimp condiment, which is eaten as an accompaniment to most meals. It may also be eaten as an unusual sandwich filling. A word of warning – Ngapi-gyaw smells strongly during cooking! It will keep for up to 6 months in a screw-top jar in the refrigerator.

METRIC/IMPERIAL

1 tablespoon dried tamarind pulp* (optional)
200 ml/⅓ pint vegetable oil
1 medium onion, peeled and sliced
8 garlic cloves, peeled and sliced crossways
2.5 cm/1 inch piece of fresh root ginger,* peeled and sliced into strips
1 teaspoon chilli powder
1 teaspoon turmeric powder
200 g/7 oz dried shrimps,* pounded
2 teaspoons shrimp paste*

AMERICAN

1 tablespoon dried tamarind pulp* (optional)
1 cup vegetable oil
1 medium onion, peeled and sliced
8 garlic cloves, peeled and sliced crossways
1 inch piece of fresh ginger root,* peeled and sliced into strips
1 teaspoon chili powder
1 teaspoon turmeric powder
2⅓ cups dried pounded shrimp*
2 teaspoons shrimp paste*

If using tamarind, place in a bowl, cover with 3 tablespoons hot water, then knead to extract the flavour. Strain the liquid, discarding the tamarind pulp.

Heat the oil in a wok or deep frying pan (deep-fat fryer), then fry the onion, garlic and ginger separately over brisk heat until golden and crisp. Remove from the pan with a slotted spoon and drain on kitchen paper towels.

Add the chilli powder to the pan and fry for 30 seconds, then add the turmeric and shrimps. Stir-fry until the shrimps are crisp and have absorbed most of the oil, then remove from the pan and drain off any excess oil.

Add the shrimp paste to the pan with the tamarind liquid, if using. Fry over low heat for about 3 minutes, stirring constantly to prevent burning. Return the shrimps to the pan, mix quickly together, then remove from the heat and stir in the onions, garlic and ginger. Allow to cool.

Serve cold in individual dishes, as an accompaniment.

MAKES 450 g/1 lb

Coconut Rice

Òn Htamìn

Coconut rice makes a pleasant change from plain boiled rice as an accompaniment to a main course. It goes particularly well with *Burmese Chicken Curry* (see page 91). For a variation, add 1 piece of cinnamon stick, 1 bay leaf, 2 cloves and 2 whole cardamoms – these will give the rice a delicious, slightly spicy flavour.

METRIC/IMPERIAL

*450 g/1 lb long-grain rice, washed
  thoroughly.*
75 g/3 oz creamed coconut, roughly
  chopped*
1 medium onion, peeled and quartered
½ teaspoon salt
1 teaspoon vegetable oil

AMERICAN

*2¼ cups long-grain rice, washed
  thoroughly*
6 tablespoons thick coconut milk*
1 medium onion, peeled and quartered
½ teaspoon salt
1 teaspoon vegetable oil

METHOD

Measure the rice into cups, then transfer to a large pan. Measure 2 cups water for every cup of rice and add to the pan.

Add the remaining ingredients and bring to the boil over high heat. Cover the pan, lower the heat to a minimum and cook for about 20 minutes, until the rice is tender. Remove the lid and stir the rice once – the liquid should have been absorbed completely and the rice grains should be fluffy. Serve hot.

SERVES 6

Tomato Salad; Cucumber Salad

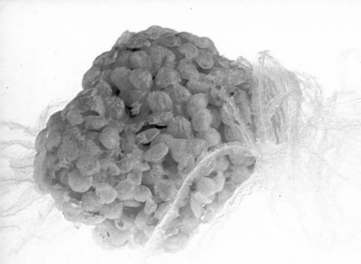

Seaweed Jelly

Kyauk-kyàw

This is a very firm jelly with an unusual coconut flavour. It sets in two layers – a creamy layer on top, with a cloudy layer underneath.

METRIC/IMPERIAL

25 g/1 oz dried agar-agar*
100 g/4 oz creamed coconut,* roughly chopped
225 g/8 oz granulated sugar

AMERICAN

1 oz dried agar-agar*
½ cup thick coconut milk*
1 cup granulated sugar

METHOD

Put the agar-agar in a bowl; add just enough cold water to cover and leave to soak for 2 to 3 hours.

Strain the agar-agar, discarding the water, then measure the agar-agar. For each measure of agar-agar, use double the amount of fresh water. (25 g/1 oz soaked agar-agar should fill a 600 ml/ 1 pint/2 cup measure, so the required amount of water will be about 1.2 litres/ 2 pints/5 cups.)

Put one quarter of the creamed coconut (coconut milk) in a small bowl. If using creamed coconut, bring 7 tablespoons of the measured water to the boil, pour over the coconut and stir until melted. Set aside.

Put the remaining creamed coconut (coconut milk) in a pan with the agar-agar and sugar. Bring the remaining water to the boil, add to the pan and simmer gently for about 10 minutes, until the mixture is smooth, stirring occasionally.

Pour the mixture into a shallow square dish. Leave to cool slightly, then pour over the reserved coconut. Leave in a cool place for about 1 hour until set, then cut into diamond shapes and arrange on a serving plate.

SERVES 6 to 8

Tapioca Pudding

Tha-gu Món

In Burma, palm sugar is used in this pudding; soft dark brown sugar can be used instead.

METRIC/IMPERIAL

225 g/8 oz tapioca
225 g/8 oz soft dark brown sugar
½ teaspoon salt
900 ml/1½ pints water
100 g/4 oz desiccated or freshly grated coconut
2 teaspoons caster sugar

AMERICAN

1½ cups tapioca
1 cup dark brown sugar, firmly packed
½ teaspoon salt
3¾ cups water
1⅓ cups shredded or freshly grated coconut
2 teaspoons superfine sugar

METHOD

Put the tapioca, brown sugar, salt and water in a pan and bring to the boil. Lower the heat and simmer for about 10 minutes until the tapioca becomes soft and transparent and the mixture is thick, stirring constantly.

Remove from the heat, pour into a greased shallow dish and leave until cold.

Scoop out the mixture in tablespoonfuls, then roll in the coconut and caster (superfine) sugar. Arrange on a serving plate.

SERVES 6 to 8

Tapioca Pudding; Sesame Semolina
Pudding; Seaweed Jelly

Sesame Semolina Pudding

Sanwìn-makìn

The secret of the flavour of this pudding
is the dry cooking of the semolina.

METRIC/IMPERIAL

225 g/8 oz semolina
225 g/8 oz soft dark brown or
  demerara sugar
½ teaspoon salt
175 g/6 oz creamed coconut,* roughly
  chopped
1.2 litres/2 pints boiling water
50 g/2 oz butter or margarine
2 teaspoons vegetable oil
2 medium eggs, beaten
75 g/3 oz seedless raisins
4 tablespoons sesame seeds* or poppy
  seeds

AMERICAN

1⅓ cups semolina
1 cup dark brown sugar, firmly packed
½ teaspoon salt
¾ cup thick coconut milk*
5 cups boiling water
¼ cup butter or margarine
2 teaspoons vegetable oil
2 medium eggs, beaten
½ cup seedless raisins
4 tablespoons sesame seeds* or poppy
  seeds

METHOD

Put the semolina in a large heavy pan and
cook over low heat for about 10 minutes,
stirring occasionally. The semolina
should become scorched or 'toasted',
but not burnt.

Remove from the heat and stir in the
brown sugar, salt, creamed coconut (coconut milk) and water. Leave to stand for
at least 30 minutes, then cook over low
heat for about 15 minutes or until quite
thick, stirring occasionally.

Remove from the heat, add the butter
or margarine and stir until melted. Stir in
the oil, leave to cool slightly, then stir in
the eggs.

Return to the heat and cook gently for 5
minutes, stirring constantly. Stir in the
raisins and cook for 5 to 10 minutes until
the mixture is thick, but not solid.

Pour into a greased shallow ovenproof
square dish and sprinkle with the sesame
or poppy seeds. Bake in a preheated
moderately hot oven (200°C/400°F, Gas
Mark 6) for about 1½ hours until the
pudding has begun to shrink away from
the sides of the dish and the seeds are
brown.

Leave until cold, then cut into squares
or diamond shapes to serve.
SERVES 6 to 8

Thailand

Ornsiri Selby-Lowndes

'*Nai nam mee pla, Nai nar mee Kow*': 'In the water there is fish, in the field there is rice', so wrote King Ramkhamkaeng, son of the founder of Siam in AD 1292. This statement characterizes Thailand even today, for the word 'hunger' does not exist in the Thai language!

The modern name 'Thailand' or '*Moeng Tai*' means 'Land of Freedom', and it is the only country in South-East Asia which has never been a colony. Thailand has always been a monarchy, and although the king no longer has absolute power, he still forms a focal point for the people and, by his example, perpetuates the lifestyle set by his ancestors.

Because of their independence, the Thai people, their customs and cuisine, have hardly been affected by outside influences through the centuries. The majority of people are Buddhists and there are no religious restrictions in their basic diet. Different kinds of meat are eaten, as well as fresh fruit and vegetables. The favourable climate in Southern Thailand allows two or three rice harvests each year, and ensures a steady supply of many varieties of *pak* (green vegetables), *tua* (green beans) and *fuk* (squash).

Thai cooking favours the use of fresh rather than dried herbs and spices, and these are available throughout the year. Fruit is generally plentiful, but some varieties are restricted to special seasons. Raw vegetables also play an important part in the Thai diet.

Cooking Utensils and Equipment

A simple charcoal stove is traditionally used for cooking. In urban areas, this has been replaced in recent years by rings fed by bottled gas, but these can only be used for boiling and frying. The most important utensil in Thai cooking is the wok, which is used for boiling, steaming and frying. For steaming, the food is placed in a covered bamboo sieve (strainer) which is suspended over boiling water in the wok. Food is often wrapped in banana leaves or stuffed into green bamboo before steaming to give it a special flavour.

Standard western kitchen equipment is suitable for preparing simple Thai dishes, but a few special items are needed for traditional cooking. One of these is a pestle and mortar. In Thailand these are made from granite with a rough interior, which makes it easier to grind fibrous materials such as prawns (shrimp) and meat. A large porcelain pestle and mortar is, however, generally satisfactory. Two other important items are the wok, now easily available, and a small charcoal stove for grilled (broiled) dishes. A Chinese steamboat is excellent for cooking Thai soups and keeping them hot at the table.

Serving

Rice is the staple diet in Thailand, as it is in most of Asia. Noodles may be eaten at noon or as a snack, but all main meals are based on rice. At least four dishes are served with the rice to form a meal. For example; a soup, a curry, a meat or fish dish and a raw vegetable salad with a spicy sauce.

Sweet dishes are not usually served as part of a meal, but are eaten as snacks; these are usually bought from street vendors rather than cooked at home. Fruit is plentiful in Thailand and is frequently served after meals. Pineapple and mangoes are particularly popular. Often the fruit is cut into small pieces, chilled and then served with a bowl of salt or spiced salt for dipping.

Rice

Long-grain or Patna rice may be used, but if you can obtain real Thai rice, it is well worth buying. The best rice, often called 'fragrant rice', comes from Nakorn Pratom, famous for its huge pagoda. If the rice is fresh (the previous season's harvest), it will absorb about one and a half times its volume in water during cooking. As the rice becomes older and drier, the amount of water needed can increase to a volume twice that of the rice. Salt is never added.

Soups

The two main types of soup eaten are *Kang Chud*, which is similar to consommé, and *Tom Yum*, which usually contains pieces of prawn (shrimp), pork, beef, chicken or fish. The flavour of *Tom Yum* is typically Thai – a blend of lemon grass,* lime juice and fish sauce. Both soups can be served along with other dishes during a meal.

Salads

Thai salads are unusual in that they can be very hot to the taste. Small green chillis (bird's eye chillis) are concealed amongst the fresh vegetables and these can take one by surprise! Thais often include a sprig of flowers and tender young mango leaves in a salad. Leaves and young shoots from various other trees and shrubs are also added, according to the season. Lettuce and cauliflower make perfectly acceptable substitutes.

Curries

In Thailand, curries are prepared with a spicy paste made from fresh ingredients, rather than a powdered dried spice base. This is because many of the ingredients, including lemon grass,* garlic, shallots, *kapi*,* *kha*,* *pak chee*,* lime peel and chillis have a superior flavour and have a much better flavour when used fresh. Unfortunately, the individual spices used in many of the Thai curries are not obtainable fresh outside Thailand and the dried equivalents, or the prepared curry pastes sold in Oriental food stores, must be used instead.

Fish

Fish is plentiful in Thailand and normally at least one fish dish is included in every Thai meal. The commonest fish is *Pla Tu*, a small mackerel which is sold ready-steamed in the markets. Mackerel is suitable for most Thai dishes where the fish is unspecified. If a whole fish is required, use *Pla Jelamed* if possible. Known in this country as Pomfret, this fish has a flat, roundish body, and can often be found in the freezer section of Chinese supermarkets. Where fish is to be pounded to a fibrous pulp, cod fillets are fairly satisfactory, but will take a little longer to grind than the native fish.

Boiled *Pla Muek* (squid) is widely used in salads; it is also fried, stewed or grilled (broiled) and added to many other dishes. Choose young small squid for preference, as they respond well to a short cooking time, and do not take on the rubbery texture of the larger squid and octopus.

Drinks to Accompany Thai Food

In Thailand, a meal is always accompanied by iced water or iced weak tea. Alcoholic drinks are less common as they are not really compatible with the hot spices used in cooking; any drink with a concentration of alcohol greater than 5 per cent is unsuitable. Thus beer should be chosen, rather than wine. Lager is particularly good; 'Singha' and 'Amarit' are the famous Bangkok brands. Alternatively, a glass of whisky heavily diluted with water is quite a pleasant accompaniment to Thai food.

Prawns (Shrimp) and Squid Hot Soup

Tom Yum Kung Lae Pla Muk

Ideally, the stock for this soup should be made with pork bones. If these are not available, however, use chicken stock (bouillon) cubes instead.

METRIC/IMPERIAL

225 g/8 oz squid
1.2 litres/2 pints stock
3 lime leaves*
1 stalk lemon grass,* crushed
225 g/8 oz prawns, peeled and
    deveined
nam pla* to taste
2–4 fresh chillis, sliced into rounds
2 garlic cloves, peeled and crushed
juice of 1 lime or lemon, or to taste
chopped coriander leaves,* to garnish

AMERICAN

½ lb squid
5 cups stock
3 lime leaves*
1 stalk lemon grass,* crushed
½ lb shrimp, shelled and deveined
nam pla* to taste
2–4 fresh chilis, sliced into rounds
2 garlic cloves, peeled and crushed
juice of 1 lime or lemon, or to taste
chopped coriander leaves,* to garnish

METHOD

Clean the squid, cut off and chop the tentacles, then cut the body into rings.

Put the stock, lime leaves and lemon grass in a pan, bring to the boil, then lower the heat and simmer for 5 minutes. Add the prawns (shrimp), squid and nam pla. Cook until the prawns (shrimp) have turned pink, then add the chillis.

Pour the soup into 4 warmed individual bowls. Mix together the garlic and lime or lemon juice to taste, then stir into the soup. Sprinkle with coriander. Serve hot.
SERVES 4

Transparent Vermicelli Soup
Kang Ron

Dried squid is an acquired taste; if you do not like its rubbery texture omit it from this recipe. It is available from Chinese food stores.

METRIC/IMPERIAL

100 g/4 oz wun sen,* soaked in water
   for 10 minutes
2 coriander roots,* finely chopped
2 garlic cloves, peeled and chopped
1 teaspoon freshly ground black
   pepper
100 g/4 oz pork, minced
1.2 litres/2 pints water
100 g/4 oz prawns, peeled and
   deveined
25 g/1 oz dried prawns* (optional)
25 g/1 oz dried squid, sliced (optional)
½ onion, peeled and sliced
2 tablespoons dried jelly mushrooms,*
   soaked in warm water for 20 minutes
pinch of monosodium glutamate*
1 egg
few spring onions, finely chopped, to
   garnish

AMERICAN

¼ lb wun sen,* soaked in water for 10
   minutes
2 coriander roots,* finely chopped
2 garlic cloves, peeled and chopped
1 teaspoon freshly ground black
   pepper
½ cup ground pork, firmly packed
5 cups water
3 large shrimp, shelled and deveined
⅓ cup dried shrimp* (optional)
1 oz dried squid, sliced (optional)
½ onion, peeled and sliced
2 tablespoons tree ears,* soaked in
   warm water for 20 minutes
pinch of msg*
1 egg
few scallions, finely chopped, to
   garnish

METHOD

Drain the wun sen, then cut into 5 cm/2 inch lengths.

Put the coriander roots, garlic and pepper in a mortar and pound to a paste. Add the pork and continue pounding to a smooth paste. Shape the mixture into 10 to 12 balls, about 1 cm/½ inch in diameter.

Bring the water to the boil in a pan, then drop in the pork balls and cook for 5 minutes. Add the prawns (shrimp) and skim off any scum that comes to the surface with a slotted spoon. Simmer for a few minutes, stirring constantly.

Add the dried prawns (shrimp) and squid, if using, the onion, mushrooms, monosodium glutamate (msg) and the drained wun sen. Simmer for a few minutes, then stir the egg slowly into the soup and remove from the heat.

Pour into a warmed tureen and sprinkle with the spring onions (scallions). Serve hot.
SERVES 4

Prawns (Shrimp) and Squid Hot Soup; Transparent Vermicelli Soup

Chicken Rice Porridge
Kow Tom Kai

This dish is popular for breakfast or as a late supper; it is often served with chilli pickle. If possible, make the stock with pork bones. If these are not available, however, use chicken stock (bouillon) cubes instead.

METRIC/IMPERIAL

1.2 litres/2 pints stock
2 large chicken breasts, skinned,
   boned and cut into 1 cm/½ inch cubes
100 g/4 oz boned pork loin, cut into
   1 cm/½ inch cubes
350 g/12 oz rice, cooked
2 celery sticks, with leaves, chopped
   into 1 cm/½ inch lengths
2 spring onions, chopped
nam pla,* to taste
freshly ground black pepper
To garnish:
1 tablespoon vegetable oil
4 garlic cloves, peeled and finely
   chopped
100 g/4 oz bacon, derinded and cut
   into 1 cm/½ inch squares

AMERICAN

5 cups stock
2 large boneless chicken breasts,
   skinned and cut into ½ inch cubes
¼ lb boneless pork loin, cut into ½ inch
   cubes
1½ cups rice, cooked
2 celery stalks, with leaves, chopped
   into ½ inch lengths
2 scallions, chopped
nam pla,* to taste
freshly ground black pepper
To garnish:
1 tablespoon vegetable oil
4 garlic cloves, peeled and finely
   chopped
¼ lb bacon, cut into ½ inch squares

METHOD

Bring the stock to the boil in a pan, then add the chicken and pork. Cook until the meat turns white, then add the rice. Remove from the heat, add the celery and spring onions (scallions), then add nam pla and pepper to taste. Set aside.

Heat the oil in a frying pan (skillet), add the garlic and fry until golden brown. Remove from the pan with a slotted spoon and set aside. Add the bacon to the pan and fry until brown and crisp.

Pour the soup into 4 warmed individual bowls and sprinkle with the garlic and bacon. Serve hot.
SERVES 4

Deep-fried Rice Vermicelli with Sauce
Pad Mee Krob

METRIC/IMPERIAL

vegetable oil for deep-frying
175 g/6 oz rice vermicelli,* broken into
    pieces
Sauce:
1 tablespoon vegetable oil
1 onion, peeled and finely chopped
2 garlic cloves, peeled and finely
    chopped
225 g/8 oz prawns, peeled and
    deveined
75 g/3 oz crabmeat
2 teaspoons brown sugar
2 tablespoons tamarind water*
1 teaspoon salt
1 tablespoon soy sauce
To garnish:
2 teaspoons finely grated orange rind
2 red chillis, shredded
chopped coriander leaves*
100 g/4 oz fresh bean sprouts

AMERICAN

vegetable oil for deep-frying
6 oz rice noodles,* broken into pieces
Sauce:
1 tablespoon vegetable oil
1 onion, peeled and finely chopped
2 garlic cloves, peeled and finely
    chopped
½ lb shrimp, shelled and deveined
½ cup crabmeat
2 teaspoons brown sugar
2 tablespoons tamarind water*
1 teaspoon salt
1 tablespoon soy sauce
To garnish:
2 teaspoons finely grated orange rind
2 red chilis, shredded
chopped coriander leaves*
2 cups fresh bean sprouts

METHOD

Heat the oil in a deep-fat fryer and fry the rice vermicelli (noodles), in batches, for about 30 seconds until the strands swell and float. Drain and set aside.

To make the sauce: Heat the oil in a wok or deep frying pan (deep-fat fryer), add the onion and garlic and fry until lightly brown. Add the prawns (shrimp) and crab and cook until they turn pink.

Stir in the remaining ingredients, with the fried vermicelli (noodles). Taste and adjust the seasoning. Heat through, then transfer to a warmed serving dish.

Garnish with the orange rind, chillis and coriander, and arrange the bean sprouts around the edge of the dish. Serve hot.

SERVES 4

Fried Mackerel with Tamarind Sauce
Pla Prio Wan

METRIC/IMPERIAL

4 medium mackerel
2 tablespoons vegetable oil
3 garlic cloves, peeled and finely
    chopped
2 tablespoons shredded fresh root
    ginger*
3 tablespoons water
1 teaspoon sugar
3 tablespoons tamarind water*
To serve:
few spring onions, chopped
1 cucumber, skinned and cut into
    1 cm/½ inch slices

AMERICAN

4 medium mackerel
2 tablespoons vegetable oil
3 garlic cloves, peeled and finely
    chopped
2 tablespoons shredded fresh ginger
    root*
3 tablespoons water
1 teaspoon sugar
3 tablespoons tamarind water*
To serve:
few scallions, chopped
1 cucumber, skinned and cut into
    ½ inch slices

METHOD

Clean the fish, but do not remove the skin. Wrap the fish together in well-buttered foil, then bake in a preheated cool oven (150°C/300°F, Gas Mark 2) for 45 minutes or until tender. Unwrap the fish, then leave until cool and dry.

Heat the oil in a wok or deep frying pan (deep-fat fryer), add the fish and fry gently until golden brown. Remove from the pan carefully and drain. Transfer to a warmed serving dish and keep hot.

To make the sauce: Add the garlic to the pan in which the fish was fried and fry over high heat until light brown. Add the ginger and fry for a further 1 minute. Stir in the water, sugar and tamarind water. Heat through, then pour over the fish.

Sprinkle with the spring onions (scallions). Serve hot, with the cucumber as a side dish.

SERVES 4

Fried Hot Fish Balls
Tod Mun Pla

METRIC/IMPERIAL

4 garlic cloves, peeled and chopped
20 peppercorns
4 coriander roots,* finely chopped
pinch of sugar
3 dried chillis
750 g/1½ lb cod fillets, skinned
1 tablespoon plain flour
1 tablespoon soy sauce
5 tablespoons vegetable oil
To serve:
½ cucumber, peeled and thinly sliced
1 teaspoon distilled vinegar
2 tablespoons water
1 teaspoon sugar
2 shallots, peeled and finely chopped
1 small carrot, peeled and grated

AMERICAN

4 garlic cloves, peeled and chopped
20 peppercorns
4 coriander roots,* finely chopped
pinch of sugar
3 dried chilis
1½ lb cod fillets, skinned
1 tablespoon all-purpose flour
1 tablespoon soy sauce
⅓ cup vegetable oil
To serve:
½ cucumber, peeled and thinly sliced
1 teaspoon distilled vinegar
2 tablespoons water
1 teaspoon sugar
2 shallots, peeled and finely chopped
1 small carrot, peeled and grated

METHOD

Put the garlic, peppercorns, coriander, sugar and chillis in a mortar and pound to a paste. Add the fish a little at a time and continue pounding to a smooth paste. Add the flour and soy sauce. Pound the mixture for a further 1 minute, then shape into 20 to 25 balls, about 2.5 cm/1 inch in diameter.

Heat the oil in a wok or deep frying pan (deep-fat fryer) and fry the fish balls, a few at a time, until golden brown all over. Remove from the pan with a slotted spoon, drain and arrange on a serving dish. Keep hot while frying the remainder.

Arrange the cucumber slices in a separate serving dish. Mix together the vinegar, water, sugar, shallots and carrot. Sprinkle over the cucumber. Serve the fish balls hot, with the cucumber salad as a side dish.

SERVES 4

Dry Chicken Curry
Kai P'Anang

METRIC/IMPERIAL

150 g/5 oz creamed coconut,* roughly
   chopped
150 ml/¼ pint water
2–3 large chicken breasts, skinned,
   boned and cut into serving pieces

Curry paste:
½ teaspoon caraway seeds
2 large chillis, seeded and chopped
½ teaspoon coriander seeds
2 teaspoons shredded lemon grass*
3 shallots, peeled
1 teaspoon finely chopped coriander
   root*
5 garlic cloves, peeled
3 slices kha*
½ teaspoon makrut peel,* grated
½ teaspoon kapi*

AMERICAN

1⅓ cups thick coconut milk*
2–3 large boneless chicken breasts,
   skinned, cut into serving pieces

Curry paste:
½ teaspoon caraway seeds
2 large chilis, seeded and chopped
½ teaspoon coriander seeds
2 teaspoons shredded lemon grass*
3 shallots, peeled
1 teaspoon finely chopped coriander
   root*
5 garlic cloves, peeled
3 slices kha*
½ teaspoon makrut peel,* grated
½ teaspoon kapi*

Put the creamed coconut (coconut milk) in
a large pan. If using creamed coconut,
add the water and heat gently until the
coconut has melted, stirring frequently.

Add the chicken to the coconut and
cook for about 10 minutes until almost
tender. Remove the chicken from the pan.
Boil the liquid for a few minutes until it
becomes oily.

Meanwhile, make the curry paste:
Pound the caraway seeds in a mortar. Add
the remaining ingredients one at a time,
pounding between each addition, to
obtain a smooth paste. Add the paste to the
coconut liquid and heat gently, stirring
constantly. Return the chicken to the pan
and reheat, turning to coat with the sauce.
Transfer to a warmed serving dish. Serve
hot.
SERVES 4

Fried Mackerel with Tamarind Sauce;
Deep-Fried Rice Vermicelli with Sauce

Stuffed Pancakes (Crêpes)
Kai Yad Sai

METRIC/IMPERIAL

225 g/8 oz minced pork
2 tablespoons tung chai*
1 teaspoon sugar
2 tablespoons soy sauce
2 onions, peeled and finely chopped
2 tablespoons vegetable oil
6 eggs, beaten
coriander leaves* to garnish

AMERICAN

1 cup ground pork
2 tablespoons tung chai*
1 teaspoon sugar
2 tablespoons soy sauce
2 onions, peeled and finely chopped
2 tablespoons vegetable oil
6 eggs, beaten
coriander leaves* to garnish

METHOD

Put the pork, tung chai, sugar, soy sauce and onions in a bowl and mix well. Heat 1 tablespoon oil in a wok or frying pan (skillet), add the pork mixture and fry gently for 3 minutes. Remove from the pan and set aside.

Add the remaining oil to the cleaned pan and tilt to coat the entire surface with oil. Pour off any excess oil, then heat the pan until smoking. Pour in half the beaten eggs to make a thin omelet. Spoon half the pork mixture into the centre, then fold over the edges. Turn the omelet over and cook quickly on the underside until lightly browned. Remove from the pan and keep hot while cooking the remaining eggs and pork in the same way. Cut the pancakes (crêpes) into slices and arrange in a serving dish. Garnish with coriander. Serve immediately.
SERVES 4

Beef with Hot Salad
Nua Nam Toak

Braising steak can be used instead of fillet steak for a more economical meal; after slicing the meat treat it with meat tenderizer, then leave for about 10 minutes before cooking. In Thailand, papaya (pawpaw) peel is used to make the meat tender.

The flavour of this dish is greatly improved if the onion, chillis and beef are grilled (broiled) over glowing charcoals rather than using a conventional grill (broiler).

METRIC/IMPERIAL

450 g/1 lb fillet steak
1 large onion, peeled and sliced into
*   rings*
2 fresh chillis
2 garlic cloves, peeled and crushed
½ teaspoon sugar
1 teaspoon salt
½ teaspoon soy sauce
juice of 1 lime or lemon
1 teaspoon chopped mint
To serve:
fresh green seasonal vegetables
*   (cucumber, tomatoes, Chinese*
*   cabbage, bean sprouts, etc.),*
*   chopped*

AMERICAN

1 lb fillet steak
1 large onion, peeled and sliced into
*   rings*
2 fresh chilis
2 garlic cloves, peeled and crushed
½ teaspoon sugar
1 teaspoon salt
½ teaspoon soy sauce
juice of 1 lime or lemon
1 teaspoon chopped mint
To serve:
fresh green seasonal vegetables
*   (cucumber, tomatoes, bok choy,*
*   bean sprouts, etc.), chopped*

METHOD

Cut the beef along the grain into strips about 6 cm/2½ inches long, 2.5 cm/1 inch wide and 1 cm/½ inch thick. Put the onion rings and chillis on a skewer and grill (broil) until soft. Remove from the skewer, then mash together.

Grill (broil) the beef until just cooked to taste, then mix with the mashed onion and chillis. Add the remaining ingredients and mix well.

Arrange the chopped vegetables around the edge of a warmed serving dish, then pile the beef mixture in the centre. Alternatively, toss the vegetables quickly with the beef and pile into a warmed serving dish. Serve hot.
SERVES 4

Fried Beef and Horapa
Pad Ho-ra-pa kub Nua

METRIC/IMPERIAL

2 tablespoons plus 1 teaspoon
*   vegetable oil*
750 g/1½ lb braising steak, thinly sliced
2 onions, peeled and sliced
3 garlic cloves, peeled and finely
*   chopped*
3 tablespoons freshly chopped horapa
*   leaves**
3 fresh chillis, sliced
nam pla* to taste
monosodium glutamate* to taste
few chopped spring onions to garnish

AMERICAN

2 tablespoons plus 1 teaspoon
*   vegetable oil*
1½ lb chuck steak, thinly sliced
2 onions, peeled and sliced
3 garlic cloves, peeled and finely
*   chopped*
3 tablespoons freshly chopped horapa
*   leaves**
3 fresh chilis, sliced
nam pla* to taste
msg* to taste
few chopped scallions to garnish

METHOD

Heat 1 teaspoon of the oil in a wok or frying pan (skillet), add the beef and fry until the juices are extracted from the meat. Stir twice and cook for about 3 minutes, then remove from the pan and set aside.

Heat the remaining oil in the pan, add the onions and garlic and fry over brisk heat until brown. Stir in the horapa, then return the beef to the pan. Add the chillis, fry for a further 1 minute, then add nam pla and monosodium glutamate (msg) to taste.

Transfer to a serving dish and garnish with the chopped spring onions (scallions). Serve hot.
SERVES 4

Son-in-Law Eggs
Kai Look Koei

METRIC/IMPERIAL

2 tablespoons vegetable oil
5 shallots, peeled and finely chopped
4 hard-boiled eggs, shelled and
*   quartered*
2 tablespoons tamarind water*
1 tablespoon water
2 teaspoons brown sugar
nam pla* to taste

AMERICAN

2 tablespoons vegetable oil
5 shallots, peeled and finely chopped
4 hard-cooked eggs, shelled and
*   quartered*
2 tablespoons tamarind water*
1 tablespoon water
2 teaspoons brown sugar
nam pla* to taste

METHOD

Heat the oil in a wok or deep frying pan (deep-fat fryer). Add the shallots and fry until brown. Remove from the pan with a slotted spoon and set aside.

Add the eggs to the pan and fry until crisp and blistered on the outside, then remove from the pan with a slotted spoon and set aside.

Add the remaining ingredients to the pan and cook for 5 minutes, stirring constantly. Return the eggs to the pan and heat gently for 2 minutes, stirring carefully. Transfer to a warmed serving dish and garnish with the fried shallots. Serve hot.
SERVES 4

Left: Beef with Hot Salad; Fried Beef and Horapa
Below: Stuffed Pancakes (Crêpes)

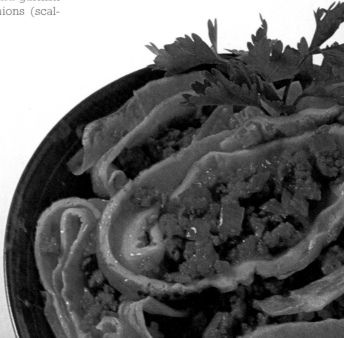

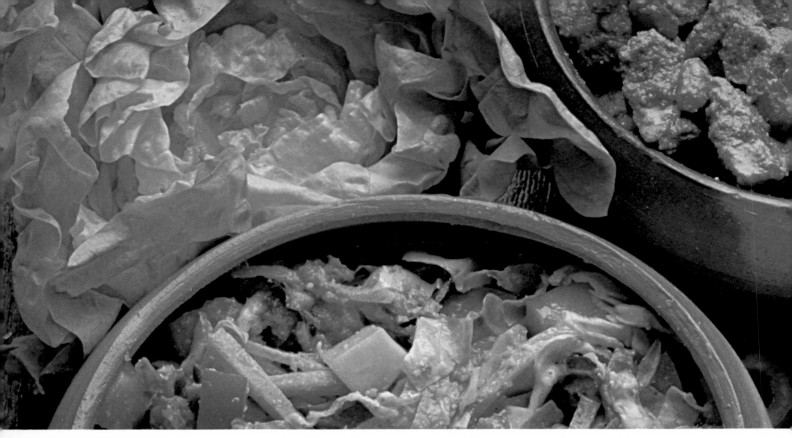

Thai Salad
Som Tum

In Thailand, papaya (pawpaw) is normally used in this salad, together with vegetables such as tomatoes and lettuce. It is a good side dish to serve with *Fried Pork Balls* (see page 106) and *Fried Chicken with Garlic* (see page 107).

METRIC/IMPERIAL

75 g/3 oz cabbage, shredded
1 large carrot, peeled and shredded
25 g/1 oz peanuts, roasted and crushed
  (see page 129)
25 g/1 oz dried prawns,* ground
Dressing:
1 tablespoon nam pla*
2 teaspoons sugar
freshly ground black pepper
2 garlic cloves, peeled and crushed
2 tablespoons lime or lemon juice

AMERICAN

1 cup shredded cabbage
½ cup shredded carrots
3 tablespoons peanuts, roasted and
  crushed (see page 129)
⅓ cup dried shrimp,* ground
Dressing:
1 tablespoon nam pla*
2 teaspoons sugar
freshly ground black pepper
2 garlic cloves, peeled and crushed
2 tablespoons lime or lemon juice

METHOD

Put all the salad ingredients in a bowl and stir well. Mix together the dressing ingredients, pour over the salad and toss well to coat. Serve cold.
SERVES 4

Masaman Curry
Kang Masaman

This is an unusual Thai curry in that it contains peanuts and tamarind water* and there are many variations. It is equally good prepared with chicken, rather than beef.

King Rama VI said in one of his poems, 'A lady who makes a good *masaman* will never be short of suitors'.

METRIC/IMPERIAL

1 kg/2–2¼ lb braising steak, cut into
  2.5 cm/1 inch squares
1.2 litres/2 pints water
200 g/7 oz creamed coconut,* roughly
  chopped
100 g/4 oz peanuts, roasted (see page
  129)
nam pla* to taste
3 tablespoons tamarind water*
coconut sugar,* to taste
Curry paste:
7 dried chillis, deseeded and finely
  chopped
½ teaspoon freshly ground black
  pepper
2 tablespoons coriander seeds
2 tablespoons cumin seeds
1 tablespoon shredded lemon
  grass*
1 cinnamon stick
5 cardamom seeds
¼ whole nutmeg, grated
1 teaspoon salt
7 shallots, peeled and grilled
5 garlic cloves, peeled
½ teaspoon kapi*

AMERICAN

2¼ lb chuck steak, cut into 1 inch
  squares
5 cups water
1 cup coconut milk*
1 cup peanuts, roasted (see page 129)
nam pla* to taste
3 tablespoons tamarind water*
coconut sugar,* to taste
Curry paste:
7 dried chilis, deseeded and finely
  chopped
½ teaspoon freshly ground black
  pepper
2 tablespoons coriander seeds
2 tablespoons cumin seeds
1 tablespoon shredded lemon
  grass*
1 cinnamon stick
5 cardamom seeds
¼ whole nutmeg, grated
1 teaspoon salt
7 shallots, peeled and broiled
5 garlic cloves, peeled
½ teaspoon kapi*

METHOD

Put the steak and water in a pan and bring to the boil. Lower the heat, cover and simmer for about 1 hour or until the meat is tender.

To make the curry paste: Put the chillis in a pan with the pepper, coriander, cumin, lemon grass, cinnamon, cardamom and nutmeg. Cook over low heat until the mixture browns, stirring constantly. Transfer to a mortar and pound to a smooth paste. Add the remaining ingredients and pound the mixture until smooth.

Remove the meat from the pan with a slotted spoon and set aside. Add the coconut cream (coconut milk) to the liquid in the pan and heat gently, stirring frequently. Add the peanuts and a little nam pla. Boil the liquid until reduced in volume by one third. Add the prepared curry paste and simmer for about 5 minutes, stirring constantly.

Return the meat to the pan and cover with a tight-fitting lid. Bring back to the boil and continue cooking until the meat is very tender. Add the tamarind water with coconut sugar and nam pla to taste. Serve hot.
SERVES 6

Soya Bean and Coconut Dip
Tao Chiew Lon

Serve this dip with a salad of chopped fresh vegetables according to availability. Cucumber, red and green peppers, chicory (Belgian endive) or celery, and crisp lettuce make a good combination.

METRIC/IMPERIAL

100 g/4 oz creamed coconut,* roughly chopped
300 ml/½ pint water
3 tablespoons tao chiew*
1 tablespoon finely chopped shallots or onion
50 g/2 oz cooked peeled prawns
50 g/2 oz mashed potato
2 chillis, finely chopped
1 teaspoon brown sugar
3 tablespoons tamarind water*
chillis to garnish

AMERICAN

1¾ cups thick coconut milk*
3 tablespoons tao chiew*
1 tablespoon finely chopped shallots or onion
2 cooked shelled shrimp
¼ cup mashed potato
2 chilis, finely chopped
1 teaspoon brown sugar
3 tablespoons tamarind water*
chilis to garnish

METHOD

If using creamed coconut, place in a pan with the water and heat gently until the coconut has melted, stirring frequently.

Work the tao chiew and shallots to a paste, using an electric blender or a pestle and mortar then add to the coconut liquid with the prawns (shrimp) and potato.

Cook until the fat from the coconut floats to the surface of the sauce, stirring constantly to prevent sticking. Stir in the remaining ingredients and bring to the boil.

Transfer to a serving dish and garnish with chillis. Serve hot, as a dip with a crisp salad.
SERVES 4

Thai Salad; Masaman Curry; Soya Bean and Coconut Dip

Sweet Mung Beans with Coconut; Sticky Rice with Black Beans; Sticky Rice and Custard

Sweet Mung Beans with Coconut
Maled Khanun

METRIC/IMPERIAL

150 g/5 oz mung beans*
150 g/5 oz creamed coconut,* roughly
  chopped
450 ml/¾ pint water
225 g/8 oz sugar
4 egg yolks, beaten

AMERICAN

1 cup mung beans*
1¼ cups thick coconut milk*
1⅓ cups water
1 cup sugar
4 egg yolks, beaten

METHOD

Crush the beans, using a pestle and mortar, then leave to soak in cold water overnight.

Drain the beans and wash to remove the green skins. Put the beans in a pan, add enough water to cover, then simmer, covered, for about 20 minutes or until soft. Drain, then return to the cleaned pan and heat gently until the beans are dry and completely cooked, stirring occasionally. Mash to a smooth paste.

Put the creamed coconut (coconut milk) in a pan. If using creamed coconut, add 150 ml/¼ pint/⅓ cup of the water and heat gently until melted, stirring frequently.

Add 150 g/5 oz/⅔ cup of the sugar to the coconut liquid, then stir in the mashed beans. Bring to the boil, then boil, uncovered, for about 30 minutes until the mixture is thick, stirring frequently with a wooden spoon. Remove from the heat and leave until completely cold.

Form the paste into about 50 small balls, approximately 1 cm/½ inch in diameter. Put the remaining sugar and water in a pan. Heat gently until the sugar has dissolved, then boil until a thin syrup is formed.

Dip each ball into beaten egg yolk to coat, then immerse in the hot syrup and cook for about 30 seconds. Remove with a slotted spoon and arrange in a single layer on a serving dish, taking care that the balls are not touching or they will stick together. Chill in the refrigerator for at least 3 hours before serving. Serve very cold.
SERVES 4

Sticky Rice with Black Beans
Kow Neo Tua Dom

In Thailand, this dish is cooked and sold in hollow sticks of green bamboo which have been cooked over charcoal. This recipe has been adapted for a domestic oven. Dried black beans are available at Chinese, Indian and Italian supermarkets.

METRIC/IMPERIAL

150 g/5 oz creamed coconut,* roughly
  chopped
600 ml/1 pint water
50 g/2 oz dried black beans, soaked in
  cold water for 12 hours
40 g/1½ oz glutinous (sweet) rice*
25 g/1 oz coconut sugar*

AMERICAN

1¼ cups thick coconut milk*
1¾ cups water
½ cup dried black beans, soaked in
  cold water for 12 hours
¼ cup glutinous (sweet) rice*
2 tablespoons coconut sugar*

METHOD

Put the creamed coconut (coconut milk) and water in a pan and heat gently, stirring frequently.

Drain the beans, then mix with the rice, sugar and coconut milk. Pour into a baking dish, cover and bake in a preheated very cool (120°C/250°F, Gas Mark ½) for about 3 hours, stirring after 2 hours. Serve hot.
SERVES 4

Sticky Rice and Custard
Kow Neo Sang Kaya

METRIC/IMPERIAL

Custard:
159 g/5 oz creamed coconut,* roughly
  chopped
300 ml/½ pint water
2 tablespoons rose water
2 tablespoons brown sugar
4 eggs, beaten
Sticky rice:
175 g/6 oz glutinous (sweet) rice*
100 g/4 oz creamed coconut,* roughly
  chopped
300 ml/½ pint water
1 teaspoon salt
1 tablespoon sugar
To decorate:
lime slices

AMERICAN

Custard:
2 tablespoons rose water
2 tablespoons brown sugar
1¾ cups thick coconut milk*
4 eggs, beaten
Sticky rice:
1 cup glutinous (sweet) rice*
1¾ cups coconut milk*
1 teaspoon salt
1 tablespoon sugar
To decorate:
lime slices

METHOD

To make the custard: If using creamed coconut, place in a pan, add the water and heat gently until the coconut has melted, stirring frequently.

Add the rose water and sugar to the coconut milk. Stir well, then beat in the eggs. Strain into a heatproof bowl and steam for about 1½ hours or until the custard has set. Alternatively, place the bowl in a baking dish of water and bake in a preheated cool oven (140°C/275°F, Gas Mark 1).

Meanwhile, make the sticky rice: Put the rice in a bowl in the top of a steamer or double boiler. If using creamed coconut, place in a pan, add the water and heat gently until the coconut has melted, stirring frequently. Mix the coconut milk with the salt and sugar, then pour over the rice. Steam for 30 minutes or until the rice is cooked.

To serve: Place the cooked custard on top of the rice and decorate with lime slices. Serve hot or cold.

SERVES 4

Kampuchea, Laos and Vietnam

Gloria Zimmerman
Bach Ngo

Few cultures of the world have been as misunderstood in the West as those of South-East Asia. Among them, the lands of Vietnam, Kampuchea and Laos are probably the least understood. Variously dismissed as a conglomeration of Chinese, Indian and French influence, these countries essentially have cultures of their own. Recent research indicates that such basic words as plough and seed, kiln and pottery, axe and boat, iron and gold, went from South-East Asian language into Chinese. Archaeological finds point to the probability that rice was first domesticated here 1,000 years earlier than in India or China; the same appears to be true in the making of polished stone tools, pottery and bronze implements. Scholars now ask themselves if the Chinese and Indians learned from the South-East Asians, rather than the other way round.

Vietnamese culture, after centuries of struggle against Chinese domination, has maintained its own distinct, sophisticated and highly complex identity. Despite 1,000 years of Chinese occupation and repeated attempts at conquest, this ancient culture – dating back over 4,000 years – has retained its own language, folklore, customs and arts. The University of Hanoi is older than any university in Europe.

Although there are overtones which reflect Chinese, Indian and a later French influence, authentic Vietnamese cuisine is unique. Craig Claiborne, leading food critic of the 'New York Times', acclaims the Vietnamese kitchen as 'one of the most outstanding on earth'. In France, home of *haute cuisine*, Vietnamese restaurants far outnumber Chinese. Vietnamese chefs have earned so enviable a reputation that soon after John F Kennedy became president, a Vietnamese chef was invited to take charge of the White House kitchen.

The diversity of Vietnamese cuisine is at least partially explained by the country's geography The extensive coastline, stretching over 1,400 miles along the eastern seaboard of South-East Asia, provides all kinds of fish and shellfish. Most of the population is concentrated in the north and south, which are connected by a narrow stretch of mountainous country in the centre. The Red River Delta of the north and the Mekong River Delta in the south provide very fertile, low lying country.

In the hot, humid south a much broader range of vegetables, fruits and other foods are grown than in the cooler north. The highlands of the centre, with their temperate climate, provide a variety of vegetables, including asparagus, cauliflower, potatoes and artichokes. As might be expected, the regional cuisines are divided in the same way: Hanoi in the north, Hue in the centre and Saigon in the south.

Laos is a small, landlocked country which is relatively undeveloped and sparsely populated by a collection of tribes without a national history. Neighbouring China and Thailand have had the greatest influence on the Laotian culture.

Kampuchea, previously known as Cambodia, was a centre of power in South-East Asia about

1,000 years ago. With its capital at Angkor, the Khmer kingdom of Cambodia developed a great civilization. The remains of this can be seen today, with such enormous structures as the Temple at Angkor Wat, the world's largest religious building. From the twelfth century, the Khmer culture and power gradually declined.

Rice, staple food of the vast majority of Asian kitchens, is no less important in the cooking of Vietnam, Kampuchea and Laos. Prepared in infinite variety, it appears at every meal and is, indeed, the 'bread' of life. The most unusual feature of Laotian food is the emphasis on glutinous (sweet) rice* at every meal. In this respect, the Laotian cuisine is unique. In Vietnam, Kampuchea and other Asian countries, glutinous (sweet) rice* is normally only used for sweets or snacks. For all-round use, the Vietnamese prefer rice that is very dry and flaky.

All three cuisines make good use of home-grown fruits and vegetables. The markets are a feast to Western eyes with their colourful display of unfamiliar fruits, vegetables and fresh herbs. A variety of mints, lemon grass* and coriander* are used in dishes.

Fish, both fresh and dried, are a major source of protein. In landlocked Laos, freshwater fish from the many streams and rivers predominate. Likewise Kampuchea, with its Tonle Sap (Great Lake), the Mekong river and the sea, has a plentiful supply of fish and shellfish. The long coastline of Vietnam, the Red river in the north and the Mekong in the south, similarly supply an abundance of seafood and freshwater fish.

Meat is less widely used than fish and seafood, primarily because it is relatively expensive. Lamb and mutton are not seen at all. Pork is cheaper than other types of meat and is therefore more frequently eaten. Vietnamese pigs, fed on chopped banana tree trunks, produce a superior pork that is much prized. Chicken and duck, much leaner than their Western counterparts, are seen on special occasions. Beef is very expensive and is served only at very special feasts. In Laos, deer and other game are hunted in the mountains and forests; these are eaten on festive occasions, rather than beef.

Nuoc Cham (see page 125), also known as Nuoc Mam, is a universal condiment, used in many different ways. This clear, salty liquid is prepared by layering fresh anchovies, sardines and other small fish, with salt, in large barrels; these are then set out in the sun. As salt is to the Western cuisine and soy sauce is to the Chinese cuisine, so Nuoc Cham is to these cuisines. It is added to all kinds of dishes during preparation; it also serves as the base for sauces to be sprinkled on prepared dishes or served as a dip. In Vietnam, Nuoc Cham is combined with garlic, lime or lemon juice, sugar and fresh chillis, and used to enhance flavours of other foods. In Kampuchea and Laos, roasted peanuts are added and, in Laos, Nuoc Cham is also mixed with anchovy paste.

The hallmarks of Vietnamese cuisine are lightness and subtlety, with a delicacy and clarity of flavour. Although Chinese influences are apparent, they have been so assimilated that even a stir-fried dish which looks somewhat Chinese will have a taste and aroma unmistakably Vietnamese, while their curry is quite unlike any Indian curry. The Vietnamese aversion to fats is apparent in their stir-frying technique in which even less oil is used than in Chinese cooking. Their dislike of fat is probably one reason why the Vietnamese simmer so many of their dishes. The light and delicate nature of this cuisine can be attributed to this limited use of fats and the emphasis on fresh, raw vegetables.

The food of the north is not as spicy as that of the south, although black pepper is widely used as a condiment. Northerners like their vegetables cooked and tend to prefer more complex and delicate flavours. Fish is not as important in the north, but shellfish, such as crab, is exceedingly popular. Stir-fried dishes are seen more often in the north than in the centre and south – undoubtedly because of the proximity of the Chinese border.

The centre mountainous neck of land connecting the north and south, is where Hue, the ancient capital of the kings of Vietnam is located. Here the influence of the royal palate is evident in the emphasis on food presentation. Small portions of a variety of dishes are served at each meal and spicy foods predominate, with the frequent use of hot chilli peppers and Nuoc Cham.*

The hot climate and fertile fields of the south provide a great variety of vegetables, fruit, meat and game. Large quantities of fresh fruits and raw vegetables are consumed. A tropical people, the South Vietnamese traditionally prefer spicy food; they also make good use of locally grown coconut and sugar cane. The influence of the French is more evident here – in the use of Western vegetables, such as potatoes and asparagus, though prepared in Vietnamese style.

Kampuchea and Laos are relatively underdeveloped countries with very low per capita incomes. In addition, they do not have the extensive range of foods that are available to the Vietnamese and this is reflected in their relatively limited cuisines. The Kampuchean diet is largely based on rice, freshwater and dried fish. It is heavily spiced and tends to be somewhat strong in flavour for Western tastes. Barbecuing over charcoal is a favourite way of preparing meat or fish, which is generally served with a raw Vegetable Platter (see page 125). Laotian dishes

are more influenced by the Thai kitchen, although their prolific use of glutinous rice* clearly distinguishes them from others. Here, too, barbecuing is very popular, though frequently it is only the first step in the preparation of a dish. The liberal use of red chilli peppers makes for many fiery dishes.

Serving

In neither Laos or Kampuchea are there restaurants serving the national cuisine. The foreigner must be invited to a family meal to sample the food. Meals are served in very simple fashion and the family are seated on straw mats on the floor, as compared to Vietnam where even simple family meals are served at the table. Chopsticks are not used in Laos and Kampuchea, but food is generally eaten with the fingers. Soup is eaten with a soup spoon out of a large communal bowl placed in the centre of the serving area. In Vietnam, the Chinese influence is evident in the universal use of chopsticks, but the Vietnamese use metal spoons rather than the ceramic soup spoons favoured by the Chinese.

Cooking Utensils and Equipment

All three cuisines tend to use the same kitchen equipment, although with a different emphasis. The mortar and pestle, the wok, a sharp chopper and chopping board are common items. In Laos, the glutinous rice* is cooked in a steamer made of woven bamboo, whereas in Vietnam and Kampuchea the steamers are metal. In all three countries, cooking in the cities is generally done over kerosene or bottled gas, whereas in rural areas charcoal is most commonly used.

Rice Noodle
Fish Soup

Num Banh Choc
Kampuchea

This soup is usually served at breakfast in Kampuchea. *Khcheay* (white turmeric) is available in dried powdered form at oriental groceries.

METRIC/IMPERIAL

1.5 litres/2½ pints water
1 fish (carp, mackerel, sea bass, etc);
  weighing 1.5 kg/3–3½ lb
3 tablespoons khcheay
2 garlic cloves, peeled
5 lemon grass leaves,* thinly sliced
1 teaspoon turmeric powder
2 tablespoons fish paste*
2 tablespoons fish sauce*
1 teaspoon salt
pinch of monosodium glutamate*
1 teaspoon sugar
250 ml/8 fl oz coconut milk*
To serve:
225 g/8 oz medium rice vermicelli*
40 g/1½ oz fresh bean sprouts
50 g/2 oz cucumber, shredded
50 g/2 oz green papaya, shredded
2 tablespoons chopped dill
50 g/2 oz cabbage, shredded
50 g/2 oz fresh or canned banana
  blossoms, shredded (optional)

Chicken Soup

Môn Sngôr
Kampuchea

METRIC/IMPERIAL

1 chicken, weighing 1–1.25 kg/2–2½ lb
2 litres/3½ pints water
3 tablespoons fish sauce*
1 teaspoon sugar
pinch of monosodium glutamate*
juice of 1 lime
2 spring onions, chopped
4 tablespoons shredded culantro*
1 red chilli, sliced

AMERICAN

1 chicken, weighing 2–2½ lb
4½ pints water
3 tablespoons fish sauce*
1 teaspoon sugar
pinch of msg*
juice of 1 lime
2 scallions, chopped
¼ cup shredded culantro*
1 red chili, sliced

METHOD

Put the chicken and water in a large pan and bring to the boil. Boil for 20 minutes or until the chicken is cooked. Remove the chicken from the pan and tear the meat from the bones in bite-sized pieces. Return the meat and bones to the pan and bring back to the boil. Boil for 5 minutes, then remove from the heat.

Put the fish sauce, sugar, monosodium glutamate (msg) and lime juice in a warmed soup tureen. Pour the hot soup into the tureen and stir well, then sprinkle over the spring onions (scallions), culantro and chilli. Serve hot with rice as part of a family dinner.
SERVES 4

AMERICAN

6¼ cups water
1 fish (bluefish, catfish, etc.), weighing
  3–3½ lb
3 tablespoons khcheay
2 garlic cloves, peeled
5 lemon grass leaves,* thinly sliced
1 teaspoon turmeric powder
2 tablespoons fish paste*
2 tablespoons fish sauce*
1 teaspoon salt
pinch of msg*
1 teaspoon sugar
1 cup coconut milk*
To serve:
½ lb medium rice vermicelli*
¾ cup fresh bean sprouts
½ cup shredded cucumber
½ cup shredded green papaya
2 tablespoons chopped dill
¾ cup shredded cabbage
½ cup fresh or canned banana
  blossoms, shredded (optional)

METHOD

Bring the water to the boil in a large pan. Add the fish and bring back to the boil, then simmer for about 15 minutes or until the fish flakes easily. Remove the fish from the pan and reserve the cooking liquid.

Remove all the flesh from the fish and discard the carcass. Put the khcheay, garlic, lemon grass and turmeric in a mortar and pound to a paste. Add the fish and pound again to a smooth paste.

Bring the reserved cooking liquid to the boil. Add the fish paste, fish sauce, salt, monosodium glutamate (msg), sugar and coconut milk. Bring back to the boil, add the pounded fish mixture, then boil for 10 to 15 minutes.

Boil the rice vermicelli in about 2 litres/3½ pints/4½ pints water for 5 minutes, then drain and rinse under cold running water. Drain again.

Pour the hot soup into a warmed soup tureen. Divide the rice vermicelli between 4 individual warmed soup bowls, add the remaining ingredients and ladle the soup over the top. Serve hot.
SERVES 4

Stir-Fried Chicken with Ginger

Sach Môn Chha Khnhei
Kampuchea

METRIC/IMPERIAL

2.5 cm/1 inch piece of fresh root
   ginger,* peeled and shredded
salt
2 tablespoons pork fat or vegetable oil
2 garlic cloves, peeled and chopped
4 chicken thighs, chopped into
   2.5 cm/1 inch squares
1 tablespoon fish sauce*
1 teaspoon sugar
1 tablespoon water
2 spring onions, cut into 5 cm/2 inch
   pieces
coriander leaves* or parsley sprigs to
   garnish

AMERICAN

1 inch piece of fresh ginger root,*
   peeled and shredded
salt
2 tablespoons pork fat or vegetable oil
2 garlic cloves, peeled and chopped
4 chicken thighs, chopped into 1 inch
   squares
1 tablespoon fish sauce*
1 teaspoon sugar
1 tablespoon water
2 scallions, cut into 2 inch pieces
coriander leaves* or parsley sprigs to
   garnish

METHOD

Sprinkle the ginger with a little salt, leave to stand for a few minutes, then squeeze and discard the liquid. Rinse the ginger with water and squeeze out the liquid again.

   Heat the pork fat or oil in a frying pan (skillet). Add the garlic and stir-fry until lightly browned. Add the ginger and stir-fry for 1 minute, then add the chicken. Stir in the remaining ingredients, except the spring onions (scallions), then cover and cook over moderate heat for 10 minutes or until the chicken is completely cooked. Stir in the spring onions (scallions).

   Transfer to a serving dish and garnish with coriander or parsley. Serve hot with rice as part of a family dinner.
SERVES 4

Stir-Fried Chicken with Ginger; Fried
Pork Spareribs; Sour Beef Stew

Sour Beef Stew

Somlâr Mochu Sachko

Kampuchea

METRIC/IMPERIAL

2 stalks lemon grass,* thinly sliced
3 garlic cloves, peeled
5 fresh or dried lime leaves,* shredded
4 tablespoons tamarind paste*
1 tablespoon turmeric powder
2 tablespoons dried galingale,* soaked
   in hot water for 1 hour
1 red chilli
2 tablespoons fish paste*
2 tablespoons pork fat or vegetable oil
2 tablespoons fish sauce*
1 kg/2–2¼ lb stewing beef, cut into
   2.5 cm/1 inch cubes
120 ml/4 fl oz water
To garnish:
2 tablespoons chopped spring onion,
   green part only

AMERICAN

2 stalks lemon grass,* thinly sliced
3 garlic cloves, peeled
5 fresh or dried lime leaves,* shredded
¼ cup tamarind paste*
1 tablespoon turmeric powder
2 tablespoons dried galingale,* soaked
   in hot water for 1 hour
1 red chili
2 tablespoons fish paste*
2 tablespoons pork fat or vegetable oil
2 tablespoons fish sauce*
2–2¼ lb stewing beef, cut into 1 inch
   cubes
½ cup water
To garnish:
2 tablespoons chopped scallion, green
   part only

METHOD

Put all the ingredients except the beef, fish sauce, paste and pork fat in a mortar and pound to a paste.

Work the fish paste through a sieve (strainer) and discard the pulp remaining in the sieve.

Heat the pork fat or oil in a pan. Add the fish paste, stir-fry for a few seconds, then add the pounded ingredients. Stir again, then add the fish sauce. Stir in the meat and water. Bring to the boil and simmer, uncovered, for 15 minutes.

Add more water as necessary to ensure the meat is just covered with liquid. Cover and simmer for 1 hour or until the meat is tender, adding more water if necessary during cooking.

Transfer to a serving dish and garnish with spring onion (scallion). Serve hot with rice as a main dish for a family dinner.
SERVES 6

Fried Pork Spareribs

Choeeng Chomni Chrouc Chean

Kampuchea

These spareribs can alternatively be cooked over charcoal.

METRIC/IMPERIAL

1 kg/2–2¼ lb pork spareribs, cut into
   separate pieces
2 tablespoons fish sauce*
1 tablespoon sugar
3 garlic cloves, peeled and chopped
pinch of freshly ground black pepper
3 tablespoons pork fat or vegetable oil
To garnish: (optional)
thinly pared strip of chilti
parsley sprig

AMERICAN

2–2¼ lb pork spareribs, cut into
   separate pieces
2 tablespoons fish sauce*
1 tablespoon sugar
3 garlic cloves, peeled and chopped
pinch of freshly ground black pepper
3 tablespoons pork fat or vegetable oil
To garnish: (optional)
thinly pared strip of chili
parsley sprig

METHOD

Put the spareribs in a bowl, cover with the remaining ingredients except the fat or oil; leave to marinate for 30 minutes.

Heat the pork fat or oil in a frying pan (skillet). Add the spareribs and fry gently for about 10 minutes on each side until golden brown and cooked through.

Drain the spareribs and arrange on a serving dish. Garnish with red chilli and parsley, if liked, arranged to resemble a flower head. Serve hot with rice.
SERVES 4

Chicken Lap

Lap Kay

Laos

A dish of Lap Kay, a bowl of chicken soup, a bamboo steamer containing glutinous (sweet) rice* and a *Vegetable Platter* (see page 125) – all of these are placed in the centre of the table. (In Laos, this would be a straw mat on the floor.)

Each diner is given a plate and a spoon. He then picks up about 1 tablespoon rice, squeezes it into a ball, presses it against the mound of Chicken Lap, then eats the rice and the food that adheres to it. A spoonful of soup is eaten after each mouthful, followed by a few pieces of vegetable from the platter.

METRIC/IMPERIAL

225 g/8 oz boned chicken meat,
   skinned and finely diced
100 g/4 oz chicken livers, finely diced
100 g/4 oz chicken gizzards, finely
   diced (optional)
2 teaspoons anchovy paste
2 teaspoons fish sauce*
1 tablespoon whole dried red chillis
2 tablespoons dried galingale,* soaked
   in hot water for 1 hour and finely
   chopped
4 teaspoons lime juice
$\frac{1}{4}$ teaspoon salt
$\frac{1}{4}$ teaspoon freshly ground black
   pepper
To garnish:
2 tablespoons chopped spring onion,
   green part only
coriander leaves*

AMERICAN

$\frac{1}{2}$ lb skinned boneless chicken meat,
   finely diced
$\frac{1}{4}$ lb chicken livers, finely diced
$\frac{1}{4}$ lb chicken gizzards, finely diced
   (optional)
2 teaspoons anchovy paste
2 teaspoons fish sauce*
1 tablespoon whole dried red chilis
2 tablespoons dried galingale,* soaked
   in hot water for 1 hour and finely
   chopped
4 teaspoons lime juice
$\frac{1}{4}$ teaspoon salt
$\frac{1}{4}$ teaspoon freshly ground black
   pepper
To garnish:
2 tablespoons chopped scallion, green
   part only
coriander leaves*

METHOD

Mix together the chicken, livers and gizzards, if using. Place in a 20 cm/8 inch square baking tin (pan) and press the mixture down firmly until about 1 cm/$\frac{1}{2}$ inch thick. Bake in a preheated moderate oven (180°C/350°F, Gas Mark 4) for 20 minutes.

Allow to cool slightly, then add the remaining ingredients and work into the mixture, with the hands, squeezing out all the excess liquid.

Arrange on a warmed serving dish and garnish with the spring onion (scallion) and coriander. Serve hot or allow to cool before serving.
SERVES 4

Chicken Soup

Ken Kay

Laos

This is always served as an accompaniment to *Lap Kay*.

METRIC/IMPERIAL

1 tablespoon dried tamarind pulp*
750 g/1$\frac{1}{2}$ lb chicken, chopped into
   5 cm/2 inch pieces, with the bones
1.6 litres/2$\frac{3}{4}$ pints water
2 tomatoes, cut into wedges
6 lime leaves*
2 tablespoons fish sauce*
$\frac{1}{2}$ teaspoon salt
pinch of freshly ground black pepper
To garnish:
2 tablespoons chopped spring onion,
   green part only
2 tablespoons chopped coriander
   leaves*

AMERICAN

1 tablespoon dried tamarind pulp*
1$\frac{1}{2}$ lb chicken, chopped into 2 inch
   pieces, with the bones
7 cups water
2 tomatoes, cut into wedges
6 lime leaves*
2 tablespoons fish sauce*
$\frac{1}{2}$ teaspoon salt
pinch of freshly ground black pepper
To garnish:
2 tablespoons chopped scallion, green
   part only
2 tablespoons chopped coriander
   leaves*

METHOD

Soak the tamarind pulp in 120 ml/4 fl oz/
½ cup hot water for 10 minutes, then knead
to extract the flavour. Strain the liquid,
discarding the pulp.

Put the chicken, water, tomatoes, tamarind water and lime leaves in a pan and
bring to the boil. Skim, then lower the heat
and simmer, uncovered, for 20 minutes or
until the chicken is tender. Add the fish
sauce, salt and pepper.

Pour the hot soup into a warmed tureen
and garnish with the spring onion (scallion) and coriander. Serve hot.
SERVES 4

Sour Carrot

Tam Sôm

Laos

Tam Sôm appears as an appetizer at all
social occasions. It has an amalgam of
flavours – sour, salty, sweet and very hot.
If pork stomach cannot be obtained, it
may be omitted.

METRIC/IMPERIAL

225 g/8 oz pork stomach
5 garlic cloves, peeled
5 dried red chillis
2 tomatoes
1 teaspoon monosodium glutamate*
2 tablespoons fish sauce*
3 medium carrots, peeled and shredded

AMERICAN

½ lb pork stomach
5 garlic cloves, peeled
5 dried red chilis
2 tomatoes
1 teaspoon msg*
2 tablespoons fish sauce*
3 medium carrots, peeled and shredded

METHOD

Put the pork stomach in a pan, cover with
water and boil for about 30 minutes.

Meanwhile, pound the garlic, chillis,
tomatoes and monosodium glutamate
(msg) in a mortar. Stir in the fish sauce.

Place the shredded carrot on a serving
dish and pour over the sauce. Drain the
pork stomach, slice thinly and arrange
on top of the salad. Mix well with chopsticks just before serving. Serve cold.
SERVES 4

**Chicken Lap, served with Chicken
Soup, Glutinous Rice (see page 122)
and Vegetable Platter (see page 125)**

Glutinous (Sweet) Rice*

In Laos, rice is always served in the bamboo basket in which it has been steamed. In the West, however, it can be steamed by putting a layer of cheese-cloth (muslin) on one of the layers of an oriental aluminium steamer, and placing the soaked glutinous (sweet) rice* on the cheesecloth (muslin). For this method of cooking rice, no measurements are necessary: every cup of glutinous (sweet) rice* doubles in volume when cooked.

METHOD

Soak the rice in water to cover for at least 6 hours, then drain. Bring water to the boil in the lower level of a steamer, making sure that the water does not touch the steaming level. Place the rack containing the rice on top of the boiling water, then cover and steam for about 15 minutes until the rice looks clear and is soft to the touch. The longer the soaking period, the shorter the cooking time.

Barbecued Pork with Mushrooms and Beans

Ocklam

Laos

This is the national dish of Laos. Beef or chicken may be substituted for the pork used here. Fresh pork skin is easily obtainable at butchers' shops while dried pork skin can be obtained at Vietnamese grocery stores – it should be soaked in warm water for 30 minutes before use.

METRIC/IMPERIAL

225 g/8 oz pork, sliced into strips 2.5 cm/1 inch wide and 5 mm/¼ inch thick
250 g/9 oz glutinous (sweet) rice*
2 tablespoons fish sauce*
½ teaspoon salt
1 aubergine, weighing about 450 g/1 lb
1 tablespoon whole dried red chillis
100 g/4 oz French beans or Chinese long beans, cut into 2.5 cm/1 inch pieces
8 large Chinese dried mushrooms,* soaked in warm water for 30 minutes and shredded
3 bay leaves
10 cm/4 inch square piece of fresh or dried pork skin, shredded into thin strips

To garnish:
few lemon slices
thinly pared strip of chilli
2.5 cm/1 inch piece of spring onion

Barbecued Pork with Mushrooms and Beans, served with Vegetable Platter (see page 125)

AMERICAN

½ lb pork, sliced into strips 1 inch wide and ¼ inch thick
1½ cups glutinous (sweet) rice*
2 tablespoons fish sauce*
½ teaspoon salt
1 eggplant, weighing about 1 lb
1 tablespoon whole dried red chilis
¼ lb string beans or Chinese long beans, cut into 1 inch pieces
8 large Chinese dried mushrooms,* soaked in warm water for 30 minutes and shredded
3 bay leaves
4 inch square piece of fresh or dried pork skin, shredded into thin strips

To garnish:
few lemon slices
thinly pared strip of chili
1 inch piece of scallion

METHOD

Roast the pork in a preheated moderate oven (180°C/350°F, Gas Mark 4) for 15 minutes. Meanwhile, put the glutinous rice in a mortar, add just enough water to cover, then crush with a pestle.

Pour 1.75 litres/3 pints/7½ cups water into a pan and bring to the boil. Add the fish sauce and salt, then the pork, aubergine (eggplant) and chillis. Boil for 10 minutes or until the aubergine (eggplant) is soft, then remove from the pan together with the chillis.

Pound the aubergine (eggplant) and chillis, using a pestle and mortar, then return to the pan. Add the beans, mushrooms and bay leaves. Bring to the boil, then add the glutinous rice with its soaking liquid and the pork skin. Boil for 20 minutes or until the glutinous rice is cooked.

Transfer to a serving dish and garnish with lemon slices, chilli and spring onion (scallion), coiling the chilli around the onion (scallion) to resemble a flower head. Serve hot with boiled rice and a *Vegetable Platter* (see page 125).
SERVES 4

Spicy Beef

Shin Ngoa Lap

Laos

METRIC/IMPERIAL

3 tablespoons glutinous rice*
450 g/1 lb beef topside, cut into 3 pieces
1 tablespoon fish sauce*
2 teaspoons anchovy paste
1 teaspoon monosodium glutamate* (optional)
1 tablespoon dried galingale,* soaked in hot water for 1 hour and finely chopped
1 tablespoon chopped coriander leaves*
1 tablespoon chopped spring onion, green part only

To finish:
1 red chilli, sliced into rings
juice of ½ lime

AMERICAN

3 tablespoons glutinous rice*
1 lb beef top round, cut into 3 pieces
1 tablespoon fish sauce*
2 teaspoons anchovy paste
1 teaspoon msg* (optional)
1 tablespoon dried galingale,* soaked in hot water for 1 hour and finely chopped
1 tablespoon chopped coriander leaves*
1 tablespoon chopped scallion, green part only

To finish:
1 red chili, sliced into rings
juice of ½ lime

METHOD

Fry the glutinous rice in a hot, dry frying pan (skillet) until brown, then pound to a powder in a mortar or electric blender.

Roast the beef in a preheated moderately hot oven (200°C/400°F, Gas Mark 6) for 15 minutes. Leave until cool enough to handle, then shred into thin strips and mix with the powdered rice.

Combine the fish sauce and anchovy paste in a pan, then cook over moderate heat until smooth. Add to the beef with the monosodium glutamate (msg), if using, the galingale, coriander and spring onion (scallion); stir well.

Arrange the meat mixture on a warmed serving dish and garnish with the chilli. Sprinkle with the lime juice just before serving. Serve hot, or at room temperature.
SERVES 4

Chicken Spring Rolls

Cha Gio Ga

Vietnam

Cha Gio Ga is the most popular dish in Vietnamese cuisine, for both rich and poor. It is usually filled with pork and crab, but a combination of any meat or seafood may be used. Serve as an appetizer with a bowl of *Nuoc Cham* or as a main course accompanied by a *Vegetable Platter* with *Nuoc Cham* served separately as a dip.

Cooked spring rolls can be frozen, then reheated in a moderate oven (180°C/350°F, Gas Mark 4). Alternatively they can be partially cooked, refrigerated for 1 day, then completed the following day.

METRIC/IMPERIAL

Filling:

50 g/2 oz transparent noodles,* soaked in water for 10 minutes, then cut into 2.5 cm/1 inch pieces

450 g/1 lb chicken breast meat, skinned and cut into thin strips

2 tablespoons dried wood ears,* soaked in warm water for 20 minutes, then finely chopped

3 garlic cloves, peeled and finely chopped

3 shallots, finely chopped

225 g/8 oz crabmeat

½ teaspoon freshly ground black pepper

Wrappers:

4 eggs, beaten

20 dried rice papers*

450 ml/¾ pint vegetable oil

To garnish:

shredded spring onion

AMERICAN

Filling:

2 oz cellophane noodles,* soaked in water for 10 minutes, then cut into 1 inch pieces

1 lb skinned and boned chicken breast meat, cut into thin strips

2 tablespoons tree ears,* soaked in warm water for 20 minutes, then finely chopped

3 garlic cloves, peeled and finely chopped

3 shallots, finely chopped

½ lb crabmeat

½ teaspoon freshly ground black pepper

Wrappers:

4 eggs, beaten

20 dried rice papers*

2 cups vegetable oil

To garnish:

shredded scallion

METHOD

To make the filling: Put all the ingredients in a bowl and mix well, using the hands.

Brush beaten egg over the entire surface of each piece of rice paper. Leave for a few seconds until soft and flexible. Place 1 teaspoon filling in a rectangular shape along the curved edge of the paper, roll once, then fold over the sides to enclose the filling and continue rolling. (The beaten egg not only makes the wrapper flexible, it also holds it together.)

Pour the cold oil into a 30 cm/12 inch frying pan (skillet), then add about one third of the spring rolls. Fry over moderate heat for about 30 minutes until golden brown, then remove with a slotted spoon and drain on absorbent kitchen paper towels. Fry the remaining spring rolls in the same way. Serve hot or at room temperature, garnished with shredded spring onion (scallion).

MAKES ABOUT 20

Chicken Spring Rolls, served with Nuoc Cham

Nuoc Cham

Vietnam

No Vietnamese meal is served without Nuoc Cham – a hot, tangy sauce which is sprinkled on food as desired. If you do not have a pestle and mortar, mash the ingredients with the back of a spoon. Do not use an electric blender – it will not give the right consistency. Nuoc Cham can be made in larger quantities and stored in the refrigerator for up to 1 week.

METRIC/IMPERIAL

2 garlic cloves, peeled
4 dried red chillis, or 1 fresh red chilli
5 teaspoons sugar
juice and pulp of $\frac{1}{4}$ lime
4 tablespoons fish sauce*
5 tablespoons water

AMERICAN

2 garlic cloves, peeled
4 dried red chilis, or 1 fresh red chili
5 teaspoons sugar
juice and pulp of $\frac{1}{4}$ lime
$\frac{1}{4}$ cup fish sauce*
$\frac{1}{3}$ cup water

METHOD

Pound the garlic, chillis and sugar using a pestle and mortar. Add the lime juice and pulp, then the fish sauce and water. Mix well to combine the ingredients. Use as required.
SERVES 4

Vegetable Platter

Dia Rau Song

A platter of raw vegetables is an important part of almost every Laotian, Cambodian or Vietnamese meal. In South-East Asia, a variety of vegetables and different herbs are used. A satisfactory vegetable platter can however be made with fewer ingredients.

METRIC/IMPERIAL/AMERICAN

soft lettuce leaves
mint leaves
coriander leaves*
cucumber, partially peeled and thinly
    sliced into half-moon shapes

METHOD

Pile the lettuce in a mound in the centre of a serving dish, then place the mint and coriander around the lettuce in separate mounds. Arrange the cucumber slices overlapping around the rim of the dish. Serve cold.
SERVES 4

125

Crabmeat and Tapioca Pearl Soup
Cua Nâú Bôt Báng
Vietnam

Fresh, frozen or canned crabmeat can be used for this soup. If using live fresh crabs, boil 1 or 2 crabs in just enough water to cover for 10 minutes, then drain and remove the meat. Reserve the cooking liquid and use in place of the chicken stock listed in the ingredients.

METRIC/IMPERIAL

1 tablespoon vegetable oil
4 shallots, peeled
225 g/8 oz crabmeat
1.2 litres/2 pints chicken stock
2 tablespoons fish sauce*
125 g/4½ oz tapioca pearls, soaked in water for 10 minutes

To garnish:
freshly ground black pepper
2 tablespoons chopped coriander leaves*
2 tablespoons chopped spring onion, green part only

AMERICAN

1 tablespoon vegetable oil
4 shallots, peeled
½ lb crabmeat
5 cups chicken stock
2 tablespoons fish sauce*
⅔ cup tapioca pearls, soaked in water for 10 minutes

To garnish:
freshly ground black pepper
2 tablespoons chopped coriander leaves*
2 tablespoons chopped scallion, green part only

METHOD

Heat the oil in a pan, add the shallots and fry gently until lightly browned. Add the crabmeat and stir-fry until beginning to brown, then add the stock and fish sauce.

Drain the tapioca, add to the pan and boil for 5 minutes or until the tapioca pearls are clear. Pour into warmed individual soup bowls and sprinkle with pepper, coriander and spring onions (scallions). Serve hot.

SERVES 4

Chrysanthemum Soup with Minced (Ground) Pork
Canh Tân Ô Thit Heo
Vietnam

Chrysanthemum choy is a cultivated edible chrysanthemum, eaten before it blooms. The tough stems are discarded and only the top, tender stems and leaves are eaten. It is available at Oriental groceries.

METRIC/IMPERIAL

100 g/4 oz minced pork
freshly ground black pepper
2 tablespoons plus 1 teaspoon fish sauce*
1 shallot, peeled and finely chopped
1.5 litres/2½ pints chicken stock
450 g/1 lb chrysanthemum choy
2 spring onions, cut into 5 cm/2 inch lengths

AMERICAN

½ cup ground pork
freshly ground black pepper
2 tablespoons plus 1 teaspoon fish
  sauce*
1 shallot, peeled and finely chopped
6¼ cups chicken stock
1 lb chrysanthemum choy
2 scallions, cut into 2 inch lengths

METHOD

Put the pork in a bowl with a pinch of black pepper, 1 teaspoon fish sauce and the shallot. Mix well, then leave to stand for about 15 minutes. Shape the mixture into about 24 small balls, using about 1 teaspoonful for each.

Put the stock in a pan and bring to the boil. Add the pork balls and boil for 12 minutes, then add the remaining fish sauce and black pepper to taste.

Put the chrysanthemum choy and spring onions (scallions) in a warmed large soup tureen. Pour over the boiling stock and meatballs. Serve hot with rice and fish sauce.

SERVES 4

Duck Soup with Dried Bamboo Shoot

Vit Xáo Măng

Vietnam

At some stage during the New Year celebrations, every Vietnamese home will serve a dish containing dried bamboo shoots.* This soup is substantial enough to be served as a complete meal.

METRIC/IMPERIAL

1 duck, weighing 1.5–2 kg/3–4¾ lb
1 tablespoon salt
¼ teaspoon freshly ground black pepper
5 shallots, peeled and crushed
25 g/1 oz dried bamboo shoot,* soaked
  in hot water for 2 hours
1 lump rock sugar*
4 tablespoons fish sauce*
225 g/8 oz medium rice vermicelli*
To serve:
1 tablespoon chopped spring onion,
  green part only
1 tablespoon chopped coriander
  leaves*
Nuoc Cham (see page 125)

AMERICAN

1 duck, weighing 3–4¾ lb
1 tablespoon salt
¼ teaspoon freshly ground black
  pepper
5 shallots, peeled and crushed
1 cup dried bamboo shoot,* soaked in
  hot water for 2 hours
1 lump rock sugar*
¼ cup fish sauce*
½ lb medium rice vermicelli*
To serve:
1 tablespoon chopped scallion, green
  part only
1 tablespoon chopped coriander
  leaves*
Nuoc Cham (see page 125)

METHOD

Sprinkle the duck with the salt and pepper, then rub all over with the crushed shallots. Leave to marinate for 1 hour.

Pour 1.2 litres/2 pints/5 cups water into a large pan and bring to the boil. Add the duck and bamboo shoot, bring back to the boil and simmer for 15 minutes, skimming frequently until no further scum is formed.

Add the rock sugar, cover and simmer for 1 hour. Add the fish sauce, cover and simmer for 30 minutes or until the bamboo shoot is tender; it should have a chewy texture.

Meanwhile, cook the rice vermicelli in about 2 litres/3½ pints/4½ pints boiling water for 5 minutes, then drain and rinse under cold running water.

Cut the duck into 8 pieces. Divide the vermicelli between 8 individual warmed soup bowls. Place a piece of duck and a few pieces of bamboo shoot on top, then cover with the hot soup. Sprinkle with the spring onion (scallion) and coriander. Serve hot with the Nuoc Cham as an accompaniment.

SERVES 8

Crabmeat and Tapioca Pearl Soup;
Chrysanthemum Soup with Minced
(Ground) Pork; Duck Soup with Dried
Bamboo Shoot

Simmered Pineapple with Fish

Cá Kho Thòm
Vietnam

METRIC/IMPERIAL

2 tablespoons vegetable oil
450 g/1 lb fish steaks (halibut, sea
    bass, etc.)
1 shallot, peeled and sliced
150 g/5 oz fresh pineapple, cut into
    2.5 cm/1 inch squares about 5 mm/
    ¼ inch thick
6 tablespoons fish sauce*
4 tablespoons sugar
1 tablespoon Caramelized Sugar (see
    opposite)
freshly ground black pepper

AMERICAN

2 tablespoons vegetable oil
1 lb fish steaks (bluefish, king
    mackerel, blackfish, etc.)
1 shallot, peeled and sliced
1 cup fresh pineapple, cut into 1 inch
    squares about ¼ inch thick
6 tablespoons fish sauce*
¼ cup sugar
1 tablespoon Caramelized Sugar (see
    opposite)
freshly ground black pepper

METHOD

Heat 1 tablespoon of the oil in a frying pan (skillet). Add the fish and fry gently until lightly browned on both sides, turning once.

Heat the remaining oil in a separate pan, add the shallot and fry gently until lightly browned. Add the pineapple and fry for about 3 minutes, then remove from the pan, using a slotted spoon. Discard the liquid.

Put half the fried pineapple and shallot in a small flameproof casserole. Place the fish steaks on top, then cover with the remaining pineapple and shallot. Add the remaining ingredients, cover with a tight-fitting lid and simmer for about 20 to 30 minutes until there is about 120 ml/ 4 fl oz/½ cup liquid remaining in the pan. Serve hot with rice.
SERVES 4

Caramelized Sugar

Put 1 tablespoon sugar in a small frying pan (skillet) with 4 tablespoons (¼ cup) water. Stir well, then cook over high heat until the mixture turns brown, stirring constantly; remove from the heat when it turns a very dark brown colour and steam forms. Stir well and add 2 table-spoons water. Return to a high heat and cook for about 5 minutes, stirring all the time, then add a squeeze of lemon juice. Stir rapidly, remove from heat and leave to cool. Store in a screwtop jar until required.

Barbecued Prawns (Shrimp)

Tôm Nùóng Bánh Hòi
Vietnam

METRIC/IMPERIAL

450 g/1 lb uncooked prawns, unpeeled
175 g/6 oz very thin rice vermicelli*
2 teaspoons vegetable oil
3 spring onions, chopped
20 roasted peanuts (see below)
To serve:
few lemon slices, quartered
coriander leaves*
Nouc Cham (see page 125)

AMERICAN

1 lb large raw shrimp, unpeeled
6 oz very thin rice vermicelli*
2 teaspoons vegetable oil
3 scallions, chopped
20 roasted peanuts (see below)
To serve:
few lemon slices, quartered
coriander leaves*
Nuoc Cham (see page 125)

METHOD

Cook the prawns (shrimp) over charcoal, for about 7 minutes, turning once. Alternatively, bake them in a preheated moderately hot oven (200°C/400°F, Gas Mark 6) for 10 minutes. Peel the prawns (shrimp), then cut each one in half and set aside.

Add the rice vermicelli to about 2 litres/3½ pints/9 cups boiling water and boil for 2 minutes, then drain and rinse under cold running water. Drain again.

Heat the oil in a frying pan (skillet), add the spring onions (scallions) and fry gently until softened.

Arrange the rice vermicelli on a warmed serving plate, top with prawns (shrimp), then sprinkle with spring onions (scallions) and peanuts. Garnish with lemon slices and coriander. Serve hot with Nuoc Cham.
SERVES 4

Chopped Roasted Peanuts

Heat a small frying pan (skillet) until very hot, then add shelled red-skinned peanuts. Fry over dry heat until the skins turn black, stirring constantly, then transfer to a colander. Leave to cool for about 3 minutes, then rub between the hands to loosen the skins. Discard the skins. Chop the peanuts coarsely using a pestle and mortar or electric blender, if required.

Fried Chicken with Coconut Milk and Lemon Grass

Gà Xào Sã Nùòć Dùà

Vietnam

METRIC/IMPERIAL

4 chicken thighs, or 2 legs and 2
   thighs, chopped into small pieces
2 garlic cloves, peeled and chopped
1 shallot, peeled and chopped
½ teaspoon sugar
¼ teaspoon salt
pinch of freshly ground black pepper
½ teaspoon curry powder
pinch of crushed dried red chillis, or
   more to taste
1 tablespoon fish sauce*
1 tablespoon vegetable oil
1 stalk lemon grass,* very finely
   chopped
250 ml/8 fl oz coconut milk*
To garnish:
2 tablespoons chopped roasted
   peanuts
1 spring onion, cut into 5 cm/2 inch
   pieces
4 lime slices, halved (optional)

AMERICAN

4 chicken thighs, or 2 legs and 2
   thighs, chopped into small pieces
2 garlic cloves, peeled and chopped
1 shallot, peeled and chopped
½ teaspoon sugar
¼ teaspoon salt
pinch of freshly ground black pepper
½ teaspoon curry powder
pinch of crushed dried red chilis,
   or more to taste
1 tablespoon fish sauce*
1 tablespoon vegetable oil
1 stalk lemon grass,* very finely
   chopped
1 cup coconut milk*
To garnish:.
2 tablespoons chopped roasted
   peanuts
1 scallion, cut into 2 inch pieces
4 lime slices, halved (optional)

METHOD

Put the chicken in a bowl with half the garlic, the shallot, sugar, salt, black pepper, curry powder, crushed chillis and fish sauce. Stir well, then leave to marinate for 30 minutes.

Heat the oil in a wok or deep frying pan (deep-fat fryer). Add the remaining garlic and the lemon grass, stir-fry for a few seconds, then add the chicken. Stir-fry for about 10 minutes until the chicken is lightly browned, then add the coconut milk. Simmer, uncovered, for 10 minutes or until the chicken is tender and the liquid is reduced to a thick sauce.

Place the chicken on a warmed serving plate. Top with the peanuts and spring onion (scallion). Arrange lime slices around the edge of the plate, if liked. Serve hot with rice.
SERVES 4

Fried Chicken with Coconut Milk and Lemon Grass; Barbecued Prawns (Shrimp)

Barbecued Spareribs

Sùòn Nùòng

Vietnam

In Vietnam, this dish is barbecued over charcoal, but in the West it can successfully be roasted in the oven. It is always served on a bed of plain boiled rice, as a one-dish meal.

METRIC/IMPERIAL

5 shallots, peeled
2 garlic cloves, peeled
2 tablespoons sugar
4 tablespoons fish sauce*
¼ teaspoon freshly ground black pepper
750 g/1½ lb pork spareribs

To serve:
plain boiled rice
Nuoc Cham (see page 125)
few cucumber slices

AMERICAN

5 shallots, peeled
2 garlic cloves, peeled
2 tablespoons sugar
¼ cup fish sauce*
¼ teaspoon freshly ground black pepper
1½ lb pork spareribs

To serve:
plain boiled rice
Nuoc Cham (see page 125)
few cucumber slices

METHOD

Pound the shallots, garlic and sugar to a paste, using a pestle and mortar. Add the fish sauce and black pepper and stir well. Place the spareribs in a roasting pan and pour the pounded mixture over them. Turn to coat thoroughly. Leave to marinate for at least 1 hour.

Roast in a preheated moderate oven (180°C/350°F, Gas Mark 4) for 45 minutes until the spareribs are well browned. Cut the ribs into separate pieces.

Put the rice in a serving dish, arrange the spareribs on top and sprinkle with a little Nuoc Cham. Arrange cucumber slices around the edge of the dish. Serve hot, with a bowl of Nuoc Cham handed separately.
SERVES 4

Barbecued Beef with Lime Juice

Thit Bò Nùòng Vi 'Săt

Vietnam

The literal translation of the name of this dish is 'Beef Barbecued on a 'Steel Griddle'. The dish is usually served in restaurants, where each diner is given a very small charcoal burner, a small steel griddle and a portion of food to cook for himself at the table. At home, use an electric or ordinary frying pan (skillet), or griddle over an electric hotplate or gas burner.

METRIC/IMPERIAL

450 g/1 lb slice beef topside, about 2.5 cm/1 inch thick
2 tablespoons vegetable oil
1 tablespoon fish sauce*
freshly ground black pepper
1 onion, peeled and thinly sliced into rings

To serve:
12 dried rice papers*
Vegetable Platter (see page 125)
few lime wedges
Nuoc Cham (see page 125)

AMERICAN

1 × 1 lb slice beef top round, about 1 inch thick
2 tablespoons vegetable oil
1 tablespoon fish sauce*
freshly ground black pepper
1 onion, peeled and thinly sliced into rings

To serve:
12 dried rice papers*
Vegetable Platter (see page 125)
few lime wedges
Nuoc Cham (see page 125)

METHOD

Slice the beef thinly against the grain, then arrange in overlapping circles on a serving dish. Sprinkle with 1 tablespoon of the oil, the fish sauce and pepper to taste, then arrange the onion slices on top.

To serve, each diner should place a rice paper on an individual serving plate and brush the surface with water. Leave for about 1 minute until the rice paper is soft and flexible, then place a lettuce leaf, a few pieces of cucumber and a sprig each of coriander and mint on the paper.

Meanwhile, heat the frying pan (skillet) at the table and, when very hot, add the remaining oil. Let each person put in a few slices of beef and a slice of onion. Cook for a few seconds, then turn over and squeeze a little lime juice onto the meat.

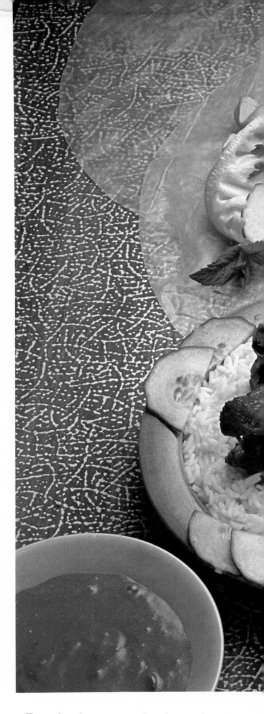

Transfer the meat and onion to the top of the salad vegetables, then fold over the sides of the rice paper to enclose the food and roll up. Serve Nuoc Cham in individual bowls as a dip. Continue with the remaining ingredients until all are used up, eating the food as soon as it is cooked.
SERVES 4

Barbecued Spareribs, served with Nuoc Cham (see page 125); Barbecued Beef with Lime Juice, served with Vegetable Platter (see page 125), Nuoc Cham and rice papers

Orange-shaped Cakes
Bánh Cam
Vietnam

METRIC/IMPERIAL

Filling:
100 g/4 oz yellow mung beans*
175 ml/6 fl oz water
100 g/4 oz sugar
Wrapping:
225 g/8 oz glutinous (sweet) rice flour*
1 teaspoon baking powder
½ teaspoon salt
100 g/4 oz sugar
2 medium potatoes, boiled, peeled and
    mashed
120 ml/4 fl oz boiling water
To finish:
50 g/2 oz toasted sesame seeds* (see
    opposite)
450 ml/¾ pint vegetable oil for deep-
    frying

AMERICAN

Filling:
¾ cup yellow mung beans*
¾ cup water
½ cup sugar
Wrapping:
2 cups glutinous (sweet) rice flour*
1 teaspoon baking powder
½ teaspoon salt
½ cup sugar
2 medium potatoes, boiled, peeled and
    mashed
½ cup boiling water
To finish:
½ cup toasted sesame seeds* (see
    below)
2 cups vegetable oil for deep-frying

METHOD

To make the filling: Rinse the mung beans thoroughly under cold running water. Put the beans and water in a small pan and bring to the boil. Lower the heat, cover and simmer for about 30 minutes until the water has evaporated completely and the beans are tender and dry. Remove from the heat and mash the beans, then add the sugar and mix well.

To make the wrapping: Put all the ingredients in a bowl, except the boiling water. Mix well, then gradually stir in the boiling water. Knead the mixture until it forms a smooth ball.

Roll 2 tablespoons of the wrapping mixture into a small ball, then flatten into a 7.5 cm/3 inch circle. Place 1 teaspoon of the filling mixture in the centre of the circle and gather the wrapping together to enclose the filling, shaping it into a ball. Repeat with the remaining wrapping and filling mixture until all the ingredients are used up, making about 12 balls.

Put the toasted sesame seeds on a plate or piece of greaseproof (waxed) paper and roll the balls in the seeds until completely coated.

Heat the oil in a small pan to 190°C/375°F. Drop one ball at a time into the hot oil and, with the bottom of a soup ladle, press against the ball and move the ladle against it, using a circular motion. Deep-fry the balls, a few at a time, for about 10 minutes until golden brown, then remove from the pan with a slotted spoon and drain on kitchen paper towels, while frying the remainder. Serve hot.
MAKES ABOUT 12

Toasted Sesame Seeds
Heat a frying pan (skillet) until very hot. Add the sesame seeds and stir-fry in the dry pan until well browned. It is essential to use a very hot pan or the seeds will become oily and not stick to the dough.

China

Deh-ta Hsiung

Most people who enjoy eating Chinese food will not attempt to cook it themselves because they think there is a great mystery surrounding this oriental art, while those whose experience of Chinese food is limited to 'chop suey' and 'sweet and sour pork' may well wonder what is so special about this cuisine. You may be surprised to learn that 'chop suey' has never even been heard of in China, and the soggy 'sweet and sour pork' often served in restaurants would never be cooked in China.

There is really no mystery about the art of Chinese cooking: once you have learnt a few basic facts, you will discover that authentic Chinese food can be cooked even without using unusual and exotic ingredients. Essentially, there are three fundamental principles in Chinese cooking: flavour, texture and colour.

Flavour

The essential elements for seasoning and bringing out subtle flavours are: soy sauce, rice wine* (medium or dry sherry is an excellent substitute), sugar, vinegar, fresh root ginger and spring onions (scallions). Garlic, peppers and chillis are also used occasionally, but discreetly, for their purpose is to enhance the flavour of the food rather than overpower it. Cornflour (cornstarch) is used in moderation for thickening sauces and for coating meat, particularly when this is finely sliced and shredded, as it helps to preserve flavour and tenderness. Cornflour (cornstarch) should never be used to excess, however, otherwise the food will look unappetizing and taste starchy.

The practice of blending different flavours in one dish is quite common in China. The idea is to give the dish contrasting tastes as well as promote an exchange of flavours between ingredients. Each item in the dish acts as a seasoning agent, imparting a little flavour to the other ingredients.

It is therefore important to choose the ingredients to be blended with care, with the emphasis on harmonized contrast.

Above all else, the Chinese believe in the freshness of their food: vegetables should be dawn-picked, or ideally picked just before they are cooked; meats are never hung; poultry and fish are always bought still alive! The Chinese claim that loss of freshness is loss of flavour.

Texture and Colour

Every dish in a Chinese meal should include two or more of the following textures: tenderness, crispness, crunchiness, smoothness and softness. Ingredients should also be chosen to complement each other in colour.

Ingredients are therefore chosen to obtain a harmony of flavours, colours and textures. For example, the main ingredient in *Jieca chao jiding* (see page 155) is chicken, which is white and tender. Mushrooms (soft and black) and celery (crisp and pale green) are used as the subsidiary ingredients to give the dish a harmonized texture. A colourful red pepper is also added for contrast and bamboo shoot (smooth in texture) for extra flavour. This combination, with the addition of salt, egg white, cornflour (cornstarch), fresh ginger root, spring onions (scallions), soy sauce and sherry makes the dish a unique experience for the palate. Apart from the Chinese dried mushrooms,* which can be substituted by fresh mushrooms, nothing out of the ordinary is used in the way of ingredients and everything can easily be obtained in any quality grocer or supermarket.

Cooking Techniques and Preparation

Chinese cooking techniques are quite simple, and one of the most important aspects is the preparation before cooking.

Cutting

Most Chinese foods are cut into very small pieces before cooking; therefore only a short cooking time is required and this helps to preserve the natural flavours. The Chinese attach great importance to the various methods of cutting.

Slicing: The ingredients are cut into thin slices, normally not much larger than a postage stamp, and as thin as cardboard. When slicing meat, always cut across the grain, which makes it more tender when cooked. Vegetables, such as carrots, are often cut on the slant so that the slices have a larger surface area to absorb flavourings.

Shredding: The ingredients are first sliced, then stacked like a pack of cards and cut into thin strips about the size of matchsticks.

Dicing: The ingredients are first cut into strips as wide as they are thick, then cut at right angles to the same width to make cubes, usually about 1cm/½ inch.

Mincing (grinding): The ingredients are very finely chopped in a mincer (grinder).

Diagonal cutting: This method is normally used for cutting vegetables, such as carrots and celery. A diagonal cut is made straight down, then the vegetable is rolled a half-turn and sliced diagonally again, in order to obtain a diamond-shaped piece.

Chopping: A heavy cleaver is used to cut through the bones and flesh of a chicken or duck. The normal method of cutting up a chicken is as follows: (1) Chop off the 'parson's nose' and either discard or, if it is to be served, split in half. (2) Disjoint the two wings. (3) Remove the legs and thighs. (4) Turn the body on its side, then separate the breast from the backbone. (5) Divide the breast into two sections, then cut each half crossways into three or four pieces. (6) Cut each wing into three pieces, and each leg and thigh into five pieces.

Marinating

After cutting, the next step is to prepare the meat for cooking by marinating it. Salt, egg white and cornflour (cornstarch) are normally used for chicken and fish; soy sauce, sugar, sherry and cornflour (cornstarch) are used for meat.

Cooking Methods

The various cooking methods can be divided into four basic categories:

Water cooking: Boiling and simmering.
Oil cooking: Frying and braising.
Fire cooking: Roasting and barbecuing.
Steam cooking: Steaming.

The most important factor in cooking Chinese food is the degree of heat. The actual timing, although important, is governed by the heat. It is therefore very difficult for most Chinese recipes to give a precise cooking time as so much depends on the size of the ingredients and the type of stove and utensils used. For this reason, cooking times for the recipes in this chapter are intended as a guide, rather than a strict rule.

Beef and Egg-Flower Soup
Niurou Danhua Tang

METRIC/IMPERIAL

1.2 litres/2 pints hot chicken stock or
    water
100 g/4 oz beef steak, coarsely
    chopped
2 teaspoons salt
1 celery stick, coarsely chopped
1 egg, beaten
freshly ground black pepper
few spring onions, sliced, to garnish

AMERICAN

5 cups hot chicken stock or water
½ cup coarsely chopped round steak
2 teaspoons salt
1 celery stalk, coarsely chopped
1 egg, beaten
freshly ground black pepper
few scallions, sliced, to garnish

METHOD

Bring the stock or water to the boil in a
pan, then add the beef, salt and celery.
Bring back to the boil, then add the egg, a
little at a time, stirring vigorously to
achieve the 'egg-flower' effect. Add
pepper to taste.

    Sprinkle with spring onions (scallions)
before serving. Serve hot.

Sliced Carrot and Pork Soup
Luopu Roupian Tang

METRIC/IMPERIAL

100 g/4 oz boned lean pork, very
    thinly sliced
1 tablespoon soy sauce
1 tablespoon sesame seed oil*
1 teaspoon cornflour
225 g/8 oz carrots, scraped and sliced
1.2 litres/2 pints chicken stock
2 teaspoons salt
chopped coriander leaves* to garnish

AMERICAN

½ cup very thinly sliced boneless
    pork loin
1 tablespoon soy sauce
1 tablespoon sesame seed oil*
1 teaspoon cornstarch
1½ cups sliced carrots
5 cups chicken stock
2 teaspoons salt
chopped coriander leaves* to garnish

METHOD

Put the pork in a bowl with the soy sauce,
oil and cornflour (cornstarch). Stir well,
then leave to marinate for 10 minutes.

    Meanwhile, place the carrots, stock
and salt in a pan, bring to the boil and
simmer for 5 minutes. Add the pork and
simmer for 8 to 10 minutes until the pork
and carrots are tender.

    Pour into a warmed soup tureen and
sprinkle with coriander. Serve hot.

Pork and Tomato Soup
Fanqie Roupian Tang

METRIC/IMPERIAL

100 g/4 oz boned lean pork, very
    thinly sliced
1 teaspoon soy sauce
1 teaspoon medium or dry sherry
2 tablespoons vegetable oil
1 small onion, peeled and chopped
2 tomatoes, chopped
1.2 litres/2 pints chicken stock
2 teaspoons salt
freshly ground black pepper
1 egg, beaten
chopped coriander leaves* to garnish

AMERICAN

½ cup very thinly sliced boneless pork
1 teaspoon soy sauce
1 teaspoon medium or pale dry sherry
2 tablespoons vegetable oil
1 small onion, peeled and chopped
2 tomatoes, chopped
5 cups chicken stock
2 teaspoons salt
freshly ground black pepper
1 egg, beaten
chopped coriander leaves* to garnish

METHOD

Put the pork in a bowl with the soy sauce
and sherry. Stir well, then leave to marinate for about 20 minutes.

    Heat the oil in a wok or frying pan
(skillet), add the onion and pork and stir-
fry for 2 minutes. Add the tomatoes and
stock and bring to the boil. Add salt and
pepper to taste and simmer for a few
minutes.

    Stir in the egg, then immediately pour
into a warmed soup tureen and sprinkle
with coriander. Serve hot.

Sliced Pork and Szechuan Preserved Vegetable Soup

Zhacai Roupian Tang

METRIC/IMPERIAL

225 g/8 oz boned lean pork, very
   thinly sliced
1 teaspoon soy sauce
1 teaspoon medium or dry sherry
1 tablespoon cornflour
40 g/1½ oz transparent noodles,*
   soaked in water for 10 minutes
1 tablespoon vegetable oil
1.5 litres/2½ pints hot chicken stock
½ cucumber, sliced into thin strips
1 teaspoon salt
freshly ground black pepper
50 g/2 oz Szechuan preserved
   vegetable,* thinly sliced

AMERICAN

1 cup very thinly sliced boneless pork
   loin
1 teaspoon soy sauce
1 teaspoon medium or pale dry sherry
1 tablespoon cornstarch
1½ oz cellophane noodles,* soaked in
   water for 10 minutes
1 tablespoon vegetable oil
6¼ cups hot chicken stock
½ cucumber, sliced into thin strips
1 teaspoon salt
freshly ground black pepper
½ cup thinly sliced Szechuan preserved
   vegetable*

METHOD

Put the pork in a bowl with the soy sauce,
sherry and cornflour (cornstarch). Stir
well, then leave to marinate for about 20
minutes.

Meanwhile, cut the noodles into man-
ageable lengths with scissors.

Heat the oil in a wok or frying pan
(skillet). Add the pork and stir-fry until it
changes colour.

Bring the stock to a rolling boil in a
separate pan. Add the cucumber, salt
and pepper to taste. Return to the boil,
then add the pork, preserved vegetable
and noodles. Boil for a few seconds, then
pour into a warmed soup tureen. Serve
hot.

**Sliced Carrot and Pork Soup; Beef and
Egg-Flower Soup; Pork and Tomato
Soup**

Meatballs in Soup
Rouwan Tang

METRIC/IMPERIAL

225 g/8 oz boned lean pork, finely
   minced
2½ teaspoons salt
1 slice fresh root ginger,* peeled and
   finely chopped
½ egg, beaten
2 tablespoons cornflour
1.5 litres/2½ pints hot chicken stock
15 g/½ oz dried wood ears,* soaked in
   warm water for 20 minutes
½ cucumber, cut into diamond-shaped
   chunks
1 tablespoon medium or dry sherry
freshly ground black pepper

AMERICAN

1 cup finely ground pork loin
2¼ teaspoons salt
1 slice fresh ginger root,* peeled and
   finely chopped
½ egg, beaten
2 tablespoons cornstarch
6¼ cups hot chicken stock
½ cup tree ears,* soaked in warm water
   for 20 minutes
½ cucumber, cut into diamond-shaped
   chunks
1 tablespoon medium or pale dry
   sherry
freshly ground black pepper

METHOD

Mix the pork with ½ teaspoon salt, the
ginger, egg and cornflour (cornstarch).
Form the mixture into about 20 small
meatballs.

  Bring the stock to the boil in a pan. Add
the meatballs, wood (tree) ears and the
remaining salt, then add the cucumber
and sherry. Simmer until the meatballs
float to the surface. Pour into a warmed
soup tureen and sprinkle with pepper to
taste. Serve hot.

Chicken and Mushroom Soup
Donggu Dun Ji

This soup can be eaten as a complete
meal because the chicken is served
whole in its cooking liquid. The meat
should be very tender so that it can easily
be torn into pieces with chopsticks or a
soup spoon.

METRIC/IMPERIAL

25 g/1 oz Chinese dried mushrooms,*
   soaked in warm water for 30 minutes
1 chicken, weighing 1 kg/2–2¼ lb
1 tablespoon medium or dry sherry
1 spring onion
1 slice fresh root ginger,* peeled
1½ teaspoons salt

AMERICAN

8 medium Chinese dried mushrooms,*
   soaked in warm water for 30 minutes
1 chicken, weighing 2–2¼ lb
1 tablespoon medium or pale dry
   sherry
1 scallion
1 slice fresh ginger root,* peeled
1½ teaspoons salt

METHOD

Drain the mushrooms, then squeeze dry,
reserving the soaking liquid. Discard the
mushroom stalks.

  Put the chicken in a large pan of boiling
water. Boil rapidly for 2 to 3 minutes,
then remove the chicken and rinse
thoroughly under cold running water.

  Put the chicken and mushrooms in a
pan or casserole with a tight-fitting lid.
Add just enough water to cover the
chicken, then add the sherry, spring
onion (scallion), ginger and reserved
soaking liquid from the mushrooms.

  Bring to the boil, then lower the heat,
cover and simmer gently for at least
2 hours.

  Just before serving, remove any impurities that float to the surface of the
soup and discard the spring onion (scallion) and ginger if wished. Stir in the salt
and pour into a warmed soup tureen.
Serve hot.

Cauliflower Gruel
Caihua Geng

Do not be put off by the term 'gruel'; this is in fact a delicious thick soup and a very colourful dish.

METRIC/IMPERIAL

1 small cauliflower, finely chopped
100 g/4 oz chicken meat, coarsely
  chopped
1 litre/1¾ pints chicken stock
2 eggs, beaten
1 teaspoon salt
50 g/2 oz lean ham, finely chopped
chopped coriander leaves* to garnish

AMERICAN

1 small cauliflower, finely chopped
½ cup coarsely chopped chicken
4¼ cups chicken stock
2 eggs, beaten
1 teaspoon salt
¼ cup finely chopped lean ham
chopped coriander leaves* to garnish

METHOD

Put the cauliflower, chicken and stock in a pan and cook gently for 15 to 20 minutes.

Pour the eggs into the soup, then stir in the salt. Add the ham, pour into a warmed soup tureen and sprinkle with coriander. Serve hot.

Duck and Cabbage Soup
Yagu Baicai Tang

METRIC/IMPERIAL

1 duck carcass, with giblets
2 slices fresh root ginger,* peeled
450 g/1 lb Chinese cabbage, sliced
salt
freshly ground black pepper

AMERICAN

1 duck carcass, with giblets
2 slices fresh ginger root,* peeled
1 lb bok choy, sliced
salt
freshly ground black pepper

METHOD

Break up the carcass, then place in a large pan. Add the giblets and any other meat left over from the duck.

Cover with water, add the ginger, then bring to the boil. Skim, then lower the heat and simmer gently for at least 30 minutes.

Add the cabbage (bok choy) and salt and pepper to taste. Continue cooking for about 20 minutes.

Discard the duck carcass and ginger, taste and adjust the seasoning. Pour into a warmed soup tureen. Serve hot.

Shredded Pork and Noodles in Soup
Rousi Tangmian

METRIC/IMPERIAL

3–4 Chinese dried mushrooms,*
  soaked in warm water for 30 minutes
225 g/8 oz boned lean pork, shredded
1 tablespoon soy sauce
1 tablespoon medium or dry sherry
1 teaspoon sugar
2 teaspoons cornflour
350 g/12 oz egg noodles
3 tablespoons vegetable oil
2 spring onions, cut into 2.5 cm/1 inch
  lengths
100 g/4 oz bamboo shoot, shredded
salt
600 ml/1 pint boiling chicken stock

AMERICAN

3–4 Chinese dried mushrooms,*
  soaked in warm water for 30 minutes
1 cup shredded pork loin
1 tablespoon soy sauce
1 tablespoon medium or pale dry
  sherry
1 teaspoon sugar
2 teaspoons cornstarch
¾ lb egg noodles
3 tablespoons vegetable oil
2 scallions, cut into 1 inch lengths
1 cup shredded bamboo shoot
salt
2½ cups boiling chicken stock

METHOD

Drain the mushrooms, then squeeze dry, reserving the soaking liquid. Discard the hard stalks, then slice the caps into thin strips.

Put the pork in a bowl with the soy sauce, sherry, sugar and cornflour (cornstarch). Stir well, then leave to marinate for about 20 minutes.

Cook the noodles in boiling water for about 5 minutes, then drain.

Heat half the oil in a wok or frying pan (skillet), add the pork and stir-fry until it changes colour. Remove from the pan with a slotted spoon and drain.

Heat the remaining oil in the pan, add the spring onions (scallions), then the mushrooms and bamboo shoot. Stir, then add a little salt. Return the pork to the pan together with the soaking liquid from the mushrooms.

Place the noodles in a large serving bowl, pour over the boiling stock then add the pork and vegetables. Serve hot.

Duck and Cabbage Soup; Shredded Pork and Noodles in Soup; Cauliflower Gruel

Bean Curd and Spinach Soup
Bocai Doufu Tang

METRIC/IMPERIAL

1 cake bean curd*
750 ml/1¾ pints chicken stock
100 g/4 oz fresh spinach leaves, torn
  into pieces
1 spring onion, chopped (optional)
2 teaspoons salt
½ teaspoon monosodium glutamate*
freshly ground black pepper

AMERICAN

1 cake bean curd*
2 cups chicken stock
¼ lb fresh spinach leaves, torn into
  pieces
1 scallion, chopped (optional)
2 teaspoons salt
½ teaspoon msg*
freshly ground black pepper

METHOD

Cut the bean curd into 1 cm/½ inch cubes.
Bring the stock to the boil in a saucepan,
add the spinach and spring onion (scallion) if using. Simmer for 5 minutes then
add the bean curd and simmer for 2 to 3
minutes.

Skim the soup, then add the salt, monosodium glutamate (msg) and pepper to
taste. Pour into a warmed soup tureen.
Serve hot.

Crab Omelet
Xierou Chao Dan

METRIC/IMPERIAL

2 spring onions
4 eggs, beaten
salt
3 tablespoons vegetable oil
2 slices of fresh root ginger,* peeled
*   and shredded*
175 g/6 oz fresh, frozen or canned
*   crabmeat*
1 tablespoon medium or dry sherry
1½ tablespoons soy sauce
2 teaspoons sugar
To garnish:
shredded lettuce
tomato and grape (optional)

AMERICAN

2 scallions
4 eggs, beaten
salt
3 tablespoons vegetable oil
2 slices of fresh ginger root,* peeled
*   and shredded*
6 oz fresh, frozen or canned crabmeat
1 tablespoon medium or pale dry
*   sherry*
1½ tablespoons soy sauce
2 teaspoons sugar
To garnish:
shredded lettuce
tomato and grape (optional)

METHOD

Cut the white part of the spring onions (scallions) into 2.5 cm/1 inch lengths. Chop the green parts finely and beat into the eggs, with salt to taste.

Heat the oil in a wok or frying pan (skillet). Add the white spring onions (scallions) and the ginger, then the crab and sherry.

Stir-fry for a few seconds then add the soy sauce and sugar. Lower the heat, pour in the egg mixture and cook for a further 30 seconds.

Transfer to a serving plate and garnish with shredded lettuce. To finish, place a serrated-cut tomato half and a grape in the centre to resemble a flower head, if liked. Serve immediately.

Stir-Fried Squid with Mixed Vegetables; Crab Omelet

Stir-Fried Squid with Mixed Vegetables
Zajin Chao Xianyou

Do not overcook the squid or it will be tough and chewy.

METRIC/IMPERIAL

400 g/14 oz squid
2 slices of fresh root ginger,* peeled
*   and finely chopped*
1 tablespoon medium or dry sherry
1 tablespoon cornflour
15 g/½ oz dried wood ears,* soaked in
*   warm water for 20 minutes*
4 tablespoons vegetable oil
2 spring onions, white part only, cut
*   into 2.5 cm/1 inch lengths*
225 g/8 oz cauliflower or broccoli,
*   divided into florets*
2 medium carrots, peeled and cut into
*   diamond-shaped chunks*
1 teaspoon salt
1 teaspoon sugar
1 teaspoon sesame seed oil*

AMERICAN

1 lb squid
2 slices of fresh ginger root,* peeled
*   and finely chopped*
1 tablespoon medium or pale dry
*   sherry*
1 tablespoon cornstarch
½ cup tree ears,* soaked in warm water
*   for 20 minutes*
¼ cup vegetable oil
2 scallions, white part only, cut into
*   1 inch lengths*
½ lb cauliflower or broccoli, divided
*   into florets*
2 medium carrots, peeled and cut into
*   diamond-shaped chunks*
1 teaspoon salt
1 teaspoon sugar
1 teaspoon sesame seed oil*

METHOD

Clean the squid, discarding the head, transparent backbone and ink bag. Cut the flesh into thin slices or rings. Place in a bowl with half the ginger, the sherry and cornflour (cornstarch). Mix well, then leave to marinate for about 20 minutes.

Meanwhile, drain the wood (tree) ears and break into small pieces, discarding the hard bits.

Heat 2 tablespoons of the oil in a wok or frying pan (skillet). Add the spring onions (scallions) and remaining ginger, then the cauliflower or broccoli, carrots and wood (tree) ears. Stir, then add the salt and sugar and continue cooking until the vegetables are tender, adding a little water if necessary. Remove from the pan with a slotted spoon and drain.

Heat the remaining oil in the pan, add the squid and stir-fry for about 1 minute. Return the vegetables to the pan, add the sesame seed oil and mix all the ingredients well together. Serve hot.

Steamed Eggs
Zheng Jidan

Dry the spinach leaves thoroughly after rinsing them.

METRIC/IMPERIAL

6 eggs, beaten
250 ml/8 fl oz hot water
1 teaspoon salt
2 teaspoons medium or dry sherry
50 g/2 oz fresh spinach leaves
50 g/2 oz cooked ham, chopped
50 g/2 oz peeled prawns
To garnish:
1 tablespoon soy sauce
1 teaspoon sesame seed oil*

AMERICAN

6 eggs, beaten
1 cup hot water
1 teaspoon salt
2 teaspoons medium or pale dry
*   sherry*
¾ cup fresh spinach leaves
¼ cup chopped cooked ham
1 large shrimp, peeled
To garnish:
1 tablespoon soy sauce
1 teaspoon sesame seed oil*

METHOD

Put the eggs in a heatproof bowl, add the water, salt and sherry and stir well.

Arrange the spinach, ham and prawns (shrimp) on top of the egg mixture, then lower the uncovered bowl into a large pan of boiling water.

Cover the pan, lower the heat so the water in the pan is just simmering and steam the eggs gently for 20 minutes. Sprinkle with the soy sauce and sesame seed oil. Serve hot.

Abalone in Oyster Sauce

Haoyou Baoyu

METRIC/IMPERIAL

3 Chinese dried mushrooms,* soaked
   in warm water for 30 minutes
2 tablespoons vegetable oil
1 × 425 g/15 oz can abalone, sliced
50 g/2 oz bamboo shoot, sliced
1 teaspoon medium or dry sherry
1 tablespoon oyster sauce*
1 teaspoon sugar
½ teaspoon salt
2 teaspoons cornflour, mixed to a paste
   with a little water
1 teaspoon sesame seed oil*

AMERICAN

3 Chinese dried mushrooms,* soaked
   in warm water for 30 minutes
2 tablespoons vegetable oil
1 × 15 oz can abalone, sliced
½ cup bamboo shoot, sliced
1 teaspoon medium or pale dry sherry
1 tablespoon oyster sauce*
1 teaspoon sugar
½ teaspoon salt
2 teaspoons cornstarch, mixed to a
   paste with a little water
1 teaspoon sesame seed oil*

METHOD

Squeeze the mushrooms dry, discard the
stalks, then slice the caps.

Heat the vegetable oil in a wok or
frying pan (skillet). Add the abalone with
the juice from the can, the mushrooms,
bamboo shoot, sherry, oyster sauce,
sugar and salt. Stir-fry for about 2 minutes, then add the cornflour (cornstarch) mixture and cook until the sauce
thickens.

Add the sesame seed oil, then serve
hot.

**Bean Curd and Prawns (Shrimp);
Abalone in Oyster Sauce; Deep-Fried
Prawns (Shrimp) in Shells**

Bean Curd and Prawns (Shrimp)

Xiaren Shao Doufu

METRIC/IMPERIAL

6 cakes bean curd*
50 g/2 oz peeled prawns
3 tablespoons vegetable oil
½ teaspoon salt
1 teaspoon sugar
1 teaspoon medium or dry sherry
2 tablespoons soy sauce
shredded spring onions, green part
   only, to garnish

AMERICAN

6 cakes bean curd*
⅓ cup shelled shrimp
3 tablespoons vegetable oil
½ teaspoon salt
1 teaspoon sugar
1 teaspoon medium or pale dry sherry
2 tablespoons soy sauce
shredded scallions, green part only, to
   garnish

METHOD

Cut each bean curd cake into 5 mm/¼ inch
thick slices, then cut each slice into 6 to 8
pieces. Cut any large prawns (shrimp) in
half, leaving the small ones whole.

Heat the oil in a wok or frying pan
(skillet). Add the bean curd and stir-fry
until golden on all sides. Add the salt,
sugar, sherry and soy sauce and stir-fry
for a few seconds.

Add the prawns (shrimp), stir gently
and cook for 1 to 2 minutes.

Serve hot, garnished with shredded
spring onion (scallion).

Deep-Fried Prawns (Shrimp) in Shells
Youbao Xianxia

METRIC/IMPERIAL

450 g/1 lb fresh prawns in shell
2 slices of fresh root ginger,* peeled
  and finely chopped
1 teaspoon medium or dry sherry
1½ teaspoons cornflour
450 ml/¾ pint vegetable oil for deep-
  frying
1 teaspoon salt
1 teaspoon chilli sauce (optional)
To garnish:
coriander leaves*
lemon peel (optional)

AMERICAN

1 lb fresh shrimp, unshelled
2 slices of fresh ginger root,* peeled
  and finely chopped
1 teaspoon medium or pale dry sherry
1½ teaspoons cornstarch
2 cups vegetable oil for deep-frying
1 teaspoon salt
1 teaspoon chili sauce (optional)
To garnish:
coriander leaves*
lemon peel (optional)

METHOD

Place the unshelled prawns (shrimp) in a bowl with the ginger, sherry and corn-flour (cornstarch). Stir gently to mix, then leave to marinate in the refrigerator for about 20 minutes.

Heat the oil in a wok or deep-fat fryer to 180°C/350°F. Lower the heat, add the prawns (shrimp) and deep-fry for about 1 minute. Remove the prawns (shrimp) with a slotted spoon and drain.

Pour off the oil, then return the prawns (shrimp) to the pan. Add the salt and chilli sauce if using; mix well. Serve hot, garnished with coriander and lemon peel, if liked.

Stir-Fried Prawns (Shrimp) and Peas
Qingdou Xiaren

If fresh peas are unobtainable, frozen ones may be used for this recipe, but they should be thawed first and stir-fried for 1 minute only.

METRIC/IMPERIAL

225 g/8 oz peeled prawns
1 egg white
2 teaspoons cornflour
3 tablespoons vegetable oil
2 spring onions, white part only, finely
  chopped
1 slice of fresh root ginger,* peeled
  and finely chopped
225 g/8 oz shelled peas
1 teaspoon salt
1 tablespoon medium or dry sherry

AMERICAN

1 lb shelled shrimp
1 egg white
2 teaspoons cornstarch
3 tablespoons vegetable oil
2 scallions, white part only, finely
  chopped
1 slice of fresh ginger root,* peeled
  and finely chopped
1½ cups shelled peas
1 teaspoon salt
1 tablespoon medium or pale dry
  sherry

METHOD

Put the prawns (shrimp) in a bowl with the egg white and cornflour (cornstarch). Mix well, then leave to marinate in the refrigerator for about 20 minutes.

Heat the oil in a wok or frying pan (skillet), add the prawns (shrimp) and stir-fry over moderate heat for about 1 minute. Remove from the pan with a slotted spoon and drain.

Increase the heat, add the spring onions (scallions), ginger, peas and salt and stir-fry for 2 minutes.

Return the prawns (shrimp) to the pan, add the sherry and continue cooking for a further 1 minute. Serve hot.

Carp with Sweet and Sour Sauce

Tangcu Liyu

Carp is a symbol of good fortune, so it is served at New Year and other festivities.

METRIC/IMPERIAL

15 g/½ oz dried wood ears,* soaked in warm water for 20 minutes
1 carp, weighing 750 g–1 kg/1½–2 lb
2 teaspoons salt
3 tablespoons flour
4 tablespoons vegetable oil
2–3 spring onions, shredded
2 slices of fresh root ginger,* peeled and shredded
1 garlic clove, peeled and finely chopped
15 g/½ oz bamboo shoot, thinly sliced
50 g/2 oz water chestnuts,* thinly sliced
1 red pepper, cored, seeded and shredded
3 tablespoons wine vinegar

Sauce:
3 tablespoons sugar
2 tablespoons soy sauce
2 tablespoons medium or dry sherry
2 teaspoons cornflour
150 ml/¼ pint chicken stock or water
1 teaspoon chilli sauce

AMERICAN

½ cup tree ears,* soaked in warm water for 20 minutes
1 carp, weighing 1½–2 lb
2 teaspoons salt
3 tablespoons flour
¼ cup vegetable oil
2–3 scallions, shredded
2 slices of fresh ginger root,* peeled and shredded
1 garlic clove, peeled and finely chopped
2 tablespoons thinly sliced bamboo shoot
¼ cup water chestnuts,* thinly sliced
1 red pepper, cored, seeded and shredded
3 tablespoons wine vinegar

Sauce:
3 tablespoons sugar
2 tablespoons soy sauce
2 tablespoons medium or pale dry sherry
2 teaspoons cornstarch
⅔ cup chicken stock or water
1 teaspoon chili sauce

METHOD

Drain the wood (tree) ears and slice very thinly, discarding the hard bits.

Clean the fish thoroughly and remove the fins and tail but leave the head on. Make diagonal slashes through to the bone along both sides of the fish at 5 mm/¼ inch intervals. Dry thoroughly, then rub the fish inside and out with 1 teaspoon salt. Coat with the flour from head to tail.

Heat the oil in a large wok or frying pan (skillet) until very hot. Lower the heat a little, add the fish and fry for about 3 to 4 minutes on each side until golden and crisp, turning the fish carefully. Drain, then transfer carefully to a warmed serving dish. Keep hot.

Mix the sauce ingredients together. Add the spring onions (scallions), ginger and garlic to the oil remaining in the pan. Stir in the wood (tree) ears, bamboo shoot, water chestnuts and red pepper, then the remaining salt and the vinegar. Add the sauce mixture and cook, stirring, until thickened. Pour over the fish. Serve immediately.

Prawn (Shrimp) Balls with Broccoli; Braised Fish with Spring Onions (Scallions) and Ginger

Braised Fish with Spring Onions (Scallions) and Ginger
Jiangcong Shao Yu

The skin of a whole fish must be scored before cooking, to prevent it from bursting and to allow the heat to penetrate more quickly. It will also make it easier for the flesh to absorb the flavours of the seasoning and sauce.

METRIC/IMPERIAL

1 fish (mullet, bream etc.), weighing 750 g/1½ lb
1 teaspoon salt
2 tablespoons flour
3 tablespoons vegetable oil
3–4 spring onions, cut into 2.5 cm/1 inch lengths
2–3 slices of fresh root ginger,* peeled and shredded
Sauce:
2 tablespoons soy sauce
2 tablespoons medium or dry sherry
150 ml/¼ pint chicken stock or water
1 teaspoon cornflour
freshly ground black pepper
To garnish:
tomato halves
coriander leaves*
cherries

AMERICAN

1 fish (mullet, sea bass etc.), weighing 1½ lb
1 teaspoon salt
2 tablespoons flour
3 tablespoons vegetable oil
3–4 scallions, cut into 1 inch lengths
2–3 slices of fresh ginger root,* peeled and shredded
Sauce:
2 tablespoons soy sauce
2 tablespoons medium or pale dry sherry
⅔ cup chicken stock or water
1 teaspoon cornstarch
freshly ground black pepper
To garnish:
tomato halves
coriander leaves*
cherries

METHOD

Clean the fish thoroughly, leaving the fins, tail and head on. Slash both sides of the fish diagonally with a sharp knife at 5 mm/¼ inch intervals as far as the bone. Rub the fish inside and out with the salt, then coat with the flour from head to tail.

Heat the oil in a large wok or frying pan (skillet) until very hot. Lower the heat a little, add the fish and fry for about 2 minutes on each side or until golden and crisp, turning the fish carefully. Remove from the pan.

Mix the sauce ingredients together. Increase the heat and add the spring onions (scallions) and ginger to the oil remaining in pan. Stir-fry for a few seconds, then stir in the sauce mixture and return the fish to the pan.

Simmer for a few minutes, then carefully transfer the fish to a warmed serving dish and pour over the sauce.

If liked, garnish the dish with tomato halves, trimmed with coriander leaves and cherries. Serve hot.

Prawn (Shrimp) Balls with Broccoli
Jielan Chao Xiaqiu

Do not overcook the prawns (shrimp) or they will lose their delicate flavour.

METRIC/IMPERIAL

225 g/8 oz Dublin Bay or Pacific (King) prawns in shell
1 slice of fresh root ginger,* peeled and finely chopped
1 teaspoon medium or dry sherry
1 egg white
1 tablespoon cornflour
3 tablespoons vegetable oil
2 spring onions, finely chopped
225 g/8 oz broccoli, cut into small pieces
1 teaspoon salt
1 teaspoon sugar

AMERICAN

½ lb unshelled jumbo shrimp
1 slice of fresh ginger root,* peeled and finely chopped
1 teaspoon medium or pale dry sherry
1 egg white
1 tablespoon cornstarch
3 tablespoons vegetable oil
2 scallions, finely chopped
½ lb broccoli, cut into small pieces
1 teaspoon salt
1 teaspoon sugar

METHOD

Wash the unshelled prawns (shrimp), dry thoroughly with kitchen paper towels, then use a sharp knife to make a shallow incision down the back of the prawn (shrimp) and pull out the black intestinal vein. Split each prawn (shrimp) in half lengthways, then cut into small pieces so that they become little round balls when cooked.

Put the prawns (shrimp) in a bowl with the ginger, sherry, egg white and cornflour (cornstarch). Stir well, then leave to marinate in the refrigerator for about 20 minutes.

Heat 1 tablespoon of the oil in a wok or frying pan (skillet), add the prawns (shrimp) and stir-fry over moderate heat until they change colour. Remove from the pan with a slotted spoon.

Heat the remaining oil in the pan, add the spring onions (scallions) and broccoli, stir, then add the salt and sugar. Cook until the broccoli is just tender, then add the prawns (shrimp) and stir well. Serve hot.

Fish Steaks in Bean Sauce

Jian Doubian Yu

METRIC/IMPERIAL

400 g/14 oz fish steaks (cod or halibut)
1 tablespoon yellow bean sauce*
3 tablespoons soy sauce
1 tablespoon medium or dry sherry
1 tablespoon sugar
1 teaspoon chilli sauce (optional)
3 tablespoons chicken stock or water
$\frac{1}{2}$ teaspoon monosodium glutamate* (optional)
2 tablespoons vegetable oil

AMERICAN

1 lb fish steaks (cod or halibut)
1 tablespoon bean sauce*
3 tablespoons soy sauce
1 tablespoon medium or pale dry sherry
1 tablespoon sugar
1 teaspoon chili sauce (optional)
3 tablespoons chicken stock or water
$\frac{1}{2}$ teaspoon msg* (optional)
2 tablespoons vegetable oil

METHOD

Cut each fish steak into 2 or 3 pieces and remove any bones. Put the fish in a bowl, then add the remaining ingredients, except the oil. Toss gently to mix, then leave to marinate for about 20 minutes.

Heat the oil in a wok or frying pan (skillet), add the fish and fry over moderate heat until golden on all sides. Add the marinade remaining in the bowl. Increase the heat and cook until almost all of the sauce has been absorbed. Serve hot.

Braised Chicken Wings

Hongmen Jichi

METRIC/IMPERIAL

12 chicken wings
4 Chinese dried mushrooms,* soaked in warm water for 30 minutes
2 tablespoons vegetable oil
2 spring onions, finely chopped
2 slices of fresh root ginger,* peeled and finely chopped
2 tablespoons soy sauce
2 tablespoons medium or dry sherry
1 tablespoon sugar
$\frac{1}{2}$ teaspoon five spice powder*
350 ml/12 fl oz water
175 g/6 oz bamboo shoot, cut into chunks
2 teaspoons cornflour, mixed to a paste with a little water

AMERICAN

12 chicken wings
4 Chinese dried mushrooms,* soaked in warm water for 30 minutes
2 tablespoons vegetable oil
2 scallions, finely chopped
2 slices of fresh ginger root,* peeled and finely chopped
2 tablespoons soy sauce
2 tablespoons medium or pale dry sherry
1 tablespoon sugar
$\frac{1}{2}$ teaspoon five spice powder*
1$\frac{1}{2}$ cups water
1$\frac{1}{2}$ cups bamboo shoot, cut into chunks
2 teaspoons cornstarch, mixed to a paste with a little water

METHOD

Trim and discard the tips of the chicken wings, then cut each wing into 2 pieces by breaking the joint.

Squeeze the mushrooms dry, discard the stalks, then cut the caps into small pieces.

Heat the oil in a wok or frying pan (skillet) until it reaches smoking point. Add the spring onions (scallions) and ginger, then the chicken wings. Stir-fry until the chicken changes colour, then add the soy sauce, sherry, sugar, five spice powder and water.

Lower the heat and cook gently until the liquid has reduced by about half. Add the mushrooms and bamboo shoot and continue cooking until the juice has almost completely evaporated. Remove the bamboo shoot chunks, rinse, drain and arrange around the edge of a warmed serving dish.

Add the cornflour (cornstarch) paste to the pan and cook, stirring constantly, until thickened. Place the chicken mixture on the centre of the bamboo shoot. Serve hot.

Chicken Wings and Broccoli Assembly

Jichi Hui Jielan

METRIC/IMPERIAL

12 chicken wings
4 spring onions, finely chopped
2 slices of fresh root ginger,* peeled and finely chopped
1 tablespoon lemon juice
1 tablespoon soy sauce
1$\frac{1}{2}$ teaspoons salt
1 tablespoon medium or dry sherry
4 tablespoons vegetable oil
225 g/8 oz broccoli, divided into florets
50 g/2 oz tomatoes, chopped
1 tablespoon cornflour, mixed to a paste with a little water

AMERICAN

12 chicken wings
4 scallions, finely chopped
2 slices of fresh ginger root,* peeled and finely chopped
1 tablespoon lemon juice
1 tablespoon soy sauce
1$\frac{1}{2}$ teaspoons salt
1 tablespoon medium or pale dry sherry
$\frac{1}{4}$ cup vegetable oil
$\frac{1}{2}$ lb broccoli, divided into florets
$\frac{1}{4}$ cup chopped tomatoes
1 tablespoon cornstarch, mixed to a paste with a little water

METHOD

Trim and discard the tips of the chicken wings, then cut each wing into 2 pieces by breaking the joint.

Put the chicken in a bowl with the spring onions (scallions), ginger, lemon juice, soy sauce, $\frac{1}{2}$ teaspoon salt and the sherry. Stir well, then leave to marinate for about 20 minutes.

Heat 2 tablespoons of the oil in a large wok or frying pan (skillet). Add the broccoli and remaining salt and stir-fry until tender but still crisp. Arrange the broccoli neatly around the edge of a warmed serving dish and keep hot.

Remove the chicken pieces, reserving the marinade. Heat the remaining oil in the pan, add the chicken and fry until golden. Remove from the pan with a slotted spoon and drain.

Add the tomatoes to the pan and stir-fry until reduced to a pulp. Return the chicken to the pan and add the marinade. Cook for about 2 minutes, then add the cornflour (cornstarch) paste and cook, stirring constantly, until thickened. Spoon into the centre of the serving dish. Serve immediately.

Braised Chicken Wings; Chicken Wings and Broccoli Assembly

White-Cut Chicken
Baiqie Ji

This famous Cantonese dish is very simple to cook. It makes an ideal starter for a banquet, or it can be served as part of a buffet.

METRIC/IMPERIAL

1 chicken, weighing 1.5 kg/3–3½ lb
Sauce:
2–3 spring onions, finely chopped
2 slices of fresh root ginger,* peeled and finely chopped
1 teaspoon salt
1 tablespoon soy sauce
1 tablespoon sesame seed oil*
freshly ground black pepper

AMERICAN

1 chicken, weighing 3–3½ lb
Sauce:
2–3 scallions, finely chopped
2 slices of fresh ginger root,* peeled and finely chopped
1 teaspoon salt
1 tablespoon soy sauce
1 tablespoon sesame seed oil*
freshly ground black pepper

METHOD

Put the chicken in a large pan, add cold water to cover, then cover the pan with a tight-fitting lid. Bring to the boil, then lower the heat and simmer for exactly 7 minutes. Turn off the heat and leave the chicken to cook in the hot water for at least 30 minutes, without removing the lid.

About 1 hour before serving, remove the chicken from the water and chop it into small pieces, using a cleaver. Re-assemble the chicken pieces on a serving dish.

Mix together the sauce ingredients and pour over the chicken. Serve warm or cover and leave in the refrigerator for at least 30 minutes before serving chilled.

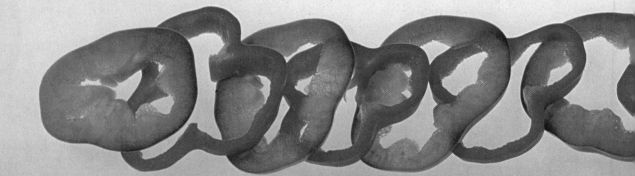

Oil-Basted Chicken
Youlin Ji

METRIC/IMPERIAL

1 chicken, weighing 1.5 kg/3–3½ lb
2 tablespoons soy sauce
1 tablespoon medium or dry sherry
1.2 litres/2 pints vegetable oil for
   deep-frying
Sauce:
2 spring onions, finely chopped
2 slices of fresh root ginger,* peeled
   and finely chopped
1 garlic clove, peeled and finely
   chopped
2 tablespoons vinegar
1½ tablespoons sugar
1 tablespoon yellow bean sauce*

AMERICAN

1 chicken, weighing 3–3½ lb
2 tablespoons soy sauce
1 tablespoon medium or pale dry
   sherry
5 cups vegetable oil
Sauce:
2 scallions, finely chopped
2 slices of fresh ginger root,* peeled
   and finely chopped
1 garlic clove, peeled and finely
   chopped
2 tablespoons vinegar
1½ tablespoons sugar
1 tablespoon bean sauce*

METHOD

Wash and clean the chicken thoroughly, then plunge into a large pan of boiling water. Boil rapidly for 2 to 3 minutes, then remove and drain.

Mix together the soy sauce and sherry, then brush over the chicken. Leave to marinate for about 20 minutes. Meanwhile, mix together the sauce ingredients in a small pan.

Heat the oil in a large wok or deep-fat fryer. Add the chicken and cook over moderate heat for 20 to 30 minutes until browned on all sides, basting constantly.

Remove the chicken from the pan, chop into small pieces, then arrange neatly on a warmed serving dish. Add any remaining marinade to the sauce mixture, heat through, then pour over the chicken. Serve hot.

Soy Chicken
Chiyou Ji

This dish can be served hot as a main course, or cold as a starter. Do not discard the cooking sauce; it can be stored in the refrigerator for future use.

METRIC/IMPERIAL

1 chicken, weighing 1.5 kg/3–3½ lb
1 teaspoon freshly ground black
   pepper
2 teaspoons finely chopped fresh root
   ginger*
5 tablespoons soy sauce
3 tablespoons medium or dry sherry
1 tablespoon brown sugar
3 tablespoons vegetable oil
300 ml/½ pint chicken stock or water
coriander leaves* to garnish

AMERICAN

1 chicken, weighing 3–3½ lb
1 teaspoon freshly ground black
   pepper
2 teaspoons finely chopped fresh
   ginger root*
⅓ cup soy sauce
3 tablespoons medium or pale dry
   sherry
1 tablespoon brown sugar
3 tablespoons vegetable oil
1¼ cups chicken stock or water
coriander leaves* to garnish

METHOD

Wash the chicken, dry thoroughly and rub inside and out with the pepper and ginger. Mix together the soy sauce, sherry and sugar. Spoon over the chicken and leave to marinate for at least 3 hours, turning the chicken occasionally.

Heat the oil in a large pan, add the whole chicken and fry, turning, until lightly browned on all sides.

Dilute the marinade with the stock or water. Add to the pan, bring to the boil, then lower the heat. Cover and simmer for 45 minutes, turning the chicken several times during cooking taking care to avoid breaking the skin.

Chop the chicken into small pieces. Arrange on a serving dish and baste with 2 tablespoons of the sauce. Garnish with coriander leaves. Serve hot.

Soy Chicken; Shredded Chicken with Peppers

Shredded Chicken with Peppers
Chijiao Chao Jisi

This is a very colourful dish with a piquant taste.

METRIC/IMPERIAL

225 g/8 oz chicken breast meat,
   skinned and shredded
½ teaspoon salt
1 tablespoon soy sauce
1 egg white
1 tablespoon cornflour
5 tablespoons vegetable oil
2 slices of fresh root ginger,*
   peeled and shredded
2–3 spring onions, shredded
1 hot chilli, shredded
1 green pepper, cored, seeded and
   shredded
1 red pepper, cored, seeded and
   shredded
2–3 celery sticks, shredded
2 tablespoons black bean sauce*

AMERICAN

1 cup shredded, skinned chicken
   breast meat
½ teaspoon salt
1 tablespoon soy sauce
1 egg white
1 tablespoon cornstarch
⅓ cup vegetable oil
2 slices of fresh ginger root,* peeled
   and shredded
2–3 scallions, shredded
1 hot chili, shredded
1 green pepper, cored, seeded and
   shredded
1 red pepper, cored, seeded and
   shredded
2–3 celery stalks, shredded
2 tablespoons salted black beans*

METHOD

Put the chicken in a bowl with the salt, soy sauce, egg white and cornflour (cornstarch) and mix well.

Heat the oil in a wok or frying pan (skillet), add the chicken and stir-fry over moderate heat until half-cooked. Remove from the pan with a slotted spoon.

Increase the heat to high. When the oil starts to smoke, add the ginger to the pan with the spring onions (scallions), chilli, peppers and celery. Stir well, then add the black bean sauce (salted black beans) and continue cooking for a few seconds.

Return the chicken to the pan, mix well, then stir-fry for about 1 to 1½ minutes until the meat is tender, but the vegetables are still crisp and crunchy. Serve hot.

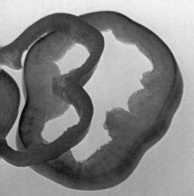

Steamed Chicken with Chinese Dried Mushrooms
Donggu Zheng Ziji

METRIC/IMPERIAL

450 g/1 lb boned chicken (breasts and thighs), cut into small pieces
1½ tablespoons soy sauce
1 tablespoon medium or dry sherry
1 teaspoon sugar
1 teaspoon cornflour
4 Chinese dried mushrooms, soaked in warm water for 30 minutes*
1 tablespoon vegetable oil
2 slices of fresh root ginger, peeled and shredded*
freshly ground black pepper
*1 teaspoon sesame seed oil**

AMERICAN

1 lb boneless chicken (breasts and thighs), cut into small pieces
1½ tablespoons soy sauce
1 tablespoon medium or pale dry sherry
1 teaspoon sugar
1 teaspoon cornstarch
4 Chinese dried mushrooms, soaked in warm water for 30 minutes*
1 tablespoon vegetable oil
2 slices of fresh ginger root, peeled and shredded*
freshly ground black pepper
*1 teaspoon sesame seed oil**

METHOD

Put the chicken in a bowl with the soy sauce, sherry, sugar and cornflour (cornstarch). Mix well, then leave to marinate for about 20 minutes.

Squeeze the mushrooms dry, discard the stalks, then cut the caps into pieces, roughly the same size as the chicken.

Brush a heatproof plate with the vegetable oil. Place the chicken pieces on the plate, top with the mushrooms, then sprinkle with the ginger, pepper to taste and the sesame seed oil.

Place in a steamer or over a pan of simmering water and cover the plate with a lid. Steam over high heat for 25 to 30 minutes. Serve hot.

Shredded Chicken with 'Fish Sauce'
Yuxiang Jisi

Fish is not used in this recipe; the sauce is normally used for cooking fish dishes, hence the name.

Shredded Chicken with 'Fish Sauce';
Golden Flower and Jade Tree Chicken

METRIC/IMPERIAL

350 g/12 oz chicken breast meat, skinned and shredded
½ teaspoon salt
½ egg white
1 teaspoon cornflour
4 tablespoons vegetable oil
2 spring onions, cut into 2.5 cm/1 inch lengths
1 slice of fresh root ginger, peeled and shredded*
1 small green pepper, cored, seeded and cut into rings
1 small red pepper, cored, seeded and cut into rings
3 celery sticks, sliced
1 tablespoon soy sauce
1 teaspoon sugar
1 teaspoon vinegar
1 teaspoon chilli sauce (optional)

Golden Flower and Jade Tree Chicken
Zinhua Yushu Ji

This is a very colourful dish, as its name implies; 'Golden Flower' refers to the ham from King-hua, 'Jade' is the chicken, and 'Tree' is the greens. It can be served as a starter at formal dinners, or as a main course for an informal dinner.

METRIC/IMPERIAL

1 chicken, weighing 1.5 kg/3–3½ lb
2 slices of fresh root ginger,* peeled
2 spring onions
3 tablespoons vegetable oil
450 g/1 lb broccoli or other greens, divided into small florets or pieces
2 teaspoons salt
250 ml/8 fl oz chicken stock
225 g/8 oz cooked ham
1 tablespoon cornflour, mixed to a paste with a little water

AMERICAN

1 chicken, weighing 3–3½ lb
2 slices of fresh ginger root,* peeled
2 scallions
3 tablespoons vegetable oil
1 lb broccoli or other greens, divided into small florets or pieces
2 teaspoons salt
1 cup chicken stock
½ lb cooked ham
1 tablespoon cornstarch, mixed to a paste with a little water

METHOD

Put the chicken in a large pan and cover with cold water. Add the ginger and spring onions (scallions), cover with a tight-fitting lid and bring to the boil. Lower the heat and simmer for exactly 3 minutes. Turn off the heat and leave the chicken to cook in the hot water for at least 3 hours, without removing the lid.

Heat the oil in a wok or frying pan (skillet). Add the broccoli or greens and 1 teaspoon salt and stir-fry for 3 to 4 minutes, until cooked to taste, moistening with a little of the stock if necessary. Remove from the pan and arrange around the edge of a large serving dish.

Remove the chicken from the pan, then carefully remove the meat from the bones, keeping the skin on the meat. Cut the chicken and ham into thin rectangular slices and arrange in alternating, overlapping layers in the centre of the broccoli.

Just before serving, heat the remaining stock with the remaining salt in a small pan. Add the cornflour (cornstarch) paste and cook, stirring, until thickened. Pour over the chicken and ham to form a thin glaze, resembling jade. Serve hot.

AMERICAN

1½ cups shredded, skinned chicken breast meat
½ teaspoon salt
½ egg white
1 teaspoon cornstarch
¼ cup vegetable oil
2 scallions, cut into 1 inch lengths
1 slice of fresh ginger root,* peeled and shredded
1 small green pepper, cored, seeded and cut into rings
1 small red pepper, cored, seeded and cut into rings
3 celery stalks, sliced
1 tablespoon soy sauce
1 teaspoon sugar
1 teaspoon vinegar
1 teaspoon chili sauce (optional)

METHOD

Put the chicken in a bowl with the salt, egg white and cornflour (cornstarch). Mix well, then leave to stand for about 20 minutes.

Heat 2 tablespoons oil in a wok or frying pan (skillet), add the chicken and stir-fry over moderate heat for about 2 minutes. Remove from the pan with a slotted spoon and drain.

Heat the remaining oil in the pan and add the spring onions (scallions), ginger, peppers and celery. Stir in the soy sauce, sugar, vinegar and chilli sauce, if using. Return the chicken to the pan and combine all the ingredients together. Serve hot.

Fried Chicken Legs
Zha Jitui

METRIC/IMPERIAL

6 chicken legs
2 tablespoons soy sauce
1 tablespoon medium or dry sherry
½ teaspoon freshly ground black
    pepper
2 tablespoons cornflour
600 ml/1 pint vegetable oil for deep-
    frying
1 tablespoon finely chopped spring
    onion

AMERICAN

6 chicken legs
2 tablespoons soy sauce
1 tablespoon medium or pale dry
    sherry
½ teaspoon freshly ground black
    pepper
2 tablespoons cornstarch
2½ cups vegetable oil for deep-frying
1 tablespoon finely chopped scallion

METHOD

Chop each chicken leg into 2 or 3 pieces, then mix with the soy sauce, sherry and pepper. Leave to marinate for about 20 minutes, turning occasionally.

Coat each piece of chicken with cornflour (cornstarch). Heat the oil in a wok or deep-fat fryer to 180°C/350°F. Lower the heat, add the chicken pieces and deep-fry until golden. Remove from the pan with a slotted spoon and drain.

Pour off all but 1 tablespoon oil, then add the spring onion (scallion) to the pan with the drained chicken pieces. Stir-fry over moderate heat for about 2 minutes. Serve hot.

Chicken in Silver Foil
Yinxiang Bao Ji

This is a variation of the traditional 'paper-wrapped chicken'. Prawns (shrimp) or other meat can be used instead of chicken.

METRIC/IMPERIAL

450 g/1 lb skinned chicken breast meat
3 spring onions, white part only
¼ teaspoon salt
1 tablespoon soy sauce
1 teaspoon sugar
1 teaspoon medium or dry sherry
1 teaspoon sesame seed oil*
4 tablespoons vegetable oil
To garnish:
shredded spring onion
finely chopped red pepper

AMERICAN

1 lb chicken breast meat, skinned
3 scallions, white part only
¼ teaspoon salt
1 tablespoon soy sauce
1 teaspoon sugar
1 teaspoon medium or pale dry sherry
1 teaspoon sesame seed oil*
¼ cup oil
To garnish:
shredded scallion
finely chopped red pepper

METHOD

Cut the chicken into 12 roughly equal-sized pieces. Cut each spring onion (scallion) into 4 pieces. Combine the chicken and spring onions (scallions) with the salt, soy sauce, sugar, sherry and sesame seed oil in a bowl. Leave to marinate for about 20 minutes.

Cut 12 squares of foil large enough to wrap around the chicken pieces 4 times. Brush the pieces of foil with oil, then place a piece of chicken on each. Top with a slice of spring onion (scallion), then wrap the foil around the chicken to make a parcel, making sure that no meat is exposed.

Heat the oil in a wok or frying pan (skillet). Add the chicken parcels and fry over moderate heat for about 2 minutes on each side. Remove and leave to drain on a wok rack or in a strainer for a few minutes; turn off the heat.

Reheat the oil. When it is very hot, return the chicken parcels to the pan and fry for 1 minute only. Serve hot in the silver foil, garnished with shredded spring onion (scallion) and red pepper.

Chicken in Silver Foil; Fried Chicken
Legs; Lotus-White Chicken

Lotus-White Chicken
Furong Ji

METRIC/IMPERIAL

5 egg whites
120 ml/4 fl oz chicken stock
1 teaspoon salt
1 teaspoon medium or dry sherry
2 teaspoons cornflour
100 g/4 oz chicken breast meat,
  skinned and finely chopped
oil for deep-frying
To garnish:
1–2 tablespoons cooked green peas
25 g/1 oz cooked ham, shredded

AMERICAN

5 egg whites
½ cup chicken stock
1 teaspoon salt
1 teaspoon medium or pale dry sherry
2 teaspoons cornstarch
½ cup finely chopped, skinned chicken
  breast meat
oil for deep-frying
To garnish:
1–2 tablespoons cooked green peas
1 slice cooked ham, shredded

METHOD

Put the egg whites in a bowl. Stir in 3 tablespoons of the chicken stock, the salt, sherry and half the cornflour (cornstarch). Add the chicken and mix well.

Heat the oil in a wok or deep-fat fryer to 180°C/350°F, then gently pour in about one third of the egg and chicken mixture. Deep-fry for 10 seconds until the mixture begins to rise to the surface, then carefully turn over. Deep-fry until golden, then remove from the pan with a slotted spoon, drain and place on a warmed serving dish. Keep hot while cooking the remaining chicken mixture in the same way.

Heat the remaining stock in a small pan. Mix the remaining cornflour (cornstarch) to a paste with a little cold water add to the stock and simmer, stirring, until thickened. Pour over the chicken.

Garnish with the peas and ham. Serve hot.

Onion Duck

Congyou Ya

METRIC/IMPERIAL

4 Chinese dried mushrooms,* soaked
  in warm water for 30 minutes
1 duckling, weighing 2–2.25 kg/4½–5¼ lb
120 ml/4 fl oz soy sauce
3 tablespoons sugar
100 g/4 oz bamboo shoot, sliced
25 g/1 oz lard
3 spring onions, finely chopped

AMERICAN

4 Chinese dried mushrooms,* soaked
  in warm water for 30 minutes
1 duckling, weighing 4½–5¼ lb
½ cup soy sauce
3 tablespoons sugar
1 cup sliced bamboo shoot
2 tablespoons lard
3 scallions, finely chopped

METHOD

Squeeze the mushrooms dry, then discard the stalks.

Put the duckling in a large pan, cover with cold water and bring to the boil. Remove the duckling from the pan and rinse under cold running water. Skim the surface of the cooking water, then return the duckling to the pan. Add more fresh water to cover the duckling if necessary and bring back to the boil.

Add the soy sauce, sugar and mushrooms to the pan. Cover and cook gently for 2½ hours, turning the duckling halfway through cooking. Add the bamboo shoot and simmer for 30 minutes. Transfer the duckling to a warmed serving dish. Drain the mushrooms and bamboo shoot and arrange around the duckling.

Heat the lard in a separate pan, add the spring onions (scallions) and fry for 1 to 2 minutes. Pour over the duckling and serve hot.

**Pan-Fried Chicken Breast; Diced
Chicken with Celery**

154

Diced Chicken with Celery
Jiecai Chao Jiding

METRIC/IMPERIAL

3–4 Chinese dried mushrooms,*
    soaked in warm water for 30 minutes
225 g/8 oz chicken breast meat,
    skinned and diced
½ teaspoon salt
1 egg white
1 tablespoon cornflour
5 tablespoons vegetable oil
2 slices of fresh root ginger,* peeled
    and finely chopped
2–3 spring onions, finely chopped
1 small head celery, diced
100 g/4 oz bamboo shoot, diced
1 red pepper, cored, seeded and
    diced
3 tablespoons soy sauce
1 teaspoon medium or dry sherry
chopped coriander leaves* or parsley
    to garnish

AMERICAN

3–4 Chinese dried mushrooms,*
    soaked in warm water for 30 minutes
1 cup diced, skinned chicken breast
    meat
½ teaspoon salt
1 egg white
1 tablespoon cornstarch
⅓ cup vegetable oil
2 slices of fresh ginger root,* peeled
    and finely chopped
2–3 scallions, finely chopped
1 small bunch celery, diced
1 cup diced bamboo shoot
1 red pepper, cored, seeded and
    diced
3 tablespoons soy sauce
1 teaspoon medium or pale dry sherry
chopped coriander leaves* or parsley
    to garnish

METHOD

Squeeze the mushrooms dry, discard the stalks then dice the caps.

Sprinkle the chicken with the salt, dip into the egg white, then coat with the cornflour (cornstarch).

Heat the oil in a wok or frying pan (skillet). Add the chicken and stir-fry over moderate heat until half-cooked, then remove with a slotted spoon.

Increase the heat to high and add the ginger and spring onions (scallions) to the pan. Add the mushrooms and remaining vegetables and stir-fry for 1 minute.

Return the chicken to the pan, add the soy sauce and sherry and cook for a further 1 minute until the liquid thickens, stirring constantly. Serve hot, garnished with chopped coriander or parsley.

Pan-Fried Chicken Breast
Ganjian Jipu

METRIC/IMPERIAL

1 large chicken breast, skinned and
    boned
1–2 spring onions, chopped
1 slice of fresh root ginger,* peeled
    and finely chopped
1 tablespoon medium or dry sherry
2 teaspoons salt
1 egg, beaten
2 teaspoons cornflour
3 tablespoons vegetable oil
1 small lettuce
Sauce:
1 tablespoon tomato purée
1 teaspoon sugar
1 teaspoon sesame seed oil*
1 tablespoon water

AMERICAN

1 large chicken breast, skinned and
    boned
1–2 scallions, chopped
1 slice of fresh ginger root,* peeled
    and finely chopped
1 tablespoon medium or pale dry
    sherry
2 teaspoons salt
1 egg, beaten
2 teaspoons cornstarch
3 tablespoons vegetable oil
1 small head of lettuce
Sauce:
1 tablespoon tomato paste
1 teaspoon sugar
1 teaspoon sesame seed oil*
1 tablespoon water

METHOD

Cut the chicken into thin rectangular slices and place in a bowl. Add the spring onion (scallion), ginger, sherry and salt and mix well. Leave to marinate for about 20 minutes.

Stir the egg into the marinated chicken, then sprinkle with the cornflour (cornstarch) and toss to coat thoroughly. Heat the oil in a wok or frying pan (skillet). Add the chicken mixture and fry until tender and golden on all sides. Remove from the pan with a slotted spoon and arrange on a bed of lettuce.

Mix together the sauce ingredients. Add to the pan in which the chicken was cooked and heat through, then either pour over the chicken, or serve as a dip. Serve hot.

Roast Duck Peking-Style

Beijing Kao Ya

Peking-style duck is unique in Chinese cuisine, not only for the way in which it is cooked, but also for the specially reared species of duck used. The ducks are brought to exactly the right degree of plumpness and tenderness by several stages of force-feeding and care.

If liked, the sauce given here may be replaced by 6 tablespoons commercially prepared hoi sin sauce.*

Spring onion (scallion) flowers are the traditional garnish for Peking-style duck. To prepare these: Make several cuts from top to bottom along each spring onion (scallion), without cutting right through the base. Leave in a bowl of iced water to open.

The traditional way to serve this dish is to arrange all the separate dishes of food on the table and allow the guests to help themselves.

METRIC/IMPERIAL

1 duckling, weighing
  1.5–1.75 kg/3–4¼ lb
1 tablespoon sugar
1 teaspoon salt
300 ml/½ pint water
Sauce:
3 tablespoons yellow bean sauce*
2 tablespoons sugar
1 tablespoon sesame seed oil*
To serve:
24 Mandarin Pancakes (see opposite)
10–12 spring onion flowers
4 leeks, cut into 7.5 cm/3 inch strips
½ cucumber, cut into 7.5 cm/3 inch
  strips
½ red pepper, cored, seeded and
  shredded

AMERICAN

1 duckling, weighing 3–4¼ lb
1 tablespoon sugar
1 teaspoon salt
1¼ cups water
Sauce:
3 tablespoons bean sauce*
2 tablespoons sugar
1 tablespoon sesame seed oil*
To serve:
24 Mandarin Pancakes (see opposite)
10–12 scallion flowers
4 leeks, cut into 3 inch strips
½ cucumber, cut into 3 inch strips
½ red pepper, cored, seeded and
  shredded

Roast Duck Peking-Style, served with traditional accompaniments: Mandarin Pancakes, dipping sauce and raw vegetables

Oil-Braised Duck

Yashao Ya

METRIC/IMPERIAL

1 duckling, weighing 1.75–2 kg/4–4¾ lb
4 tablespoons orange juice
2 tablespoons sugar
4 tablespoons soy sauce
4 teaspoons salt
4 tablespoons medium or dry sherry
1 tablespoon vinegar
½ teaspoon five spice powder*
1 slice of fresh root ginger,* peeled
600 ml/1 pint chicken stock
1.2 litres/2 pints vegetable oil for deep-frying

AMERICAN

1 duckling, weighing 4–4¾ lb
¼ cup orange juice
2 tablespoons sugar
¼ cup soy sauce
4 teaspoons salt
¼ cup medium or pale dry sherry
1 tablespoon vinegar
½ teaspoon five spice powder*
1 slice of fresh ginger root,* peeled
2½ cups chicken stock
5 cups vegetable oil for deep-frying

METHOD

Plunge the duckling into a pan of boiling water. Leave for a few minutes, then drain and place in a clean pan with all the remaining ingredients. Bring to the boil, then lower the heat. Cover with a tight-fitting lid and simmer gently for 45 minutes, turning the duckling at least twice during cooking. Remove the duckling from the pan, drain and dry thoroughly. Leave the cooking liquid simmering over low heat to reduce and thicken.

Heat the oil in a wok or deep-fat fryer. Add the duckling to the oil and cook over moderate heat until browned on all sides.

Return the duckling to the simmering liquid and turn it several times to coat with the sauce.

Remove from the pan and cut into small pieces. Re-arrange the duckling on a warmed serving dish and pour the remaining sauce over the top. Serve hot.

Mandarin Pancakes

Bo Bing

METRIC/IMPERIAL

450 g/1 lb plain flour
300 ml/½ pint boiling water
little vegetable oil

AMERICAN

4 cups all-purpose flour
1¼ cups boiling water
little vegetable oil

METHOD

Sift the flour into a bowl. Mix the water with 1 teaspoon oil, then slowly stir into the flour, using chopsticks or a wooden spoon.

Knead the mixture into a firm dough, then divide into 3 equal portions. Roll each portion into a long 'sausage', then cut each sausage into 8 equal pieces.

Press each piece into a flat pancake with the palm of the hand. Brush one pancake with a little oil, then place another on top to form a 'sandwich'; repeat with the remaining dough to make 12 sandwiches.

Flatten each 'sandwich' on a lightly floured surface with a rolling-pin into a 15 cm/6 inch circle.

Place an ungreased frying pan (skillet) over moderate heat. When it is very hot, fry the 'sandwiches', one at a time. Turn the pancakes as soon as air bubbles appear on the surface. Cook the other side until little brown spots appear underneath. Remove the 'sandwich' from the pan and peel the 2 layers apart very gently. Fold each pancake into four to serve.

MAKES 24 PANCAKES

Note: Cold pancakes can be reheated in a steamer or hot oven for 5 to 10 minutes.

METHOD

Clean the duck and hang it up to dry thoroughly, preferably overnight in a cool, well-ventilated room.

The next day, dissolve the sugar and salt in the water and rub all over the duck. Leave for several hours until dry.

Place the duck on a rack in a roasting pan and roast in the centre of a preheated moderately hot oven (200°C/400°F, Gas Mark 6) for 1 hour.

Place the sauce ingredients in a pan and heat gently for 2 to 3 minutes, stirring constantly, then pour into a serving bowl.

Carve the duck into neat slices and arrange on a serving dish. Arrange the Mandarin pancakes on a separate dish and garnish both dishes with spring onion (scallion) flowers. Put the leeks, cucumber, and pepper on another dish.

To eat: Spread each pancake with a little sauce, then place a little leek and cucumber in the middle. Top with 1 or 2 slices of duck. Roll up the pancake.

Stir-Fried 'Three Whites'

Chao Sanbai

METRIC/IMPERIAL

100 g/4 oz chicken breast meat, skinned and diced
100 g/4 oz pork fillet, diced
1 teaspoon salt
1 egg white
1 tablespoon cornflour
3 tablespoons vegetable oil
2 spring onions, white part only, finely chopped
2 garlic cloves, peeled and finely chopped
100 g/4 oz bamboo shoot, diced
1 tablespoon medium or dry sherry
1 tablespoon yellow bean sauce*

AMERICAN

½ cup diced, skinned chicken breast meat
½ cup diced pork loin
1 teaspoon salt
1 egg white
1 tablespoon cornstarch
3 tablespoons vegetable oil
2 scallions, white part only, finely chopped
2 garlic cloves, peeled and finely chopped
1 cup diced bamboo shoot
1 tablespoon medium or pale dry sherry
1 tablespoon bean sauce*

METHOD

Put the chicken and pork in separate bowls. Mix together the salt, egg white and cornflour (cornstarch); divide equally between the chicken and pork and mix well.

Heat 1 tablespoon oil in a wok or frying pan (skillet), add the chicken and stir-fry until half-cooked. Remove from the pan with a slotted spoon and drain. Add another tablespoon oil to the pan and stir-fry the pork until half-cooked. Remove and drain.

Increase the heat and add the remaining oil to the pan. Add the spring onions (scallions), garlic and bamboo shoot, then return the chicken and pork to the pan. Stir in the sherry and bean sauce, then add a little stock or water to moisten if necessary.

Cook, stirring, until the meats and bamboo shoot are well coated with sauce and most of the liquid has been absorbed. Serve hot.

Braised Eggs with Pork

Lu Jidan Zhurou

If you happen to have any sauce left over from *Braised Tripe* (see page 165) or *Soy Chicken* (see page 149), add it to the sauce with the pork and eggs, as it will greatly improve the flavour of this dish.

METRIC/IMPERIAL

6 eggs
225 g/8 oz boned lean pork, in one piece
Sauce:
4 tablespoons soy sauce
2 tablespoons sugar
1 teaspoon salt
1 teaspoon five spice powder*
1.2 litres/2 pints water

AMERICAN

6 eggs
½ lb boneless pork loin, in one piece
Sauce:
¼ cup soy sauce
2 tablespoons sugar
1 teaspoon salt
1 teaspoon five spice powder*
5 cups water

METHOD

Cook the unshelled eggs in boiling water for 5 minutes, plunge into cold water, then carefully remove the shells.

Add the pork to a pan of boiling water. Remove when it changes colour, drain and dry on kitchen paper towels.

To make the sauce: Put all the ingredients in a pan, bring to the boil, stirring, then lower the heat and simmer for about 1 hour. Add the pork and eggs and simmer for 15 minutes, then turn off the heat and leave the eggs and pork to cool in the sauce for at least 50 minutes.

Remove the eggs and pork from the sauce. Cut the eggs into halves or quarters and thinly slice the pork. Arrange the eggs around the edge of a serving plate and place the pork in the centre. Serve cold.
Note: Keep the sauce in the refrigerator for future use.

Bean Sprouts with Shredded Pork
Douya Chao Rousi

METRIC/IMPERIAL

225 g/8 oz fresh bean sprouts
350 g/12 oz boned lean pork, shredded
2 tablespoons soy sauce
1 teaspoon medium or dry sherry
2 teaspoons cornflour
3 tablespoons vegetable oil
2 spring onions, shredded
1 slice of fresh root ginger,* peeled
   and shredded
1 teaspoon salt
50 g/2 oz leeks, shredded

AMERICAN

½ lb fresh bean sprouts
¾ cup shredded pork loin
2 tablespoons soy sauce
1 teaspoon medium or pale dry sherry
2 teaspoons cornstarch
3 tablespoons vegetable oil
2 scallions, shredded
1 slice of fresh ginger root,* peeled
   and shredded
1 teaspoon salt
1 small leek, shredded

METHOD

Rinse the bean sprouts in cold water, discarding any husks that float to the surface.

Put the pork in a bowl. Sprinkle with the soy sauce, sherry and cornflour (cornstarch). Mix well, then leave to marinate for about 20 minutes.

Heat 1 tablespoon of the oil in a wok or frying pan (skillet). Add the spring onions (scallions) and ginger, then the pork. Stir-fry until the pork changes colour, then remove the pork from the pan with a slotted spoon and drain.

Heat the remaining oil in the pan. Add the salt, then the bean sprouts and leeks. Stir-fry for about 1 minute. Return the pork to the pan, stir well and cook for a further 1 minute. Serve hot.

Pork Slices with Cauliflower; Bean Sprouts and Shredded Pork

Pork Slices with Cauliflower
Caihua Chao Roupian

METRIC/IMPERIAL

4 Chinese dried mushrooms,* soaked
   in warm water for 30 minutes
225 g/8 oz boned lean pork, sliced
2 tablespoons soy sauce
1 tablespoon medium or dry sherry
1 tablespoon cornflour
1 medium cauliflower, divided into
   florets
salt
3 tablespoons vegetable oil
2 spring onions, cut into 2.5 cm/1 inch
   lengths
1 slice of fresh root ginger,* peeled
   and cut into strips

AMERICAN

4 Chinese dried mushrooms,* soaked
   in warm water for 30 minutes
½ lb pork loin, sliced
2 tablespoons soy sauce
1 tablespoon medium or pale dry
   sherry
1 tablespoon cornstarch
1 medium cauliflower, divided into
   florets
salt
3 tablespoons vegetable oil
2 scallions, cut into 1 inch lengths
1 slice of fresh ginger root,* peeled
   and cut into strips

METHOD

Squeeze the mushrooms dry, discard the stalks, then cut the mushroom caps into halves or quarters, according to size.

Put the pork in a bowl and sprinkle with the soy sauce, sherry and 1 teaspoon of the cornflour (cornstarch). Mix well, then leave to marinate for about 20 minutes.

Meanwhile, blanch the cauliflower in boiling salted water for 1 to 2 minutes, then drain and set aside.

Heat the oil in a large wok or frying pan (skillet). Add the spring onions (scallions) and ginger, then the pork. Stir-fry until the pork changes colour, then add the mushrooms and 1 teaspoon salt. Stir-fry for a further 1 minute, then add the cauliflower and stir well.

Mix the remaining cornflour (cornstarch) to a paste with a little water, add to the pan and cook, stirring, until thickened.

Arrange the cauliflower around the edge of a serving dish and pile the pork mixture into the centre. Serve hot.

Red-Cooked Pork Leg or Shoulder
Hongshao Zhuti

Red-cooked pork should be so tender that it can easily be pulled off the bone with chopsticks or a fork.

METRIC/IMPERIAL

4 Chinese dried mushrooms,* soaked in warm water for 30 minutes
1 leg or shoulder of pork, weighing 1.5 kg/3–3½ lb
1 garlic clove, peeled and crushed
6 tablespoons soy sauce
3 tablespoons medium or dry sherry
3 tablespoons crystallized or brown sugar
1 teaspoon five spice powder*
To garnish:
1 carrot, thinly sliced into rounds
shredded spring onion

AMERICAN

4 Chinese dried mushrooms,* soaked in warm water for 30 minutes
1 pork leg or shoulder, weighing 3–3½ lb
1 garlic clove, peeled and crushed
6 tablespoons soy sauce
3 tablespoons medium or pale dry sherry
3 tablespoons rock or brown sugar
1 teaspoon five spice powder*
To garnish:
1 carrot, thinly sliced into rounds
shredded scallion

METHOD

Squeeze the mushrooms dry, then discard the stalks.

Put the pork in a large pan of cold water. Bring to the boil, boil for a few minutes, then drain. Rinse the pork under cold running water, then drain again.

Return the pork to the cleaned pan. Add the mushrooms, garlic, soy sauce, sherry, sugar and five spice powder. Cover with a tight-fitting lid and bring to the boil.

Lower the heat and simmer gently for 2 to 3 hours, turning the pork several times during cooking. There should be very little liquid left at the end of the cooking time; if necessary, increase the heat and simmer, uncovered, until the liquid has reduced and thickened.

Serve the pork hot or cold, garnished with carrot slices and shredded spring onion (scallion).

Steamed Spareribs in Black Bean Sauce
Chizhi Zheng Paigu

METRIC/IMPERIAL

450 g/1 lb pork spareribs, chopped into small pieces
1 garlic clove, peeled and crushed
1 slice of fresh root ginger,* peeled and finely chopped
1 tablespoon vegetable oil
Sauce:
2 tablespoons black bean sauce*
1 tablespoon soy sauce
1 teaspoon sugar
1 teaspoon medium or dry sherry
1 teaspoon cornflour
To garnish:
1 small green or red pepper, cored, seeded and shredded
1 teaspoon sesame seed oil* (optional)

AMERICAN

1 lb pork spareribs, chopped into small pieces
1 garlic clove, peeled and crushed
1 slice of fresh ginger root,* peeled and finely chopped
1 tablespoon vegetable oil
Sauce:
2 tablespoons salted black beans*
1 tablespoon soy sauce
1 teaspoon sugar
1 teaspoon medium or pale dry sherry
1 teaspoon cornstarch
To garnish:
1 small green or red pepper, cored, seeded and shredded
1 teaspoon sesame seed oil* (optional)

METHOD

Put the spareribs in a bowl with the garlic, ginger and sauce ingredients. Mix well, then leave to marinate for about 20 minutes.

Brush a heatproof plate with the vegetable oil, then put the sparerib mixture on the plate. Place in a steamer, or over a pan of boiling water and cover with a lid. Steam over high heat for 30 minutes. Sprinkle with the green or red pepper and sesame seed oil, if using. Serve hot.

Braised Meatballs
Hongshao Rouwan

METRIC/IMPERIAL

3 Chinese dried mushrooms,* soaked
   in warm water for 30 minutes
225 g/8 oz boned pork, finely
   minced
1 egg white
2 tablespoons soy sauce
1 tablespoon medium or dry sherry
1 teaspoon sugar
1 tablespoon cornflour
3 tablespoons vegetable oil
1 slice of fresh root ginger,* peeled
   and finely chopped
2 spring onions, white part only, finely
   chopped
225 g/8 oz Chinese cabbage,
   shredded
1 teaspoon salt
450 ml/¾ pint chicken stock
   (approximately)
50 g/2 oz transparent noodles,* soaked
   in water for 10 minutes and drained

AMERICAN

3 Chinese dried mushrooms,* soaked
   in warm water for 30 minutes
1 cup ground pork
1 egg white
2 tablespoons soy sauce
1 tablespoon medium or pale dry
   sherry
1 teaspoon sugar
1 tablespoon cornstarch
3 tablespoons vegetable oil
1 slice of fresh ginger root,* peeled
   and finely chopped
2 scallions, white part only, finely
   chopped
½ lb bok choy, shredded
1 teaspoon salt
2 cups chicken stock (approximately)
2 oz cellophane noodles, soaked in
   water for 10 minutes and drained

METHOD

Squeeze the mushrooms dry, then discard the hard stalks.

Mix the pork with the egg white, soy
sauce, sherry, sugar and cornflour
(cornstarch). Form the mixture into about
8 meatballs.

Heat the oil in a pan, add the meatballs
and fry until golden. Remove from the
pan with a slotted spoon. Add the ginger
and spring onions (scallions) to the pan,
then stir in the cabbage (bok choy),
mushrooms and salt. Return the meatballs to the pan and pour in just enough
stock to cover. Bring to the boil, then
lower the heat and simmer for 25
minutes.

Stir in the noodles and simmer for
about 3 minutes. Serve hot.

Stir-Fried Pork
with Bamboo Shoot
Dongsun Chao Rousi

METRIC/IMPERIAL

225 g/8 oz boned lean pork, thinly
   sliced
1 teaspoon dry sherry
2 tablespoons soy sauce
3 tablespoons vegetable oil
1 garlic clove, peeled and chopped
275 g/10 oz bamboo shoot, thinly sliced
2 teaspoons vinegar
shredded spring onion and tomato to
   garnish

AMERICAN

1 cup thinly sliced pork loin
1 teaspoon pale dry sherry
2 tablespoons soy sauce
3 tablespoons vegetable oil
1 garlic clove, peeled and chopped
2½ cups thinly sliced bamboo shoot
2 teaspoons vinegar
shredded scallion and tomato to
   garnish

METHOD

Put the pork in a bowl with the sherry and
½ tablespoon of the soy sauce. Mix well,
then leave to marinate for about 20
minutes.

Heat the oil in a wok or frying pan
(skillet), add the garlic and fry until
golden brown. Remove from the pan
with a slotted spoon and discard.

Add the pork to the pan and stir-fry
until it changes colour. Add the bamboo
shoot, the remaining soy sauce and the
vinegar. Stir-fry for about 30 seconds.
Serve hot, garnished with shredded
spring onion (scallion) and tomato.

**Red-Cooked Pork Leg; Stir-Fried Pork
with Bamboo Shoot**

Mu-Hsu Pork; 'Ants Cimbing Trees'

'Ants Climbing Trees'

Mayi Shangshu

This strangely named dish is quite simply minced (ground) pork with transparent (cellophane) noodles.

METRIC/IMPERIAL

225 g/8 oz boned pork, minced
2 tablespoons soy sauce
1 tablespoon sugar
1 teaspoon cornflour
½ teaspoon chilli sauce
3 tablespoons vegetable oil
1 small red chilli, chopped
2 spring onions, chopped
75 g/3 oz transparent noodles,* soaked
   in water for 30 minutes
120 ml/4 fl oz chicken stock or water
shredded spring onion to garnish

AMERICAN

1 cup ground pork
2 tablespoons soy sauce
1 tablespoon sugar
1 teaspoon cornstarch
½ teaspoon chili sauce
3 tablespoons vegetable oil
1 small red chili, chopped
2 scallions, chopped
3 oz cellophane noodles,* soaked in
   water for 30 minutes
½ cup chicken stock or water
shredded scallion to garnish

METHOD

Put the pork in a bowl with the soy sauce, sugar, cornflour (cornstarch) and chilli sauce. Mix well, then leave to marinate for about 20 minutes.

Heat the oil in a wok or frying pan (skillet), add the chilli and spring onions (scallions). Stir-fry for a few seconds, then add the pork. Stir-fry until the pork changes colour.

Drain the noodles, then add to the pan. Blend well, then add the stock or water and continue cooking until all the liquid has been absorbed.

Serve hot, garnished with shredded spring onion (scallion).

Mu-Hsu Pork

Chao Muxu Rou

Mu-Hsu is the Chinese for laurel, which has bright yellow fragrant flowers in autumn. This dish owes its name to the bright yellow colour of the scrambled eggs which is mixed with the pork. Traditionally, this dish is often used as a filling for *Mandarin pancakes* (see page 157).

METRIC/IMPERIAL

25 g/1 oz tiger lily,* soaked in warm
    water for 20 minutes
15 g/½ oz wood ears,* soaked in warm
    water for 20 minutes
4 eggs
salt
3 tablespoons vegetable oil
4 spring onions, shredded
225 g/8 oz pork fillet, shredded
1 tablespoon soy sauce
1 teaspoon medium or dry sherry
1 teaspoon sesame seed oil*

AMERICAN

¾ cup lily flowers,* soaked in warm
    water for 20 minutes
½ cup tree ears,* soaked in warm water
    for 20 minutes
4 eggs
salt
3 tablespoons vegetable oil
4 scallions, shredded
1 cup shredded pork loin
1 tablespoon soy sauce
1 teaspoon medium or pale dry sherry
1 teaspoon sesame seed oil*

METHOD

Drain the tiger lily (lily flowers) and wood (tree) ears, discard any hard bits and shred finely.

Beat the eggs with a little salt. Heat 1 tablespoon of the oil in a wok or frying pan (skillet). Add the eggs and scramble lightly, removing them from the pan before they set too hard.

Heat the remaining oil in the same pan. Add the spring onions (scallions) and pork and stir-fry until the pork changes colour. Add the tiger lily (lily flowers) and wood (tree) ears, 1 teaspoon salt, the soy sauce and sherry. Stir-fry for about 2 minutes, then add the scrambled eggs and sesame seed oil. Mix all the ingredients well together. Serve hot.

Pork Cooked in Barbecue Sauce

Cha Shao

METRIC/IMPERIAL

675 g/1½ lb pork fillet, cut into thick
    strips
2 tablespoons medium or dry sherry
3 tablespoons sugar
2 tablespoons soy sauce
½ teaspoon five spice powder*
1 teaspoon salt
3 tablespoons vegetable oil
2 spring onions, finely chopped
1 slice of fresh root ginger,* peeled
    and finely chopped
1 garlic clove, peeled and finely
    chopped

AMERICAN

1½ lb pork loin, cut into thick strips
2 tablespoons medium or pale dry
    sherry
3 tablespoons sugar
2 tablespoons soy sauce
½ teaspoon five spice powder*
1 teaspoon salt
3 tablespoons vegetable oil
2 scallions, finely chopped
1 slice of fresh ginger root,* peeled
    and finely chopped
1 garlic clove, peeled and finely
    chopped

METHOD

Put the pork in a bowl with the sherry, sugar, soy sauce, five spice powder and salt. Mix well, then leave to marinate for at least 2 hours, turning the pork occasionally.

Heat the oil in a wok or frying pan (skillet). Add the spring onions (scallions), ginger and garlic and stir-fry for a few seconds.

Drain the pork, reserving the marinade, then add to the pan and fry until brown. Remove the pork and vegetables from the pan, pour off the excess oil, then add the reserved marinade and heat through. Return the pork and vegetables to the pan and cook gently until almost all the juice has been absorbed.

Leave to cool, then cut the pork into thin slices. Serve cold.

Aubergines (Eggplant) and Pork in Hot Sauce

Yuxiang Qiezi

METRIC/IMPERIAL

175 g/6 oz boned lean pork, shredded
2 spring onions, finely·chopped
1 slice of fresh root ginger,* peeled
  and finely chopped
1 garlic clove, peeled and finely
  chopped
1 tablespoon soy sauce
1 teaspoon medium or dry sherry
1½ teaspoons cornflour
600 ml/1 pint vegetable oil for deep-
  frying
225 g/8 oz aubergine, cut into
  diamond-shaped chunks
1 tablespoon chilli sauce
3–4 tablespoons chicken stock or water
chopped spring onion to garnish

AMERICAN

¾ cup shredded pork loin
2 scallions, finely chopped
1 slice of fresh ginger root,* peeled
  and finely chopped
1 garlic clove, peeled and finely
  chopped
1 tablespoon soy sauce
1 teaspoon medium or pale dry sherry
1½ teaspoons cornstarch
2½ cups vegetable oil for deep-frying
½ lb eggplant, cut into diamond-
  shaped chunks
1 tablespoon chili sauce
3–4 tablespoons chicken stock or water
chopped scallion to garnish

METHOD

Put the pork in a bowl with the spring onions (scallions), ginger, garlic, soy sauce, sherry and cornflour (cornstarch). Mix well, then leave to marinate for about 20 minutes.

Heat the oil in a wok or deep-fat fryer to 180°C/350°F. Lower the heat, add the aubergine (eggplant) and deep-fry for about 1½ minutes. Remove from the pan with a slotted spoon and drain.

Pour off all but 1 tablespoon oil from the pan, then add the pork and stir-fry for about 1 minute. Add the aubergine (egg-plant) and chilli sauce and cook for about 1½ minutes, then moisten with the stock or water. Simmer until the liquid has almost completely evaporated. Serve hot, garnished with chopped spring onion (scallion).

Braised Tripe
Lu Zhudu

This dish can either be served cold as a starter, or hot as a main course. Reserve the cooking liquid from the tripe; it will keep in the refrigerator and can be used in other dishes, such as *Braised Eggs with Pork* (see page 158).

METRIC/IMPERIAL

1 kg/2 lb tripe
salt
2 tablespoons vegetable oil
2 slices of fresh root ginger,* peeled
2 spring onions
1 teaspoon five spice powder*
2 tablespoons medium or dry sherry
4 tablespoons soy sauce
1 teaspoon sugar
1 litre/1¾ pints chicken stock or water
To finish:
1 teaspoon sesame seed oil*
chopped coriander leaves*

AMERICAN

2 lb tripe
salt
2 tablespoons vegetable oil
2 slices of fresh ginger root,* peeled
2 scallions
1 teaspoon five spice powder*
2 tablespoons medium or pale dry sherry
¼ cup soy sauce
1 teaspoon sugar
4¼ cups chicken stock or water
To finish:
1 teaspoon sesame seed oil*
chopped coriander leaves*

METHOD

Wash the tripe thoroughly. Rub all over with salt, then rinse well. Put the tripe in a pan of boiling water. Lower the heat, cover and simmer for 20 minutes. Drain thoroughly.

Heat the vegetable oil in a heavy pan, add the tripe and brown lightly. Add the remaining ingredients and bring to the boil. Lower the heat, cover with a tight-fitting lid, then simmer gently for 2 hours.

Remove the tripe from the cooking liquid and cut into small slices. Arrange on a serving dish and sprinkle with the sesame seed oil. Serve hot or cold, garnished with chopped coriander.

Stir-Fried Liver with Spinach
Bocai Chao Zhugan

Avoid overcooking the liver or it will be tough.

METRIC/IMPERIAL

350 g/12 oz pig's liver, cut into thin triangular slices
2 tablespoons cornflour
4 tablespoons vegetable oil
450 g/1 lb fresh spinach leaves, rinsed and drained thoroughly
1 teaspoon salt
2 slices of fresh root ginger,* peeled
1 tablespoon soy sauce
1 tablespoon medium or dry sherry
shredded spring onion to garnish

AMERICAN

¾ lb pork liver, cut into thin triangular slices
2 tablespoons cornstarch
¼ cup vegetable oil
1 lb fresh spinach leaves, rinsed and drained thoroughly
1 teaspoon salt
2 slices of fresh ginger root,* peeled
1 tablespoon soy sauce
1 tablespoon medium or pale dry sherry
shredded scallion to garnish

METHOD

Blanch the liver for a few seconds in boiling water, then drain and coat the slices with the cornflour (cornstarch).

Heat 2 tablespoons of the oil in a wok or frying pan (skillet). Add the spinach and salt and stir-fry for 2 minutes. Remove from the pan, then arrange around the edge of a warmed serving dish and keep hot.

Heat the remaining oil in the pan until it reaches smoking point. Add the ginger, liver, soy sauce and sherry. Stir well, then pour over the spinach.

Serve immediately, garnished with shredded spring onion (scallion).

Aubergines (Eggplant) and Pork in Hot Sauce; Stir-Fried Liver with Spinach

Mange-Tout (Snow Peas) and Beef

Xuedo Niurou

METRIC/IMPERIAL

225 g/8 oz beef steak, thinly sliced
2 tablespoons oyster sauce*
1 tablespoon medium or dry sherry
1 teaspoon cornflour
4 tablespoons vegetable oil
2 spring onions, cut into 2.5 cm/1 inch
　lengths
1 slice of fresh root ginger,* peeled
　and cut into strips
225 g/8 oz mange-tout, topped and
　tailed
1 tablespoon salt
1 teaspoon sugar

AMERICAN

1 cup thinly sliced flank or round steak
2 tablespoons oyster sauce*
1 tablespoon medium or pale dry
　sherry
1 teaspoon cornstarch
¼ cup vegetable oil
2 scallions, cut into 1 inch lengths
1 slice of fresh ginger root,* peeled
　and cut into strips
½ lb snow peas, topped and tailed
1 tablespoon salt
1 teaspoon sugar

METHOD

Put the beef in a bowl with the oyster sauce, sherry and cornflour (cornstarch). Mix well, then leave to marinate for about 20 minutes.

Heat half the oil in a wok or frying pan (skillet). Add the spring onions (scallions) and ginger. Stir-fry for a few seconds, then add the beef. Stir-fry until evenly browned, then transfer to the mixture to a warmed serving dish and keep hot.

Heat the remaining oil in the pan. Add the mange-tout (snow peas), salt and sugar and stir-fry for about 2 minutes. (Do not overcook, or the mange-tout (snow peas) will lose their texture and colour.)

Add the mange-tout (snow peas) to the beef and mix well. Serve hot.

Stir-Fried Beef with Broccoli

Jielan Chao Niurou

METRIC/IMPERIAL

225 g/8 oz lean beef steak, thinly sliced
2 teaspoons salt
1 teaspoon medium or dry sherry
1 tablespoon cornflour
4 tablespoons vegetable oil
225 g/8 oz broccoli, divided into small
　florets
little chicken stock or water (optional)
2 spring onions, cut into 2.5 cm/1 inch
　lengths
100 g/4 oz button mushrooms, sliced
1 tablespoon soy sauce

AMERICAN

½ lb flank or round steak, thinly sliced
2 teaspoons salt
1 teaspoon medium or pale dry sherry
1 tablespoon cornstarch
¼ cup vegetable oil
½ lb broccoli, divided into small florets
little chicken stock or water (optional)
2 scallions, cut into 1 inch lengths
1 cup button mushrooms, sliced
1 tablespoon soy sauce

METHOD

Put the steak in a bowl with ½ teaspoon salt, the sherry and cornflour (cornstarch); mix well. Leave for 20 minutes.

Heat 2 tablespoons of the oil in a wok or frying pan (skillet). Add the broccoli and remaining salt and stir-fry for a few minutes, adding a little stock or water to moisten if necessary. Remove from the pan with a slotted spoon and drain.

Heat the remaining oil in the pan. Add the spring onions (scallions) and fry for a few seconds. Add the steak and stir-fry until evenly browned. Stir in the mushrooms, soy sauce and broccoli. Serve hot.

Beef and Carrot Stew

Luopu Men Niunan

METRIC/IMPERIAL

2 tablespoons vegetable oil
1 garlic clove, peeled and crushed
1 slice of fresh root ginger,* peeled
   and chopped
1 spring onion, chopped
750 g/1½ lb stewing beef, cut into
   1 cm/½ inch squares
4 tablespoons soy sauce
1 tablespoon sugar
1 tablespoon medium or dry sherry
½ teaspoon five spice powder*
450 g/1 lb carrots, peeled

AMERICAN

2 tablespoons vegetable oil
1 garlic clove, peeled and crushed
1 slice of fresh ginger root,* peeled
   and chopped
1 scallion, chopped
1½ lb stewing beef, cut into ½ inch
   squares
¼ cup soy sauce
1 tablespoon sugar
1 tablespoon medium or dry sherry
½ teaspoon five spice powder*
1 lb carrots, peeled

METHOD

Heat the oil in a heavy pan or flameproof casserole. Add the garlic, ginger and spring onion (scallion) and fry until golden brown. Add the beef and the remaining ingredients, except the carrots. Add just enough cold water to cover. Bring to the boil, lower the heat and simmer for about 1½ hours.

   Cut the carrots diagonally into diamond shapes. Add to the beef and simmer for 30 minutes or until the beef and carrots are tender. Serve hot.

Beef and Carrot Stew; Mange-Tout
(Snow Peas) and Beef; Stir-Fried
Beef with Broccoli

Mongolian Lamb Hot Pot

Shua Yangrou

This is the famous Peking dish that ranks almost as high as Roast Duck. It is not quite as popular because the Chinese generally prefer pork, beef or poultry to lamb; this is particularly true in the South.

If the meat is sliced when half-frozen, it will be much easier to obtain the very thin slices required.

The Hot Pot – sometimes known as a Mongolian Fire Pot or Chafing Pot – is placed in the centre of the table with the other ingredients arranged around it. A fondue set can be used instead.

METRIC/IMPERIAL

1 boned shoulder, loin or leg of lamb, weighing 1.5 kg/3–3½ lb
450 g/1 lb fresh spinach leaves, cut into large pieces
1 kg/2 lb Chinese cabbage, cut into large pieces
3 cakes bean curd,* each cut into 8–10 slices
100 g/4 oz transparent noodles,* soaked in water for 10 minutes and drained

Sauces:
3 tablespoons hoi sin sauce*
3 tablespoons chilli sauce
2 tablespoons soy sauce
1 tablespoon sesame seed oil*
2 tablespoons chopped spring onions
1 tablespoon chopped fresh root ginger*
2–3 garlic cloves, peeled and finely chopped

To serve:
2.25 litres/4 pints chicken stock or water

AMERICAN

1 boned shoulder, loin or leg of lamb, weighing 3–3½ lb
1 lb fresh spinach leaves, cut into large pieces
2 lb bok choy, cut into large pieces
3 cakes bean curd,* each cut into 8–10 slices
¼ lb cellophane noodles,* soaked in water for 10 minutes and drained

Sauces:
3 tablespoons hoi sin sauce*
3 tablespoons chili sauce
2 tablespoons soy sauce
1 tablespoon sesame seed oil*
2 tablespoons chopped scallions
1 tablespoon chopped fresh ginger root*
2–3 garlic cloves, peeled and finely chopped

To serve:
5 pints chicken stock or water

METHOD

Cut the lamb into fairly large, very thin slices and arrange on a serving plate. Arrange the spinach, cabbage (bok choy), bean curd and noodles on another serving plate.

Put the hoi sin sauce and chilli sauce in separate bowls. Combine the soy sauce and sesame seed oil in a third bowl. Mix the spring onions (scallions), ginger and garlic in another bowl.

Place the meat, vegetables and sauces on the table. Stand the Hot Pot in the middle and pour in the stock or water.

When the diners are seated, bring the stock to the boil. Meanwhile, allow guests to prepare their own sauces by mixing the different ingredients together according to taste.

When the stock is boiling vigorously, each guest should pick up a piece of lamb with chopsticks and cook it in the stock until just tender; this should take no longer than 20 to 30 seconds, depending on the thickness of the meat. The meat is then dipped into a sauce before eating.

The vegetables can be cooked and eaten in the same way, adding more stock or water to the Hot Pot as necessary. When all the meat is eaten, put the remaining vegetables in the pot. Boil vigorously for a few minutes, then serve as a soup in individual bowls.

Mongolian Lamb Hot Pot

Ten-Variety Fried Rice
Shijin Chaofan

METRIC/IMPERIAL

3 Chinese dried mushrooms,* soaked in warm water for 30 minutes
225 g/8 oz long-grain rice
3 eggs
salt
3 tablespoons vegetable oil
4–5 spring onions, finely chopped
100 g/4 oz peeled prawns
50 g/2 oz cooked ham, diced
50 g/2 oz cooked chicken or pork, diced
50 g/2 oz bamboo shoot, diced
25 g/1 oz shelled peas
2 tablespoons soy sauce

AMERICAN

3 Chinese dried mushrooms,* soaked in warm water for 30 minutes
1 cup long-grain rice
3 eggs
salt
3 tablespoons vegetable oil
4–5 scallions, finely chopped
2 large shrimp, shelled
¼ cup diced cooked ham
¼ cup diced cooked chicken or pork
½ cup diced bamboo shoot
¼ cup shelled peas
2 tablespoons soy sauce

METHOD

Squeeze the mushrooms dry, discard the hard stalks, then dice the caps.

Wash the rice in cold water once only, then place in a saucepan and cover with enough cold water to come about 2.5 cm/1 inch above the surface of the rice.

Bring to the boil, then stir once with a spoon to prevent the rice sticking to the bottom of the pan during cooking. Cover with a tight-fitting lid, reduce the heat to as low as possible and cook for 15 to 20 minutes.

Meanwhile, beat the eggs with a little salt. Heat 1 tablespoon of the oil in a frying pan (skillet) over low heat. Add the eggs and cook to make an omelet. Remove from the pan and leave to cool.

Heat the remaining oil in the pan, add the spring onions (scallions), then stir in the prawns (shrimp), ham, chicken or pork, mushrooms, bamboo shoot and peas. Add the soy sauce and cooked rice. Cook, stirring, for about 1 minute. Break the omelet into pieces and fold into the rice mixture. Serve hot.

Bean Sprout·Salad
Laingban Douyar

METRIC/IMPERIAL

450 g/1 lb fresh bean sprouts
salt
2 eggs
1 tablespoon vegetable oil
100 g/4 oz cooked ham, cut into thin
  strips
Sauce:
2 tablespoons soy sauce
2 tablespoons vinegar
1 tablespoon sesame seed oil*
freshly ground black pepper
To garnish:
thinly pared strip of red pepper
parsley sprig

AMERICAN

1 lb fresh bean sprouts
salt
2 eggs
1 tablespoon vegetable oil
½ cup thinly sliced cooked ham
Sauce:
2 tablespoons soy sauce
2 tablespoons vinegar
1 tablespoon sesame seed oil*
freshly ground black pepper
To garnish:
thinly pared strip of red pepper
parsley sprig

METHOD

Wash and rinse the bean sprouts in cold water, discarding any husks that float to the surface. Cook in boiling salted water for 3 minutes. Drain, rinse in cold water, then drain again and set aside.

Beat the eggs with a little salt. Heat the oil in a frying pan (skillet) over low heat. Add the eggs and cook to make a thin omelet. Remove from the pan, leave to cool, then cut into thin strips.

Combine all the sauce ingredients together, then mix with the bean sprouts. Transfer to a serving plate and arrange the ham and omelet strips on top. Garnish with the red pepper, coiled to resemble a flower head, with the parsley in the middle. Serve cold.

Kidney-Flower Salad
Liangban Yaohua

The kidneys are scored and cut before cooking so that they will open up – hence the name kidney flowers.

METRIC/IMPERIAL

350 g/12 oz pigs' kidneys, skinned and split in half lengthways
1 medium head celery, sliced diagonally
2 slices of fresh root ginger,* peeled and finely shredded
2 spring onions, finely chopped
Sauce:
2 tablespoons soy sauce
1 tablespoon vinegar
1 tablespoon sesame seed oil*
1 teaspoon chilli sauce
½ teaspoon sugar
To garnish: (optional)
pineapple chunks
radish slices
grapes

AMERICAN

¾ lb pork kidney, skinned and split in half lengthways
1 medium bunch celery, sliced diagonally
2 slices of fresh ginger root,* peeled and finely shredded
2 scallions, finely chopped
Sauce:
2 tablespoons soy sauce
1 tablespoon vinegar
1 tablespoon sesame seed oil*
1 teaspoon chili sauce
½ teaspoon sugar
To garnish: (optional)
pineapple chunks
radish slices
grapes

METHOD

Score the surface of the kidneys in a criss-cross pattern, then cut them into pieces.

Cook the kidneys in boiling water for 2 minutes. Drain, rinse in cold water then drain again and transfer to a serving plate. Arrange the celery around the kidneys.

Combine all the sauce ingredients together, then mix with half the ginger and the spring onions (scallions). Pour the sauce over the kidneys, then leave to marinate for about 30 minutes before serving.

Top with the remaining ginger. Garnish with pineapple, radish and grapes, if liked. Serve cold.

Kidney Flower Salad; Bean Sprout Salad

Celery and Giblet Salad
Qincai Ban Zhengan

Gizzards need thorough cleaning before cooking. Make sure the dark green gall bladder is not broken when removing it from the liver or it will give a sharp, bitter taste to the salad.

METRIC/IMPERIAL

giblets (gizzard and liver) from 2 chickens, cut into small pieces
1 teaspoon dry or medium sherry
½ teaspoon salt
½ teaspoon cornflour
25 g/1 oz wood ears,* soaked in warm water for 20 minutes
1 slice of fresh root ginger,* peeled and finely shredded
1 small head celery, sliced diagonally
Sauce:
2 tablespoons soy sauce
2 tablespoons vinegar
1 tablespoon sesame seed oil*
freshly ground black pepper

AMERICAN

giblets (gizzard and liver) from 2 chickens, cut into small pieces
1 teaspoon pale dry or medium sherry
½ teaspoon salt
½ teaspoon cornstarch
1 cup tree ears,* soaked in warm water for 20 minutes
1 slice of fresh ginger root,* peeled and finely shredded
1 small bunch celery, sliced diagonally
Sauce:
2 tablespoons soy sauce
2 tablespoons vinegar
1 tablespoon sesame seed oil*
freshly ground black pepper

METHOD

Put the giblets in a bowl and sprinkle with the sherry, salt and cornflour (cornstarch). Mix well, then leave to marinate for 30 minutes.

Drain the wood (tree) ears, discard the hard parts and cook in boiling water for 1 minute. Drain, rinse under cold running water and drain again.

Cook the giblets in boiling water for 2 minutes, then drain. Combine all the sauce ingredients together and mix with half the ginger.

Arrange the giblets, celery and wood (tree) ears on a serving plate and pour over the sauce. Garnish with the remaining ginger. Serve cold.

Ten-Variety Fried Noodles (Chow Mein)
Shijin Chaomian

METRIC/IMPERIAL

175 g/6 oz boned lean pork, shredded
1 tablespoon soy sauce
1 teaspoon sugar
2 teaspoons cornflour
350 g/12 oz egg noodles
2 eggs
salt
4 tablespoons vegetable oil
2 spring onions, cut into 2.5 cm/1 inch lengths
100 g/4 oz bamboo shoot, shredded
100 g/4 oz fresh spinach leaves or other green vegetable, shredded
100 g/4 oz peeled prawns
little chicken stock or water (optional)

AMERICAN

¾ cup shredded pork loin
1 tablespoon soy sauce
1 teaspoon sugar
2 teaspoons cornstarch
¾ lb egg noodles
2 eggs
salt
¼ cup vegetable oil
2 scallions, cut into 1 inch lengths
1 cup shredded bamboo shoot
1½ cups shredded fresh spinach leaves or other green vegetable
2 large shrimp, shelled
little chicken stock or water (optional)

METHOD

Put the pork in a bowl with the soy sauce, sugar and cornflour (cornstarch). Mix well, then leave to marinate for about 20 minutes.

Cook the noodles in boiling water for about 5 minutes, drain and rinse under cold running water, then drain again.

Beat the eggs with a little salt. Heat a little of the oil in a frying pan (skillet) over low heat. Add the eggs and cook to make a thin omelet. Remove from the pan and cut into thin strips.

Heat a little more oil in the pan, add the pork and stir-fry until it changes colour. Remove from the pan with a slotted spoon and drain.

Heat the remaining oil in the pan. Add the spring onions (scallions), then the bamboo shoot, spinach and a little salt. Stir, then add the prawns (shrimp) and return the pork to the pan with the egg strips.

Mix the ingredients thoroughly, adding a little chicken stock or water to moisten if necessary. Stir in the noodles, heat through and stir-fry until there is no liquid remaining in the pan. Serve hot.

Non-Stick Three Ways

San Buzhan

This dessert is so called because it should not stick to the pan, nor the chopsticks, nor the teeth!

METRIC/IMPERIAL

5 egg yolks
175 g/6 oz sugar
2 tablespoons cornflour
150 ml/¼ pint water
5 tablespoons vegetable oil or 65 g/
  2½ oz lard

AMERICAN

5 egg yolks
¾ cup sugar
2 tablespoons cornstarch
⅔ cup water
5 tablespoons vegetable oil or lard

METHOD

Put the egg yolks in a bowl, add the sugar, cornflour (cornstarch) and water and mix well.

  Heat the oil or lard in a frying pan (skillet) until it reaches smoking point. Pour about half into a cup and reserve. Add the egg mixture to the pan, tilting the pan in order to hold the mixture together. Stir continuously for 2 minutes, adding the reserved oil or lard little by little around the edges. Cook until golden. Serve immediately.

Steamed Dumplings with Sweet Filling

Sweet Bean Paste Pancakes (Crêpes)

Dousha Shao Bing

Sweet red bean paste – also called sweet soy bean paste – is a thick bean paste sold in cans in Chinese foodstores. It is often used as a base for sweet sauces.

METRIC/IMPERIAL

100 g/4 oz plain flour
1 egg, beaten
150 ml/¼ pint water
6–8 tablespoons sweet red bean paste
  or finely chopped dates
vegetable oil for deep-frying

AMERICAN

1 cup all-purpose flour
1 egg, beaten
⅔ cup water
6–8 tablespoons sweet red bean paste
  or ground dates
vegetable oil for deep-frying

METHOD

Put the flour into a large bowl, make a well in the centre and add the egg. Add the water gradually, beating constantly, to make a smooth batter.

  Lightly oil an 18 cm/7 inch frying pan (skillet) and place over moderate heat. When the pan is very hot, pour in just enough batter to cover the bottom thinly, tilting the pan to spread it evenly. Cook for 30 seconds or until the underside is just firm, then carefully remove from the pan. Repeat with the remaining batter.

  Divide the sweet red bean paste or dates equally between the pancakes (crêpes), placing it in the centre of the uncooked side of each one. Fold the bottom edge over the filling, then fold the sides towards the centre, to form an envelope. Brush the edge of the top flap with a little water, fold down and press the edges together firmly to seal.

  Heat the oil in a deep-fat fryer and fry the pancakes (crêpes) for 1 minute or until crisp and golden. Remove and drain on kitchen paper towels.

  Cut each pancake (crêpe) into 6 or 8 slices. Serve hot, with Chinese tea.

Steamed Dumplings with Sweet Filling
Dousha Bao

If liked, you can make these dumplings with a cooked savoury filling, such as finely chopped pork and mushrooms.

METRIC/IMPERIAL

Pastry:
1½ tablespoons dried yeast
2½ teaspoons sugar
3 tablespoons lukewarm water
450 g/1 lb plain flour
300 ml/½ pint lukewarm milk
Filling:
1 × 225 g/8 oz can sweetened chestnut purée, or yellow bean sauce*

AMERICAN

Pastry:
1½ tablespoons active dry yeast
2½ teaspoons sugar
3 tablespoons lukewarm water
4 cups all-purpose flour
1¼ cups lukewarm milk
Filling:
1 × ½ lb can chestnut purée, or bean sauce*

METHOD

To make the pastry: Dissolve the yeast and sugar in the water. Sift the flour into a large bowl, then gradually stir in the yeast mixture and the milk. Mix to a firm dough.

Turn the dough out onto a lightly floured surface and knead well for at least 5 minutes. Transfer to a bowl, cover with a damp cloth and leave in a warm place for 1½ to 2 hours or until doubled in bulk.

To make the dumplings: Knead the dough on a lightly floured surface for about 5 minutes, then roll into a long 'sausage' about 5 cm/2 inches in diameter. Slice the 'sausage' with a sharp knife into 2.5 cm/1 inch rounds. Flatten each round with the palm of the hand, then roll out until 10 cm/4 inches in diameter.

Place 1 teaspoon chestnut purée or bean sauce in the centre of each round, then gather up the dough around the filling to meet at the top. Twist the top of the dough to enclose the filling tightly. Leave to rest for at least 20 minutes.

Place the dumplings on a damp cloth in the bottom of a steamer, leaving 2.5 cm/1 inch space between each one. Steam for 15 to 20 minutes. Serve hot.
MAKES ABOUT 24 DUMPLINGS

Plum-Blossom and Snow Competing for Spring
Meixue Zhengchun

METRIC/IMPERIAL

2 dessert apples
2 bananas
juice of ½ lemon
2 eggs, separated
100 g/4 oz sugar
3 tablespoons milk
3 tablespoons water
3 tablespoons cornflour

AMERICAN

2 dessert apples
2 bananas
juice of ½ lemon
2 eggs, separated
½ cup sugar
3 tablespoons milk
3 tablespoons water
3 tablespoons cornstarch

METHOD

Peel and core the apples and slice thinly. Peel the bananas and slice thinly. Arrange the apple and banana slices in alternate layers on an ovenproof dish, sprinkling each layer with lemon juice.

Put the egg yolks in a pan with the sugar, milk, water and cornflour (cornstarch). Heat very gently, stirring, until smooth, then pour over the fruit.

Beat the egg whites until stiff, then spoon over the top. Bake in a preheated hot oven (220°C/425°F, Gas Mark 7) for about 5 minutes until the top is crisp and golden. Serve hot or cold.

Japan

Kay Shimizu

Under the cherry-trees,
On soup, and fish-salad and all,
Flower petals.
                    Basho

This Japanese *haiku* (poem) is most appropriate as an introduction to Japanese cuisine. Even in poetry, food is given dignity and beauty.

Japan is a country with a very small area, but because of its length it encompasses a wide range of climatic conditions and geographic differences. There is an endless assortment of foods, but this does not mean that the food is so plentiful that it is inexpensive!

For centuries, Japan was a closed port and was not subject to foreign influence until quite recently, which is most probably why this country developed such a unique, elegant style of cooking. Despite the proximity to China and the use of many similar ingredients, the Japanese approach to cooking, and the flavours, are entirely different from the Chinese.

Japanese cuisine is exquisite, aesthetic and sophisticated. Visual feasting is part of the traditional Japanese meal – you feed your eyes as well as your stomach. Japanese food is made pleasing by the artistic way in which the food is arranged and garnished on beautiful ceramic plates or bowls. The Japanese have a strong sensitivity and awareness for natural colour, symmetry and general appearance of each prepared food. Indeed, there is probably no other cuisine in the world which practises 'culinary art' to the same extent as the Japanese. Hand-crafted serving dishes and bowls, often specially created by a potter, are carefully selected for each food. The Japanese have a talent of arranging the food and garnish to display contrast of colour, shapes and textures. Seasonal fresh flowers and leaves are a common garnish.

Each food is prepared separately and thus, even when served together, the individual flavours and colourings are retained. Seasonings are delicate and fragrant. The Japanese have a great reverence for food; they appreciate Nature for her ability to produce such a fabulous array of edibles according to season. Japan is probably one of the few countries in the world where people will pay any price to savour the very 'first' sweet strawberry, fragrant *matsutake* (pine mushroom) or juicy melon of the season. These are often packed individually in special boxes, with elaborate cushioning, and sold as gifts. A great deal of time and effort goes into producing these gourmet delights.

Certain holidays are celebrated in grand style: New Year is probably the most important. Food is prepared and placed in beautiful tiered, lacquered boxes. Friends, relatives and neighbours come to greet each other and food and drink are served. A rice patty made from glutinous (sweet) rice* is dropped into *ozoni* (a special New Year's soup). So sacred is this holiday that the 'o' is put before the word '*zoni*' to

for only the freshest marine life; in hand massaging their cattle and feeding them beer to produce the world's most expensive and beautifully marbled tender beef. The average housewife makes a daily trip to the market to buy the choicest fresh foods for her table, even if she has a refrigerator. Menus are kept fairly simple with an entrée, a few side dishes, pickles, soup and always rice and green tea.

The traditional Japanese meal is served on a low table with the diners sitting on cushions placed on the *tatami* (straw mat) floor. In the entrance of every home, shoes are removed and slippers put on, so dining at floor level is a very clean custom. In many homes, however, meals are now served at normal table height and chairs are used.

There are no matching place settings in Japan; after a traditional dinner there is a mountain of little dishes and plates to be cleared. Knives are not used for eating; the food is cut into small pieces during preparation and eaten with chopsticks, unless it is something like a whole fish which can be separated easily with chopsticks when cooked.

Japanese cooking is relatively simple. Most dishes are cooked in advance and served at room temperature, since sometimes there are only two burners on the gas stove. In the past, few Japanese kitchens had ovens, but, in recent years, portable ones have become available. In fact, Japan was the first country to introduce microwave ovens for domestic use.

Medium-grain rice is served at all meals. So valued is this 'staff of life' grain, that the Japanese have an old saying, '*Tsukiyo ni kome no meshi*'. Translated, this is 'Moonlight and boiled rice' – one never tires of eating even a simple meal of boiled rice by moonlight. When you have become acquainted with the delights of Japanese cuisine you will appreciate the full meaning of this ancient proverb. Plain boiled rice does have a special satisfying flavour, and is delicious by itself.

Be sure to use *shoyu* (Japanese light soy sauce)* in these recipes; to use Chinese soy sauce instead would ruin the flavour of the dish. The same applies to *miso* (Japanese soy bean paste),* which is entirely different from Chinese soy bean paste.*

Sake (rice wine)* is the traditional accompaniment to Japanese food. It is served warm and enjoyed throughout the meal. Green tea is a national 'habit'; it is served frequently during the day and at meal times in fragile ceramic tea cups without handles. Green tea has a very delicate flavour, and is therefore most suited to Japanese cuisine.

This chapter provides a selection of the more popular Japanese recipes; essentially they are simple, light, delicious and beautifully presented – truly representative of an exquisite cuisine.

specify the honorific form of the word. *Osechi ryori* is a carefully planned combination of foods for the New Year feast. During this period, of almost one week's celebrating, the shops are closed and virtually all of Japan is at a standstill.

Children's Day in May (formerly Boy's Day) is celebrated with fragrant cherry leaves wrapped around special rice cakes. The Japanese still observe these ancient traditions, despite the influences of the Western world in recent years.

The Japanese take extreme care and pride in growing the best fruit and vegetables; in fishing

Harusame Soup
Spring Rain Soup

This light soup has a wonderful aroma and a chewy texture. It can be prepared at the table if wished, in which case each guest has a bowl of stock and adds ingredients to taste.

METRIC/IMPERIAL

100 g/4 oz dehydrated mung bean threads* or harusame,* soaked in boiling water for 30 minutes
2–3 shiitake,* soaked in boiling water for 20 minutes
1 litre/1¾ pints dashi (see opposite) or chicken stock
pinch of monosodium glutamate* (optional)
1 tablespoon sake*
salt
100 g/4 oz peeled prawns
6–8 mange tout
1 gobo*, par-boiled (optional)
4–6 spring onions
2 carrots
few cucumber strips
100 g/4 oz napa*
few spinach leaves

To garnish:
1 teaspoon grated fresh root ginger*
1 spring onion, finely shredded
2 teaspoons puréed daikon*

AMERICAN

1 cup dehydrated mung bean threads* or harusame,* soaked in boiling water for 30 minutes
2–3 shiitake,* soaked in boiling water for 20 minutes
4 cups dashi (see opposite) or chicken stock
pinch of msg* (optional)
1 tablespoon sake*
salt
⅔ cup shelled shrimp
6–8 snow peas
1 gobo*, par-boiled (optional)
4–6 scallions
2 carrots
few cucumber strips
¼ lb napa*
few spinach leaves

To garnish:
1 teaspoon grated fresh ginger root*
1 scallion, finely shredded
2 teaspoons grated daikon*

METHOD

Drain the mung bean threads and cut into 5 cm/2 inch lengths. Drain the mushrooms, reserving the liquid, and discard the stems.

Put the stock in a pan. Carefully pour in the reserved mushroom liquid, leaving any sandy sediment at the bottom – this should be discarded. Bring to the boil, then lower the heat and simmer for about 2 minutes. Add the monosodium glutamate (msg) if using, the sake and salt to taste.

Divide the stock between 4 warmed individual soup bowls. Arrange the other ingredients attractively on a serving dish, cutting the vegetables to make interesting shapes, if liked. Place the garnish ingredients on separate dishes. Serve immediately.
SERVES 4

Miso Shiru
Bean Soup

This is a traditional thick bean soup which can be served at any meal. Years ago it was the basic hot soup that was served for breakfast as a mainstay, but nowadays more and more people are turning to the Western-style breakfast and giving up the Japanese-style meal. Made with soya beans, this soup is very nutritious, especially when served with rice. For a stronger flavour, substitute akamiso* for the shiromiso* and adjust the quantity according to taste.

METRIC/IMPERIAL

225 g/8 oz shiromiso*
1.2 litres/2 pints dashi (see page 179)
1 block tofu,* cut into bite-sized pieces
pinch of monosodium glutamate* (optional)
finely shredded spring onion, green part only, to garnish

AMERICAN

½ cup shiromiso*
5 cups dashi (see page 179)
1 block tofu,* cut into bite-sized pieces
pinch of msg* (optional)
finely shredded scallion, green part only, to garnish

METHOD

Put the shiromiso and dashi in a pan and heat gently until dissolved, stirring constantly. Bring to the boil, add the tofu and heat through, then stir in the monosodium glutamate (msg) if using.

Pour into warmed individual soup bowls and garnish with the spring onion (scallion). Serve hot.
SERVES 4

Harusame Soup (above); Miso Shiru (below)

Dashi

Japanese Basic Stock

Dashi is indispensable in Japanese cooking. Chicken stock or broth occasionally makes a suitable substitute, but to cook truly 'Japanese', one should always use dashi where stock or broth is called for in a recipe. Dashi is a light fish and seaweed stock. It is usually made as a 'first dashi' and generally used for the delicate flavouring of soups. The same basic ingredients are saved for making a 'second dashi', to which *katsoubushi** (dried bonito fish) and water are added. This second type of dashi is used for sauces and pan-fried dishes.

To save time, you may use one of the many excellent instant dashi powders which are available in foil packets.

METRIC/IMPERIAL

1 × 10 cm/4 inch square kombu*
1.2 litres/2 pints water
15 g/½ oz flaked katsuobushi*
1½ teaspoons salt
1 teaspoon shoyu*
pinch of monosodium glutamate*
  (optional)

AMERICAN

1 × 4 inch square kombu*
5 cups water
½ cup flaked katsuobushi*
1½ teaspoons salt
1 teaspoon shoyu*
pinch of msg* (optional)

METHOD

Rinse the kombu and wipe with a damp cloth. Put the kombu and water in a pan and bring to the boil. Remove the kombu, add the katsuobushi to the pan and remove from the heat; leave to stand for 2 minutes. Strain, then add the remaining ingredients.

MAKES 1.2 litres/2 pints/5 cups

Note: The seaweed need not be wasted; cook it with a little shoyu and sugar, then slice and serve as a 'nibble'.

179

Tempura
Assorted Fritters

Japanese deep-fried foods are noted for their delicacy, and extreme care is taken to use the lightest vegetable oils. The crisp batter is almost as thin as gauze, so the colour and texture of the ingredients show through faintly and look most attractive. Best results are obtained if all the ingredients for the batter are ice cold and the batter should be made just before using.

Fish fillets, strips of carrot, *shiitake*,* asparagus stalks, parsley and slices of yellow courgette (baking squash) can be substituted for the prawns (shrimp) and vegetables suggested here. The dipping sauce reduces the oiliness of the tempura and adds a delicate seasoning to the crispy coating.

METRIC/IMPERIAL

450 g/1 lb prawns
*1 medium sweet potato, peeled and
    sliced into 5 mm/¼ inch rounds*
*1 small aubergine, cut lengthways into
    5 mm/¼ inch slices*
8 mange tout
12 mushrooms, whole or sliced
*1 onion, peeled and thinly sliced into
    rings*
*12 French or runner beans, cut into
    5 cm/2 inch lengths*
vegetable oil for deep-frying
Tentsuyu (Dipping sauce):
450 ml/¾ pint dashi (see page 179)
*2 tablespoons shoyu**
*3 tablespoons mirin**
pinch of salt
pinch of monosodium glutamate
    (optional)*
Batter:
50 g/2 oz plain flour
50 g/2 oz cornflour
1½ teaspoons baking powder
½ teaspoon salt
*1 teaspoon monosodium glutamate
    (optional)*
1 egg, lightly beaten
200 ml/⅓ pint iced water
1 ice cube
To garnish:
*4 tablespoons puréed daikon**
*3 tablespoons grated fresh root
    ginger**

AMERICAN

1 lb shrimp
*1 medium sweet potato, peeled and
    sliced into ¼ inch rounds*
*1 small eggplant, cut lengthways into
    ¼ inch slices*
8 snow peas
12 mushrooms, whole or sliced
*1 onion, peeled and thinly sliced into
    rings*
12 string beans, cut into 2 inch lengths
vegetable oil for deep-frying
Tentsuyu (Dipping sauce):
2 cups Dashi (see page 179)
*2 tablespoons shoyu**
*3 tablespoons mirin**
pinch of salt
pinch of msg (optional)*
Batter:
½ cup flour
½ cup cornstarch
1½ teaspoons baking powder
½ teaspoon salt
1 teaspoon msg (optional)*
1 egg, lightly beaten
1 cup ice water
1 ice cube
To garnish:
*¼ cup puréed daikon**
*3 tablespoons grated fresh ginger
    root**

METHOD

Peel (shell) and devein the prawns (shrimp), leaving the last segment of the shell and tail intact. Pat the prawns (shrimp) and vegetables dry with kitchen paper towels. Arrange on a large serving dish, cover with plastic wrap and chill in the refrigerator until required.

To make the tentsuyu: Put all the ingredients in a pan and stir well to combine. Heat through, then keep hot while making the batter.

To make the batter: Put the dry ingredients in a chilled bowl and stir well. Mix together the beaten egg and water, then stir gently into the dry ingredients, taking care not to overmix. Add the ice cube.

Heat the oil in a deep-fat fryer to 180°C/350°F. Dip the prawns (shrimp) and vegetables into the batter, a piece at a time, then fry a few pieces at a time in the hot oil until light golden. Drain on kitchen paper towels, then serve immediately in a folded napkin.

Pour the hot sauce into individual bowls and arrange the garnish on individual plates. Diners should then mix together the sauce and garnish according to taste, using it as a dip for the fritters. Serve hot.
SERVES 4

Nuta Negi
Spring Onions (Scallions) with Miso

Spring onions (scallions) make a delectable cooked vegetable – not pungent and piquant-flavoured as in their raw state.

METRIC/IMPERIAL

*2 bunches of spring onions, root ends
    removed*
3 strips of wakame (optional)*
*15 fresh scallops, boiled and chopped
    into large pieces*
Sauce:
*3 tablespoons shiromiso**
3 tablespoons dashi (see page 179)
*1 tablespoon su**
1 tablespoon water
1 teaspoon dry mustard

AMERICAN

*2 bunches of scallions, root ends
    removed*
3 strips of wakame (optional)*
*15 fresh scallops, boiled and chopped
    into large pieces*
Sauce:
*3 tablespoons shiromiso**
3 tablespoons dashi (see page 179)
*1 tablespoon su**
1 tablespoon water
1 teaspoon dry mustard

METHOD

Drop the spring onions (scallions) into a pan of boiling water. Boil for 2½ minutes, then drain and squeeze out the excess moisture. Cut into 5 cm/2 inch lengths.

Soak the wakame in water to cover for 10 minutes. Drain, rinse under cold running water, then drain and cut into thin strips.

To make the sauce: Put all the ingredients in a pan and stir well. Cook for 3 minutes until quite thick, stirring constantly.

Put the spring onions (scallions), wakame and prepared scallops in a bowl, pour over the sauce, then fold gently to mix. Transfer to individual serving dishes and serve at room temperature.
SERVES 4

Shashimi

Sashimi
Sliced Raw Fish

Sashimi is a culinary miracle – raw fish without a fishy smell or taste! Always use absolutely fresh fish; check for firm flesh, clear, bright eyes if the head is still attached, and no odour.

Octopus (parboiled), squid, abalone, sea bass, bream, sea urchin, cuttlefish, red clam, striped bass, prawns and shrimps are some of the raw seafoods which can be prepared in this way; raw chicken breasts, sprinkled with lemon juice, can be treated in the same way.

METRIC/IMPERIAL

750 g/1½ lb sea bass, tuna or other
   saltwater fish, filleted
175 g/6 oz daikon,* shredded
1 carrot, shredded
4–5 spring onions, shredded
few mange tout
few cooked, unshelled giant prawns
1 tablespoon wasabi*
few lemon wedges
1 tablespoon freshly grated root
   ginger*
shoyu* to taste

AMERICAN

1½ lb sea bass, tuna or other saltwater
   fish, filleted
2 cups shredded daikon*
1 carrot, shredded
4–5 scallions, shredded
few snow peas
few cooked, unshelled king shrimp
1 tablespoon wasabi*
few lemon wedges
1 tablespoon freshly grated ginger
   root*
shoyu* to taste

METHOD

Remove any skin, blood and dark sections from the fish. Cut the flesh diagonally with a sharp knife into slices about 2.5 cm/1 inch long and 5 mm/¼ inch thick.

Arrange the shredded daikon, carrot and spring onions (scallions) in mounds on a serving platter, together with the mange tout (snow peas). Arrange the raw fish slices and cooked shrimp (prawns) on the platter.

Mix the wasabi to a thick paste with a little water. Place on the platter, with the lemon wedges and ginger.

To serve: Pour shoyu into individual bowls, then allow each diner to add wasabi and ginger to his own bowl of shoyu according to taste. The fish and vegetables are then dipped into the sauce before eating. Serve with Japanese-style medium-grain rice.
SERVES 4

Kyuri To Kani
No Sunomono

Crab and Cucumber
with Vinegar Sauce

This is an ideal dish for a buffet because it will keep well for several hours. If liked, prawns (shrimp) or abalone can be used instead of crab. Score the cucumber using a canelling knife, or fork, to give an attractive serrated edge.

METRIC/IMPERIAL

1 small cucumber, 18–20 cm/7–8 inches
   long
¼ teaspoon salt
100 g/4 oz fresh crabmeat
Sauce:
5 tablespoons su*
4 tablespoons sugar
½ teaspoon salt
pinch of monosodium glutamate*
   (optional)
To garnish:
1 tablespoon sesame seeds,* toasted
few strips of lemon rind

AMERICAN

1 small cucumber, 7–8 inches long
¼ teaspoon salt
½ cup fresh crabmeat
Sauce:
5 tablespoons su*
¼ cup sugar
½ teaspoon salt
pinch of msg* (optional)
To garnish:
1 tablespoon sesame seeds,* toasted
few strips of lemon rind

METHOD

Score the cucumber lengthwise, slice into paper-thin rounds and sprinkle with the salt. Leave for 20 minutes.

Meanwhile, to make the sauce: Put all the ingredients in a bowl and stir well.

Squeeze the cucumber slices and discard the juice. Pour the sauce over the cucumber, add the crab and toss lightly.

Transfer to individual serving bowls and garnish with the sesame seeds and lemon rind. Serve cold.
SERVES 4

Shake No Kasuzuke
Salmon with Sake Lees

When fresh salmon is plentiful, this is an excellent way to preserve some for later use. This dish makes a quick entrée and will keep for several months in the refrigerator. The flavour of *kasu** goes well with salmon, but it is strongly flavoured and should therefore be eaten in small quantities – until you acquire a taste for it, that is!

METRIC/IMPERIAL

4 fresh salmon steaks
1½ tablespoons salt
Marinade:
*450 ml/¾ pint kasu**
225 g/8 oz sugar
To serve:
1 small lettuce, shredded
½ small daikon, puréed*

AMERICAN

4 fresh salmon steaks
1½ tablespoons salt
Marinade:
*2 cups kasu**
1 cup sugar
To serve:
1 small head of lettuce, shredded
½ small daikon, puréed*

METHOD

Put the salmon in a bowl and sprinkle both sides with the salt. Cover with plastic wrap or foil and leave in the refrigerator for 4 days to allow the flesh of the salmon to become firm.

Drain the fish well, then pat dry with kitchen paper towels. Mix together the marinade ingredients and use to coat both sides of the salmon. Place in a dish, cover and keep in the refrigerator for 7 days before serving.

Remove most of the marinade from the salmon, then grill (broil) for about 7 minutes on one side only until the fish flakes easily when tested with a fork. Take care not to overcook as the marinade causes the fish to char easily.

Serve hot, with small mounds of shredded lettuce and puréed daikon.
SERVES 4

Shio Yaki
Salt Grilled (Broiled) Fish

This method of preparing protein-rich fish is surprisingly simple – the fat in the skin of the fish oozes out during cooking and the salt creates moisture so that the flesh is deliciously moist. Hot steamed rice and green tea make good accompaniments.

METRIC/IMPERIAL

1 mackerel or red snapper, weighing 750 g/1½ lb
salt
To serve:
few lemon wedges
shoyu (optional)*

AMERICAN

1 mackerel or red snapper, weighing 1½ lb
salt
To serve:
few lemon wedges
shoyu (optional)*

METHOD

Remove the scales from the fish, leaving the skin intact. Clean the fish thoroughly and remove the head if wished, then sprinkle lightly inside and out with salt. Leave to stand for about 30 minutes.

Make 3 diagonal slashes on the surface of the fish. Grill (broil) under a preheated grill (broiler) for about 5 minutes on each side, until the fish flakes easily when tested with a fork; do not overcook.

Serve hot with lemon wedges and shoyu. Hand shoyu separately, if liked.
SERVES 4

Nizakana
Braised Fish

This dish makes a quick, simple meal with plenty of flavour. Serve with rice and a green vegetable, with *shichimi** and *sansho** as condiments, if liked.

METRIC/IMPERIAL

1 tablespoon vegetable oil
1 kg/2–2¼ lb fresh salmon, cut into serving pieces
1 medium onion, peeled, halved and cut into 1 cm/½ inch thick slices
*1½ tablespoons sake**
2 tablespoons water
*4 tablespoons shoyu**
2½ tablespoons sugar
*1 teaspoon freshly grated root ginger**
pinch of monosodium glutamate (optional)*

AMERICAN

1 tablespoon vegetable oil
2 lb fresh salmon, butterfish or yellowtail, cut into serving pieces
1 medium onion, peeled, halved and cut into ½ inch thick slices
*1½ tablespoons sake**
2 tablespoons water
*¼ cup shoyu**
2½ tablespoons sugar
*1 teaspoon freshly grated ginger root**
pinch of msg (optional)*

METHOD

Place a frying pan (skillet), over moderate heat, add the oil, then the fish and onion. Mix the remaining ingredients

Shio Yaki, Shake No Kasuzuke

Chiri Nabe
Fish Stew

This dish can be prepared at the table like a fondue, if wished. Guests should eat from the pan, dipping the cooked morsels into the sauce.

METRIC/IMPERIAL

15 cm/6 inch piece of kombu*
1.75 litres/3 pints water
225 g/8 oz filleted red snapper, cod or other white fish, cut into serving pieces
1 bunch of spring onions, sliced diagonally.
4 fresh shiitake,* stems removed, or button mushrooms
1 block tofu,* cut into 2.5 cm/1 inch chunks
4 large napa* leaves, cut into 5 cm/2 inch pieces
Dipping sauce:
120 ml/4 fl oz shoyu*
175 ml/6 fl oz lemon juice
seasoning suggestions: minced spring onions, toasted sesame seeds,* freshly grated root ginger,* grated white daikon,* shichimi*

AMERICAN

6 inch piece of kombu*
7½ cups water
½ lb filleted red snapper, cod or other white fish, cut into serving pieces
1 bunch of scallions, sliced diagonally
4 fresh shiitake,* stems removed, or button mushrooms
1 block tofu,* cut into 1 inch chunks
4 large napa* leaves, cut into 2 inch pieces
Dipping sauce:
½ cup shoyu*
¾ cup lemon juice
seasoning suggestions: ground scallions, toasted sesame seeds,* freshly grated ginger root,* grated white daikon,* shichimi*

METHOD

Rinse the kombu, wipe with a damp cloth and place in a fondue pan or electric frying pan (skillet). Add the water, bring to the boil, then add the fish. Bring back to the boil and add the spring onions (scallions), mushrooms, tofu and napa. Bring back to the boil, stirring constantly. The vegetables should then be crisp and tender and the fish cooked through.

To make the dipping sauce: Mix together the shoyu and lemon juice, then add suggested seasonings according to taste. Divide between individual dishes.

Serve the fish stew hot, with the dipping sauce and steamed rice.
SERVES 4

together, then pour into the pan. Cover and simmer for about 10 minutes until the fish flakes easily when tested with a fork. Serve hot.
SERVES 4 to 6

Chawanmushi

Hot Chicken and Egg Soup

Chawanmushi can be served as a soup course or light luncheon dish. Do not overcook the custard or steam over too high a heat, or the eggs will curdle and become tough.

Special ceramic *chawanmushi* cups with lids are available, but individual heatproof bowls or custard cups may be used instead.

METRIC/IMPERIAL

½ boned chicken breast, cut into 8
   slices
2 teaspoons shoyu*
450 ml/¾ pint dashi (see page 179)
1½ teaspoons mirin*
½ teaspoon salt
pinch of monosodium glutamate*
   (optional)
3 eggs, lightly beaten
4 slices kamaboko*
4 mushrooms, sliced
25 g/1 oz bamboo shoot, sliced
4 mange tout or watercress sprigs to
   garnish

AMERICAN

½ boned chicken breast, cut into 8
   slices
2 teaspoons shoyu*
2 cups dashi (see page 179)
1½ teaspoons mirin*
½ teaspoon salt
pinch of msg* (optional)
3 eggs, lightly beaten
4 slices kamaboko*
4 mushrooms, sliced
¼ cup sliced bamboo shoot
4 snow peas or watercress sprigs to
   garnish

METHOD

Put the chicken slices in a bowl, sprinkle with half the shoyu and leave to marinate.

Meanwhile, put the dashi in a separate bowl. Add the mirin, remaining shoyu, salt, monosodium glutamate (msg) if using and the eggs. Mix well.

Divide the chicken slices equally between 4 individual bowls. Add 1 slice each of kamaboko, mushroom and bamboo shoot to each bowl. Pour the egg mixture carefully over the top and garnish with the mange tout (snow peas) or watercress.

Cover the bowls with lids or foil and place in a steamer or saucepan containing about 2.5 cm/1 inch boiling water. Cover and steam over medium heat for 12 to 15 minutes until set. Serve immediately.
SERVES 4

Mizutaki

Chicken in Broth

Literally translated, mizutaki means 'water cooking'. This dish is traditionally cooked in a pan shaped like an angel cake pan with a chimney in the centre where hot charcoals are buried to provide the heat supply for the cooking. An electric frying pan (skillet) or fondue dish can be used instead, so that guests can cook their own chicken and vegetables at the table.

Appearance plays a very important part in the art of Japanese cooking. Try to arrange the vegetables as artistically as possible on the serving dish – they should look like a beautiful picture.

Mizutaki

METRIC/IMPERIAL

8 dried shiitake,* soaked in warm
   water for 20 minutes
1 chicken, weighing 1.25 kg/2½–2¾ lb,
   boned and cut into 2.5 cm/1 inch
   chunks
1 green pepper, cored, seeded and
   cut into long strips
½ cucumber, cut into strips
few carrots, trimmed
few mange tout
1 block tofu,* cut into 2.5 cm/1 inch
   cubes (optional)
1 medium napa,* sliced into
   2.5 cm/1 inch strips
few spring onions, cut into 5 cm/2 inch
   lengths
1 litre/1¾ pints dashi (see page 179)
1 tablespoon sake*
1 small piece of kombu* (optional)
Gomatare (Sesame sauce):
1 tablespoon shiromiso*
4 tablespoons sesame seeds,* toasted
   and crushed
3 tablespoons mirin*
1 tablespoon sugar
2½ tablespoons shoyu*
120 ml/4 fl oz dashi (see page 179)
½ teaspoon salad oil

AMERICAN

8 dried shiitake,* soaked in warm
   water for 20 minutes
1 chicken, weighing 2½–2¾ lb, boned
   and cut into 1 inch chunks
1 green pepper, cored, seeded and
   cut into long strips
½ cucumber, cut into strips
few carrots, trimmed
few snow peas
1 block tofu,* cut into 1 inch cubes
   (optional)
1 medium napa,* sliced into 1 inch
   strips
few scallions, cut into 2 inch lengths
4¼ cups dashi (see page 179)
1 tablespoon sake*
1 small piece of kombu* (optional)
Gomatare (Sesame sauce):
1 tablespoon shiromiso*
¼ cup sesame seeds,* toasted and
   crushed
3 tablespoons mirin*
1 tablespoon sugar
2½ tablespoons shoyu*
½ cup dashi (see page 179)
½ teaspoon salad oil

METHOD

Drain the mushrooms, squeeze dry, then discard the stems and slice the caps into thin strips.

Arrange the chicken and vegetables artistically on a large serving plate. Mix together all the sauce ingredients and divide between individual serving bowls.

Put the dashi in a pan and stand in the centre of the table. Bring the dashi to the boil, add the sake, kombu if using, and chicken and cook for 15 minutes. Let guests help themselves to chicken and vegetables, cooking the vegetables in the bubbling broth as required. Serve the sauce as a dip.
SERVES 4

Oyako Domburi
Chicken and Eggs with Rice

The literal translation of this recipe title is 'parent (chicken) and child (egg) in a bowl'. It makes a very filling meal for lunch. Try to keep the bowl covered until serving time to retain the heat.

METRIC/IMPERIAL

250 ml/8 fl oz dashi (see page 179)
3 tablespoons shoyu*
2 tablespoons sake*
100 g/4 oz chicken breast meat, thinly
   sliced
½ medium onion, peeled and sliced
100 g/4 oz mushrooms, sliced
350 g/12 oz medium-grain rice,
   cooked, hot
5 eggs, lightly beaten
pinch of monosodium glutamate*
   (optional)
few spring onions, chopped, to garnish

AMERICAN

1 cup dashi (see page 179)
3 tablespoons shoyu*
2 tablespoons sake*
½ cup thinly sliced chicken breast meat
½ medium onion, peeled and sliced
1 cup sliced mushrooms
1½ cups medium-grain rice, cooked, hot
5 eggs, lightly beaten
pinch of msg* (optional)
few scallions, chopped, to garnish

METHOD

Put the dashi in a pan and bring to the boil. Add the shoyu, sake, chicken, onion and mushrooms and cook for about 5 minutes.

Meanwhile, divide the hot rice between 4 warmed large serving bowls, cover and set aside.

Add the eggs to the pan and stir gently. Add the monosodium glutamate (msg) if using, and cook until the eggs are half set. Pour the mixture over the hot rice in the bowls, sprinkle with the spring onions (scallions) and cover with lids.
Serve immediately.
SERVES 4

Yakitori
Grilled (Broiled) Chicken

This is one of the most popular of all Japanese grilled (broiled) dishes. A charcoal grill (broiler) imparts a flavour which is unsurpassed, but the dish can be cooked under an ordinary grill (broiler). Use bamboo skewers if possible; these should be soaked in water for about 15 minutes before using.

METRIC/IMPERIAL

1 kg/2–2¼ lb boned chicken, cut into
    chunks
1 bunch of spring onions, cut into
    5 cm/2 inch lengths
2 green peppers, cored, seeded and
    cut into 5 cm/2 inch chunks
Marinade:
175 ml/6 fl oz shoyu*
50 g/2 oz sugar
175 ml/6 fl oz sake*
pinch of monosodium glutamate*
    (optional)
To serve:
pinch of powdered sansho*

AMERICAN

2–2¼ lb boneless chicken, cut into
    chunks
1 bunch of scallions, cut into 2 inch
    lengths
2 green peppers, cored, seeded and
    cut into 2 inch chunks
Marinade:
¾ cup shoyu*
¼ cup sugar
¾ cup sake*
pinch of msg* (optional)
To serve:
pinch of powdered sansho*

METHOD

Thread the chicken, spring onions (scallions) and green peppers alternately on 4 skewers. Mix together the marinade ingredients and brush over the skewers. Leave to marinate for 30 minutes, basting occasionally.

Grill (broil) for 3 minutes, then dip the skewers in the marinade again, turn and grill (broil) for 2 minutes; do not overcook.

Serve hot with a pinch of sansho pepper.
SERVES 4

Buta Teriyaki
Pork on Skewers

Pork marinated in Teriyaki sauce has an exquisite flavour, especially if cooked over a charcoal grill (broiler). If this is not available, an ordinary grill (broiler) may be used, although the flavour will not be quite so good.

If liked, spring onions (scallions), mushroom caps and strips of green pepper can be added to the skewers, alternating with the pork. Use bamboo skewers if possible; these should be soaked in water for about 15 minutes before use.

As a variation, chicken, beef, prawns (shrimp) or fish may be used instead of pork.

METRIC/IMPERIAL

1 kg/2–2¼ lb pork fillet, thinly sliced
1 teaspoon grated fresh root ginger*
1 medium onion, peeled and finely
    chopped
½ teaspoon monosodium glutamate*
    (optional)
5 tablespoons shoyu*
4 tablespoons sugar
4 tablespoons sake*

AMERICAN

2–2¼ lb pork loin, thinly sliced
1 teaspoon grated fresh ginger root*
1 medium onion, peeled and finely
    chopped
½ teaspoon msg* (optional)
⅓ cup shoyu*
¼ cup sugar
¼ cup sake*

METHOD

Put all the ingredients in a bowl, mix well, then leave to marinate for at least 1 hour.

Thread the pork on 4 skewers, reserving the marinade. Grill (broil) for 3 minutes on each side, basting frequently with the marinade. Serve immediately.
SERVES 4

Tonkatsu
Pork Cutlets

This dish was probably introduced to the Japanese by foreign traders some centuries ago. It is very popular and most suitable for anyone trying Japanese food for the first time, since it is similar to Western dishes. It is equally good served cold, or in sandwiches.

METRIC/IMPERIAL

4–6 boned loin or chump pork chops,
    or fillet steaks
salt
freshly ground black pepper
flour for coating
2 eggs, beaten
panko* or breadcrumbs for coating
vegetable oil for deep-frying
To serve:
175 g/6 oz cabbage, finely shredded
few parsley sprigs
tonkatsu sauce* (optional)

AMERICAN

4–6 boneless loin or butterfly pork
    chops or tenderloin steaks
salt
freshly ground black pepper
flour for coating
2 eggs, beaten
panko* or breadcrumbs for coating
vegetable oil for deep-frying
To serve:
2 cups finely shredded cabbage
few parsley sprigs
tonkatsu sauce* (optional)

METHOD

Pound the pork with a mallet to flatten it slightly, then sprinkle lightly with salt and pepper. Coat with flour, dip in the egg, then coat with panko or breadcrumbs.

Heat the oil in a deep-fat fryer to 180°C/350°F. Deep-fry the pork for 10 minutes, turning down the heat a little so that the pork cooks thoroughly; turn the pork once during frying to brown both sides.

Test the pork to make sure the meat is no longer pink, then remove from the pan with a slotted spoon and drain on kitchen paper towels. Cut each piece of pork into 3 to 4 slices, then re-shape on a warmed serving dish.

Arrange the cabbage around the pork and garnish with parsley. Serve hot with tonkatsu sauce, if liked.
SERVES 4 to 6

Buta Teriyaki

Niku No Miso Yaki

Meat with Miso

Akamiso is Japanese red soybean paste. It gives meat an entirely different flavour. Served with hot steamed rice and salad, this dish makes a quick family meal.

METRIC/IMPERIAL

750 g/1½ lb beef flank steak, in one piece

Marinade:

4 tablespoons akamiso*
2 tablespoons shoyu*
1½ tablespoons sugar
1 teaspoon grated fresh root ginger*
1 spring onion, chopped
2 tablespoons vegetable oil
toasted sesame seeds* to garnish

AMERICAN

1½ lb beef flank steak, in one piece

Marinade:

¼ cup akamiso*
2 tablespoons shoyu*
1½ tablespoons sugar
1 teaspoon grated fresh ginger root*
1 scallion, chopped
2 tablespoons vegetable oil
toasted sesame seeds* to garnish

METHOD

Cut the meat lengthways through the middle, then cut into thin slices across the grain. Place the slices in a bowl with the akamiso, shoyu, sugar, ginger and spring onion (scallion). Mix well, then leave to marinate for 10 minutes.

Place a frying pan (skillet) over high heat. Add the oil, then the meat and marinade. Stir-fry for about 2 minutes. Serve hot, sprinkled with toasted sesame seeds.

SERVES 4

Teppanyaki
Mixed Grill

Teppan means 'iron', and *yaki* means 'to fry'. Any combination of meat, seafood or poultry can be used with vegetables in season for this dish. As illustrated, vegetables, such as radishes, chopped fresh spinach leaves, sliced green or red peppers, mange tout (snow peas), French (green) beans and spring onions (scallions) are all suitable. Traditionally, a heavy iron griddle is used at the table, but an electric frying pan (skillet) may be used instead.

At Japanese speciality restaurants, talented cooks bow before the diners and act out a 'show', waving sharp knives in the air while they prepare this scrumptious meal before your very eyes.

METRIC/IMPERIAL

4 sirloin or fillet steaks, or 4 boned
   chicken breasts, cut into chunks
8 cooked, unshelled prawns
2 medium courgettes, sliced into
   julienne strips
2 medium onions, peeled and finely
   sliced
225 g/8 oz fresh bean sprouts
225 g/8 oz button mushrooms
1 tablespoon vegetable oil
Ponzu (Tart sauce):
120 ml/4 fl oz shoyu*
120 ml/4 fl oz lime or lemon juice
4 tablespoons mirin*
Karashi jyoyu (Mustard sauce):
2 teaspoons dry mustard
2 teaspoons hot water
3 tablespoons shoyu*
2 tablespoons su*
1 teaspoon sesame seed oil*
pinch of monosodium glutamate*
   (optional)

AMERICAN

4 top sirloin or fillet beef steaks, or 4
   boned chicken breasts, cut into chunks
8 cooked, unshelled shrimp
2 medium zucchini, sliced into julienne
   strips
2 medium onions, peeled and finely
   sliced
4 cups fresh bean sprouts
2 cups button mushrooms
1 tablespoon vegetable oil
Ponzu (Tart sauce):
½ cup shoyu*
½ cup lime or lemon juice
¼ cup mirin*
Karashi jyoyu (Mustard sauce):
2 teaspoons dry mustard
2 teaspoons hot water
3 tablespoons shoyu*
2 tablespoons su*
1 teaspoon sesame seed oil*
pinch of msg* (optional)

METHOD

Arrange the beef or chicken, prawns (shrimp) and vegetables artistically on a large serving plate.

To make the ponzu sauce: Mix together all the ingredients and pour into individual dishes. To make the karashi jyoyu sauce: Mix the mustard and water to a paste, then add the remaining ingredients. Pour into individual dishes.

Heat a griddle or electric frying pan (skillet) at the table. Add the oil, then some of the meat and prawns (shrimp). As the meat becomes tender, add a few vegetables to the pan and cook until they are tender but still crisp.

Serve the meat, prawns (shrimp) and vegetables as they are ready, letting the guests dip them into their sauces while more teppanyaki is cooking.
SERVES 4

Sukiyaki
Meat with Vegetables

This extraordinary combination of ingredients with its tasty sauce is a delectable meal-in-one. It is especially good prepared at the table – the guests eat it little by little as it cooks, and more ingredients are added to the pan. Towards the end, as the juices blend together, the flavour is unsurpassed.

Be sure to serve Sukiyaki with hot steamed rice. Vary the vegetables, according to season and taste.

METRIC/IMPERIAL

100 g/4 oz dried shiitake,* soaked in
   warm water for 20 minutes, or button
   mushrooms
1 × 75 g/3 oz can shirataki,* or 100 g/
   4 oz mung bean threads,* soaked in
   boiling water for 30 minutes
few pieces of beef suet
1 kg/2–2¼ lb sirloin or fillet steak, thinly
   sliced
1 medium onion, peeled and sliced
   into rings
2 bunches of spring onions, cut into
   5 cm/2 inch lengths
1 carrot, thinly sliced into squares
150 g/5 oz water chestnuts* or bamboo
   shoot, sliced
few spinach and/or napa* leaves, cut
   into 3.5 cm/1½ inch slices
1 block tofu,* diced
Sauce:
120 ml/4 fl oz shoyu*
4 tablespoons sugar
120 ml/4 fl oz dashi (see page 179)
¾ teaspoon monosodium glutamate*
   (optional)
120 ml/4 fl oz mirin*
To serve:
4 eggs (optional)
shoyu,* to taste (optional)

1 cup shiitake,* soaked in warm water
   for 20 minutes, or button mushrooms
1 × 3 oz can shirataki,* or 1 cup mung
   bean threads,* soaked in boiling
   water for 30 minutes
few pieces of beef suet
2–2¼ lb top sirloin, fillet or rib eye
   beef, thinly sliced
1 medium onion, peeled and sliced
   into rings
2 bunches of scallions, cut into 2 inch
   lengths
1 carrot, thinly sliced into squares
1 cup water chestnuts* or bamboo
   shoot, sliced
few spinach and/or napa* leaves, cut
   into 1½ inch slices
1 block tofu,* diced
Sauce:
½ cup shoyu*
¼ cup sugar
½ cup dashi (see page 179)
¾ teaspoon msg* (optional)
½ cup mirin*
To serve:
4 eggs (optional)
shoyu,* to taste (optional)

METHOD

If using shiitake, drain, squeeze dry, then discard the stems and slice the caps. If using mung bean threads, drain, then cut into 5 cm/2 inch lengths.

Heat an electric frying pan (skillet) at the table. Add the suet and render some of the fat, then remove. Add half the meat and cook for a few minutes.

Mix together the sauce ingredients, then add a little sauce to the pan and mix with the meat. Push this mixture to one side of the pan, then arrange half the remaining ingredients in the other side of the pan. Pour over half the remaining sauce.

Cook over high heat for 3 to 4 minutes, turning the ingredients gently to cook both the top and bottom; do not overstir as the ingredients should still remain whole after cooking.

Push the cooked ingredients carefully to one side of the pan, then continue adding more ingredients and sauce to the pan while the guests are helping themselves to the cooked half.

If liked, provide each diner with an individual bowl into which he may crack an egg. The diner then mixes the egg with shoyu according to taste and dips morsels of hot food into this mixture; the heat of the food will cook the egg slightly.
SERVES 4 to 6

Hijiki To Aburage
Seaweed with Fried Bean Cake

Japan is surrounded by water, so it is hardly surprising that seaweeds have become one of the major foodstuffs to the Japanese. These seaweeds are high in protein, starch, sugar, fat, vitamins A, B_1, B_2, calcium, phosphorus, iron and trace elements.

METRIC/IMPERIAL

5 tablespoons dry hijiki*
2 aburage*
1 teaspoon vegetable oil
150 ml/¼ pint dashi (see page 179)
1 tablespoon mirin*
2½ teaspoons sugar
2 tablespoons shoyu*

AMERICAN

5 tablespoons dry hijiki*
2 aburage*
1 teaspoon vegetable oil
⅔ cup dashi (see page 179)
1 tablespoon mirin*
2½ teaspoons sugar
2 tablespoons shoyu*

METHOD

Pick out as much sediment as possible from the hijiki, then wash and soak in cold water for 1 hour. Drain, then rinse thoroughly under cold running water to remove the sand. Strain in a fine sieve (strainer).

Wash the aburage in boiling water to remove excess oil then cut lengthways into 5 mm/¼ inch slices.

Heat a frying pan (skillet), add the oil, then the hijiki. Fry for about 2 minutes, then add the aburage and dashi. Simmer, uncovered, for 5 minutes.

Add the remaining ingredients, stir well and cook for 7 minutes or until all the liquid has evaporated. Serve hot in warmed individual serving dishes.
SERVES 4

Above: Teppanyaki
Left: Sukiyaki

Shiitake No Amanie
Sweet Black Mushrooms

*Shiitake** is the legendary Black Forest mushroom so favoured by the Japanese and Chinese for its health-giving vitamins.

Shiitake is available in dehydrated form in speciality shops and markets and, although it is possible to buy fresh *shiitake*, it is the dehydrated form that should be used in this recipe. Chew the succulent pieces slowly to appreciate their fabulous taste!

METRIC/IMPERIAL

15 dried shiitake, with large caps,*
   soaked in warm water for 20 minutes
450 ml/¾ pint water
1½ teaspoons sugar
*1–2 tablespoons mirin**
pinch of salt
*2 teaspoons shoyu**
*pinch of monosodium glutamate**
   (optional)
shredded spring onion and carrot
   slices to garnish

AMERICAN

15 dried shiitake, with large caps,*
   soaked in warm water for 20 minutes
2 cups water
1½ teaspoons sugar
*1–2 tablespoons mirin**
pinch of salt
*2 teaspoons shoyu**
pinch of msg (optional)*
shredded scallion and carrot slices to
   garnish

METHOD

Drain the mushrooms, reserving the soaking liquid, then discard the mushroom stems. Leave the caps whole or slice each one into 5 pieces.

Pour the mushroom liquid slowly into a pan, taking care to avoid including the sandy sediment at the bottom which should be discarded. Add the mushrooms and boil for 5 minutes. Add the remaining ingredients and cook for 5 minutes. If liked, sprinkle in a little more mirin.

Remove from the heat, then leave to stand for 10 minutes. Arrange the mushrooms in an attractive pattern on a serving plate. Garnish with the spring onion (scallion) and carrot slices, placed in the centre to resemble a flower head. Serve at room temperature, as an appetizer or side dish.
SERVES 4

Kimpira
Chilli-Flavoured Burdock

This can be served as an appetizer or as an accompaniment to any meal. Burdock is considered a nuisance weed in the West, but in Japan *gobo,** the root, is used as a vegetable. It is an acquired taste, however, and you may have to try it several times before you like it. The chilli pepper gives the dish its name and zip.

METRIC/IMPERIAL

3 long gobo, skinned*
1 small carrot, peeled
1 tablespoon vegetable oil
*1 tablespoon shoyu**
1 tablespoon sugar
pinch of salt
*pinch of monosodium glutamate**
   (optional)
pinch of dried chilli pepper flakes

AMERICAN

3 long gobo, skinned*
1 small carrot, peeled
1 tablespoon vegetable oil
*1 tablespoon shoyu**
1 tablespoon sugar
pinch of salt
pinch of msg (optional)*
pinch of dried chili pepper flakes

METHOD

Cut the gobo and carrot into paper-thin 1 cm/½ inch wide strips, using a vegetable peeler. Place in a bowl of cold water until ready for use, then drain and pat dry with kitchen paper towels.

Heat a frying pan (skillet). When hot, add the oil, then the vegetables and stir-fry for about 2 minutes until tender but still crisp.

Add the remaining ingredients and stir-fry for 2 minutes. Serve hot or at room temperature.
SERVES 4

Shitake No Amanie; Shira Ae

Shimeji
Tree Oyster Mushrooms

The *shimeji** (tree oyster) mushroom has been cultivated in Japan for years as a fresh fungi 'vegetable'. It is now becoming more widely available because it can be grown easily under controlled conditions. In damp woods, one can find the wild species of *shimeji** – *Pleurotus ostreatus*; this mushroom is occasionally referred to as the 'shellfish of the forest' since it has a slight shellfish flavour.

METRIC/IMPERIAL

*225 g/8 oz fresh shimeji**
1½ teaspoons butter
1 garlic clove, peeled and crushed
*1 teaspoon sake**
3 tablespoons chicken stock
salt
freshly ground black pepper
*pinch of monosodium glutamate**
  (optional)

AMERICAN

*½ lb fresh shimeji**
1½ teaspoons butter
1 garlic clove, peeled and ground
*1 teaspoon sake**
3 tablespoons chicken stock
salt
freshly ground black pepper
pinch of msg (optional)*

METHOD

Tear the shimeji into bite-sized pieces. Melt the butter in a frying pan (skillet) over low heat. Add the garlic and stir-fry for 30 seconds, then add the shimeji and sake. Stir-fry for 1 minute, then add the remaining ingredients and cook for 2 minutes. Serve immediately, as a side dish.
SERVES 4

Shira Ae
Vegetables with Tofu Sauce

This is a most interesting tangy white dressing for cooked vegetables.

METRIC/IMPERIAL

*6 aburage**
2 pieces konnyaku, cut into*
  5 cm/2 inch strips
3 small carrots, peeled and cut into
  5 cm/2 inch strips
250 ml/8 fl oz dashi (see page 179)
*1 block tofu**
*5 tablespoons white sesame seeds,**
  toasted and crushed
*2 tablespoons shiromiso**
3 tablespoons sugar
1 teaspoon salt
*pinch of monosodium glutamate**
  (optional)
cucumber strips and carrot slice to
  garnish

AMERICAN

*6 aburage**
2 pieces konnyaku, cut into 2 inch*
  strips
3 small carrots, peeled and cut into
  2 inch strips
1 cup dashi (see page 179)
*1 block tofu**
*5 tablespoons white sesame seeds,**
  toasted and crushed
*2 tablespoons shiromiso**
3 tablespoons sugar
1 teaspoon salt
pinch of msg (optional)*
cucumber strips and carrot slice to
  garnish

METHOD

Wash the aburage in boiling water to remove the excess oil, then cut lengthways into 5 mm/¼ inch slices. Cook the konnyaku in boiling salted water for 2 minutes, then drain.

Cook the aburage, konnyaku and carrots in the dashi for about 5 minutes until the carrots are tender but still crisp and most of the dashi has evaporated. Leave to cool, then cut the vegetables into small pieces and place in a large serving bowl.

Wrap the tofu in a cloth and press down to squeeze out as much water as possible. Crush the tofu. Add the remaining ingredients, mix well, then pour the tofu dressing over the vegetables. Mix together, taking care not to crush the vegetables.

Garnish with cucumber strips and a carrot slice. Serve at room temperature, as a side dish.
SERVES 4

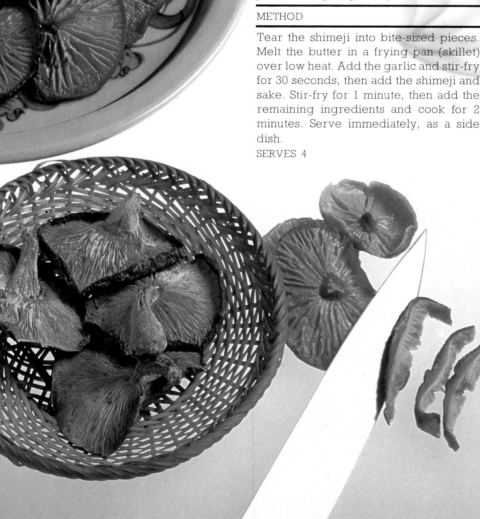

Horenso Tamago Maki

Omelet Spinach Roll

This dish presents spinach and egg together in an interesting way. The colourful green spinach encircled by the yellow of the omelet resembles a pretty flower.

METRIC/IMPERIAL

350 g/12 oz fresh spinach leaves,
washed
¾ teaspoon shoyu*
2 eggs, lightly beaten
pinch of salt
1 teaspoon sugar
little vegetable oil
shoyu* to taste

AMERICAN

¾ lb fresh spinach leaves, washed
¾ teaspoon shoyu*
2 eggs, lightly beaten
pinch of salt
1 teaspoon sugar
little vegetable oil
shoyu* to taste

METHOD

Drop the spinach into a pan of rapidly boiling water and boil for about 1½ minutes until the leaves are wilted and bright green. Drain and rinse twice in cold water.

Hold the spinach leaves, stems together, then squeeze out the water and trim off any hard stems. Sprinkle with the shoyu. Divide in half and shape into 2 long rolls.

Put the eggs, salt and sugar in a bowl and mix well (do not overbeat or the eggs will become frothy).

Heat a 20 cm/8 inch frying pan (skillet). Coat the base of the pan with oil, then add half the egg mixture, twirling the pan so that the egg mixture coats the base. Cook over moderate heat, until the egg sets and the surface is dry to the touch.

Transfer to a *sudare* (bamboo mat) or clean cloth.

Place one of the spinach rolls on the edge of the omelet. Roll up the omelet firmly, enclosing the spinach, using the mat or cloth as an outer support. Repeat with the remaining egg mixture and spinach.

Leave the rolls to rest for a few minutes, then carefully cut into 2.5 cm/1 inch slices. Arrange on a serving plate. Serve cold, with a bowl of shoyu as a dip.
SERVES 4

Nasu No Karashi

Mustard-Pickled Aubergine (Eggplant)

This spicy pickle will add spark to any dinner. It is an unusual way to blend ingredients.

METRIC/IMPERIAL

1 medium aubergine, or 6 small
Japanese elongated aubergines
750 ml/1¼ pints water
1 tablespoon salt
Dressing:
1 teaspoon dry mustard
3 tablespoons shoyu*
3 tablespoons mirin*
3 tablespoons sugar
pinch of monosodium glutamate*
(optional)

AMERICAN

1 medium eggplant, or 6 small
Japanese elongated eggplants
3 cups water
1 tablespoon salt
Dressing:
1 teaspoon dry mustard
3 tablespoons shoyu*
3 tablespoons mirin*
3 tablespoons sugar
pinch of msg* (optional)

METHOD

Cut the aubergine (eggplant) crossways into slices about 2.5 mm/⅛ inch thick, then cut the slices into quarters. Soak in the water, with the salt added, for 1 hour.

Meanwhile, make the dressing: Put all the ingredients in a bowl and stir well.

Drain the aubergine (eggplant) and pat dry with kitchen paper towels. Arrange in a glass serving bowl and pour over the dressing.

Cover with plastic wrap and chill in the refrigerator for several hours or overnight before serving, to allow the flavours to develop.
SERVES 4

Napa No Tsukemono

Cabbage Pickles

Pickles appear on every Japanese menu; they go especially well with the blandness of the rice and tea and they also help to clear the palate of lingering tastes such as fish. Many methods of preserving vegetables are used, including brine, rice bran, soya bean paste and mustard.

This recipe, using brine, is one of the simplest ways of preserving. If kept in the brine in the refrigerator, the *napa** will keep for about 1 week.

METRIC/IMPERIAL

1 large head of napa,* quartered
3 tablespoons coarse salt
4 tablespoons seedless raisins or
stoned prunes
250 ml/8 fl oz water
3 dried chillis

AMERICAN

1 large head of napa,* quartered
3 tablespoons coarse salt
¼ cup seedless raisins or pitted prunes
1 cup water
3 dried chilis

METHOD

Put the napa in a glass bowl, sprinkling the layers with the salt. Add the remaining ingredients and mix well until the salt has dissolved.

Place a saucer on top of the cabbage, put a heavy weight on top, then leave to marinate for 12 hours.

Discard the raisins or prunes and wash the cabbage quickly. Squeeze out the excess moisture, then slice the cabbage into bite-sized pieces. Serve cold.
SERVES 4 to 6
Note: For extra flavour, add a little shoyu,* monosodium glutamate (msg)* and freshly grated root ginger* mixed with a little sugar, before serving.

Horenso Tomago Maki; Nasu No Karashi (centre)

Gyoza Yaki
Fried Dumplings

METRIC/IMPERIAL

3 napa* leaves
225 g/½ lb boned lean pork, minced
2 spring onions, chopped
1 garlic clove, peeled and crushed
½ teaspoon grated fresh root ginger*
2 tablespoons shoyu*
½ teaspoon salt
1 tablespoon sesame seed oil*
½ packet round gyoza skins*
2 tablespoons vegetable oil
Dipping sauce:
2 tablespoons su*
2 tablespoons dry mustard
2 tablespoons shoyu*
pinch of monosodium glutamate*
  (optional)

AMERICAN

3 napa* leaves
1 cup lean ground pork
2 scallions, chopped
1 garlic clove, peeled and ground
½ teaspoon grated fresh ginger root*
2 tablespoons shoyu*
½ teaspoon salt
1 tablespoon sesame seed oil*
½ package round gyoza skins*
2 tablespoons vegetable oil
Dipping sauce:
2 tablespoons su*
2 tablespoons dry mustard
2 tablespoons shoyu*
pinch of msg* (optional)

METHOD

Blanch the napa quickly in boiling water, drain, then squeeze out excess moisture. Mince (grind) coarsely, then combine with the remaining ingredients, except the gyoza skins and vegetable oil.

Put 1 spoonful of the mixture on one half of a gyoza skin. Fold in half, enclosing the filling. Brush the inside edges with water and press together to seal. (For an authentic finish, pleat the top side as you seal the skin.) Repeat with the remaining filling mixture and skins.

Heat a frying pan (skillet), add the vegetable oil, then the gyoza, overlapping them slightly in a neat pattern, with the pleated sides on top. Cover and cook over moderate heat for about 5 minutes.

Add just enough hot water to cover the gyoza, then cover with a lid and cook until all the water has evaporated.

To make the dipping sauce: Combine all the ingredients together and divide between individual dishes.

Serve the gyoza hot, with the dipping sauce.

SERVES 4

Gohan
Plain Steamed Rice

The Japanese prefer medium- or short-grain rice because it cooks into a fluffy mass that clings together but is not sticky. This type of rice has an entirely different texture from long-grain rice, which has a tendency to be drier with separate grains.

In Japan, a bowl of rice is usually eaten with every meal. It is generally served plain, with the entrée and side dishes. However, there are speciality dishes using rice with various combinations of meat, fish, poultry and vegetables.

The amount of water required to cook the rice will vary according to its origin and the length of time it has been stored since the harvest; the quantity given in this recipe is therefore only an approximate guide. If you are lucky enough to have an electric rice steamer, it will produce perfect rice every time you use it! No salt is added to plain rice in the cooking stage.

METRIC/IMPERIAL

575 g/1¼ lb short- or medium-grain rice
750 ml/1¼ pints water

AMERICAN

3 cups short- or medium-grain rice
3 cups water

METHOD

Wash the rice thoroughly under cold running water, rubbing it well between the palms of the hands. Drain and repeat this process about 3 times until the rinsing water is clear. Leave to drain in a colander for about 20 minutes.

Put the rice in a heavy pan, add the water, then cover and bring quickly to the boil. Lower the heat and simmer for 20 minutes, by which time most of the water will have been absorbed; do not remove the lid at any stage. Increase the heat and cook for about 20 seconds, then remove the pan from the heat. Leave to stand for 10 minutes, without removing the lid.

Fluff up the rice with a wet rice paddle or a fork. Serve hot in individual rice bowls or on a large serving plate.

SERVES 4 to 6

Nigiri Zushi; Shushi

Sushi

Basic Vinegared Rice

The basic recipe for making all kinds of sushi is to combine medium-grain rice with a vinegared sauce, but the variations are endless. It can be made into *Nigiri Zushi* (see opposite), or *Chirashi Zushi*, a kind of rice salad in which the sushi is tossed with salad ingredients. Another variation is *Makizushi*, a rice roll covered with *nori** and filled with layers of different seasoned ingredients.

When making sushi, add a 15 cm/6 inch piece of *kombu** – if available – to the pan of rice. Cook for 3 minutes, then remove. This will impart a more traditional flavour.

METRIC/IMPERIAL

575 g/1¼ lb medium-grain rice
750 ml/1¼ pints water
Vinegar sauce:
*6 tablespoons su**
4½ tablespoons sugar
2 teaspoons salt
*1 teaspoon monosodium glutamate**
  (optional)
To garnish:
*1–2 tablespoons toasted sesame seeds**
*beni-shoga** or sansho* (optional)*

AMERICAN

3 cups medium-grain rice
3 cups water
Vinegar sauce:
*6 tablespoons su**
4½ tablespoons sugar
2 teaspoons salt
1 teaspoon msg (optional)*
To garnish:
*1–2 tablespoons toasted sesame seeds**
*beni-shoga** or sansho* (optional)*

METHOD

Wash the rice thoroughly under cold running water, rubbing it well between the palms of the hands. Drain and repeat this process about 3 times until the rinsing water is clear. Drain.

Put the rice in a heavy pan, add the water and leave to soak for 1 hour. Cover the pan and bring quickly to the boil, then reduce the heat to very low and simmer for 15 minutes; do not remove the lid at any stage.

Turn off the heat and leave the rice to steam in its own heat for 10 minutes, then remove from the heat and leave to stand for 10 minutes.

Meanwhile, make the vinegar sauce: Put the sauce ingredients in a small pan (not aluminium) and heat until the sugar has dissolved, stirring constantly. Set aside until required.

Fluff up the rice with a wet rice paddle or fork, then transfer to a large stainless steel or ceramic bowl. Pour the vinegar sauce over the hot rice. Toss lightly, lifting the rice from the bottom up with the wet rice paddle or fork to produce the desired lustre.

Serve hot, sprinkled with toasted sesame seeds and garnished with beni-shoga or sansho, if liked.
SERVES 4 to 6

Nigiri Zushi

Rice Balls with Topping

This is the Japanese snack which is prepared at the popular *sushi* bars.

The tuna or sea bass topping given here can be replaced with shrimps. These should be peeled, deveined and boiled briefly, with a toothpick inserted along the underside to prevent them curling. Cut them in half, keeping the back side intact, then place on top of the *wasabi.**

Another variation is to serve the rice ovals topped with rectangular pieces of thin omelet. These make marvellous hors d'oeuvre.

METRIC/IMPERIAL

1 tablespoon su (approximately)*
575 g/1¼ lb sushi (see left)
1 tablespoon wasabi (approximately),*
  mixed to a paste with water
30 small slices of raw fresh tuna or sea
  bass (approximately)
To serve:
few parsley sprigs
*few slices beni-shoga**
shoyu to taste*

AMERICAN

1 tablespoon su (approximately)*
3 cups sushi (see left)
1 tablespoon wasabi (approximately),*
  mixed to a paste with water
30 small slices of raw fresh tuna or sea
  bass (approximately)
To serve:
few parsley sprigs
*few slices beni-shoga**
shoyu to taste*

METHOD

Moisten the hands with a little su. Scoop up 2 tablespoons rice in one hand then, with the other hand, squeeze the rice into an egg-shaped oval, about 5 cm/2 inches long. Dab the top with wasabi paste, then cover with a slice of fish, pressing it down firmly. Repeat with the remaining rice, wasabi paste and fish, to make about 30 rice ovals.

Arrange the rice ovals on a tray and garnish with the parsley and beni-shoga. Hand shoyu separately as a dip for the fish. Serve cold with plenty of green tea.
MAKES ABOUT 30

Sekiyan; Hiyashi Somen; Tsukimi Udon

Hiyashi Somen

Chilled Noodles

This is a most unusual way to eat noodles; it is very refreshing in the summer and looks most attractive. Guests help themselves to the somen, then use individual bowls of sauce as a dip. If liked, you can top the somen with boiled fresh shrimps or seasoned *shiitake.** Grated fresh root ginger* or *wasabi** can also be served as an accompaniment.

METRIC/IMPERIAL

*450 g/1 lb somen**
Sauce:
450 ml/¾ pint dashi (see page 179)
*120 ml/4 fl oz shoyu**
*4 tablespoons sake**
1 tablespoon sugar
To garnish:
few ice cubes
few small tomatoes, quartered
few spring onions, shredded

AMERICAN

*1 lb somen**
Sauce:
2 cups dashi (see page 179)
*½ cup shoyu**
*¼ cup sake**
1 tablespoon sugar
To garnish:
few ice cubes
few cherry tomatoes, quartered
few scallions, shredded

METHOD

Cook the somen in plenty of boiling water for about 5 minutes until *al dente.* Drain, rinse thoroughly under cold running water and drain again. Place in a large shallow glass serving bowl and chill in the refrigerator.

Put the sauce ingredients in a pan and stir well. Bring to the boil, then lower the heat and simmer for 2 minutes. Leave to cool, then pour into individual glass bowls and chill in the refrigerator.

Garnish the chilled somen with ice cubes, tomatoes and spring onions (scallions). Serve the sauce separately.
SERVES 4

Tsukimi Udon
Noodles with Broth

Noodles are consumed in large quantities, and with great relish, in Japan. 'Slurping' is good etiquette and everyone eats noodles with their meals or as a snack. There are many varieties of noodle in Japan – thick and wide ones, coloured ones and ones made from buckwheat. This recipe uses the traditional thick, wide udon,* and the egg on top is like a full moon – the title literally translated means 'seeing the moon noodles'.

METRIC/IMPERIAL

*450 g/1 lb udon**
900 ml/1½ pints dashi (see page 179)
1 tablespoon sugar
1½ teaspoons salt
*1 tablespoon shoyu**
4 eggs
To garnish:
2 spring onions, thinly sliced
*13 cm/5 inch square piece of nori,**
*   toasted and finely shredded*

AMERICAN

*1 lb udon**
3¾ cups dashi (see page 179)
1 tablespoon sugar
1½ teaspoons salt
*1 tablespoon shoyu**
4 eggs
To garnish:
2 scallions, thinly sliced
5 inch square piece of nori, toasted and finely shredded*

METHOD

Add the noodles to a large pan of boiling water, stirring constantly. Bring back to the boil, then add 250 ml/8 fl oz/1 cup cold water. Bring back to the boil again, then cook the noodles for 10 to 12 minutes until *al dente*. Drain, then rinse thoroughly under cold running water and drain again.

Put the dashi, sugar, salt and shoyu in a large pan and stir well. Bring to the boil over high heat, then add the noodles. Bring back to the boil, stirring constantly, then cook until the noodles are heated through.

Pour into warmed individual bowls, then break 1 egg over each bowl. Cover the bowls with lids and the heat from the noodles will cook the eggs. Garnish with spring onions (scallions) and nori shreds. Serve hot.
SERVES 4

Sekihan

Steamed Pink Rice with Beans

This pale pink rice is a celebration dish, prepared for special occasions such as birthdays. For the rice to acquire a pink colour, preparation must be started the day before the dish is required.

METRIC/IMPERIAL

*200 g/7 oz azuki**
*750 g/1¾ lb mochigome**
goma jio, made with 1 teaspoon black sesame seeds* and 2 teaspoons salt*

AMERICAN

*¾ cup azuki**
*4 cups mochigome**
goma jio, made with 1 teaspoon black sesame seeds* and 2 teaspoons salt*

METHOD

Pick over and wash the azuki, then put them in a pan and cover with water. Bring to the boil, then drain, cover with fresh cold water and bring to the boil again. Lower the heat, cover with a lid and simmer gently for about 40 minutes, adding more water to keep the beans covered during cooking. Drain and reserve the cooking liquid.

Wash the mochigome thoroughly, drain and place in a bowl. Cover with the reserved azuki liquid and leave to stand overnight to allow the rice to acquire a pinkish colour.

Drain the rice and reserve the liquid. Mix the mochigome and azuki together, taking care not to crush the beans. Line a steamer plate, or other heatproof plate, with a piece of cheesecloth (muslin). Bring the water in the steamer to the boil, then spread the rice and bean mixture on the cloth, patting it smooth and making a few vent holes in it. Steam over high heat for about 50 minutes until the rice is cooked, basting every 12 minutes with the reserved azuki liquid.

Divide between warmed individual serving bowls and sprinkle with goma jio. Serve hot or at room temperature.
SERVES 8 to 10

Zenzai or Shiruko

Red Bean Soup with Rice Dumplings

This soup is served as a sweet snack, rather than as a dessert. The rice used in these little dumplings is glutinous rice* – sticky and satisfying – for true rice eaters!

METRIC/IMPERIAL

*225 g/8 oz azuki**
275 g/10 oz sugar
½ teaspoon salt
Dango (dumplings):
*½ package mochiko**

AMERICAN

*1 cup azuki**
1¼ cups sugar
½ teaspoon salt
Dango (dumplings):
*½ package mochiko**

METHOD

Pick over and wash the azuki, then put them in a pan with 1.5 litres/2½ pints/6¼ cups water. Bring to the boil, then lower the heat and simmer for 2 hours until the beans are soft.

Add more water to the pan to make the liquid up to 1.2 litres/2 pints/5 cups (some of the water will have evaporated during cooking). Add the sugar and salt and cook for 15 minutes, stirring occasionally.

Meanwhile, make the dumplings: Mix the mochiko with enough water to make a stiff dough. Knead well, then pinch off tiny portions to form small balls, about the size of marbles. Make a small indentation in the side of each dumpling.

Bring the azuki soup back to the boil, then drop the dumplings into the soup. Cook until the dumplings rise to the surface. Divide between warmed individual bowls. Serve hot.
SERVES 4

Kasutera

Sponge Cake

This light cake is not normally baked in Japanese kitchens – it is usually purchased from one of the many pastry shops in Japan. It was originally introduced several centuries ago by the Dutch traders who came to the port of Nagasaki. In recent years, small electric ovens have become part of the Japanese kitchen, and these have made it possible for cakes such as this one to be baked at home.

METRIC/IMPERIAL

5 eggs, beaten
150 g/5 oz sugar
75 g/3 oz honey
75 g/3 oz plain flour
¾ teaspoon baking powder
2 tablespoons icing sugar to decorate

AMERICAN

5 eggs, beaten
⅔ cup sugar
¼ cup honey
¾ cup all-purpose flour
¾ teaspoon baking powder
2 tablespoons confectioners' sugar to decorate

METHOD

Put the eggs in a bowl, then gradually beat in the sugar and honey. Beat for about 10 minutes until thick and pale, using an electric beater if possible. Sift the flour and baking powder together, then fold gently into the egg mixture.

Pour the mixture into a greased and floured 23 cm/9 inch square cake tin (pan). Bake in a preheated moderate oven (180°C/350°F, Gas Mark 4) for 30 minutes. Leave the cake in the tin (pan) for 10 minutes, then transfer to a wire rack and leave to cool completely.

Sprinkle with icing (confectioners') sugar. Cut into squares before serving.
MAKES ONE 23 cm/9 inch CAKE

Matcha Ice Cream; Momo No Kanten

Momo No Kanten
Peach 'Gelatin'

Serve with tea, either as a snack or a dessert. Unsweetened crushed pineapple may be substituted for the peach pulp, if liked.

METRIC/IMPERIAL

1 long block kanten*
450 ml/¾ pint water
350 g/12 oz sugar
120 ml/4 fl oz fresh peach pulp
juice of ½ lemon
2 egg whites

AMERICAN

1 long block kanten*
2 cups water
1½ cups sugar
½ cup fresh peach pulp
juice of ½ lemon
2 egg whites

METHOD

Wash the kanten under cold running water, then put in a pan, cover with the water and leave to soak for 20 to 30 minutes. Bring to the boil over moderate heat until completely melted, then add the sugar and stir until dissolved. Strain through a very fine sieve (strainer), then stir in the peach pulp and lemon juice and leave to cool.

Beat the egg whites until stiff, then gradually fold in the cooled liquid. Pour into a shallow tin (pan) and chill in the refrigerator until set. Cut into 2.5 cm/1 inch squares or diamond shapes. Serve chilled.

MAKES ABOUT 24

Matcha Ice Cream
Green Tea Ice Cream

This ice cream, with its pale, minty colour, makes a beautiful ending to a Japanese meal.

METRIC/IMPERIAL

600 ml/1 pint vanilla ice cream,
    softened
1 tablespoon matcha*
1 can sweetened azuki beans* (optional)

AMERICAN

2½ cups vanilla ice cream, softened
1 tablespoon matcha*
1 can sweetened azuki beans* (optional)

METHOD

Blend together the ice cream and matcha, then freeze until required. Scoop into individual serving dishes and top with sweetened azuki beans, if liked.

SERVES 4

The Philippines

Kay Shimizu

Philippine cuisine is a happy marriage of many fine foods from many countries. The Filipinos are a very hospitable people; they love to eat with friends and they love their fiestas and the related pageantry. Their fiestas date back to ancient Malay rites, probably as early as A.D. 1300 when the Malays came to the Philippine Islands. Since then the Spanish, Americans, Chinese and Japanese have all influenced the Filipino-Asian tropical diet, and Philippine cuisine has subsequently emerged as a rather unique, international one.

The use of certain vegetables, spices and cooking methods is reminiscent of the early strong Spanish influence, yet other foods definitely display the Chinese style of cooking. Being in the tropical zone, there is a great similarity to other South-Eastern Asian countries in the abundance of tropical fruits, such as bananas, mangoes, coconuts and pineapples.

The Filipinos are not such avid tea drinkers as the Japanese and the Chinese; they have their own favourite drinks made from fermented coconut juice or fermented sugar-cane juice. They also enjoy coffee, rich hot chocolate and milk. The Spanish custom of *meriendas* is observed in the Philippines. During these morning or afternoon coffee breaks, cakes, tarts and sweet fritters are served. Glutinous (sweet) rice* is the basis of many of the sweet delicacies.

Everyday food is fairly simple. Rice, fish and vegetables, fried or combined with meat, is the standard diet. The Phlippine Islanders enjoy the taste of their famous *bagoong* (fish paste)* as well as *patis* (clear fish liquid sauce).* *Patis* is extracted from fish which has been mixed with salt and fermented for several days. *Bagoong* and *patis* appear at every Filipino meal – rather like the salt and pepper which we use. The cool tangy flavour of vinegar is most characteristic in the *adobo* style of cooking pork, chicken and beef. The slight tartness of the dish results in a distinctive combination of flavours.

Filipino recipes do not yet have the universal appeal or variety of Chinese or Japanese foods, but the recipes in this chapter provide an introduction to this unusual cuisine.

Escabeche

Hot Pickled Fish

Fish is plentiful in the seas surrounding the Philippine Islands. This method of preparing fish is the most common in Philippine cuisine, which has many different foreign influences.

METRIC/IMPERIAL

1 kg/2–2¼ lb cleaned red snapper, sea bass or other white fish
salt
flour for coating
3 tablespoons vegetable oil
3 garlic cloves, peeled and crushed
1 teaspoon grated fresh root ginger*
1 large onion, peeled and thinly sliced into rings
1 large green pepper, cored, seeded and sliced into 5 mm/¼ inch strips
1 tablespoon cornflour
300 ml/½ pint water
3 tablespoons cider vinegar
1½ tablespoons brown sugar

AMERICAN

2–2¼ lb cleaned red snapper, sea bass or other white fish
salt
flour for coating
3 tablespoons oil
3 garlic cloves, peeled and ground
1 teaspoon grated fresh ginger root*
1 large onion, peeled and thinly sliced into rings
1 large green pepper, cored, seeded and sliced into ¼ inch strips
1 tablespoon cornstarch
1¼ cups water
3 tablespoons cider vinegar
1½ tablespoons brown sugar

METHOD

Wash the fish and pat dry with kitchen paper towels. Leave the fish whole or slice into steaks, then sprinkle lightly with salt and flour.

Heat a frying pan (skillet) over moderate heat. Add 2 tablespoons oil, then add the fish. Fry until the fish is crisp and brown on all sides, then remove from the pan and set aside.

Add the remaining oil to the pan with the garlic and ginger. Fry until brown, then add the onion and green pepper. Stir-fry for 1 minute, then remove from the pan and set aside.

Mix the cornflour (cornstarch) to a paste with a little of the water, then add to the pan with the remaining water, the vinegar, sugar and ½ teaspoon salt. Bring to the boil, then lower the heat and simmer until thickened, stirring constantly. Add the fish, bring the sauce back to the boil, then cover and cook for about 5 minutes. Return the vegetables to the pan and stir-fry for 1 minute to heat through.

Carefully transfer the fish to a warmed serving dish. Arrange the vegetables around the fish. Taste and adjust the seasoning of the sauce, then pour over the fish and vegetables. Serve hot.
SERVES 4 to 6

Pancit Guisado

Noodles with Meat and Vegetables

There are many variations of pancit; it can be prepared with any kind of meat that is available. It is similar to Chinese chow mein, and no doubt the Chinese have influenced the dish.

METRIC/IMPERIAL

225 g/8 oz miti*
4 tablespoons vegetable oil
1 garlic clove, peeled and crushed
225 g/8 oz boned lean pork, thinly sliced
225 g/8 oz chicken breast meat, thinly sliced
225 g/8 oz fresh prawns, peeled, deveined and diced
1 medium onion, peeled and thinly sliced
75 g/3 oz cabbage, shredded
2 tablespoons patis*
175 ml/6 fl oz chicken stock
pinch of paprika pepper
½ teaspoon salt
freshly ground black pepper

To garnish:
2 hard-boiled eggs, shelled and quartered
2 spring onions, chopped
few lemon wedges

AMERICAN

½ lb miti*
¼ cup vegetable oil
1 garlic clove, peeled and ground
1 cup thinly sliced lean pork
1 cup thinly sliced chicken breast meat
1 cup fresh shrimp, shelled, deveined and diced
1 medium onion, peeled and thinly sliced
1 cup shredded cabbage
2 tablespoons patis*
¾ cup chicken stock
pinch of paprika pepper
½ teaspoon salt
freshly ground black pepper

To garnish:
2 hard-cooked eggs, shelled and quartered
2 scallions, chopped
few lemon wedges

METHOD

Cook the noodles in boiling water for about 2 minutes until slightly undercooked. Drain, rinse under cold running water, then drain again. Place in a bowl with 1 tablespoon of the oil and mix well.

Heat a wok or deep frying pan (skillet) over moderate heat. Add 1 tablespoon of the oil, then add the noodles. Fry until golden brown on all sides, then remove the noodles from the pan and set aside. Wipe the pan clean with kitchen paper towels, then add 1 tablespoon of the oil and the garlic. Fry until the garlic is brown, then add the pork and fry for 5 minutes. Add the chicken and prawns (shrimp), stir-fry for about 2 minutes over high heat, then remove all the ingredients from the pan and set aside.

Wipe the pan clean again with kitchen paper towels and place over high heat. When it is very hot, add the remaining oil, then the onion and cabbage. Stir-fry for about 4 minutes until the onion is translucent but the cabbage is still undercooked and crunchy.

Add the remaining ingredients, stir well, then add the cooked meat and fish mixture. Heat through for about 2 minutes until most of the juices have evaporated, stirring constantly.

Add the noodles to the pan, toss well and cook until heated through.

Pile onto a warmed serving dish. Garnish with the eggs, spring onions (scallions) and lemon wedges. Serve hot.
SERVES 4 to 6

Pancit Guisado

Chicken and Pork En Adobo
Chicken and Pork Stew

Adobo is a cooking style rather than a recipe, and there are as many variations as there are cooks who make it. This version is a spicy combination of pork and chicken, but it can be made with only one meat if preferred. It tastes better 2 to 3 days after it has been cooked, but it is so good that there is rarely any left to be kept for later!

METRIC/IMPERIAL

*1 kg/2–2¼ lb boned lean pork, cut into
  chunks*
*450 g/1 lb chicken breast meat, cut into
  chunks*
1 garlic clove, peeled and crushed
2 bay leaves
*2 medium onions, peeled and
  quartered*
120 ml/4 fl oz cider vinegar
1 tablespoon soy sauce
salt
freshly ground black pepper
350 ml/12 fl oz water
1 tablespoon lard

AMERICAN

*2–2¼ lb boneless lean pork, cut into
  chunks*
*1 lb chicken breast meat, cut into
  chunks*
1 garlic clove, peeled and ground
2 bay leaves
*2 medium onions, peeled and
  quartered*
½ cup cider vinegar
1 tablespoon soy sauce
salt
freshly ground black pepper
1½ cups water
1 tablespoon lard

METHOD

Put the pork and chicken in a pan, then add the garlic, bay leaves, onions, vinegar, soy sauce and salt and pepper to taste. Stir well, then leave to marinate for 30 minutes.

Add the water to the pan and bring to the boil. Lower the heat and simmer for 45 minutes to 1 hour, until the meat is tender and the cooking liquid has reduced to about 120 ml/4 fl oz/½ cup. Strain the cooking liquid and reserve.

Melt the lard in the cleaned pan. Add the pork and chicken and fry over brisk heat until browned. Add the reserved cooking liquid and simmer for about 5 minutes.

Serve hot with rice.
SERVES 6 to 8

Lumpia
Filled Egg Rolls

Lumpia my be eaten 'fresh' or deep-fried, and the variety of fillings is endless, depending upon the cook's culinary imagination and what happens to be available. They are always served with distinctive dipping brown sauce.

Ready-made wrappers are sold in specialist stores, but they can easily be made at home, following this recipe for 'fresh' lumpia.

Chicken and Pork En Adobo; Lumpia

METRIC/IMPERIAL

Filling:
3 tablespoons vegetable oil
1 large onion, peeled and sliced
2 garlic cloves, peeled and crushed
225 g/8 oz boned cooked pork, diced
50 g/2 oz cooked ham, chopped
*100 g/4 oz prawns, peeled and
  chopped*
100 g/4 oz cooked garbanzo beans*
*1 medium carrot, peeled and cut into
  julienne strips*
*225 g/8 oz French or runner beans,
  topped, tailed and cut into julienne
  strips*
175 g/6 oz parboiled potatoes, diced
175 g/6 oz cabbage, shredded
1 teaspoon salt, or to taste
Wrappers:
2 eggs, separated
50 g/2 oz cornflour
250 ml/8 fl oz water
vegetable oil for frying
18–20 small lettuce leaves
Dipping brown sauce:
250 ml/8 fl oz chicken stock
2 tablespoons light soy sauce
6 tablespoons brown sugar
1 teaspoon salt
2 tablespoons cornflour
1 garlic clove, peeled and crushed
To garnish:
parsley sprigs

on a serving dish.

To make the sauce: Put all the ingredients in a pan, except the garlic. Mix well and cook gently until the mixture thickens, stirring constantly. Float the garlic on top of the sauce. Arrange 2 lumpias on each serving plate, spoon a little sauce over the top and garnish with parsley. Serve at room temperature.
MAKES 18 to 20

Bombones de Arroz
Rice Fritters

As is the case in many Asian countries, rice is often used as an ingredient for desserts. These are not eaten after a meal in the Western manner, but as snacks between meals.

METRIC/IMPERIAL

150 g/5 oz cooked medium-grain rice
2 eggs, beaten
3 tablespoons sugar
½ teaspoon vanilla essence
50 g/2 oz plain flour
1 tablespoon baking powder
pinch of salt
4 tablespoons desiccated coconut
vegetable oil for deep-frying
sifted icing sugar for sprinkling

AMERICAN

1 cup cooked medium-grain rice
2 eggs, beaten
3 tablespoons sugar
½ teaspoon vanilla extract
½ cup all-purpose flour
1 tablespoon baking powder
pinch of salt
¼ cup shredded sweetened coconut
vegetable oil for deep-frying
sifted confectioners' sugar for
    sprinkling

METHOD

Put the rice, eggs, sugar and vanilla in a bowl and mix well. Sift together the flour, baking powder and salt, then stir into the rice mixture. Stir in the coconut.

Heat the oil in a deep-fat fryer to 180°C/350°F. Drop tablespoonfuls of the mixture into the hot oil, one at a time, and deep-fry until golden brown on all sides. Drain on kitchen paper towels, then sprinkle with icing (confectioners') sugar. Serve hot.
MAKES ABOUT 20

AMERICAN

Filling:
3 tablespoons vegetable oil
1 large onion, peeled and sliced
2 garlic cloves, peeled and ground
1 cup diced cooked pork
¼ cup chopped cooked ham
½ cup chopped shelled shrimp
½ cup cooked garbanzo beans*
1 medium carrot, peeled and julienne
    cut
1 cup julienne cut string beans
1 cup parboiled diced potatoes
2 cups shredded cabbage
1 teaspoon salt, or to taste
Wrappers:
2 eggs, separated
½ cup cornstarch
1 cup water
vegetable oil for frying
18–20 small lettuce or romaine leaves
Dipping brown sauce:
1 cup chicken stock
2 tablespoons light soy sauce
6 tablespoons brown sugar
1 teaspoon salt
2 tablespoons cornstarch
1 garlic clove, peeled and ground
To garnish:
parsley sprigs

METHOD

To make the filling: Heat a wok or deep frying pan (skillet) over low heat. Add the oil, then the onion and garlic. Fry gently for a few minutes, then add the pork, ham, prawns (shrimp) and beans. Cook gently for about 2 minutes.

Add the vegetables, except the cabbage, cover and simmer for about 5 minutes, then add the cabbage and salt. Cover again and cook until the vegetables are tender but still crisp. Drain off any excess liquid, then leave to cool.

To make the wrappers: Beat the egg whites until stiff. Beat the egg yolks lightly, then add to the whites. Blend the cornflour (cornstarch) and water together, then add to the egg mixture and mix well.

Heat a 20 cm/8 inch frying pan (skillet) over moderate heat and brush with oil. Pour about 2 tablespoons of the batter into the pan, tilting the pan so that the mixture spreads to cover the base thinly. Cook until set and firm, like a thin pancake (crêpe), then remove from the pan and set aside while cooking the remainder.

Put 1 lettuce leaf on each wrapper, then put a spoonful of the prepared cooled filling in the centre. Fold the bottom end over the filling, then roll up to enclose the filling completely. Arrange the lumpias

Korea

Jan Leeming

The name of Korea or *Koryo* means 'high and clear', and is symbolic of the country's rugged mountains, rushing shallow streams and clear blue skies which have earned it the nickname of the 'Switzerland of Asia'. Korea is roughly the size of Great Britain. It extends southwards from eastern Siberia and Manchuria and lies between Japan on the east and China on the west.

The Koreans are descended from several Mongol tribes dating back to prehistoric times. Despite the proximity to Japan and China and repeated invasions by these two countries, the Koreans have clung to one language, one culture and their own ancient traditions. In the past, the West thought of Korea as a cultural bridge between Japan and China, yet it is now known that many traditions of these countries were directly influenced by Korean culture.

Korea has a temperate climate of four distinct seasons. The summer is hot and humid, the winter is cold, springtime is mild with a proliferation of flowers and blossom, and the autumn is mild and wet. This climate, and the rich soil, provide good agricultural land. Traditionally, the Koreans enjoy the autumn best because it is at this time that the crops have been harvested and food is plentiful.

Korean food consists of staple grains, subsidiary dishes and special foods. The grains are rice, barley and millet, either prepared singly or mixed, but almost always cooked simply by boiling. Special foods are usually highly seasoned with red pepper, garlic, spring onions (scallions), fresh root ginger,* soy sauce, salt, sesame seed oil* and baked sesame seeds,* then served with plain boiled rice and subsidiary dishes such as the peppery-hot, fermented pickled cabbage called *Kim Chee* (see page 207). This is a unique Korean dish and one without which no Korean home would be complete. During the late autumn, making winter Kim Chee is a family event in which all activity centres around preparing and chopping the vegetables and filling the earthenware pickle pots. There is a saying in Korea that, 'When the *Kim Chee* is prepared for the winter, half the harvest is done'. So essential is this pickled cabbage to a Korean's diet, that during the Korean war the soldiers used to take tins of it into battle with them – whatever else they went without, it would not be their *Kim Chee*!

If one had to liken the taste of Korean food to any other, the choice would be Indonesian rather than Japanese or Chinese as might be expected.

Korean food has many different flavours, from chilli-hot to delicately subtle, but the overall impression for the newcomer to the Korean table is one of sweetness, found in such dishes as *Bulgogi* (see page 213) and *Thak Tuigim Jang* (see page 212). The taste of Korean food is unique, but not so remote from Western dishes which combine sweet foods, such as fruit, with meat and poultry. This sweetness, or maybe the sheer satisfaction of eating Korean food, may be the reason why desserts as we know them do not feature in a Korean meal. In fact, Koreans will often eat fruit and rice cakes before a meal, and will finish with a plate of decoratively cut fruit.

The Korean has three meals a day; these are similar in that they all usually consist of soup, rice, fish or beef and the ubiquitous *Kim Chee*. The Korean breakfast is becoming Westernized, but it used to be the main meal of the day and it was usual for guests to be invited to breakfast. Lunch is usually the leftovers from breakfast.

With the advent of the smaller Western breakfast, dinner is fast becoming the main meal of the day. For dinner, each person has a bowl of rice and a bowl of soup; in addition, there are at least five different side dishes, plus soy sauce for dipping, and *Kim Chee*. At a special dinner, at least fifteen different dishes could be offered. The food is eaten with chopsticks and a spoon and in no specific order; soup may well appear on the table halfway through the meal, for example.

There is no fixed dining room in a traditional Korean home; the meal table, small and low, is taken to whichever room is convenient. Traditionally, the men will eat first, then the women, rather like a first and second sitting. However, in some homes today you will find the family almost eating together. The men occupy

one table, the children another, and the women's table is placed closest to the kitchen!

In the past, and still found today, in the country regions, the kitchen contained a fire fuelled by logs from the mountains. This provided heat for cooking and, by means of a system of pipes under the floor, warmth for the house. This *ondol* system of heating is so much a part of Korean life, that even the most modern Western-style houses have rooms with concrete floors under which there is a heat-radiating network of pipes.

Cooking Equipment and Utensils

The basic items in a Korean kitchen are a rice kettle and a soup kettle, which are heavy lidded pots made of pig iron. Other cooking takes place in a *Sot*, which is similar to the Chinese wok, curved at the bottom so that it sits in an aperture over the flame. The Korean housewife would also have a *Shin-Sol-Lo* pot for special occasion cooking. She might also have a *Bulgogi* pan, although this is, in Korean terms, a fairly recent invention having only been around for about 60 years. (The pan almost defies description, being a conical-shaped piece of metal with lipped apertures cut into it to allow the heat through and the meat juices to drip down into a collecting rim.) Without a *Bulgogi* pan, the cook would use a special *Bulgogi* grill (broiler) (see page 213).

Other basic utensils include a chopper and several extremely sharp knives.

Preparation and Cooking

In Korean cookery, great emphasis is placed on very fine cutting. This art, coupled with the decorative cutting of vegetables for garnish and fresh fruit for pure beauty, is the first element of cuisine learned by a Korean girl. Watching a Korean cook preparing a plate of fresh fruit for the table, or making a garnish of flower-like shapes from a peeled carrot, wielding a massive sharp knife, is an experience to be remembered!

More time is often spent preparing ingredients (chopping, slicing and marinating), than cooking. In many cases, particularly vegetables, the ingredients are literally 'shown' to the pan and taken out again. The Koreans like to eat their vegetables almost raw and their meat and fish are usually so finely sliced that these too, take very little time to cook. Most cooking is over high heat for a short time, otherwise the dishes are steamed.

Nothing is ever wasted in a Korean kitchen. Beef and poultry bones are always boiled to provide stock for soup or a base for a marinade. Remains of cooked meat are sliced and added to soup dishes, such as *Neng Myun* (see page 210) and *Yuk Ke Jang* (see page 208), or form the basis of the 'dish of kings' *Shin-Sol-Lo* (see page 211).

Festive Cooking

Shin-Sol-Lo is time-consuming to prepare, but it is a special dish for special occasions such as *Hansik*, which falls during February or March and is the day on which rites to worship ancestors are observed, or on *Sol* which is New Year's Day.

Although traditional dress is rarely worn by the younger men nowadays, at New Year the women might well wear their beautifully feminine *Chima Chogori*. This comprises a long, full skirt coming up to the bust line and a very short jacket which ends just below the top of the skirt; it is usually brightly coloured and often heavily embroidered.

Ginseng

Wine or *sake** can be drunk with Korean food, but it is more usual to serve the meal with Korean tea made from barley, often with a little Ginseng added. Ginseng, or *insam* as it is called in Korea, is the best known and most firmly credited of all Oriental herb medicines. It can be grown in any temperate climate, but Korean Ginseng is acknowledged as the finest.

A glass of Ginseng brandy at the end of your Korean meal will complement and complete a unique experience.

Hobak Chun
Savoury Battered Courgettes (Zucchini)

This delicate-tasting hors d'oeuvre can be eaten hot or cold.

METRIC/IMPERIAL

400 g/14 oz large courgettes, thinly
    sliced into rounds
salt
100 g/4 oz bean curd* (optional)
100 g/4 oz beef topside, minced
2 teaspoons sesame seeds*
2 teaspoons sesame seed oil*
4 teaspoons chopped spring onions
1 teaspoon crushed garlic
pinch of monosodium glutamate*
½ teaspoon freshly ground black
    pepper
100 g/4 oz plain flour
3 small eggs, beaten
4 tablespoons vegetable oil
To serve:
boo* (optional)
parsley sprig (optional)
Korean soy sauce (see opposite)

AMERICAN

¾–1 lb zucchini, thinly sliced into
    rounds
salt
1 cake bean curd*
½ cup ground top round beef
2 teaspoons sesame seeds*
2 teaspoons sesame seed oil*
4 teaspoons chopped scallions
1 teaspoon crushed garlic
pinch of msg*
½ teaspoon freshly ground black
    pepper
1 cup all-purpose flour
3 small eggs, beaten
¼ cup vegetable oil
To serve:
boo* (optional)
parsley sprig (optional)
Korean soy sauce (see opposite)

METHOD

Put the courgettes (zucchini) in a single layer on a plate, sprinkle with salt, then set aside.

Mash the bean curd, then squeeze out the water until the bean curd is dry. Place in a bowl with the beef, sesame seeds, sesame seed oil, spring onions (scallions), garlic, monosodium glutamate (msg), pepper and salt to taste. Mix well.

Dip one side of each courgette (zucchini) slice in flour. Spread a little beef mixture on the floured side, pressing it down well and spreading it out to cover. Dip both sides of each courgette (zucchini) slice in more flour, then in the egg.

Heat the oil in a frying pan (skillet), add the courgettes (zucchini), meat side down, and fry for 2 to 3 minutes until brown. Turn the slices over and fry until the underside is golden. Remove with a slotted spoon and drain on kitchen paper towels.

Arrange on a serving dish. Garnish, if liked, with flower shapes, cut from boo, and parsley. Serve hot or cold with Korean soy sauce handed separately as a dip.
SERVES 4

Koon Mandoo
Pan-fried Meat Dumplings

These are not the type of dumplings normally found in stews – they look rather like miniature Cornish pasties and are wrapped in a very thin dough. The Koreans often pinch the *wun tun skins** decoratively, or pull the edges of the crescent down and twist them together to form a shape like a hat with a brim. Serve hot as part of a main meal, or cold as part of an hors d'oeuvre.

METRIC/IMPERIAL

225 g/8 oz beef topside, minced
½ teaspoon sesame seeds*
1 teaspoon sesame seed oil*
2 teaspoons chopped spring onions
1 teaspoon crushed garlic
½ teaspoon salt
2 pinches of monosodium glutamate*
30 wun tun skins*
4 tablespoons vegetable oil
To serve:
carrot (optional)
parsley sprig (optional)
Korean soy sauce (see opposite)

AMERICAN

1 cup ground beef top round
½ teaspoon sesame seeds*
1 teaspoon sesame seed oil*
2 teaspoons chopped scallions
1 teaspoon crushed garlic
½ teaspoon salt
2 pinches of msg*
30 wun tun skins*
¼ cup vegetable oil
To serve:
carrot (optional)
parsley sprig (optional)
Korean soy sauce (see opposite)

METHOD

Put all the ingredients in a bowl, except the wun tun skins and vegetable oil. Mix well, then put a small teaspoon of the mixture in the middle of each wun tun skin. Fold the skin over and pinch together to form a semi-circle.

Drop the dumplings into a pan of boiling water and boil for 3 minutes. Heat the vegetable oil in a frying pan (skillet). Remove the dumplings from the water with a slotted spoon, drain, then transfer to the oil. Fry until golden, turning constantly. Remove and drain.

Arrange on a serving dish. Garnish, if liked, with flower shapes, cut from carrot, and parsley. Serve hot or cold, with Korean soy sauce as a dip.
SERVES 4

Koon Mandoo, served with Korean Soy Sauce; Hobak Chun

Kim Chee

Pickled Chinese Cabbage (Bok Choy)

This famous hot pickled cabbage, made by the jarful, is something no self-respecting Korean would be without!

METRIC/IMPERIAL

1 head Chinese leaves, chopped
3 tablespoons salt
2 teaspoons hot chilli powder
2 teaspoons crushed garlic
4 spring onions, finely chopped
1 tablespoon sugar
1 hard pear, peeled, cored and grated
½ teaspoon monosodium glutamate*

AMERICAN

1 head bok choy, chopped
3 tablespoons salt
2 teaspoons hot chili powder
2 teaspoons crushed garlic
4 scallions, finely chopped
1 tablespoon sugar
1 hard pear, peeled, cored and grated
½ teaspoon msg*

METHOD

Put the Chinese leaves (bok choy) in a bowl, add the salt and leave overnight.

Remove the cabbage from the bowl and rinse under cold running water. Drain, then pat dry. Place in a large jar and stir in the remaining ingredients.

Cover with a heavy weight and leave for 1 to 2 days before using.

Korean Soy Sauce

This is a basic soy sauce which is enhanced by additional ingredients. It is served in individual bowls as a dip to accompany many of the Korean dishes in this chapter.

METRIC/IMPERIAL

3 tablespoons soy sauce
1 tablespoon chopped spring onions
1 teaspoon sesame seeds*
1 teaspoon sesame seed oil*
1 teaspoon crushed garlic
½ teaspoon sugar
1 teaspoon vinegar
pinch of chilli powder
pinch of monosodium glutamate*

AMERICAN

3 tablespoons soy sauce
1 tablespoon chopped scallions
1 teaspoon sesame seeds*
1 teaspoon sesame seed oil*
1 teaspoon crushed garlic
½ teaspoon sugar
1 teaspoon vinegar
pinch of chili powder
pinch of msg*

METHOD

Mix all the ingredients together, then divide equally between 4 individual shallow dishes.
SERVES 4

Bintatok

Korean Pizza

This dish is a cross between a pizza and a pancake (crêpe). It should be made with ground mung beans*; if these are not available, use split peas instead.

METRIC/IMPERIAL

225 g/8 oz mung beans*
4 tablespoons vegetable oil
1 large onion, peeled and finely chopped
4 spring onions, green part only, finely chopped
1 carrot, peeled and finely chopped
1 small red pepper, cored, seeded and thinly sliced
50 g/2 oz minced beef
salt
freshly ground black pepper
Korean soy sauce (see left) to serve

AMERICAN

1⅓ cups mung beans*
¼ cup vegetable oil
1 large onion, peeled and finely chopped
4 scallions, green part only, finely chopped
1 carrot, peeled and finely chopped
1 small red pepper, cored, seeded and thinly sliced
¼ cup ground beef, firmly packed
salt
freshly ground black pepper
Korean soy sauce (see left) to serve

METHOD

Put the beans in a bowl, cover with warm water and leave to soak for at least 3 hours, preferably overnight.

Transfer the beans and any remaining liquid to an electric blender and work to a thick, smooth batter. Alternatively, pound the mixture until smooth using a pestle and mortar.

Heat a quarter of the oil in a small omelet pan (about 15 cm/6 inches in diameter). Add a quarter of the batter and tilt the pan to spread the batter evenly over the base.

Sprinkle a quarter of the remaining ingredients over the top of the bintatok and fry for at least 3 minutes until the edges begin to curl. Turn the bintatok over carefully and fry the other side for 3 minutes until golden brown underneath. Transfer to a warmed serving dish and keep hot while cooking the remaining ingredients in the same way to make 4 bintatok.

Serve hot with Korean soy sauce handed separately as a dip.
SERVES 4

Solong Tang
Beef Soup with Noodles and Ginger

METRIC/IMPERIAL

100 g/4 oz fine noodles
350 g/12 oz cooked beef brisket or topside
900 ml/1½ pints beef stock
50 g/2 oz spring onions, finely chopped
2 teaspoons crushed fresh root ginger*
1 teaspoon sugar
2 teaspoons freshly ground black pepper
2–3 teaspoons salt
1 teaspoon monosodium glutamate*

AMERICAN

¼ lb fresh wheat noodles
¾ lb cooked beef brisket or top round
3¾ cups beef stock
¾ cup finely chopped scallions
2 teaspoons crushed fresh ginger root*
1 teaspoon sugar
2 teaspoons freshly ground black pepper
2–3 teaspoons salt
1 teaspoon msg*

METHOD

Cook the noodles in boiling water for 3 to 5 minutes then drain and set aside.

Cut the meat into very thin slices, then cut each slice into strips, about 5 cm/2 inches long and 1 cm/½ inch wide.

Put all the ingredients in a pan, except the noodles and beef. Bring to the boil, then add the beef and simmer for 5 minutes. Hold the noodles in a sieve (strainer) over the pan and spoon the liquid over them to reheat, allowing the liquid to strain through into the pan.

Divide the noodles equally between 4 warmed individual soup bowls, then pour over the soup, distributing the strips of beef evenly. Serve hot.
SERVES 4

Yuk Ke Jang
Spicy Hot Beef Soup with Bean Sprouts

METRIC/IMPERIAL

3 tablespoons vegetable oil
1 teaspoon chilli powder
2 teaspoons crushed garlic
1 teaspoon crushed fresh root ginger*
900 ml/1½ pints beef stock
275 g/10 oz cooked beef topside, thinly sliced
2 tablespoons chopped spring onions
100 g/4 oz fresh bean sprouts
1 teaspoon monosodium glutamate*
¼–½ teaspoon salt

AMERICAN

3 tablespoons vegetable oil
1 teaspoon chili powder
2 teaspoons crushed garlic
1 teaspoon crushed fresh ginger root*
3¾ cups beef stock
1¼ cups thinly sliced cooked beef top round
2 tablespoons chopped scallions
1 cup fresh bean sprouts
1 teaspoon msg*
¼–½ teaspoon salt

METHOD

Heat the oil in a frying pan (skillet). Add the chilli powder, garlic and ginger and stir-fry over moderate heat for 1 minute. Remove from the heat.

Put the stock in a pan and bring to the boil. Add the chilli mixture and the remaining ingredients and simmer for 10 minutes. Serve hot.
SERVES 4

Shikumchee-Taeng-Jang-Kuk
Spinach Soup with Bean Curd and Squid

Despite its lengthy name, this soup is very easy to make.

METRIC/IMPERIAL

600 ml/1 pint well-flavoured beef stock
100 g/4 oz bean curd,* diced
50 g/2 oz cleaned squid, cut into thin strips (optional)
100 g/4 oz fresh young spinach leaves, cut into thin strips
2 teaspoons crushed garlic
1 tablespoon soy bean paste*
4 tablespoons sliced spring onions
1 teaspoon monosodium glutamate*
salt

AMERICAN

2½ cups well-flavored beef stock
1 cake bean curd,* diced
¼ cup cleaned squid, cut into thin strips (optional)
¼ lb fresh young spinach leaves, cut into thin strips
2 teaspoons crushed garlic
1 tablespoon soy bean paste*
¼ cup sliced scallions
1 teaspoon msg*
salt

METHOD

Put the stock in a pan and bring to the boil. Add the remaining ingredients and boil for 2 minutes. Serve hot in warmed individual soup bowls.
SERVES 4

Maeum Tang
Spiced Fish Soup
This is a dish for those who love spicy hot food.

METRIC/IMPERIAL

750 g/1½ lb cod fillets, skinned and cut into large chunks
600 ml/1 pint water
2 tablespoons vegetable oil
1 medium onion, peeled and finely chopped
2 tablespoons chopped spring onions
2 teaspoons crushed garlic
1 teaspoon crushed fresh root ginger*
2–6 teaspoons chilli powder, according to taste
2–3 teaspoons salt
100 g/4 oz courgettes, thinly sliced
1 medium green pepper, cored, seeded and finely sliced

AMERICAN

1½ lb cod fillets, skinned and cut into large chunks
2½ cups water
2 tablespoons vegetable oil
1 medium onion, peeled and finely chopped
2 tablespoons chopped scallions
2 teaspoons crushed garlic
1 teaspoon crushed fresh ginger root*
2–6 teaspoons chili powder, according to taste
2–3 teaspoons salt
1 cup thinly sliced zucchini
1 medium green pepper, cored, seeded and finely sliced

METHOD

Put the cod in a pan with the water. Bring to the boil, then lower the heat and simmer gently for 5 minutes. Remove from the heat and set aside.

Heat the oil in a frying pan (skillet). Add the onion, spring onions (scallions), garlic. ginger and chilli powder and salt to taste. Stir-fry over moderate heat for 1 minute, then add the courgettes (zucchini) and pepper and stir-fry for 1 minute. Add to the fish and simmer gently until heated through. Serve hot.
SERVES 4

Shin-Sol-Lo (see page 211), served in a traditional cook pot; Shikumchee-Taeng-Jang-Kuk

Neng Myun
Cold Noodle Soup

METRIC/IMPERIAL

450 g/1 lb fine noodles
225 g/8 oz cooked beef brisket or
    topside
900 ml/1½ pints chicken stock
8 whole black peppercorns
5 cm/2 inch piece of fresh root
    ginger,* peeled
½ teaspoon monosodium glutamate*
1–2 teaspoons salt
1 teaspoon soy sauce
4 dried chillis
To serve:
24 cucumber slices
1 large hard pear, peeled, cored and
    thinly sliced
2 hard-boiled eggs, shelled and halved
    lengthways
prepared mustard and vinegar to taste
    (optional)

AMERICAN

1 lb fresh wheat noodles
½ lb cooked beef brisket or top round
3¾ cups chicken stock
8 whole black peppercorns
2 inch piece of fresh ginger root,*
    peeled
½ teaspoon msg*
1–2 teaspoons salt
1 teaspoon soy sauce
4 dried chilis
To serve:
24 cucumber slices
1 large hard pear, peeled, cored and
    thinly sliced
2 hard-cooked eggs, shelled and
    halved lengthways
prepared mustard and vinegar, to taste
    (optional)

METHOD

Cook the noodles in boiling water for 3 to 5 minutes, then drain and leave to cool.

Cut the meat into very thin slices, then cut each slice into strips, about 5 cm/ 2 inches long and 1 cm/½ inch wide.

Put all the ingredients in a pan, except the noodles. Bring to the boil, then simmer for 5 minutes. Remove from the heat, leave until cold, then remove the peppercorns, ginger and chillis.

Divide the noodles between 4 to 6 individual soup bowls. Divide the cucumber and pear slices between the bowls, alternating the slices in layers on top of the noodles. Top each bowl with an egg half, then gently pour over the cold soup, taking care not to disturb the layers. Add a little mustard and vinegar before serving, if liked. Serve cold.
SERVES 4 to 6

Ojingo Pokum
Squid with Vegetables in Chilli-Hot Sweet Sauce

The squid should be scored crossways to help tenderize it during cooking.

METRIC/IMPERIAL

450 g/1 lb fresh squid
2 tablespoons vegetable oil
1 small green pepper, cored, seeded
    and thinly sliced into rings
1 small red pepper, cored, seeded and
    thinly sliced into rings
1 medium onion, peeled and finely
    chopped
2 teaspoons crushed garlic
2 teaspoons sugar
1 teaspoon monosodium glutamate*
1 tablespoon kochujang*

AMERICAN

1 lb fresh squid
2 tablespoons vegetable oil
1 small green pepper, cored, seeded
    and thinly sliced into rings
1 small red pepper, cored, seeded and
    thinly sliced into rings
1 medium onion, peeled and finely
    chopped
2 teaspoons crushed garlic
2 teaspoons sugar
1 teaspoon msg*
1 tablespoon kochujang*

Ojingo Pokum

METHOD

Clean the squid, discarding the head, transparent backbone and ink bag. Cut the flesh into 2.5 cm/1 inch squares and score crossways.

Heat the oil in a frying pan (skillet). Add the vegetables and fry over brisk heat for 2 minutes, shaking the pan constantly. Remove from the heat, then add the squid, garlic, sugar and monosodium glutamate (msg).

Return to the heat and fry briskly for 2 minutes, stirring and shaking the pan constantly. Stir in the kochujang and fry for 1 minute over high heat, stirring all the time. Serve hot.

SERVES 4

Shin-Sol-Lo

Korean Celebration Firepot

Shin-Sol-Lo was once the dish of 'kings', because only the royal household could afford to eat it. Originally it would have been served in traditional Korean Royal Palace style in a Shin-Sol-Lo cook pot, and it would have contained crabs, prawns (shrimp) and many different meats. This recipe is a much simplified version, although it is still fairly time-consuming to make. Special Shin-Sol-Lo cook pots are difficult to obtain, but a fondue pot makes an acceptable substitute.

METRIC/IMPERIAL

450 g/1 lb boo*
2 tablespoons sesame seed oil*
4 medium onions, peeled and finely chopped
2 teaspoons crushed garlic
2 teaspoons sesame seeds*
175 g/6 oz liver, thinly sliced
4 tablespoons vegetable oil
175 g/6 oz cod or other firm white fish fillets, sliced
400 g/14 oz minced beef
2 eggs, beaten
salt
freshly ground black pepper
900 ml/1½ pints beef stock
1 teaspoon monosodium glutamate*
225 g/8 oz cooked beef brisket or topside, cut into thin strips
1 medium cucumber, sliced diagonally
4 mushrooms, finely sliced
2 medium carrots, peeled and sliced diagonally
8 spring onions, shredded
75 g/3 oz fresh bamboo shoot
2 tablespoons pine nuts

Batter:
100 g/4 oz plain flour
2 eggs, well beaten
2 tablespoons water (approximately)

AMERICAN

1 lb boo*
2 tablespoons sesame seed oil*
4 medium onions, peeled and finely chopped
2 teaspoons crushed garlic
2 teaspoons sesame seeds*
¾ cup thinly sliced liver
¼ cup vegetable oil
¾ cup sliced cod or other firm white fish fillets
1¾ cups ground beef
2 eggs, beaten
salt
freshly ground black pepper
3¾ cups beef stock
1 teaspoon msg*
½ lb cooked beef brisket or top round, cut into thin strips
1 medium cucumber, sliced diagonally
4 mushrooms, finely sliced
2 medium carrots, peeled and sliced diagonally
8 scallions, shredded
¾ cup fresh bamboo shoot
2 tablespoons pine nuts

Batter:
1 cup all-purpose flour
2 eggs, well beaten
2 tablespoons water (approximately)

METHOD

Cook the boo in boiling water for 20 minutes, then drain and cut into small pieces. Heat the sesame seed oil in a frying pan (skillet), add the onion and fry gently until soft. Add the garlic and sesame seeds, then remove from the heat and mix with the boo.

To make the batter: Put the flour and eggs in a bowl and beat thoroughly until smooth. Add the water gradually, stirring constantly until the batter is smooth.

Dip the liver slices in the batter. Heat 1 tablespoon of the vegetable oil in the frying pan (skillet), add the liver and fry for 5 minutes. Remove from the pan with a slotted spoon, drain on kitchen paper towels and leave to cool. Meanwhile, dip the fish slices in the remaining batter. Heat another tablespoon of the oil in the pan, add the fish and fry for 5 minutes. Drain as for the liver.

Mix the minced (ground) beef and eggs together, then add salt and pepper to taste. Roll into 1 cm/½ inch balls. Heat the remaining vegetable oil in the frying pan (skillet). Add the meatballs and fry for about 5 minutes, turning frequently, until evenly browned. Remove from the pan with a slotted spoon, then drain on kitchen paper towels.

Put the stock in a pan with 1 teaspoon each of pepper and monosodium glutamate (msg). Bring to the boil, then lower the heat and simmer gently.

Meanwhile, arrange the ingredients in layers in individual Shin-Sol-Lo pots or a fondue pot. Put a layer of beef strips in the bottom, cover with boo mixture, then arrange the liver and fish slices on top in alternate layers.

Top with the cucumber, mushroom, carrot, spring onions (scallions), bamboo shoot and meatballs; arrange decoratively clockwise so that each third of the pan is filled in the same way.

Arrange the pine nuts around the funnel of the Shin-Sol-Lo pot or heap together in the centre of the fondue pot. Pour the stock gently over the ingredients, taking care not to disturb the arrangement.

If using Shin-Sol-Lo pots, put lighted charcoal into the centre, fan until the charcoal ignites, then heat for approximately 5 minutes. If using a fondue pot, bring gently to the boil over moderate heat. Serve hot.

SERVES 4 to 6

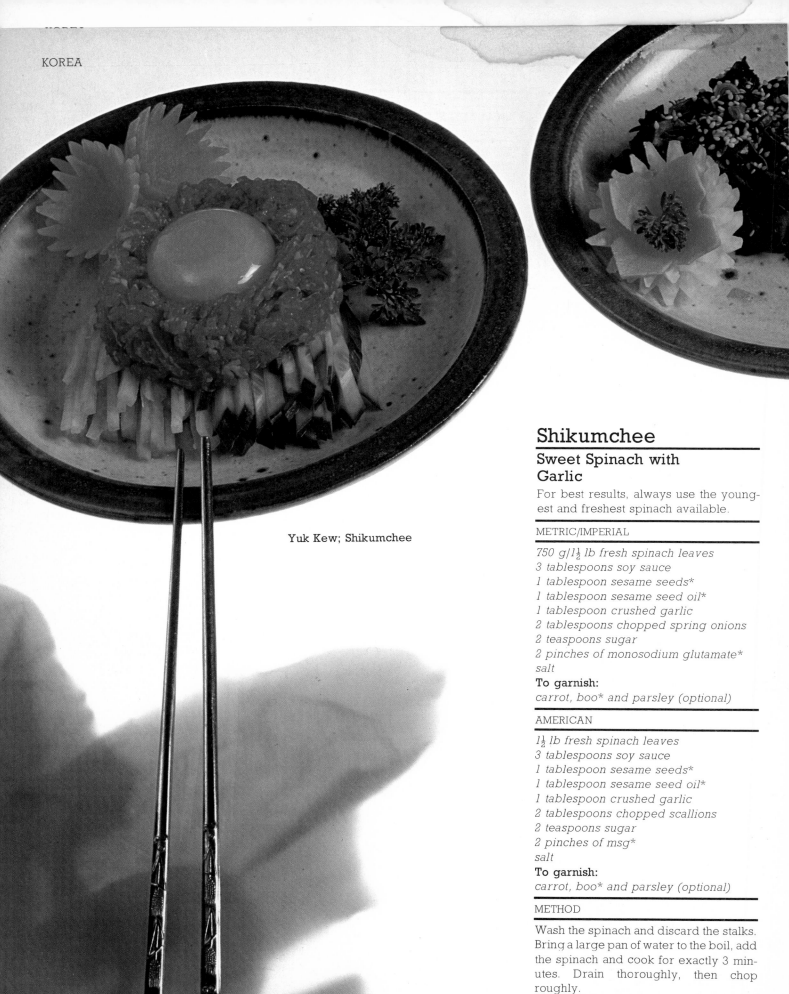

Yuk Kew; Shikumchee

Shikumchee

Sweet Spinach with Garlic

For best results, always use the young-est and freshest spinach available.

METRIC/IMPERIAL

750 g/1½ lb fresh spinach leaves
3 tablespoons soy sauce
1 tablespoon sesame seeds*
1 tablespoon sesame seed oil*
1 tablespoon crushed garlic
2 tablespoons chopped spring onions
2 teaspoons sugar
2 pinches of monosodium glutamate*
salt

To garnish:
carrot, boo* and parsley (optional)

AMERICAN

1½ lb fresh spinach leaves
3 tablespoons soy sauce
1 tablespoon sesame seeds*
1 tablespoon sesame seed oil*
1 tablespoon crushed garlic
2 tablespoons chopped scallions
2 teaspoons sugar
2 pinches of msg*
salt

To garnish:
carrot, boo* and parsley (optional)

METHOD

Wash the spinach and discard the stalks. Bring a large pan of water to the boil, add the spinach and cook for exactly 3 min-utes. Drain thoroughly, then chop roughly.

Place the spinach on a serving place and sprinkle the remaining ingredients on top. Garnish, if liked, with flower shapes, cut from carrot, boo and parsley. Serve hot.
SERVES 4

Kal Bee Jim

Beef Spareribs in Tangy Sauce with Chestnuts

METRIC/IMPERIAL

750 g/1½ lb beef spareribs trimmed of
fat and cut into pieces 5 cm/2 inches
wide
Sauce:
4 tablespoons soy sauce
450 ml/¾ pint water
2 teaspoons sesame seed oil*
2 teaspoons sesame seeds*
1 tablespoon sugar
1 teaspoon freshly ground black
pepper
1 teaspoon crushed garlic
100 g/4 oz cooked chestnuts, finely
chopped
100 g/4 oz bamboo shoot

AMERICAN

1½ lb beef ribs or back ribs, trimmed of
fat and cut into pieces 2 inches wide
Sauce:
¼ cup soy sauce
2 cups water
2 teaspoons sesame seed oil*
2 teaspoons sesame seeds*
1 tablespoon sugar
1 teaspoon freshly ground black
pepper
1 teaspoon crushed garlic
8 large cooked chestnuts, finely
chopped
1 cup bamboo shoot

METHOD

Parboil the beef for 5 minutes, then drain
and set aside.

To make the sauce: Put all the ingredients in a pan and stir well. Bring to
the boil, then add the beef and bring
back to the boil. Lower the heat and
simmer gently for 30 minutes or until the
beef is tender. Serve hot.
SERVES 4

Yuk Kwe

Spiced Raw Beef

This is the Korean version of Steak
Tartare. The egg yolk is broken at the
table and mixed with the beef, pear and
cucumber. Use either chopsticks or a
fork for mixing and eating. If partially
frozen beef is used, it will be easier to
obtain very thin slices.

METRIC/IMPERIAL

450 g/1 lb beef fillet or topside
2 teaspoons sugar
2 teaspoons sesame seeds*
1 tablespoon sesame seed oil*
1 tablespoon crushed garlic
½ teaspoon monosodium glutamate*
salt
4 egg yolks (optional)
To garnish:
2 small hard pears, peeled, cored
and sliced into matchstick strips
12 diagonal slices of cucumber, cut into
matchstick strips
parsley sprigs
carrot (optional)

AMERICAN

1 lb fillet or beef top round
2 teaspoons sugar
2 teaspoons sesame seeds*
1 tablespoon sesame seed oil*
1 tablespoon crushed garlic
½ teaspoon msg*
salt
4 egg yolks (optional)
To garnish:
2 small hard pears, peeled, cored and
sliced into matchstick strips
12 diagonal slices of cucumber, cut into
matchstick strips
parsley sprigs
carrot (optional)

METHOD

Cut the meat into very thin slices no more
than 3 mm/⅛ inch thick, then cut the slices
into matchstick strips. Place in a bowl
with the remaining ingredients, except
the egg yolks. Mix together, using the
hands (their warmth will thaw the meat),
then divide into 4 portions.

Divide the pear and cucumber strips
equally between 4 individual serving
plates, arranging them in separate piles.
Place the meat mixture on top. If using
egg yolks, mould the mixture into a neat
shape and put an egg yolk in each hollow.
Garnish with parsley sprigs and carrot
'flowers', if liked. Serve raw.
SERVES 4

Chap Chee

Spicy Vegetables

METRIC/IMPERIAL

900 ml/1½ pints water
200 g/7 oz bean threads*
3 tablespoons vegetable oil
225 g/8 oz Chinese leaves, shredded
salt
1 large carrot, peeled and cut
diagonally into matchstick strips
100 g/4 oz fresh spinach leaves,
cooked and roughly chopped
8 medium Chinese dried mushrooms
soaked in warm water for 30
minutes, then drained (optional)
Sauce:
1 tablespoon sesame seed oil*
1 tablespoon soy sauce
2 teaspoons sugar
2 teaspoons sesame seeds*
½ teaspoon salt
½ teaspoon monosodium glutamate*

AMERICAN

3¾ cups water
3 small packages bean threads*
3 tablespoons vegetable oil
½ lb bok choy, shredded
salt
1 large carrot, peeled and cut
diagonally into matchstick strips
¼ lb fresh spinach leaves, cooked and
roughly chopped
8 medium Chinese dried mushrooms,*
soaked in warm water for 30
minutes, then drained (optional)
Sauce:
1 tablespoon sesame seed oil*
1 tablespoon soy sauce
2 teaspoons sugar
2 teaspoons sesame seeds*
½ teaspoon salt
½ teaspoon msg*

METHOD

Bring the water to the boil in a pan, add
the bean threads and boil for 3 minutes.
Drain and set aside.

Heat 2 tablespoons of the oil in a pan.
When very hot, add the Chinese leaves
(bok choy) and salt to taste and fry for 2
minutes, tossing the leaves constantly.
Remove from the pan and set aside.

Heat the remaining oil in the pan. Add
the carrot and fry for 1 minute, stirring.
Return the Chinese leaves (bok choy) to
the pan, add the spinach and mushrooms
if using, and cook for a further 2 minutes,
shaking the pan constantly.

To make the sauce: Put all the ingredients in a pan and stir well. Bring to
the boil, then add to the vegetable mixture with the bean threads. Mix well and
heat through. Serve immediately.
SERVES 4

Glossary

Aburage [JAPAN]
Fried soybean cake

Agar-agar [BURMA/CHINA/ JAPAN/MALAYSIA]
Known as *kanten* in Japan. A kind of seaweed available in long white strands or powdered form. Use in very small quantities, as a little will quickly set a large volume of liquid. It has almost no taste or colour. Powdered gelatine may be substituted, allowing 4 tablespoons gelatine to 25g/1oz agar-agar. Available from Oriental stores and some health food shops.

Akamiso [JAPAN]
Soybean paste, reddish brown in colour.

Ata [INDIA]
A type of wholemeal (wholewheat) flour used in the preparation of Indian unleavened breads. Sometimes sold in the West as *chappati* flour. Available from Indian stores.

Azuki [JAPAN]
Red beans. Sweetened azuki beans are available in cans.

Bagoong [PHILIPPINES], see **Fish paste.**

Balachan [MALAYSIA], see **Terasi.**

Bamboo shoot, dried [VIETNAM]
Not a substitute for fresh or canned bamboo shoots. Dried bamboo shoots have their own special flavour and texture. Soak in hot water for at least 2 hours before using.

Bean curd [CHINA/KOREA/ INDONESIA/MALAYSIA]
Known as *tahu* or *taukwa* in Indonesia/Malaysia. Made of puréed and pressed soya beans, its texture is like soft cheese. Sold in cakes, 7.5 cm/3 inches square and 2.5 cm/1 inch thick. It will keep fresh for several days if stored in water in the refrigerator. Dried bean curd skin is also available, in packets of sheets or sticks: Soak in cold water overnight or in warm water for 1 hour before using. Available from Oriental stores and some health food shops.

Beans, salted [INDONESIA/ MALAYSIA/THAILAND]
Known as *tao chiew* in Thailand, *tauco* in Indonesia/Malaysia. Black soya beans which have been steamed, spiced and preserved in salt. Sold in cans and packets. Should be transferred to an airtight jar and stored in the refrigerator; will then keep for up to 1 year.

Bean Sauce [CHINA]
Also known as yellow bean sauce and brown or black bean sauce. Crushed yellow soya beans, mixed to a paste with flour, vinegar, spices and salt. Sold in jars and cans.

Bean threads [CHINA/JAPAN/ KOREA/THAILAND/VIETNAM], see **Mung bean threads.**

Belimbing wuluh [MALAYSIA]
A sour kind of fresh fruit. Common in South-East Asia, but unobtainable in Europe and U.S.A. Lemon, lime or rhubarb may be used as a substitute.

Beni-shoga [JAPAN]
Red salt preserved ginger.

Besan [INDIA]
A very fine flour made from from ground chick peas (garbanzos). It must be sieved before using as it tends to become lumpy on standing.

Blacan [MALAYSIA), see **Terasi.**

Boo [BURMA/KOREA]
A long white radish resembling a parsnip in appearance. It has a mild flavour and English radishes should not be used as a substitute. Available in high-class greengrocers or in areas where there are Chinese, Japanese and Korean inhabitants. If unobtainable, use tender white turnips as a substitute.

Buah keras [MALAYSIA], see **Kemiri.**

Bumbu [MALAYSIA]
A general term for any mixture of ingredients that gives a strong flavour to a dish. It can refer to the dry ingredients, or to the sauces that are made from them.

Bũn tâu [VIETNAM], see **Mung bean threads.**

Cabé rawit [MALAYSIA]
Small, very hot chillis – red, green or sometimes white in colour.

Candlenut [MALAYSIA], see **Kemiri.**

Cellophane noodles [CHINA/ JAPAN/KOREA/THAILAND/ VIETNAM], see **Mung bean threads.**

Chinese parsley, see **Cilantro,** see **Coriander.**

Citronella, see **Lemon grass.**

Cloud ear [CHINA], see **Wood ear.**

Coconut milk [INDIA/MALAYSIA/ THAILAND/VIETNAM]
Known as *narial ka doodth* in India, *santen* in Indonesia and Malaysia. Best made from fresh coconuts:– Grate the flesh of 1 coconut into a bowl, pour on 600 ml/1 pint/2½ cups boiling water, then leave to stand for about 30 minutes. Squeeze the flesh, then strain before using. This quantity will make a thick coconut milk, add more or less water as required. Desiccated (shredded) coconut can be used instead of fresh coconut:– Use 350g/12 oz/4 cups to 600 ml/1 pint/2½ cups boiling water. Use freshly made coconut milk within 24 hours. Canned coconut milk is also available.

Coconut sugar [THAILAND]
Also known as palm sugar. Brown sugar may be substituted.

Coriander [ALL COUNTRIES]
Also known as *pak chee* [Thailand], *dhania* [India], *ngô* [Vietnam], Chinese parsley and cilantro. Widely used in South-East Asian cooking in the form of leaves, roots, stems, seeds and powder. In Vietnam, Laos and Kampuchea, only the fresh leaves and stems are used and are indispensable to these cuisines. The fresh leaves are usually chopped, the roots are washed and dried, then grated. The roots will keep in an airtight jar. Can easily be grown outdoors in summer. Parsley is often substituted for fresh coriander although it does not impart the same flavour. Available at Oriental and Continental specialist stores.

Creamed coconut [BURMA/ MALAYSIA/THAILAND]
Sold in packets, tubs, slabs and cakes. More concentrated than coconut milk. Cut up roughly before using, then heat gently with water added until melted, stirring frequently. Use as coconut milk.

Culantro [VIETNAM]
Also known as *ngo tay*. A member of the coriander family. Each stem has 1 elongated leaf which grows in a dark green cluster.

Daikon [JAPAN]
A long white radish. Sometimes referred to as the 'workhorse' of the Japanese diet, it is a basic vegetable in Japanese cooking. Use both raw and cooked.

Dal [INDIA]
The general name given to a variety of pulses grown in the Indian sub-continent. Along with rice, these pulses form the staple diet of millions of peasants. There are several varieties – *moong, urhad, chenna* and, the dal which most people in the West are familiar with, the lentil. They are all interchange-able, and the cooking method is the same for each.

Daun jeruk purut [MALAYSIA]
The leaf of a fruit similar to a lime.

Daun kunyit [MALAYSIA]
Turmeric leaf.

Dhania [INDIA], see **Coriander.**

Dried mushrooms [CHINA/ JAPAN/KOREA/THAILAND/ VIETNAM], see **Mushrooms, dried.**

Ebi [MALAYSIA]
Tiny uncooked dried shrimps.

Fiddlehead ferns [MALAYSIA], see **Paku.**

Fish paste [KAMPUCHEA/ PHILIPPINES]
Known as *bagoong* in the Philippines. It is a thick paste made from fermented fish or shrimps and salt. Used in small quantities as a relish. Kampuchean fish paste is made from whole preserved anchovies which are strained when required. Available from Oriental stores.

Fish sauce [KAMPUCHEA/LAOS/ PHILIPPINES/THAILAND/ VIETNAM]
Known as *patis* in the Philippines, *nam pla* in Thailand, *nuoc cham* or *nuoc mam* in Kampuchea, Laos and Vietnam. As important to these schools of cooking as salt is in the West. Prepared from fresh anchovies and salt which are layered in wooden barrels and left to ferment. The liquid that is drained off initially is light and clear and considered to be the best quality; the two subsequent extractions are darker and of a poorer quality. Available from Oriental stores.

Five spice powder [CHINA/ MALAYSIA]
A reddish-brown aromatic powder, made from a combination of ground spices – anise, fennel, cloves, cinnamon and Szechuan pepper. These spices are also sold as 'five spices', ready-mixed but whole. Will keep indefinitely in an airtight container.

Galingale
[MALAYSIA/THAILAND/VIETNAM]
Known as *laos* in Malaysia, *kha* in Thailand. It is the root of a plant resembling ginger, creamy white in colour, with a delicate flavour. Used fresh, but only dried galingale is obtainable in the West. Soak in hot water for 1 hour before using in cooking, then remove before serving. Galingale (*laos*) powder is also available.

Garbanzo beans [PHILIPPINES]
Chick peas.

Ghee [INDIA]
Clarified butter. To make pure ghee: Heat 1.5 kg/3 lb unsalted (sweet) butter over low heat in a heavy pan. Skim off any floating impurities, then maintain the heat at just below simmering point for 1 hour. Strain through several layers of cheesecloth (muslin), then store in a cool place. It will keep for several months. Many Indian cooks use a ghee substitute derived from vegetable oil; this is available from Asian stores.

Ginger [ALL COUNTRIES]
Fresh root ginger, sometimes referred to as 'green ginger'. Peel before using, then slice, crush or chop finely. To keep fresh: Peel, then wash and place in a jar, cover with pale dry sherry, seal and store in the refrigerator. Ground ginger is not an acceptable substitute, but dried root ginger may be used, in which case the quantity should be decreased as it is sharper in taste.

Glutinous (sweet) rice
[KAMPUCHEA/LAOS/JAPAN/ MALAYSIA/THAILAND/ VIETNAM]
Known as *mochigome* in Japan. Also sometimes referred to as 'sticky rice'. Short-grain rice that becomes very sticky when cooked. Used in stuffings, cakes and puddings. In Laos it is used in place of long-grain rice and served with all meals.

Glutinous (sweet) rice flour
[KAMPUCHEA/LAOS/MALAYSIA/ JAPAN/THAILAND/VIETNAM]
Known as *mochiko* in Japan. Made from ground glutinous (sweet) rice. There is no substitute. Obtainable from Chinese supermarkets.

Gobo [JAPAN]
Edible burdock roots.

Goma [JAPAN], see **Sesame seeds.**

Goma abura [JAPAN], see **Sesame seed oil.**

Goma jio [JAPAN]
Salted sesame seeds. Dry fry 1 tablespoon black sesame seeds in a hot frying pan (skillet) until they 'jump', shaking the pan constantly. Transfer to a bowl, then sprinkle with 2 teaspoons salt.

Gula jawa [MALAYSIA]
Also known as *gula malaka*. Brown palm sugar, sold in thin blocks. Demerara or Muscovado sugar may be used as a substitute.

Gyoza skins [JAPAN]
Round in shape. *Wun tun* (wonton) skins may be used as a substitute.

Hakusai [JAPAN], see **Napa.**
Harusame [JAPAN]
Soya bean noodles. Can be used instead of mung bean threads if these are unobtainable.

Hijiki [JAPAN]
Brown algae seaweed.

Hoi sin (hosin) sauce [CHINA]
Also known as Chinese barbecue sauce. Made from soya beans, flour, sugar, spices and red food colouring. Available in jars or cans from Chinese supermarkets, it will keep for several months in the refrigerator.

Horapa [THAILAND]
A member of the *ocimum* family, like sweet basil. Use fresh rather than dried. Sweet basil may be used as a substitute.

Jelly mushrooms [THAILAND], see **Wood ear.**

Kamaboko [JAPAN]
Japanese fish cake.

Kapi [THAILAND], see **Terasi.**

Kasu [JAPAN]
Rice wine lees. Sold in 2.25 kg/5 lb blocks in Asian stores.

Katsuobushi [JAPAN]
Dried bonito fish. Used in making Dashi (basic stock).

Kecap [INDONESIA/MALAYSIA]
Soy sauce. It is darker and sweeter than Chinese dark soy sauce and quite different from Chinese light soy sauce which is very salty.

Kemiri [MALAYSIA]
Also known as *buah keras* and candlenuts. Used in many South-East Asian dishes. Pale yellow nuts, roughly the same size as chestnuts. They are usually shelled before being exported and the kernels break into fragments. If '2 kemiri' are specified in a recipe, this means the equivalent of 2 whole nuts.

Kha [THAILAND], see **Galingale.**

Kochujang [KOREA]
Hot bean mash paprika paste. Nearest equivalent is mashed onions and chilli powder fried in oil. Available in cans from Oriental stores.

Kombu [JAPAN]
Tangle or kelp seaweed. Used in making Dashi (basic stock).

Konnyaku [JAPAN]
Tuber root cake.

Laksa [MALAYSIA], see **Rice vermicelli.**

Laos [MALAYSIA], see **Galingale.**

Lemon grass [BURMA/ MALAYSIA/THAILAND/VIETNAM]
Known as *serai* or *sereh* in Malaysia, *takrai* in Thailand. Also known as *citronella*. Fresh lemon grass is available from Oriental stores. The lower third of the stalk, the bulb like portion, is the part to use when a recipe specifies 'chopped or sliced lemon grass'. Alternatively, the whole stalk may be bruised and added during cooking, but then it should be removed before serving. Dried lemon grass is a good substitute:– Soak in hot water for about 2 hours before using, then remove from the dish before serving. (1 tablespoon dried lemon grass is roughly equivalent to 1 stalk fresh.) Powdered lemon grass is also available.

Lentil flour [BURMA]
Made from ground or pounded lentils. Can be made at home using an electric blender or pestle and mortar.

Lime leaves
[THAILAND/VIETNAM]
Fresh lime leaves are preferred, but virtually unobtainable in the West. Dried lime leaves are available from Oriental stores.

Lombok [MALAYSIA]
Chilli. *Lombok merah* are red, *lombok hijau* are green, *lombok rawit* are the hottest and are available in dried form in the West.

Makrut [THAILAND]
An ugly-looking citrus fruit with very strongly flavoured peel and leaves. The peel is ground with other ingredients in curry pastes and the leaves are used in soup. Lemon leaves can be used as a substitute.

Matcha [JAPAN]
Powdered green tea used for the traditional Japanese tea ceremony. This tea is made from the most tender tea leaves of the first spring picking, and is processed by a very expensive, tedious method.

217

Mint [THAILAND], see **Saranae**.

Mirin [JAPAN]
Sweetened *sake* (rice wine) used in cooking and for seasoning. If unavailable, substitute dry sherry and sugar in the proportion of 4 tablespoons ($\frac{1}{4}$ cup) sherry to $1\frac{1}{2}$ tablespoons sugar.

Miso [JAPAN], see **Soy bean paste**.

Miti [PHILIPPINES]
Wide egg noodles. Fresh egg noodles can be used as a substitute.

Mochigome [JAPAN], see **Glutinous (sweet) rice**.

Mochiko [JAPAN], see **Glutinous (sweet) rice flour**.

Monosodium glutamate (msg) [CHINA/JAPAN/KOREA/THAILAND]
Known as *oji-no-moto* in Korea, *veh t'sin* in China. A chemical compound sometimes known as 'taste essence'. It is used to bring out the natural flavours in food, and is entirely optional in all recipes where it is specified. It is widely used in restaurants, but should be used sparingly at home: $\frac{1}{4} - \frac{1}{2}$ teaspoon is ample in any recipe. Obtainable from most Oriental stores.

Mung beans [KOREA/VIETNAM]
Dried mung beans are very small and green in colour. Dried split peas may be used as a substitute, although mung beans are usually available at good health food shops. When their green husks have been removed, dried mung beans are yellow in colour.

Mung bean threads [CHINA/JAPAN/KOREA/THAILAND/VIETNAM]
Known as *saifun* in Japan, *wun sen* in Thailand, *būn tâu* in Vietnam. Also known as Chinese bean threads or transparent (cellophane) noodles. They are very fine dried noodles made from mung bean flour. Sold in packets. Soak in water for about 10 minutes before using.

Mushrooms, dried [CHINA/JAPAN/KOREA/THAILAND/VIETNAM]
Known as dried *shiitake* in Japan. Chinese and Japanese dried mushrooms (lentinus edodes) are sold in plastic bags in Oriental stores. They are very fragrant, and will keep almost indefinitely in an airtight jar. They have an entirely different flavour from their fresh counterparts. Soak in warm water for 30 minutes before using. Ordinary mushrooms do not make a good substitute.

Mushrooms, dried jelly [THAILAND], see **Wood ear**.

Nam pla [THAILAND], see **Fish sauce**.

Napa [JAPAN]
This is *hakusai* or Chinese cabbage, sometimes referred to as celery cabbage. Not to be confused with Chinese leaves (bok choy). Napa has very delicate leaves and is used both raw and cooked. Bok choy can be used as a substitute.

Ngapi [BURMA], see **Terasi**.

Ngô [VIETNAM], see **Coriander**.

Ngô tay [VIETNAM], see **Culantro**.

Nori [JAPAN]
Dried seaweed. Often toasted, then shredded and used as a garnish.

Nuoc cham/Nuoc mam [KAMPUCHEA/LAOS/VIETNAM], see **Fish sauce**.

Oyster sauce [CHINA]
A thickish brown sauce with a rich flavour. Made from oysters and soy sauce. It keeps indefinitely in the refrigerator.

Pak chee [THAILAND], see **Coriander**.

Paku [MALAYSIA]
Also known as *pakis*. Young edible fern shoots, called 'fiddlehead ferns' in North America. Young curly kale may be used as a substitute.

Panko [JAPAN]
Coarse breadcrumbs.

Patis [PHILIPPINES], see **Fish sauce**.

Prawns, dried [THAILAND]
Sold in packets in Chinese supermarkets. Best kind are bright pink in colour because they are the freshest. Rinse before use to remove dirt and excess salt.

Radish, white Chinese [BURMA/KOREA], see **Boo**.

Rice flour [BURMA/INDIA/MALAYSIA]
Made from ground rice. Can be made at home using an electric blender, coffee mill or pestle and mortar.

Rice papers, dried [VIETNAM]
Known as *banh trang*. A thin, brittle, disc-like pancake (crêpe). Used in many ways, to make spring rolls and as a wrapper for a variety of foods. Must be moistened with water or egg to make them flexible before using. Mostly imported from Thailand and available at Oriental stores.

Rice powder [MALAYSIA]
Known as *tepung beras*. Extremely fine powdered rice. When specified in a recipe it must be assumed that rice flour may not be used.

Rice vermicelli [MALAYSIA/THAILAND/VIETNAM]
Known as *laksa* in Malaysia, rice sticks or rice noodles in North America. These are noodles made from rice flour which come in various sizes. In soups, the very thin string-like variety called *bun*, are used. The different sizes can be interchanged in recipes if it is difficult to obtain the exact type specified.

Rice wine [CHINA/JAPAN/KOREA/MALAYSIA] see **Sake**.

Rijsttafel [MALAYSIA]
Rice table. The name given by the Dutch to a variety of Indonesian dishes that are all served together.

Rock sugar [VIETNAM]
Known as rock candy in North America. It is crystallized sugar, amber in colour, which is used to give a glaze to certain dishes. 1 lump rock sugar is equivalent to 1 table-spoon granulated sugar.

Saifun [JAPAN], see **Mung bean threads**.

Sake [JAPAN/KOREA]
Rice wine. Dry sherry makes an acceptable substitute. Sold in Oriental stores.

Salam [MALAYSIA]
The leaves of this plant are used extensively in Malaysian cooking. Bay leaves can be used as a substitute.

Salt fish, dried [BURMA]
Sword fish is the commonest fish used. Rinse well to remove excess salt before using. Available at Oriental stores.

Sambal ulek [INDONESIA]
Used as an accompaniment and in cooking. Made by crushing fresh red chillis with a little salt: Remove the seeds from the chillis, chop finely, then crush with salt using a pestle and mortar. Three chillis will make about 1 tablespoon sambal ulek. Also available ready-prepared in small jars from Oriental stores and some delicatessens.

Sansho [JAPAN]
Zanthoxylum pieratum. Fresh leaves of this bush are used for fragrance and garnish. Powdered sansho, a fragrant pepper, is also available.

Santen [MALAYSIA], see **Coconut milk**.

Saranae [THAILAND]
Mint. Always use spearmint (*Mentha spicata*) in preference to other types of mint for Thai recipes.

Saté [MALAYSIA]
Also known as *satay*. A general name for any kind of meat, poultry or fish that is grilled (broiled) on a skewer.

Serai/Sereh [MALAYSIA], see **Lemon grass**.

Sesame seeds [BURMA/JAPAN/KOREA/VIETNAM]
Known as *goma* in Japan. There are 2 types – white (*kurogoma*) and black (*shirogoma*). Can be used raw or toasted. To toast sesame seeds, dry fry in a hot frying pan (skillet) until they 'jump', shaking the pan constantly.

Sesame seed oil [CHINA/JAPAN/INDIA/KOREA/THAILAND/VIETNAM]
Known as *goma abura* in Japan. A strongly-flavoured seasoning oil made from roasted sesame seeds. Used for its fragrance and the flavour it imparts to other foods. Sold in bottles. Keeps indefinitely.

Shichimi [JAPAN]
A mixture of 7 spices, ground to a spicy hot powder. Not to be confused with Five Spice Powder. Used on noodles and other cooked dishes.

Shiitake, dried [JAPAN], see **Mushrooms, dried**.

Shiitake, fresh [JAPAN]
Japanese mushrooms, which have an entirely different, more delicate flavour than their dried counterparts. Vitamin-packed and exalted 'the elixir of life' in many Asian countries. Ordinary mushrooms do not make a good substitute.

Shirataki [JAPAN]
Yam noodles. Sold in cans. Mung bean threads may be substituted.

Shiromiso [JAPAN]
White soybean paste.

Shoyu [JAPAN]
Light soy sauce prepared from fermented cooked soya beans, wheat, malt and salt. Do not substitute Chinese or other soy sauces, their flavour is completely different and will spoil Japanese dishes.

Shrimp-flavoured soy sauce [BURMA]
Also known as fish sauce. It gives a fishy taste to dishes. Ordinary soy sauce can be used as a substitute. Available from Chinese stores.

Shrimp paste [BURMA]
Made from salted dried shrimps. Greyish pink in colour. Anchovies mixed with a little vinegar may be used as a substitute, but this is not very satisfactory. Available in jars from Chinese stores.

Shrimps, dried [BURMA]
Available whole, pounded or powdered, from Oriental stores.

Silver leaf [INDIA], see **Varak.**

Somen [JAPAN]
Very thin thread-like wheat vermicelli.

Soy bean paste [CHINA/JAPAN/KOREA]
Known as *miso* in Japan. A basic seasoning made from cooked soya beans, malt and salt. Sold in plastic packs at Oriental stores and some health food shops.

Split pea flour [BURMA]
Made from ground or pounded split peas. Can be made at home using an electric blender or pestle and mortar.

Su [JAPAN]
Rice vinegar, distilled from white rice. It has a very sweet aromatic quality and is much milder than cider vinegar. If unobtainable, substitute distilled white vinegar and mix with water. Seasoned rice vinegars, with sugar and monosodium glutamate added, are also available.

Szechuan preserved vegetable [CHINA]
A root vegetable pickled in salt and chilli, which is therefore very hot and salty to the taste. Sold in cans, it should be transferred to an airtight jar once opened, then it will keep for several months in the refrigerator.

Tahu/Taukwa [INDONESIA/MALAYSIA], see **Bean curd.**

Takrai [THAILAND], see **Lemon grass.**

Tamarind [BURMA/INDIA MALAYSIA/THAILAND/VIETNAM]
Also known as *asam* or *assem*. An acid-flavoured fruit resembling a bean pod. Sold as dried tamarind pulp in blocks and is dark brown in colour. The dried tamarind pulp must be made into tamarind water before using:– Soak about 25 g/1 oz tamarind pulp in 300 ml/$\frac{1}{2}$ pint/$1\frac{1}{4}$ cups water for 5 to 10 minutes, then squeeze, strain and use the water. The longer the tamarind is left to soak, the stronger the flavour. The amount of tamarind pulp and water can be adjusted according to the thickness required; the thicker the water, the more sour it tastes. Lime, lemon or mango juice or vinegar may be used as substitutes but the flavour of the finished dish will not be the same. Tamarind paste is also available, packaged in plastic bags. It should be refrigerated once opened. in which case it will keep indefinitely. Both tamarind pulp and tamarind paste are available at Oriental stores.

Tao chiew [THAILAND], see **Beans, salted.**

Tauco [INDONESIA/MALAYSIA], see **Beans, salted.**

Tepung Beras [MALAYSIA], see **Rice powder.**

Terasi [MALAYSIA]
Also known as *balachan/blacan* (Malaysia), *kapi* (Thailand) and *ngapi* (Burma). A kind of pungent shrimp paste, used in very small quantities.

Depending on the recipe in which it is used, it can be crushed with spices to make a paste which is then sautéed in oil. Alternatively, it may be grilled (broiled) or fried first, then added to other ingredients.

Tiger lily [CHINA]
Known as lily flower in North America. Also known as yellow flower or golden needles in China. A dried bud, golden-yellow in colour and crunchy in texture. Soak in water before using. It keeps indefinitely.

Tofu [JAPAN]
Soybean cake.

Tonkatsu sauce [JAPAN]
A commerically-prepared thick brown sauce made from fruit and vegetables combined with spices and seasonings. Soy sauce or ketchup may be used as substitutes.

Transparent noodles [CHINA/JAPAN/KOREA/THAILAND/VIETNAM], see **Mung bean threads.**

Tree ear [CHINA/THAILAND/VIETNAM], see **Wood ear.**

Tung chai [THAILAND]
Tiensin preserved vegetables. Obtainable from Chinese super-markets.

Udon [JAPAN]
A thick, broad noodle made from flour and water (without eggs).

Varak [INDIA]
Known as silver leaf in the West. Used solely for decorative purposes, although it is said to aid the digestion. Available from most Indian food suppliers.

Wakame [JAPAN]
Lobe leaf seaweed. Traditionally, the heavy vein is removed. The vein can be eaten, but it is rather chewy.

Wasabi [JAPAN]
A green horseradish grated from the root of the Eutrema Wasabi. Use green horseradish powder which is very pungent and hot for convenience, as fresh wasabi is both difficult to obtain and very expensive. Dry mustard mixed to a paste with a little water may be used as a substitute.

Water chestnut [CHINA/JAPAN]
A walnut-sized bulb with brown skin; the inside flesh is white and crisp. Canned water chestnuts are ready-peeled and will keep for about 1 month in the refrigerator.

Wood ear [CHINA/THAILAND/VIETNAM]
Known as tree ear in North America, cloud ear in China, jelly mushrooms in Thailand. A dried tree fungus. Use only in small quantities. Soak in warm water for about 20 minutes before using, until they become glutinous and crinkly. The dried fungi will keep indefinitely. Available at Chinese supermarkets.

Wun sen [THAILAND], see **Mung bean threads.**

Wun tun skins [KOREA/MALAYSIA]
Known as wonton skins in North America. Paper-thin squares or circles of dough. Can be made at home, or bought ready-rolled and trimmed at Chinese supermarkets. Store in the refrigerator or freezer.

Index

Suppliers of Asian Ingredients

Denotes that they will fill mail orders.

Osaka Ltd*
   17–17a Goldhurst Tce
   Finchley Rd
   London N.W.6.
   Tel: 01-624-9805
   Chinese, Indian,
   Indonesian, Japanese

Tokyo Ya*
   234 West End Lane
   London N.W.6
   Tel: 01-435-9805
   Chinese, Indonesian,
   Indian, Japanese

Chinese Emporium
   22 Rupert St
   London W.1.
   Tel: 01-278-9061
   Chinese

Loon Moon Supermarket
   9a Gerrard St
   London W.1.
   Tel: 01-734-9940
   Chinese

Far Eastern Supermarket
   28 Willesden Rd
   London N.W.10.
   Tel: 01-459-0977
   Chinese, Indian, Malaysian

Indian Emporium Ltd*
   8 Great Russell St
   London W.1.
   Tel: 01-580-3470
   Indian

Ganesha
   6 Park Walk
   Fulham Rd
   London S.W.10.
   Indonesian, Thai

Mikadoya
   250 Upper Richmond Rd
   Putney
   London S.W.15.
   Tel: 01-789-3980
   Japanese

Mikadoya Mail Orders*
   Unit 5 Goose Green
   Trading Estate
   47 East Dulwich Rd
   London S.E.22.
   Tel: 01-299-0363
   Japanese

Chung Nam Provisions
   44 Bromsgrove Street
   Birmingham 5.
   Tel: 021-622-4542
   Chinese

Win Yit Cash and Carry Warehouse
   96 Coventry Street
   Birmingham 5.
   Tel: 021-643-2851
   Chinese, Japanese, Indian,
   Thai

Quong Tai Young and Co.*
   24/26 Nelson Street
   Liverpool 1.
   Tel: 051-709-8053
   Chinese

Win Yit Warehouse
   45/47 Faulkner Street
   Manchester.
   Tel: 061-236-4152
   Indian, Chinese, Japanese,
   Indonesian

The Edinburgh Chinese Company Ltd.
   26 Dublin Street
   Edinburgh 3.
   Tel: 031-556-2304
   Chinese, Indonesian,
   Indian, Korean

Oriental Food Stores
   25–26 Argyll Place
   Edinburgh 6.
   Indian, Chinese

Eurasian Stores
   119 Buccleuch Street
   Edinburgh 6.
   Tel: 031-667-2999
   Indian

ACKNOWLEDGMENTS
Food photography by Robert Golden
Food prepared by Caroline Ellwood
Japanese food prepared by Susumu Okado
Photographic stylist: Antonia Gaunt

The publishers would like to thank the following individuals and organisations for their kind permission to reproduce the location photographs in this book:-
Alan Hutchinson 114; Sonia Halliday Photographs (Jane Taylor) 132; Korean Embassy 204–5; Roland Michaud 204–5; Syndication International 9; Vision International (Paolo Koch) 133; Zefa (Bitsch) 86–7, (Schmidt) 55, (Starfoto) 101, (Steinhaus) 176–7.

The publishers would also like to express their gratitude to the following companies for the loan of accessories for photography:-
Ajimura Japanese Restaurant, 27 Endell St WC2; Collet's Chinese Gallery & Bookshop, 40 Great Russell St WC1; Craftsmen Potters Shop, William Blake House, Marshall St W1; Frida, 111 Long Acre WC2; Ikeda Japanese Restaurant, 30 Brook St W1; Mitsukiku, 15 Old Brompton Road SW7; New Neal Street Shop, 23 Neal St WC2; Nice Irma's Floating Carpet, 46 Goodge St W1; Paul Wu Ltd, 64 Long Acre WC2; Mr. Eric Wee, Arirang Restaurant, 31–2 Poland St W1.

PDO 82-0818